FAMOUS IN THE LAST CENTURY

POP MUSIC QUIZZES
From the 1950s, right up to 1999.

First published in this edition 2022

MRM Publications (©)

Credits for this publication are printed on page 288. Thank you to all those mentioned, and also all others who aren't, but may well have provided me with some assistance, in many ways, along the long road producing this book

The dedications for this book are on page 4.

FAMOUS IN THE LAST CENTURY

POP MUSIC QUIZZES

From the 1950s, right up to 1999.

From ABBA to ZZ Top

MIKE LEWIS

Dedicated to Jeff, Thorney and Dave* for showing total confidence in Mo and me, and providing us with an exciting new chapter in the senior section of our lives in a lovely community!

Thank you to Severn Beach Community Library for including all of my published quiz books on their shelves in the Village Hall.

FAMOUS IN THE LAST CENTURY *is also dedicated to all of my extended family, and the numerous friends, acquaintances, colleagues - and pets! - who have helped to shape my life. Starting from my first employment steps at Fry's, Somerdale, right on through my working life, including the worlds of accountancy, marketing, advertising, public relations, graphic design, retailing, travel, local government, football and entertainment.*

Sadly, many of those family members, friends, colleagues, acquaintances - and pets, have passed away. Many of them in recent times. One thing is for certain. I will never forget any of them.

* Sadly, Dave M died on 8th January 2023. Mo and I will miss him enormously, as will all his feathered friends. RIP Dave.

From the author

Do you like popular music? Do you like quizzes?

If the answer is yes to both questions, here's another question!

Is your favourite music decade the 50s, 60s, 70s, 80s or 90s?

If you prefer any of the decades above, this book covers all of them!

This is a quiz book about 20th century pop music! From ABBA to ZZ Top!

During the past few years, I have published four quiz books through Amazon. Two of them were packed with various quiz rounds that proved popular when I presented quizzes around the country for almost 30 years as the lead presenter of The Inquizitors, supported brilliantly by Rob and Mo. The other two books were on favourite topics, both for me and for many other people around the UK. One was television and the other was films. All four books remain available from Amazon.

As I have been writing this quiz book, over many months, it has prompted me to open up Amazon Unlimited Music on numerous occasions to play music by the artist about whom I have been setting questions. I hope it does the same for you, the reader! Listening to music from Frankie Laine, a giant in the 1950s right up to 1990s, and bands like Oasis certainly does broaden the mind to appreciate all types of music! So we are literally covering the best of music, from ABBA to ZZ Top.

Originally, I planned to publish this book in time for Easter 2022. Of course, the best laid plans … and all that! After a move of home to Severn Beach, where life is so laid back and enjoyable, I found it difficult to kick start myself – before now!

Apart from individual quizzes and background information upon over 200 acts, there are many general trivial rounds, puzzles, anagrams, pictures and much more about hundreds of acts. The artistes include many who have had many hits in the singles and album chart over a period of many years to the one-hit wonders.

My personal favourite decade was the sixties. During those times I was involved as a drummer in a band, so I do particularly love the music of that era. I can remember the excited crowds in those, what are now, far off times! It was certainly a ground-breaking music scene and produced so many memorable songs and acts. Of course, other decades may well be preferred by each reader – fear not, they're all covered, right from 1954 – 1999. Occasionally I may have included questions that spill over into the 21st century if acts continued to be successful.

Thank you for buying the book, I hope that it gives plenty of enjoyment, both for individual testing or as a basis for setting quizzes for family, friends or a club or community.

Mike Lewis

ABBA are a Swedish pop group, formed in 1972 in Stockholm comprising Agnetha Fältskog, Björn Ulvaeus, Benny Andersson, and Anni-Frid Lyngstad. The name is an acronym of the first letters of their first names. One of the greatest musical groups of all time. 26 Top 40 UK hits between 1974 and 1992 (including a re-release). Nine of them reached No.1 and nineteen reached the Top 10. ABBA also had 13 Top 30 albums, including 9 Number Ones.

1. In most countries, *Voulez-Vous* was released as a single A-side, but in the UK it was released as a double A-side with another track. Which one?

2. A song title in Swedish: *Väntar Inte Mamma På Dig?*. What English song?

3. Which member had a role in the Swedish version of *Jesus Christ Superstar*?

4. Which musical did Bjorn and Benny create as their first project after ABBA split?

5. In 1967, who won a national talent competition singing *En ledig dag (A Day Off)*?

6. ABBA is formed from the quartet's first initials. Before they could use the name they had to seek permission from what type of business which had the same name?

7. Who have Björn and Benny cited as a major influence on their music?

8. ABBA only reached number one in the US singles chart once - and that was only for one week in 1977. What was the song?

9. What is the very last line of the 1980 Number One, *Super Trouper*?

10. What two UK number one singles feature Agnetha on lead vocals?

You can't beat this round! How much notice have you taken of the men and women sitting behind the drum kits? Well, here's your chance to find out!

1. Arguably the most influential of all rock drummers of the 20th century. He started in the New Yardbirds in August 1968 but was better known for his subsequent group. He died tragically in 1980 aged 32. Who was he and what was the famous band?

2. Def Leppard's drummer lost his left arm in a car accident. What is the name of the one-armed drummer known as Thunder God?

3. Considered by many to be the greatest jazz drummer of all time, name the legendary icon who passed away on April 2, 1987, following surgery to remove a malignant brain tumour?

4. Which highly respected drummer, awarded the OBE in 2004, started out in Marty Wilde's Wildcats and moved into The Shadows in 1961?

5. Which female drummer, long associated with Prince, has also appeared with a long string of stars including Lionel Richie, Madonna, Diana Ross, Gloria Estefan and Marvin Gaye?

ABBA ANSWERS: *1. Angeleyes; 2. Does Your Mother Know; 3.Agnetha (Playing Mary Magdalene); 4. Chess (with Tim Rice); 5. Anna-Frid; 6.A canned fish company; 7. The Beach Boys; 8. Dancing Queen; 9. "'Cause somewhere out there in the crowd there's you";*
10. Take a Chance On Me and The Winner Takes It All. **LET THERE BE DRUMS ANSWERS:**
1. John Bonham, Led Zeppelin; 2. Rick Allen; 3. Buddy Rich; 4. Brian Bennett; 5. Sheila E.

BRYAN ADAMS *(born 5 November 1959) is a Canadian guitarist, singer, composer and record producer from Kingston, Ontario. Adams has sold over 100 million records worldwide. Everything I Do (I Do It For You) was No. 1 in the UK for a record 16 consecutive weeks. Also had another 9 Top 10 hits (3 with other artists) amongst 24 singles that featured in the Top 40. He has also had 10 albums in the UK Top 30, including 3 No 1's.*

1. Bryan appeared as a petrol station attendant in the film *Pink Cadillac* but which of his songs featured in the film? A) Pink Cadillac   B) Run To Him   C) Summer of '69

2. Lyrics: 'Look into my eyes you will see what you mean to me. Search your heart, search your soul. And when you find me there you'll search no more' Name the song.

3. What film featured Bryan Adams, Sting, and Rod Stewart singing' All For Love?

4. True or False? Bryan is also a successful photographer. His work has been published in several leading magazines.

5. Adams reached number 29 in the UK charts in 1985 with It's Only Love, a duet with which female singer?   A) Diana Ross   B) Tina Turner   C) Natalie Cole

6. Bryan has been nominated for 3 Academy Awards, in 1992 for *(Everything I Do) I Do It for You*, in 1996 for *Have You Ever Really Loved a Woman?* and in 1997 for *I Finally Found Someone*. Name the three films in which the songs were featured.

7. In a reworked 2005 version of *When You're Gone*, for his *Anthology* album, Bryan featured Pamela Anderson as his duet partner. But who was his original partner on the 1998 number 3 hit in the UK?

8. Adams stopped eating meat and dairy and became a vegan in which year?
A) 1969   B) 1979   C) 1989

9. In June 1988, Adams performed at a birthday party concert at Wembley Stadium in honour of whom?

10. Bryan didn't have another solo number one in the UK The nearest he got was a No. 2 in 1993. What was the song?   A) Have You Ever Really Loved a Woman   B) Please Forgive Me   C) Thought I'd Died and Gone To Heaven

WHEN BRYAN ADAMS CAME TO BRISTOL!

Set list at Ashton Gate Stadium, Bristol 2003: *Here I Am, 18 'til I Die, Let's Make a Night to Remember, Can't Stop This Thing We Started, Back to You, Summer of '69, It's Only Love, (Everything I Do) I Do It for You, Cuts Like a Knife, When You're Gone, Please Forgive Me, Heaven, Somebody, The Only Thing That Looks Good on Me Is You, Encore: C'mon Everybody, A Little Less Conversation, Seven Nights to Rock, Wild Thing, She's Only Happy When She's Dancin', Encore 2: Cloud Number Nine, Run to You, The Best of Me, Straight From the Heart.*

BRYAN ADAMS ANSWERS: *1. C) Summer of '69; 2. (Everything I Do)I Do It For You); 3. The Three Musketeers; 4. True; 5. B) Tina Turner; 6. Robin Hood: Prince of Thieves, Don Juan DeMarco and The Mirror Has Two Faces; 7. Melanie C; 8. C) 1989; 9. Nelson Mandela; 10. B) Please Forgive Me.*

 **AEROSMITH** are an American rock band formed in Boston in 1970. Steven Tyler (lead vocals), Joe Perry (guitar), Tom Hamilton (bass), Joey Kramer (drums) and Brad Whitford (guitar). Charted 15 times in the UK Top 40 singles chart and 10 times in the UK Top 40 albums chart (6 in Top 10) . Only had one Top 10 singles hit, I Don't Want to Miss a Thing, reached No. 4 in 1998. Perry and Whitford left Aerosmith in 1979 and 1981, but both returned in 1984. Over 150 million records sold.

1. In what year did Aerosmith perform at the Reading festival?

2. What is pictured on the back cover of the *Big Ones* album?

3. Which 1993 No.19 hit track contains these lyrics?: 'If you can judge a wise man by the colour of his skin, then mister you're a better man than I.'

4. On which film soundtrack was Aerosmith not included: *Armageddon*, *Wayne's World 2*, *Charlie's Angels* or *Top Gun*.

5. On the 1973 album *Aerosmith*, the final track is a Rufus Thomas classic, covered by many acts, but just a #36 hit for the Dennisons, what is the classic track?

6. Which founding member was the first rhythm guitarist in Aerosmith?
A) Bruce Welch   B) John Fogerty   C) Ray Tabano

7. On a 1978 'Live Bootleg' Album Aerosmith covered a Lennon / McCartney track. Which one?   A) Helter Skelter   B) I Feel Fine   C) Come Together

8. *Walk This Way* was recorded in 1986 and got to No. 8 in the UK singles chart. Who were the Rap band that successfully covered the song?

9. Which Aerosmith guitarist eventually ended up controlling the fan club and t-shirt merchandising for the band?

10. On which classic will you hear these lyrics? 'I could stay awake just to hear you breathing, Watch you smile while you are sleeping, While you're far away and dreaming, I could spend my life in this sweet surrender'.

LOOK AT THESE LYRICS AND NAME THE SONGS AND ARTISTES

1. *Candlelight and soul forever, A dream of you and me together, Say you believe it say you believe it. (1996)*

2. *Out on the wily, windy moors, We'd roll and fall in green. (1978)*

3. *Put on your red shoes and dance the blues. (1983)*

4. *Got a picture of you beside me, Got your lipstick mark still on your coffee cup. (1995)*

5. *Come on sugar, come on hear my plea, Well she looked at my Ford, we'll never agree. (1959)*

*AEROSMITH ANSWERS: 1. 1977; 2. A Sumo wrestler; 3. Livin' on the Edge; 4. Top Gun; 5. Walkin' the Dog; 6. C) Ray Tabano; 7. C) Come Together; 8. Run-DMC; 9. Ray Tabano; 10. I Don't Want To Miss A Thing. **WAXING LYRICAL ANSWERS:** 1. 2 Become 1 - Spice Girls; 2. Wuthering Heights - Kate Bush; 3. Let's Dance - David Bowie; 4. Back For Good - Take That; 5. Brand New Cadillac - Vince Taylor & Playboys (Covered 1979 by The Clash on London's Calling album).*

A-HA are a Norwegian synth-pop band formed in Oslo in 1982, comprising Morten Harket (vocals), Paul Waaktaar-Savoy (guitars) and Magne Furuholmen (keyboards/guitars). Between 1985 and 1994 A-Ha had 15 UK Top 40 singles (including a No.1 and 6 other Top 10 hits). 6 of the band's albums were highly successful - 3 reaching No. 2 in the album charts and the other three entering the top 20. The most successful global pop music act from Norway. Made comebacks in 1998 and 2015.

1. What is A-Ha's only UK number one single?
A) Take On Me   B) The Sun Always Shines on TV   C) Stay on These Roads

2. In 1987 the band reached number 5 with a Paul Waaktaar-Savoy song that was used as the theme to which James Bond film?

3. A-Ha's first 6 singles reached the Top 10 in the UK. The 7th only reached No. 13. What was it?   A) Manhattan Skyline   B) Cry Wolf   C) I've Been Losing You

4. The band were listed in the Guinness World Records for having the then biggest-paying rock concert attendance for a 1991 performance at the Maracana Stadium in Brazil. How many fans gathered?   A) 138,000   B) 168,000   C) 198,000

5. The name A-Ha derives from a song title in an early Paul Waaktaar-Savoy portfolio. True or False?

6. When they first came to London in 1982, why did A-Ha choose the studio of musician, producer, and soon-to-be-manager John Ratcliff?   A) It was next door to McDonalds   B) It had a Space Invaders machine   C) Technologically advanced

7. What song contains these lyrics? Talking away, I don't know what, I'm to say, I'll say it anyway, Today is another day to find you, Shying away, I'll be coming for your love, okay?

8. In 1994, the band unofficially entered a hiatus, and band members focused on solo projects before being invited to perform at what major event in Oslo in 1998?

9. In 1990 A-Ha had a No.13 hit with which 1963 Everly Brothers classic?
A) Crying in the Rain   B) Cathy's Clown   C) Let It Be Me

10. Approximately how many copies did Take On me sell in the UK when first released in 1984?   A) 3,000   B) 1,000   C) 300

WHO HAD THESE HITS IN THE UK?

1. Smoke Gets In Your Eyes (No. 1 in 1959)

2. Smoke on the Water (No. 21 in 1977)

3. Holy Smoke (No. 3 in 1990)

4. Smoke (No. 5 in 1998)

A-HA ANSWERS: *1. B) The Sun Always Shines on TV; 2. The Living Daylights;*
3. A) Manhattan Skyline; 4. C) 198,000; 5. True; 6. B) It had a Space Invaders machine;
7. Take On Me; 8. The Nobel Peace Prize Concert; 9. A) Crying in the Rain; 10. 300.
SMOKE WITHOUT FIRE ANSWERS: *1. The Platters; 2. Deep Purple; 3. Iron Maiden;*
4. Natalie Imbruglia.

DYNAMIC Duos

Occasionally two music acts get together and release a duet. Down the years there have been many major hit records resulting from such collaborations. Here are just a few of them. The list includes songs, artistes and years in which they were major hits. Not all of them are boy / girl pairings! All you have to do is fill in the gaps. There are a couple of novelties included here! The hit parade has always been pretty unpredictable!

SONG	ARTISTES	YEAR
1. Somethin' Stupid	?	1967
2. ?	Marc Almond featuring Gene Pitney	1989
3. You Don't Bring Me Flowers	?	1978
4. Islands in the Stream	Kenny Rogers and Dolly Parton	?
5. ?	Sarah Brightman and Steve Harley	1986
6. Tonight I Celebrate My Love	?	1983
7. Don't Let the Sun Go Down On Me	George Michael and Elton John	?
8. What Are We Gonna Get 'Er Indoors	?	1983
9. No More Tears (Enough Is Enough)	?	1979
10. ?	Windsor Davies and Don Estelle	1975
11. Especially For You	Kylie Minogue and Jason Donovan	?
12. She Means Nothing To Me	?	1983
13. ?	Puff Daddy and Faith Evans	1997
14. ?	Elton John and Kiki Dee	1993
15. Summer Nights	?	1978
16. ?	Philip Bailey and Phil Collins	1985
17. Ebony and Ivory	Paul McCartney and Stevie Wonder	?
18. The Boy Is Mine	?	1998
19. Fun, Fun, Fun	?	1996
20. Under Pressure	Queen and David Bowie	?

DYNAMIC DUOS ANSWERS: 1. Nancy Sinatra and Frank Sinatra (No. 1); 2. Something's Gotten Hold Of My Heart (No. 1); 3. Barbra Streisand and Neil Diamond (No. 5); 4. 1983 (No. 7); 5. The Phantom of the Opera (No. 7); 6. Roberta Flack and Peabo Bryson (No. 2); 7. 1991; 8. Dennis Waterman and George Cole (No. 21); 9. Donna Summer and Barbra Streisand (No. 3); 10. Whispering Grass (No. 1); 11. 1988; 12. Phil Everly and Cliff Richard (No. 9); 13. I'll Be Missing You (No. 1); 14. True Love (No. 2); 15. John Travolta and Olivia Newton John (No. 1); 16. Easy Lover (No. 1); 17. 1982; 18. Brandy and Monica (No. 2); 19. Status Quo and The Beach Boys (No. 24); 20. 1981 (No. 1).

THE ANIMALS *were a ground-breaking English rhythm-and-blues & rock band, formed in Newcastle-upon-Tyne in the early 1960s. Original line-up: Eric Burdon (vocals), Alan Price (keyboards), Hilton Valentine (guitar), John Steel (drums) and Bryan 'Chas' Chandler (bass). In 1965 Price left to pursue a solo career, followed by Steel in 1966. The Animals had 9 UK Top 40 singles including 1 No.1 and 6 Top 10 hits, also 4 Top 10 albums. Eric Burdon & The Animals then had 6 Top 40 singles.*

1. Prior to 1964, a few of the Animals line-up had played in another band. What name did that band have? A) The Kansas City Five B) War C) The Tweets

2. Mickie Most helped the band to record *The House of the Rising Sun* in just 15 minutes at a cost of just £1 10s 0d. True or False?

3. Staying with their biggest smash hit, can you complete the lyrics? "There is a house in New Orleans, they call the Rising Sun. And it's been the ruin of many a poor boy, and ...."

4. *Don't Let Me Be Misunderstood* reached No. 3 in 1965. Which jazz singer had recorded the song previously? A) Cleo Laine B) Ella Fitzgerald C) Nina Simone

5. Which Eric Burdon and The Animals song lasted 7.27 minutes and took up both sides of a single and was released in 1968?

6. Sadly two of the original line up have died. Bassist Chas Chandler in 1996 and in 2021 the man who played the memorable opus on *House of the Rising Sun* died in Connecticut aged 77. Who was he?

7. On which BBC weekend show did Status Quo make their radio debut in 1963?

8. *I'm Crying* reached No. 8 in the UK singles chart in 1964. Which two members of the band wrote the song?

9. In 1965 *We've Gotta Get Out Of This Place* was kept off the top of the chart by which Beatles record? A I Want To Hold Your Hand B) Help! C) A Hard Days Night

10. Which future Police guitarist linked up with Eric Burdon and The Animals in 1968?

NAME THESE HITS ABOUT 'HANDS'

1. Name Laurie London's solitary hit, a No. 1 in 1957.

2. A year later which top entertainer had a double sided No. Three hit, *Tulips From Amsterdam / You Need Hands*?

3. In 1990 Elton John also had a double sided No. 1. *Sacrifice* was one side, what was the flip side?

4. In 1999 who had a No. 2 hit with *If I Could Turn Back the Hands of Time*?

THE ANIMALS ANSWERS: *1. A) The Kansas City Five; 2. True; 3. "God I Know I'm One"; 4. C) Nina Simone; 5. Sky Pilot; 6. Hilton Valentine; 7. Saturday Club (hosted by Brian Matthew); 8. Eric Burdon and Alan Price; 9. B) Help!; 10. Andy Summers.*
YOU NEED HANDS ANSWERS: *1. He's Got the Whole World in His Hands; 2. Max Bygraves; 3 Healing Hands; 4. R. Kelly.*

PAUL ANKA *(born July 30, 1941) is a Canadian singer, songwriter, and actor, born in Ottawa, Ontario. His parents were both of Lebanese Christian descent. He had 134 weeks on the charts, with 13 Top 40 hits, with another couple just peaking outside the Top 40. He had a total of 7 Top 10 hits, including a major No. 1 smash hit. Toured UK with Buddy Holly in 1958 and wrote his number one smash It Doesn't Matter Anymore.*

1. Paul Anka began his singing career at just fourteen years of age. Which of these songs was his first single? A) Young and Foolish B) Every Night C) I Confess

2. In 1957 Anka had his biggest hit, aged just 14. *Diana* topped the charts in both Canada and the US as well as the UK. How many weeks was it No. 1 in Britain? A) 7 B) 8 C) 9

3. Also in 1957, Paul reached number 3 in the UK with *I Love You Baby*. Which act then got to No.13 with the song in November 1964?

4. Which No. 3 Anka song from 1959 contains these lyrics? 'I've got everything, You could think of, But all I want, Is someone to love"

5. In 1960 Paul Anka had a minor hit with a song that was revived by Donny Osmond 12 years later and became a No. 1 smash hit. What was the song?

6. When the 'British Invasion' happened in the early 1960s, Paul Anka's music style became redundant, so he bought back the rights to his music, for how much? A) $100,000 B) $250,000 C) $500,000

7. While on holiday in France, Paul Anka heard a song called *Comme d'habitude (As Usual)*. He acquired adaptation, recording, and publishing rights for the song and wrote English lyrics. So, what was the song that spent 75 weeks inside the Top 40, became Frank Sinatra's signature song and was also a Top 10 hit for Elvis Presley?

8. For which late night talk show did Paul Anka write the theme song, now estimated to have been played around 1.4 million times? A) Late Show with David Letterman B) The Tonight Show with Johnny Carson C) The Oprah Winfrey Show

9. After 12 chart-less years in the UK, Anka had a 1974 hit, *(You're) Having My Baby*, a duet with which singer? A) Odia Coates B) Kim Carnes C) Stevie Nicks

10. True or False? In 2020, Paul Anka appeared as Broccoli in the US version of *The Masked Singer* and finished 7th.

10 FEMALE ACTS WITH JUST ONE BIG UK HIT. NAME THEM!	
1. *I'm Just a Baby (1962)*	6. *There's No-one Quite Like Grandma (1980)*
2. *Uptown Top Ranking (1977)*	7. *I've Never Been to Me (1982)*
3. *One Day at a Time (1982)*	8. *99 Red Balloons (1984)*
4. *Ring My Bell (1979)*	9. *First Time (1988)*
5. *Together We Are Beautiful (1980)*	10. *Stay (I Missed You) (1994)*

PAUL ANKA ANSWERS: *1. C) I Confess; 2. C) 9; 3. Freddie and the Dreamers; 4. Lonely Boy; 5. Puppy Love; 6. B) $250,000; 7. My Way; 8. B) The Tonight Show with Johnny Carson; 9. A) Odia Coates; 10. True.* **THE GIRLS: ONE HIT WONDERS:** *1. Louise Cordet; 2. Althea & Donna; 3. Lena Martell; 4. Anita Ward; 5. Fern Kinney; 6. St Winifred's School Choir; 7. Charlene; 8. Nena; 9. Robin Beck; 10. Lisa Loeb and Nine Stories.*

THE BACHELORS (Conleth (Con) Cluskey (born 18 November 1941, died 8 April 2022), Declan (Dec) Cluskey (born 23 December 1942), and John Stokes (Sean James Stokes) (born 13 August 1940). Between 1963 / 1967 they had 17 Top 40 hits, including a No.1 and 7 other top Top 10 hits. Also 8 Top 40 hit albums. In 1984, there was an acrimonious split and various Bachelors formations appeared. No doubts though about their major chart achievements in the sixties.

1. The Bachelors started out in 1957 as a classically styled instrumental harmonica-act. What was the act's name?   A) Morton Fraser's Harmonica Gang   B) The Three Monarchs   C) The Harmonichords

2. What song, originally composed for the 1926 silent film *What Price Glory*, and subsequently a huge success for Mantovani, was The Bachelors first Top 10 hit?

3. In 1964 the trio appeared on a major Sunday TV show, hosted by Bruce Forsyth. The episode had the largest viewing audience ever for which very popular show?

4. Also in 1964, The Bachelors had their only number one hit, a song originally written as the theme song for the 1927 classic silent film *7th Heaven*. What was its title?

5. 1964 was indeed a great year for the trio. Four further Top 10 hits followed that year. *Ramona, I Wouldn't Trade You For the World* and *No Arms Can Ever Hold You were three*. But, which song that had originally been number one by Frankie Laine for 18 weeks in 1953 got The Bachelors to number 2?

6. On what label did The Bachelors record all of their hits?
A) Top Rank   B) Decca   C) Columbia

7.Despite The Bachelors' last chart single being in 1967, they continued to play the cabaret circuit, maintaining the original line-up until 1984. In this period they also moved to which new recording label to suit their easy listening style?

8. With which US chart topping Simon and Garfunkel song did The Bachelors have Top 3 success in the UK in 1966?   A) Sound of Silence   B) Bridge Over Troubled Water   C) The 59th Street Bridge Song (Feelin' Groovy)

9. The Bachelors appeared in two films, *Just for You* in 1964, and *I've Gotta Horse* the following year. Both starred which major UK pop star of the time?

10. The Bachelors achieved 9 Top 100 hits in the US. One of them was the flipside of *The Sound of Silence*. What was the track?
A) Love Me With All Your Heart   B) Everybody's Talkin'   C) Hello Dolly

1. *Here Comes Summer (1959)*	6. *Summer Breeze (1974)*
2. *Theme From a Summer Place (1960)*	7. *Summer of my Life (1976)*
3. *In Summer (1963)*	8. *Long Hot Summer (1983)*
4. *Summer In the City (1966)*	9. *The Boys of Summer (1985)*
5. *In the Summertime (1970)*	10. *Cruel Summer (1998)*

WHO HAD THESE SUMMER HITS?

THE BACHELORS ANSWERS: *1. C) The Harmonichords; 2. Charmaine; 3. Sunday Night at the London Palladium; 4. Diane; 5. I Believe; 6. B) Decca; 7. Philips; 8. A) The Sound of Silence; 9. Billy Fury; 10. A) Love Me With All Of Your Heart. **IT'S SUMMER TIME ANSWERS:** 1. Jerry Keller; 2. Percy Faith & Orchestra; 3. Billy Fury; 4. Lovin' Spoonful; 5. Mungo Jerry; 6. Isley Brothers; 7. Simon May; 8. Style Council; 9. Don Henley; 10. Ace of Base.*

BANANARAMA *are a female English group, formed in 1980 when friends Sara Dallin and Keren Woodward from Bristol moved to London and met Siobhan Fahey. Between 1982 and 1993 they had 23 Top 40 hits, including 9 Top 10 successes. Also 4 Top 40 Albums, with 2 Top 10 hits. Fahey left in 1988 and joined Shakespears Sister. Jacquie O'Sullivan replaced her until 1991. Then Dallin and Woodward continued as a duo. Bananarama have had most UK chart entries for an all-female group.*

1. Bananarama took their name, in part, from the Roxy Music song *Pyjamarama*. True or False?

2. Bananarama had a huge hit with their song *Robert De Niro's Waiting*, but which film star was originally meant to be 'waiting'?
A) Al Pacino   B) Tom Hanks   C) Michael Douglas

3. *Bananarama's version of the song* Venus *only reached number 8 in the UK, but it reached number one in how many other countries?   A) 2   B) 4   C) 8*

4. Bananarama did a cover of *Help!* with Lananeeneenoonoo for 'Comic Relief' in 1989. French and Saunders were two members of Lananeeneenoonoo, who was the third?   A) Helen Lederer   B) Kathy Burke   C) Joanna Lumley

5. For which of these Bananarama songs did the original video show six pair of male hands caressing Sara and Keren but was seen as 'too suggestive' and censored?
A) I Can't Help It   B) I Want You Back   C) Love in the First Degree

6. Lyrics: "The room has suddenly grown cold and outside in the street it's raining". What 1987 number 3 hit contains those lyrics?

7. Bananarama are known for their unique vocal style which features all members singing the same notes in unison? True or False?

8. Why was Siobhan filmed only from her shoulders and up in the *I Can't Help It* music video?

9. How many of their early albums were primarily produced and co-written with Jolley & Swain?   A) 4   B) 3   C) 2

10. Bananarama featured on which charity supergroup single in 1984, and were the only performers to repeat their appearance on the second version in 1989?

THE SONG UNCHAINED MELODY REACHED NO. 1 IN THE UK THREE TIMES IN THE TWENTIETH CENTURY

Unchained Melodies

WHO HAD THE HIT VERSIONS IN:

A) 1955

B) 1990

C) 1995

Woah, my love, my darling, I've hungered for your touch, A long, lonely time, And time goes by so slowly, And time can do so much, Are you still mine? I need your love.

BANANARAMA ANSWERS: *1. True; 2. A) Al Pacino; 3. C) 8; 4. B) Kathy Burke; 5. A) I Can't Help It; 6. Love in the First Degree; 7. True; 8. She was pregnant; 9. B) 3; 10. Do They Know It's Christmas (Band Aid/Band Aid II).* **UNCHAINED MELODY ANSWERS:** *A) Jimmy Young; B) The Righteous Brothers; C) Robson & Jerome*

THE 1960s. *A culture of groups began to emerge, often out of the declining skiffle scene in major urban centres in the UK like Liverpool, Manchester and London. In Liverpool, it has been estimated that there were around 350 active bands playing ballrooms, concert halls and clubs. Beat bands were heavily influenced by American bands such as Buddy Holly and the Crickets, as well as earlier British groups such as the Shadows. This was followed by other style bands including Blues, Folk and various shades of Rock music, Rhythm and Blues and Soul.*

1. What was the best selling single in the UK throughout the 1960s?

2. Which band had success with *Nashville Cats, Summer in the City* and *Daydream*?

3. Which band from Southend, Essex had a minor hit with *Poison Ivy* before changing name to either a wrong Latin interpretation for "far from these things", or the name of a friend's Burmese cat - depending upon your source?

4. Which Manchester band, linked up with Liverpool singer Billy J Kramer and had a string of hits with him, plus an instrumental success of their own, *The Cruel Sea*?

5. Which Trad Jazz band had a string of hits between 1961 and 1964, including *Midnight in Moscow* and three other top 10 hits?

6. Phil May was lead singer in which rock band from Sidcup in Kent who took their name from a song by blues singer Willie Dixon?

7. In which trendsetting instrumental band were Tony Meehan and Jet Harris replaced by Brian Bennett and Liquorice Locking respectively in 1961 and 1962?

8. Which band backed Wayne Fontana on a number of hits before going out on their and registering hits including a UK number two, *A Groovy Kind of Love*?

9. True or False? The Zombies' Rod Argent wrote and sung lead vocals on the 1964 number 12 UK hit *She's Not There*.

10. Which country singer played on 5 tracks of the Beach Boys *Pet Sounds* and spent four months touring with them, playing bass and singing falsetto harmonies?

11. Dave Clark Five had 17 Top 40 hits between 1963 and 1970. Dave Clark was the drummer, but who drummed on their breakthrough number one *Glad All Over*?

12. Chan Romero wrote *The Hippy Hippy Shake* in 1959 when he was just 17. However, which Liverpool band took the song to number two in the UK in 1964?

13. Which 1966 number 5 UK hit starts with these lyrics? "You think we look pretty good together, You think my shoes are made of leather...."

14. **ADAM LEMAR** is an anagram of a 60s Scottish band who started 1969 with a number one that was a cover of a Beatles *White Album* track? Who are they?

15. Alvin Stardust had 11 Top 40 hits between 1973 and 1984, however his initial success came in 1961 and 1962 when he had 4 Top 40 hits, under what name?

1960S BANDS SPOTLIGHT ANSWERS: 1. She Loves You by The Beatles; 2. The Lovin' Spoonful; 3. Procol Harum; 4. The Dakotas; 5. Kenny Ball & His Jazzmen; 6. The Pretty Things; 7. The Shadows; 8. The Mindbenders; 9. False (he wrote it but Colin Blunstone sung it!); 10. Glen Campbell (a top session guitarist); 11. Bobby Graham (another top session player); 12. The Swinging Blue Jeans; 13. Substitute by The Who; 14. Marmalade; 15. Shane Fenton & The Fentones.

BAND AID were a charity supergroup of many musicians and recording artists. It was founded in 1984 by Bob Geldof and Midge Ure to raise money for anti-famine efforts in Ethiopia. The song Do They Know It's Christmas? surpassed all hopes and was the Christmas No. 1 upon release. 3 re-recordings of the song raised further money for charity, all reached No. 1. Band Aid II in 1989, Band Aid 20 in 2004 and Band Aid 30 in 2014.

1. The original Band Aid single was recorded on 25 November 1984. Many stars of the day were at the recording, but who was late, direct from a US tour on Concorde?
A) Boy George B) Bono C) Paul McCartney

2. In 1984 what song did the Band Aid single keep from the Christmas Number One spot in the UK? A) We All Stand Together by Paul McCartney B) Last Christmas by Wham! C) Like a Virgin by Madonna

3. Who sang the opening line in 1984, "It's Christmas time, There's no need to be afraid, At Christmas time, We let in light and we banish shade"?

4. Who designed the cover for the 1984 single?
A) David Hockney B) Sir Peter Blake C) Andy Warhol

5. Who produced Band Aid II in 1989?
A) George Martin B) Midge Ure C) Stock, Aitken and Waterman

6. In a 1985 *Time Out* interview, which anti-establishment rock frontman said: "I'm not afraid to say that I think Band Aid was diabolical. Or to say that I think Bob Geldof is a nauseating character."?

7. Who were the only artists to appear on both the 1984 Band Aid single and the Band Aid 2 version five years later?
A) Sara and Keren from Bananarama B) Spandau Ballet C) Status Quo

8. Band Aid 20 was released in 2004. Which singer reprised their line from the 1984 original?: "Well tonight thank God it's them, instead of you".
A) Tony Hadley B) Bono C) Boy George

9. From the previous question, who sung the line in 1989?
A) Matt Goss B) Paul Weller C) Kylie Minogue

10. Band Aid 30 was released in 2014 to aid with the Ebola crisis. Who played the drums on this release? A) Roger Taylor B) Ringo Starr C) Phil Collins

THE 1985 LIVE AID CONCERT on Saturday 13 July 1985, was conceived as a follow-on to the successful charity single Do They Know It's Christmas?.

In London's Wembley Stadium: Bob Geldolf opens Live Aid; Status Quo; Style Council; Boomtown Rats with Adam Ant; Adam Ant; Ultravox; Spandau Ballet; Elvis Costello; Nik Kershaw with Billy Connolly; Sade; Phil Collins with Julian Lennon; Sting with Howard Jones; Bryan Ferry; Paul Young with Alison Moyet; U2; Dire Straits; Queen; David Bowie; The Who; Elton John; Wham!; Paul McCartney.

In Philadephia's JFK Stadium: Joan Baez; The Hooters; The Four Tops; Billy Ocean; Black Sabbath with Ozzy Osbourne; Run-DMC; Rick Springfield; REO Speedwagon; Crosby, Stills, Nash; Judas Priest; Bryan Adams; The Beach Boys; George Thorogood; Queens Performance from London; Music video featuring David Bowie and Mick Jagger; Simple Minds; The Pretenders; Santana with Pat Metheny; Ashford and Simpson with Teddy Pendergrass; Madonna; Rod Stewart; Tom Petty; Kenny Loggins; The Cars; Neil Young; Power Station; Thompson Twins; Eric Clapton; Phil Collins with Robert Plant and Jimmy Page; Duran Duran; Patti LaBelle; Daryl Hall and John Oates with Eddie Kendricks and David Ruffin. Mick Jagger; Tina Turner; Bob Dylan.

BAND AID ANSWERS: *1. A) Boy George; 2. B) Last Christmas by Wham!; 3. Paul Young; 4. B) Sir Peter Blake; 5. Stock, Aitken, Waterman; 6. Morrissey; 7. A) Sara and Keren from Bananarama; 8. B) Bono; 9. A) Matt Goss; 10. A) Roger Taylor (Phil Collins 1985 and 1989).*

THE BANGLES *are an American pop rock band formed in Los Angeles in 1981. The classic lineup consisted of founding members Susanna Hoffs (guitar/vocals), Debbi Peterson (drum /vocals) and Vicki Peterson (guitar vocals) with Michael Steele (bass /vocals). The Bangles had 8 Top 40 UK singles. This included a No. 1 and 2 further Top 3 hits. Additionally they had 3 Top 10 albums, including a 'Greatest Hits' compilation.*

1. What Top 3 UK single did the Bangles record for the film, *Less Than Zero*?
A) Hazy Shade of Winter   B) Walk Like An Egyptian   C) Manic Monday

2. All 4 members of The Bangles could sing. On *Walk Like An Egyptian*, which band member was not given lead vocals?
A) Susanna Hoffs   B) Debbi Peterson   C) Vicki Peterson

3. After a break up in 1989, which of The Bangles had moderate success with three singles and an album in the UK?

4. In their early years, their band name changed many times. Which of the following was NOT a past name?   A) The Colors   B) The Anklets   C) The Supersonic Bangs

5. Who wrote one of their biggest hits, *Manic Monday*?
A) Prince   B) Paul McCartney   C) Michael Jackson

6. True or False? Star Trek's Leonard Nimoy had a cameo in one of their lesser UK hits, *Going Down To Liverpool*, in 1986.

7. Susanna Hoffs trained to be a dancer for many years, and took her dancing skills to Bangles concerts. She sometimes amazed crowds by doing what?
A) Pirouette with help from the nearest band member   B) Leap over her band mates' shoulders   C) Slide into the splits while playing guitar

8. For which film soundtrack did The Bangles record *Hazy Shade Of Winter*?
A) The Goonies   B) Austin Powers The Spy Who Shagged Me   C) E.T.

9. Which Bangles album was their first Top 3 hit in 1986?
A) All Over the Place   B) Different Light   C) Everything

10. The Bangles broke up in 1989 but reformed in 1999 to perform at a tribute concert for what band?   A) The Beatles   B) The Rolling Stones   C) The Who

---

COLOURFUL HITS
Just fill in the missing colours

1. FROZEN ...... JUICE (Peter Sarsedt, No. 10 in 1969)

2. NIGHTS IN ..... SATIN (Moody Blues, No. 19, 9, & 14 in 1967, 1972 & 1979)

3. BIG ...... TAXI (Joni Mitchell, No. 11 in 1970)

4. BAND OF .... (Freda Payne, No. 1 in 1970)

5. MR .... SKY (ELO, No. 6 in 1978)

6. ..... EYED BOY (Texas, No. 5 in 1997)

7. ...... RAIN (Prince, No. 8 in 1984)

8. ..... TAMBOURINE (Lemon Pipers, No. 7 in 1968)

9. ...LIGHT SPELLS DANGER (Billy Ocean, No. 2 in 1977)

10. .... SAVANNAH (Erasure, No. 3 in 1977)

THE BANGLES ANSWERS: *1. B) Hazy Shade of Winter; 2. B) Debbi Peterson; 3. Susanna Hoffs; 4. B) The Anklets; 5. A) Prince; 6. True; 7. C) Slide into the splits while playing guitar; 8. B) Austin Powers The Spy Who Shagged Me; 9. B) Different Light; 10. A) The Beatles.*
COLOURFUL HITS ANSWERS: *1. Orange; 2. White; 3. Yellow; 4. Gold; 5. Blue; 6. Black; 7. Purple; 8. Green; 9. Red; 10. Blue.*

Popular music of the UK in the 1970s built upon new styles of music developed from blues rock towards the late 1960s, including folk rock and psychedelic rock. Several important and influential subgenres were created in Britain, including folk rock and glam rock, a process that reached its apogee in the development of progressive rock and also the most enduring subgenres of heavy metal music. The UK also began to be increasingly influenced by third world music.

1. What was the name of David Bowie's flamboyant alter ego?

2. What was the best selling single of the decade in the UK?

3. Lyrics: "Well, you can tell by the way I use my walk, I'm a woman's man, no time to talk". Name the song and the singer.

4. Errol Brown was the lead singer of which British soul band?

5. What is the name of the soul band with Chaka Khan as the lead singer, who charted in the UK with *Ain't Nobody*, before she went solo?

6. True or False? The Eagles only reached the UK singles chart Top 10 with one song, *Hotel California*, which reached number 8 in 1977.

7. Anyone who plays guitar, regardless of ability, has tried to play the classic intro to which Deep Purple song from 1977?

8. What is the third studio album by Van Morrison, released in January 1970, which established him as a major artist in popular music?

9. Which band did Paul McCartney form with his wife Linda in the '70s?

10. Who wrote, *Blinded by the Light*, a UK number 6 hit for Manfred Mann in 1977?

11. Which band covered Betty Everett's US number 1, *You're No Good*, written by Clint Ballard Jr, and sent it to number 3 in the UK in 1963?

12. What musical genre is a prime influence in the works of The Clash?
A) Punk   B) Ska   C) Disco

13. Which female singer joined Fleetwood Mac in 1975, and helped them become one of the best-selling music acts of all time, including the classic album *Rumours*?

14. Pink Floyd's most commercially successful album is…
A) The Wall   B) Dark Side of the Moon   C) Meddle

15. *Morning Has Broken* is a Christian hymn first published in 1931. It charted twice in the UK during the 20th century, in 1972 and 1992. Who were the two hitmakers?

16. Who was crowned *Queen of Disco* with hits like *Hot Stuff* and *Bad Girls* among many others?

17. Which prolific singer/songwriter had just two major UK hits, *It Might As Well Rain Until September* in 1962 and *It's Too Late* in 1971?

18. Dr. and the Medics had a number one hit with a 1986 cover version of a 1970 number one for Norman Greenbaum. What was the song?

19. Philip Bailey pursued a solo career and had a UK No. 1 with *Easy Lover*, a duet with Phil Collins. Which innovative band did he previously front?

20. Lyn Cornell and Ann Simmons had their only Top 10 UK hit with *Guilty* in 1974. What was the name of this female duo?

1970s ANSWERS: 1. Ziggy Stardust; 2. Mull of Kintyre by Wings; 3. Stayin' Alive by the Bee Gees; 4. Hot Chocolate; 5. Rufus; 6. True; 7. Smoke on the Water; 8. Moondance; 9. Wings; 10. Bruce Springsteen; 11. Swinging Blue Jeans; 12. A) Punk; 13. Stevie Nicks; 14. B) Dark Side of the Moon; 15. Cat Stevens and Neil Diamond; 16. Donna Summer; 17. Carole King; 18. Spirit in the Sky; 19. Earth, Wind & Fire; 20. The Pearls.

Since the charts were introduced in 1952 comedy songs are a rarely-seen phenomenon, often reserved for charity singles. However there are many great examples of comedy acts having unexpected hits. There are also some examples of acts, normally associated with comedy, proving to have excellent vocal skills. Here are 20 examples!

COMEDY AND MUSIC CAN MIX!

MATCH THE COMEDY ACT WITH THE CORRECT HIT SINGLE

SONG TITLE	PERFORMER(S) / YEAR
1. Dizzy	A. Billy Connolly (1975)
2. Atmosphere	B. Benny Hill (1971)
3. The Trail of the Lonesome Pine	C. Ken Dodd (1965)
4. Funky Moped / Magic Roundabout	D. Monty Python (1991)
5. Funky Gibbon / Sick Man Blues	E. Des O'Connor (1968)
6. Mad Passionate Love	F. Mike Harding (1975)
7. Tears	G. The Goodies (1975)
8. Right Said Fred	H. Windsor Davies & Don Estelle (1975)
9. Ernie (The Fastest Milkman in the West)	J. Jasper Carrott (1975)
10. I Pretend	K. Freddie Starr (1974)
11. The Rochdale Cowboy	L. Vic Reeves & The Wonder Stuff (1991)
12. Don't Jump Off The Roof Dad	M. Smokie feat Roy 'Chubby' Brown (1995)
13. Whispering Grass	N. Charlie Drake (1961)
14. It's You	P. Russ Abbott (1984)
15. My Boomerang Won't Come Back	Q. Fred Wedlock (1981)
16. You Need Hands / Tulips From Amsterdam	R. Bernard Bresslaw (1958)
17. D.I.V.O.R.C.E.	S. Max Bygraves (1958)
18. Always Look on the Bright Side of Life	T. Bernard Cribbins (1962)
19. Oldest Swinger In Town	U. Laurel & Hardy with the Avalon Boys (1975)
20. Living Next Door To Alice (Who the F**k is Alice)	V. Tommy Cooper (1961)

All Shook up

ANAGRAMS

Elvis Songs

Can you find 10 Elvis Presley hits?

1. APOLLO HUSK	6. DENTURE SNORTER
2. OUIJA SHERLOCK	7. HOMOGENOUSLY ORIENTATE
3. ANDY WOW	8. HOWEY UNDER FOOT
4. DAM MAINLY SNOWY	9. ERRS UNDER
5. HOT TEETHING	10. INVESTOR OWNER

COMEDY AND MUSIC CAN MIX ANSWERS: *1L, 2P, 3U, 4J, 5G, 6R, 7C, 8T, 9B, 10E, 11F, 12V, 13H, 14K, 15N, 16S, 17A, 18D, 19Q, 20M.* **ELVIS PRESLEY SONGS ANAGRAMS ANSWERS:** *1. All Shook Up; 2. Jailhouse Rock; 3. Way Down; 4. Always On My Mind; 5. In the Ghetto; 6. Return to Sender; 7. Are You Lonesome Tonight?; 8. The Wonder of You; 9. Surrender; 10. It's Now or Never.*

THE BARRON KNIGHTS are a British humorous pop rock group. Formed in Leighton Buzzard, Bedfordshire in 1959. Began as a straight pop group playing English dance halls before going to Hamburg, Germany. Came to fame in 1964 with Call Up the Groups (Parts 1 and 2), parodying a number of current pop groups. 7 further hits followed (5 Top 10 hits).

1. What was the band's name when they formed in 1959?
A) Once a Knight   B) Knights of the Round Table   C) Knights in Shining Armour

2. Which famous rock bassist wrote that the Barron Knights were the first group he saw with an electric bass, inspiring him to take up the instrument?
A) Bill Wyman   B) Paul McCartney   C) John Paul Jones

3. In 1963 the Barron Knights were a support act on The Beatles' Christmas show and then toured with both The Beatles and The Rolling Stones. True or False?

4. On their first hit, Call Up the Groups, a number 3 UK hit, what Dave Clark Five song was parodied as *Boots and Blisters*?

5. In 1967, the group released the single *Lazy Fat People*, a satirical song written by which top rock musician of the time?
A) Hank Marvin   B) Rick Parfitt   C) Pete Townshend

6. *An Olympic Record* was the band's 5th Top 40 hit in October 1968. How long did the group then have to wait for their next hit?   A) 10 years   B) 9 years   C) 8 years

7. For studio recordings the Barron Knights often brought in session musicians as required, including in 1968 a then unknown Elton John. True or False?

8. The Barron Knights only success across the Atlantic was a minor hit, *The Topical Song*. What Supertramp song was parodied in this song?

9. On the day Elvis passed away, the Barron Knights performed a new number in Tenby, South West Wales. The reaction was fantastic, so within days they recorded which No. 7 hit?   A) A Taste of Aggro   B) Live in Trouble   C) Agadoo

10. Where in the world did the Barron Knights perform twice for British soldiers?
A) Iraq   B) The Falkland Islands   C) Afghanistan

How many of these acts had a UK Number one record?

Janet Jackson, Bon Jovi, Shania Twain, Guns N' Roses, Dolly Parton, Bruce Springsteen, Bob Marley, Aerosmith, The Carpenters , Billy Fury, Marty Wilde, The Who, The Smiths, The Cure, Ramones, Joy Division, Bob Dylan, Bjork, Radiohead, Pulp, Johnny Cash, Beastie Boys, Depeche Mode, Tina Turner, The Ronettes, Swinging Blue Jeans, Morrissey, Green Day, Texas, Foo Fighters, The Eagles, Martha & The Vandellas, Sheryl Crow, MC Hammer, The Pointer Sisters, The Sex Pistols, James, Ultravox, The Stranglers, Yazoo, Ricky Nelson, Cyndi Lauper, Jackson Five, The Floaters.

THE BARRON KNIGHTS ANSWERS: *1. B) Knights of the Round Table; 2. A) Bill Wyman; 3. True; 4. Bits and Pieces; 5. C) Pete Townshend (The Who); 6. B) 9 years; 7. True; 8. The Logical Song; 9. B) Live in Trouble; 10. B) The Falkland Islands.*
UK NUMBER ONES ANSWER: *Just The Floaters (One hit wonders in 1977 with Float On).*

JOHN BARRY formed the **JOHN BARRY SEVEN** in 1957. They had 6 Top 40 hits before John Barry moved into film music, initially James Bond films. Two further Bond linked hits followed as the John Barry Orchestra. After numerous personnel changes including involvement by Bobby Graham, Dave Richmond and Alan Bown, the band eventually folded in 1963.

1. *Hit and Miss* was a 1960 Top 10 UK hit for the John Barry Seven. For which popular BBC music show was it the theme tune?

2. Barry was employed by EMI from 1959 -1962, arranging for its singers. Who was the main artiste for whom he arranged a string of hits, as well as composing songs and scores for movies starring the singer?

3. Who was lead guitarist in the JB7, renowned for the James Bond Theme, that is featured in every Bond film?   A) Jimmy Page   B) Big Jim Sullivan   C) Vic Flick

4. In 1960 the John Barry Seven had a battle with The Ventures for chart supremacy with which instrumental number, eventually getting to No. 11 to The Ventures No. 8?

5. Barry won five Academy Awards, including which 1966 film about an orphaned lion cub starring Bill Travers and Virginia McKenna?

6. In 1999 what award was bestowed upon John Barry at Buckingham Palace for his services to music?

7. Barry was honoured with a BAFTA Fellowship award at The Orange British Academy Film Awards in 2005. True or False?

8. What instrument did John Barry play in the John Barry Seven?
A) Bass   B) Trumpet   C) Drums

9. With which 1990 American epic Western film, starring, directed, and produced by Kevin Costner did Barry win the Academy Award?

10. John Barry was never enamoured about writing individual songs, however he did write *We Have All the Time in the World*, a 1990 #3 UK hit, for which musical legend?   A) Louis Armstrong   B) Frank Sinatra   C) Bing Crosby

CATS RULE

THE WORLD

WHO HAD THESE HIT SONGS?
1. Year of the Cat (1977)
2. Cool For Cats (1979)
3. Stray Cat Strut (1981)
4. The Cat Crept In (1974)
5. Wild Cat (1960)
6. Walking My Cat Named Dog (1966)
7. Honky Cat (1972)
8. Cleopatra's Cat (1994)
9. Cat People (Putting Out Fire) (1982)
10. Black Cat (1990)

JOHN BARRY ANSWERS: *1. Juke Box Jury; 2. Adam Faith; 3. C) Vic Flick; 4. Walk Don't Run; 5. Born Free; 6. O.B.E.; 7. True; 8. B) Trumpet; 9. Dances With Wolves; 10. A) Louis Armstrong.* **CATS RULE THE WORLD ANSWERS:** *1. Al Stewart; 2. Squeeze; 3. Stray Cats; 4. Mud; 5. Gene Vincent; 6. Norma Tanega; 7. Elton John; 8. Spin Doctors; 9. David Bowie; 10. Janet Jackson.*

DAME SHIRLEY BASSEY, DBE - *Born in Tiger Bay, Cardiff, she began performing as a teenager in 1953. In January 1959, Bassey was the first Welsh person to have a No. 1 UK single. Known for her expressive voice and for recording 3 James Bond theme songs. Had 28 Top 40 hits (+1 with Bryn Terfel) and 20 Top 40 albums. In 2000, Bassey was appointed a Dame Commander of the Order of the British Empire (DBE) for services to the performing arts. In 1977, she received the Brit Award for Best British Female Solo Artist.*

1. Shirley Bassey's first hit was a cover of *The Banana Boat Song* which reached number one in 1957. True or False?

2. Despite her success in the UK, Bassey has had just one Top 10 hit in the US. A No. 8 in 1967, with which song that ironically only reached No. 21 in the UK?
A) Something   B) Goldfinger   C) Tonight

3. Which US President invited Bassey to appear at a Washington gala celebrating his second year in office?   A) Jimmy Carter   B) George Bush   C) John F Kennedy

4. Shirley's first #1 came at the beginning of 1958. What was the song?
A) As I Love You   B) Kiss Me Honey Honey Kiss Me   C) With These Hands

5. In 2009 Bassey released her first studio album of original compositions in 30 years. Songs on the album were written specifically for Bassey by renowned writers including Rufus Wainwright, KT Tunstall, Gary Barlow, the Pet Shop Boys and the Manic Street Preachers. What was the album called?
A) The Performance   B) The Girl From Tiger Bay   C) Get the Party Started

6. Name the three James Bond theme songs featuring Shirley Bassey.

7. "The minute you walked in the joint, I could see you were a man of distinction". The opening lyrics to which Bassey signature song from *Sweet Charity*?

8. Which song from Lionel Bart's *Oliver* took Bassey to No. 2 in the UK in 1960?

9. For which TV show was Bassey surprised, firstly in November 1972 by Eamonn Andrews at Heathrow Airport, and in January 1993 by Michael Aspel at her curtain call at the Royal Albert Hall?

10. In 1997, Bassey's *History Repeating* reached number one on the UK Dance Chart and number 10 on the US Dance Chart. Which electronic music duo wrote it?

WHO HAD HITS SINGING ABOUT THE WEATHER?

1. Sunshine On A Rainy Day (No. 4 in 1991)
2. Rain or Shine (No. 2 in 1986)
3. Blame It on the Weatherman (No. 1 in 1999)
4. Sandstorm (No. 8 in 1996)
5. Weather With You (No. 7 in 1992)
6. Candle in the Wind '97 (No. 1 in 1997)
7. It's Raining Men (No. 3 in 1984)
8. Thunder in the Mountains (No. 4 in 1981)
9. Skiing in the Snow (No. 12 in 1975)
10. It's Gonna Be A Cold Cold Christmas (No. 4 in 1975)

DAME SHIRLEY BASSEY ANSWERS: 1. False (it reached No. 8, Harry Belafonte's version was No. 2); 2. B) Goldfinger; 3. C) John F Kennedy; 4. A) As I Love You; 5. A) The Performance; 6. Goldfinger, Diamonds Are Forever, Moonraker; 7. Big Spender; 8. As Long As He Needs Me; 9. This Is Your Life; 10. Propellerheads. **WEATHER FORECAST ANSWERS:** *1. Zoe; 2. Five Star; 3. B*Witched; 4. Cast; 5. Crowded House; 6. Elton John; 7. Weather Girls; 8. Toyah; 9. Wigan's Ovation; 10. Dana.*

THE BAY CITY ROLLERS were a Scottish pop rock band known for their worldwide teen idol popularity in the 1970s. They have been called the 'tartan teen sensations from Edinburgh'. The group's line-up had many changes over the years, but the classic line-up during its heyday included guitarists Eric Faulkner and Stuart Wood, singer Les McKeown, bassist Alan Longmuir, and drummer Derek Longmuir. They notched up 12 Top 40 singles in the UK including 2 number ones and 7 other top 10 hits. Also 5 Top 20 albums including 2 number ones.

1. Derek Longmuir threw a dart at a map of the US, landing first on Arkansas. A second dart landed near Bay City, Michigan. That's how their name was chosen. True or False?

2. The Rollers had a completely distinctive style of dress. What was it?
A) Bell bottomed trousers   B) Tartan trousers and scarves   C) Overalls

3. The band's manager was a former big band leader and influential local band and club manager. Who was he?   A) Ian Mitchell   B) Tam Parton   C) Gregory Ellison

4. How did the Rollers travel to the Radio 1 fun day at Mallory Park and who accompanied them?   A) Monster Truck with Sweet   B) Hot Air Balloon with the Osmonds   C) Speedboat with the Wombles

5. After signing with Bell Records, the Rollers first hit was what song?
A) Keep on Dancing   B) Remember (Sha-La-La-La)   C) Shang-a-Lang

6. Derek Longmuir retired from the music industry in 1981. For what career did he then train?   A) Nurse   B) Physiotherapist   C) Teacher

7. *Bye Bye Baby* was their first No. 1 hit in 1975. It was followed by a second chart topper. What was it?   A) Money Honey   B) Give a Little Love   C) Shang-a-Lang

8. What was the name of the Rollers own TV Programme ?

9. Who was the lead singer of the Bay City Rollers, during their most successful period in the 1970s, that sadly died of a combination of natural causes in 2021?

10. In 2016, which record label, a subsidiary of Sony, paid an out of court settlement to some of the band members over unpaid royalties?   A) Arista   B) Bell   C) Epic

Motown Records is an American record label owned by the Universal Music Group. It was founded by Berry Gordy Jr. as Tamla Records on January 12, 1959. In the 1960s Tamla Motown, produced a style of soul music with mainstream pop appeal.

1. The Temptations sang "I've got sunshine on a cloudy day / When it's cold outside / I've got the month of May." Name the hit?

2. Who had their only UK No. 1 with Reach Out I'll Be There?

3. Which singing trio featured Cindy Birdsong between 1967 and 1972?

4. Which act were first to have I Heard It Through the Grapevine, written by Norman Whitfield and Barrett Strong, released in 1966? (No. 1 in US, No. 47 in UK)

5. The song War, by Norman Whitfield and Barrett Strong, is an obvious anti-Vietnam War statement. First recorded by The Temptations, who had a No.3 hit in the UK with the song?

6. Which Stevie Wonder hit is the UK's official top Motown single, with sales of 1.1 million?

THE BAY CITY ROLLERS ANSWERS: *1.True; 2. B) Tartan trousers and scarves; 3. B) Tam Parton; 4.C) Speedboat with the Wombles; 5. A) Keep on Dancing; 6. A) Nurse; 7. B) Give a Little Love; 8. Shang-a-Lang; 9. Les McKeown; 10. A) Arista.*
MOTOWN MAGIC ANSWERS: *1. My Girl; 2. The Four Tops; 3. The Supremes; 4. Gladys Knight & The Pips; 5. Edwin Starr; 6. Superstition.*

When you look back at this decade we had a real treat from all genres of music. Try this 90s music trivia quiz, covering all sorts of great sounds from that memorable era!

1. Which US TV series had *I'll Be There For You* by The Rembrandts, a big hit in both 1995 & 1997, as its theme?

2. *Smells Like Teen Spirit* was a No. 7 hit in 1991 for which grunge band?

3. Which *Quadrophenia* actor featured as narrator on *Parklife* by Blur in 1994?

4. Which Madonna song was the world's biggest selling single of 1990, selling over 6 million copies and topping the charts in more than 30 countries?

5. Who is known for the 1990's hit songs *Cornflake Girl*, *Pretty Good Year* and *Professional Widow*?

6. Name the lead singer of the band, No Doubt on their 1997 No.1, *Don't Speak*.

7. Marshall Bruce Mathers is better known by his stage name. Who is he?

8. What was the title of Coolio's hit from the soundtrack of *Dangerous Minds*?

9. What was the best selling single of the entire decade of the 1990s, a tribute song that was a re-write of a 1974 / 1988 hit by the same artist?

10. Which 1996 Danny Boyle black-comedy film ended with Underworld's No. 2 chart hit *Born Slippy*?

11. 'Chilli' Thomas, Tionne 'T-Boz' Watkins, Lisa 'Left Eye' Lopes were members of which R&B girl group?

12. *Hard Knock Life (Ghetto Anthem)* featuring a sample from the musical *Annie*, was a hit for which rapper?

13. Which 90s dance craze originated from a 1996 No. 2 hit by Los Del Mar?

14. What did Baz Luhrmann say that *Everybody's Free To Wear* in his No.1 hit in Jun 1999?

15. *Jagged Little Pill* was the title of the debut album from which Canadian singer?

16. "I've known a few guys who thought they were pretty smart, But you've got being right down to an art". Lyrics from which No. 3 from 1999?

17. Pulp released their iconic single *Common People* in 1995, but from which UK city do the band originate?

18. What famous boy band were formed in 1993 by Irish manager Louis Walsh?

19. Who was the lead guitarist in The Stone Roses?

20. In 1995, which Bacharach-David-Dixon song, formerly a 1961 US hit for The Shirelles, was the first Beatles single to enter the UK charts for 12 years?

21. The clip art on the right represents a song title from 1997 Name the song and the singer!

BACK TO THE 90's ANSWERS: *1. Friends; 2. Nirvana; 3. Phil Daniels; 4. Vogue; 5. Tori Amos; 6. Gwen Stefani; 7. Eminem; 8. Gangsta's Paradise; 9. Candle in the Wind 1997; 10. Trainspotting; 11. TLC; 12. Jay-Z; 13. Macarena; 14. Sunscreen; 15. Alanis Morrisette; 16. That Don't Impress Me Much; 17. Sheffield; 18. Boyzone; 19. John Squire; 20. Baby It's You; 21. Torn by Natalie Imbruglia.*

THE BEACH BOYS are an American rock band, formed in Hawthorne, California, in 1961. The original lineup was brothers Brian, Dennis, and Carl Wilson, their cousin Mike Love, and friend Al Jardine. Distinguished by their vocal harmonies, adolescent-oriented themes, and musical ingenuity, they were one of the most influential acts of the rock era. The Beach Boys recorded 29 Top 40 singles in the UK, including two with other acts, 2 No. 1's and 11 other Top 10 hits. Additionally they achieved 26 Top 40 Albums listings with 2 number ones and 12 other top 10 successes.

1. Which Beach Boys album, originally meant for a James Bond film, is considered to be one of the best rock albums of all time?
A) Smiley Smile   B) Surfin' U.S.A.   C) Pet Sounds

2. Complete these lyrics from the Beach Boys first UK Top 10 hit *I Get Around*. "I'm getting bugged driving up and down this same old strip, I gotta find a new place where … …. … …"   A) The kids are hip   B) I can chill and sip   C) My friends can sit

3. Which of the original Beach Boys is deaf in one ear?

4. The only woman featured in the Beach Boys played keyboards on their 1972 tour. Who was she?   A) Pat Benatar   B) Toni Tennille   C) Linda Ronstadt

5. Which future country star was a Beach Boy in 1964/5, playing bass as well as being a prolific session guitarist?

6. Where is the monument, the Beach Boys Historic Landmark (below), located?
A) Hawthorne, California   B) Nashville, Tennessee   C) Orlando, Florida

7. Which two members hated each other, so much so that they eventually had a restraining order that kept them apart?

8. Which Beach Boys song is Paul McCartney's favourite, having the power to make him feel quite emotional?   A) Good Vibrations   B) Kokomo   C) God Only Knows

9. Which of the Beach Boys sadly drowned?
A) Dennis Wilson   B) Carl Wilson   C) Al Jardine

10. With whom did the Beach Boys cover *Fun Fun Fun* in 1996, reaching No. 24 in the UK charts?   A) The Fat Boys   B) Status Quo   C) The Surfaris

GOD ONLY KNOWS
Written by Brian Wilson & Tony Asher

I may not always love you,
But long as there are stars above you,
You never need to doubt it,
I'll make you so sure about it,
God only knows what I'd be without you.

If you should ever leave me,
Though life would still go on, believe me,
The world could show nothing to me,
So what good would living do me,
God only knows what I'd be without you.

THE BEACH BOYS ANSWERS: *1. C) Pet Sounds; 2. A) The kids are hip; 3. Brian Wilson; 4. B) Toni Tennille (Captain & Tennille); 5. B) Glen Campbell; 6. A) Hawthorne, California; 7. Dennis Wilson and Mike Love (despite being cousins); 8. C) God Only Knows; 9. A) Dennis Wilson; 10. B) Status Quo.*

THE BEATLES *were an English rock band, formed in Liverpool in 1960, whose best-known line-up comprised John Lennon, Paul McCartney, George Harrison and Ringo Starr. They are regarded as the most influential band of all time and were integral to the development of 1960s counterculture and popular music's recognition as an art form. The Beatles had 30 Top 40 hits, including 38 Top 10 hits -16 of No.1's. The Beatles also had 26 Top 40 albums, many were successfully re-released. Of those, 14 were number ones and 23 reached the Top 10. John, Paul, Ringo & George feature later in the book.*

1. Why did George Martin make the Beatles re-record *Please Please Me*?
A) Drumming was substandard   B) It was too slow   C) The lyrics were too explicit

2. Who was the only non-member of the Beatles to receive a performance credit on a record?   A) Billy Preston   B) Eric Clapton   C) Ravi Shankar

3. Which Beatle led the way on the Abbey Road zebra crossing?

4. John Lennon and Paul McCartney sang backing vocals on which Rolling Stones Top 10 single?   A) I Wanna Be Your Man   B) Not Fade Away   C) We Love You

5. The 1967 double A-side *Strawberry Fields Forever / Penny Lane* was the first Beatles single since *Love Me Do (1962)* not to reach No.1. What kept it at No. 2?
A) This Is My Song - Petula Clark   B) Edelweiss - Vince Hill   C) Release Me - Engelbert Humperdinck

6. When Ringo was hospitalised with tonsillitis on the eve of the Australasian tour in 1964, who replaced him on drums?   A) Pete Best   B) Jimmie Nicol   C) Andy White

7. What was The Beatles working title of the song *Yesterday*?
A) Fried Eggs   B) Scrambled Eggs   C) Hard-boiled Eggs

8. What was the first single by a former Beatle to reach No. 1 in the UK?

9. What Beatles album was Phil Spector brought in to salvage?
A) Let It Be   B) Help!   C) White Album

10. What was the Beatles' first single to sell a million copies?
A) Love Me Do   B) Can't Buy Me Love   C) She Loves You

11. To what did John Lennon change his middle name?
A) Winston   B) Peace   C) Ono

12. Why did the BBC ban *I Am the Walrus*?   A) Drug references
B) Use of the word 'knickers'   C) Use of the words 'pornographic priestess'

13. Which Beatles song has inspired the most cover versions?
A) Yesterday   B) Let It Be   C) Something

14. Which of the following celebrities did **NOT** appear on the cover of *Sgt. Pepper's Lonely Hearts Club Band*?   A) Marilyn Monroe   B) Edgar Allan Poe   C) Cliff Richard

15. What item from the *Sgt. Pepper's Lonely Hearts Club Band* album cover was auctioned for £670,000 in 2008?   A) French Horn   B) Bass Drum   C) Guitar

THE BEATLES ANSWERS: 1. B) It was too slow; 2. A) Billy Preston; 3. John; 4. C) We Love You; 5. C) Release Me - Engelbert Humperdinck; 6. B) Jimmie Nicol; 7. B) Scrambled Eggs; 8. My Sweet Lord by George Harrison; 9. A) Let It Be; 10. C) She Loves You; 11. C) Ono; 12. B) and C) Use of 'knickers' and 'pornographic priestess' in the lyrics; 13. A) Yesterday; 14. C) Cliff Richard; 15. B) Bass Drum (with a hand-written letter from Sir Peter Blake authenticating Joe Ephgrave artwork).

THE BEAUTIFUL SOUTH *were an English pop rock group formed in 1988 by Paul Heaton & Dave Hemingway, former members of The Housemartins, who performed lead and backing vocals. Other band members were Sean Welch (bass), Dave Stead (drums) and Dave Rotheray (guitar). Three female lead vocalists featured: Briana Corrigan (1988-92), Jacqui Abbott (1994-2000) and Alison Wheeler (2003-7). The band notched up 18 Top 40 singles, including a No. 1 and 5 other Top 10 hits. In the 20th century the band had seven Top 10 albums, including three No.1's. Sold around 15 million records worldwide.*

1. The first album released by The Beautiful South in the UK included the number one single *A Little Time*. What was the album's title?
A) Choke   B) From Hull to Eternity   C) Welcome to the Beautiful South

2. Which 1989 No. 2 hit opened with these lyrics? "I love you from the bottom, of my pencil case, I love you in the songs, I write and sing"
A) 36D   B) Good As Gold   C) Song For Whoever

3. The vast majority of all Beautiful South songs are written by the same two band members- Paul Heaton and which other member?
A) Dave Rotheray   B) Sean Welch   C) Dave Hemingway

4. How many UK singles were released from the 1998 album *Quench* and made the Top 20?   A) 2   B) 3   C) 4

5. The second Beautiful South album *Choke* had 11 tracks. One was a great instrumental. What was the track called?
A) Apache   B) The Rising of Grafton Street   C) To Hull and Back

6. The album *Blue Is The Colour* included a number 8 single for which the lyrics had to be altered as they included the 'F' word. What was the song?
A) Don't Marry Her   B) Rotterdam   C) Blackbird on the Wire

7. With which of the band's former singers did Paul Heaton performed from 2011, with the pair notching up 4 hit albums?

8. Who released a first 'solo' album on Proper Music, *The Life of Birds*, in 2010?

9. 2004's album *Golddiggas, Headnodders and Pholk Songs*, was an album of unusually arranged cover tunes. Which song from Grease was included?

10. The final Beautiful South album was released on 15 May 2006. What is it called?
A) Goodbye   B) Superbi   C) The Cat Loves the Mouse

LYRICS FROM BEAUTIFUL SOUTH SONGS - BUT WHICH ONES?

1. When he's at my gate, with a big fat eight, You wanna see the smile on my face *(1998)*

2. And the women tug their hair, Like they're trying to prove it won't fall out *(1996)*

3. Just like that murder in '73, Just like that robbery in '62 *(1989)*

4. Think of you with pipe and slippers, think of her in bed *(1996)*

5. Got one note to last all week, I'll carry on regardless *(1994)*

THE BEAUTIFUL SOUTH ANSWERS: *1. A) Choke; 2. C) Song For Whoever; 3. A) Dave Rotheray; 4. 3 (Perfect 10 (No.2), Dumb (No. 16), How Long's A Tear Take To Dry (No. 12), (The Table reached No. 47); 5. B) The Rising of Grafton Street; 6. A) Don't Marry Her; 7. Jacqui Abbott; 8. Dave Rotheray; 9. You're the One That I Want; 10. B) Superbi.*
BEAUTIFUL SOUTH LYRICS ANSWERS: *1. Perfect 10; 2. Rotterdam; 3. You Keep It All In; 4. Don't Marry Her; 5. Good as Gold (Stupid as Mud).*

THE BEE GEES *were a group formed in 1958, featuring brothers Barry, Robin, and Maurice Gibb. They were especially successful as a popular music act in late 1960s / early 1970s. Later prominent in the disco era in mid-to late 1970s. The trio sang recognisable, three-part tight harmonies; The Bee Gees wrote all of their own hits, as well as writing and producing several major hits for other artists. Recorded 37 Top 40 hits from 1967-1998, including 4 number ones and 15 other Top 10 songs. 14 Top 40 albums including a number one and 10 other Top 10 successes.*

1. On which island were the Gibb brothers all born?

2. What was the title of the Bee Gees' first No 1 single in the UK?
A) Tragedy   B) Night Fever   C) Massachusetts

3. Why was the band's seven week tour of the US cancelled in 1968?   A) Robin collapsed with nervous exhaustion   B) Air crew strike   C) They were denied visas

4. What year were the Bee Gees inducted into the Rock 'n' Roll Hall of Fame?
A) 1997   B) 1987   C) 1977

5. The title of the Bee Gees' first hit in 1967 referenced a fictional mining disaster in which state?   A) New Mexico   B) New Jersey   C) New York

6. For which major musical film did Barry Gibb write and co-produce the title track?
A) Xanadu   B) Grease   C) Rocky Horror Picture Show

7. Which 1983 Top 10 romantic duet was penned by the Bee Gees; who sung the song, usually associated with country music legends?

8. In 2018 what honour did Prince Charles bestow upon Barry Gibb?

9. What inspired the Gibb brothers to write the lyrics for *Stayin' Alive*?   A) A Daily Mail story   B) Words on Robin's Concorde ticket   C) A line from The Godfather

10. What is the song *I've Gotta Get a Message to You* about?   A) A 'Dear John' letter   B) A man awaiting execution   C) A love letter

SAVE A LIFE WITH THE AID OF THE BEE GEES!

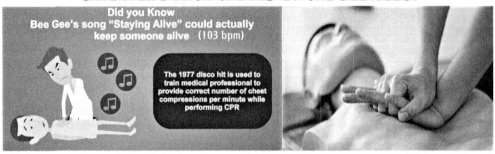

Did you Know
Bee Gee's song "Staying Alive" could actually keep someone alive (103 bpm)

The 1977 disco hit is used to train medical professional to provide correct number of chest compressions per minute while performing CPR

Begin CPR: *Place one hand on top of the other in the centre of the chest then push hard and fast. Use your body weight to give compressions at least 2 inches deep at a rate of at least 100 per minute. Tip: If counting the compressions is too tough, try compressing to the beat of the '70s disco hit Stayin' Alive (103 bpm).*

THE BEE GEES ANSWERS: *1. Isle of Man; 2. C) Massachusetts; 3. A) Robin collapsed with nervous exhaustion; 4. A) 1997; 5. C) New York; 6. B) Grease (performed by Frankie Valli); 7. Islands in the stream by Dolly Parton & Kenny Rogers; 8. He was Knighted; 9. B) Words on Robin's Concorde ticket; 10.B) A man awaiting execution.*

The 1980s saw the emergence of electronic dance music and new wave, also known as Modern Rock. Disco fell out of fashion in the early 80's, genres such as post-disco, Italo disco, Euro disco, and dance-pop became popular. Rock music remained in vogue. Soft rock, glam metal, thrash metal, shred guitar with heavy distortion, pinch harmonics, and whammy bar abuse were in. Also adult contemporary, quiet storm, and smooth jazz. In the late 1980s, glam metal became the largest, most commercially successful brand of music worldwide.

1. What was the biggest selling single of the 80s in the UK?

2. What was the theme song for the 1982 film, *Rocky III* which got to number one?

3. In 1980, which British ska band sang about their *Baggy Trousers*?

4. Mick Jagger and David Bowie had a No.1 hit together with which song in 1985?

5. Lyrics: "Loving would be easy if your colours were like my dreams" Name the hit.

6. Cyndi Lauper peaked at No. 2 with her biggest hit in 1988. What was its title?

7. MTV was launched in 1981, what was the first video shown featuring Buggles?

8. *What's Love Got To Do With It* was a No. 3 for Tina Turner in 1988. It was co-written by which former Cliff Richard guitarist and half of a hit making 1970s duo?

9. Who wrote and sang *9 to 5* as well as starring in the film of the same name?

10. What song from the soundtrack of *Batman* did Prince write and take to No. 2?

11. Which act was the most charted British female singer of the 1980s with 17 hits?

12. Which Motown legend had a No.1 with the Bee Gees written *Chain Reaction*?

13. In what year did The Bangles reach No.1 in the UK with *Eternal Flame*?

14. *The Power of Love* by Huey Lewis and The News was the theme to which blockbuster film of 1985?

15. Kylie Minogue equalled Little Eva's 1962 No. 2 with what 1988 hit?

16. Lyrics: "Tommy used to work on the docks, union's been on strike, He's down on his luck, it's tough, so tough" Name the 1986 number four hit.

17. Bobby G, Cheryl Baker, Mike Nolan and Jay Aston made up which band?

18. Which singer-songwriter with 32 Top 40 hits has the real name Michael Barratt?

19. Dexy's Midnight Runners' 1980 No.1 is a tribute to whom?

20. ZTT Records was one of the most prominent record companies in the 80s. Do you know what ZTT stands for?

BACK TO THE 80's ANSWERS: *1. Do They Know It's Christmas? – Band Aid; 2. Eye of the Tiger - Survivor; 3. Madness; 4. Dancing in the Street; 5. Karma Chameleon by Culture Club; 6. Girls Just Want To Have Fun; 7. Video Killed the Radio Star; 8. Terry Britten and Graham Lyle (Gallagher & Lyle); 9. Dolly Parton; 10. Batdance; 11. Kim Wilde; 12. Diana Ross; 13. 1989; 14. Back to the Future; 15. The Locomotion; 16. Livin' On a Prayer by Bon Jovi; 17. Bucks Fizz; 18. Shakin' Stevens; 19. Geno Washington (soul singer); 20. Zang Tuum Tumb.*

PAT BENATAR *(born January 10, 1953), is an American rock singer-songwriter and four-time Grammy Award winner. In the US, she has had two multi-Platinum albums, five Platinum albums, and 15 Billboard Top 40 singles. Pat Benatar's polished mainstream pop/rock made her a top female vocalist in the early '80s. She came on like an arena rocker with her power chords, tough sexuality, and powerful vocals, her music was straight pop/rock. In the UK she has had limited chart success, but she has recorded 9 Top 100 hits with just 3 of those reaching the Top 40. Additionally Pat Benatar has had 9 Top 100 albums with just one Top 10 success.*

1. Mike Chapman and Nicky Chinn produced records for Pat Benatar. They also produced dozens of other artists. Which of the following was **NOT** produced by one of them? A) Joan Jett & The Blackhearts   B) The Sweet C) Suzi Quatro

2. During the recording session for which 1985 hit song did Pat learn that she was pregnant with her first child? A) Love Is A Battlefield B) We Belong C) One Love

3. In 1979 Pat had a huge success with the album In the *Heat of the Night* on which she sung which Smokie No. 3 hit from 1975? A) Living Next Door to Alice B) I'll Meet You at Midnight C) If You Think You Know How To Love Me

4. What is the name of the club where Pat got discovered?
A) Catch a Rising Star B) Roaring Twenties C) The Apollo Theatre

5. Pat lived in Virginia before she became famous. How did she earn a living?
A) Waitress B) Bank Teller C) Assembly Line Worker

6. Pat performed in which original musical by Harry Chapin which really transformed her into a rock singer? A) Lucky Times B) The Zinger C) Story Songs

7. On *Precious Time*, her first album to chart in the UK, the final track is taken from The Beatles *White Album*. What is the 'loud and dirty rocker'?

8. On her 1980 album, *Crimes of Passion*, Pat memorably covered Kate Bush's self-penned debut hit from 1978. What is the song?

9. Lyrics: "This bloody road remains a mystery, this sudden darkness fills the air. What're we waitin' for? Won't anybody help us, what're we waitin' for?" Name the song from 1985. A) Invincible B) Shadows of the Night C) We Belong

10. Pat sung the film theme for *Invincible*, which tennis legend was the subject of the 1975 film? A) Jimmy Connors B) Martina Navratilova C) Billie Jean King

POP PUZZLES
CAN YOU NAME THESE 5 SONGS?

A.   B.   C.   D.   E.

PAT BENATAR ANSWERS: *1. A) Joan Jett & The Blackhearts; 2. B) We Belong; 3. C) If You Think You Know How To Love Me; 4. A) Catch a Rising Star; 5. B) Bank Teller; 6. B) The Zinger; 7. Helter Skelter; 8. Wuthering Heights; 9. A) Invincible; 10.C) Billie Jean King.*
POP PUZZLES ANSWERS: *A) Another Brick in the Wall; B) Everybody Hurts; C) A Kiss From a Rose; D). Back in the USSR; E) Shakin' All Over.*

GEORGE BENSON *(born January 10, 1943) is an American guitarist, singer, and songwriter. He began his professional career at the age of 19 as a jazz guitarist. Benson first came to prominence in the 1960s, playing soul jazz with Jack McDuff and others. He then launched a successful solo career, alternating between jazz, pop, R&B singing, and scat singing. Had 14 Top 40 hits in the UK singles chart, including 3 Top 10 records. 11 Top 40 albums, including a number one and 4 more Top 10 successes. In 1990, Benson was awarded an Honorary Doctorate of Music from the Berklee College of Music.*

1. George Benson had his first single chart success in the UK in 1975. What song reached number 30 in the charts?
A) Supership   B) Nature Boy   C) The Greatest Love of All

2. *The Other Side of Abbey Road* is a 1970 studio album by George Benson, covering songs from the Beatles' 1969 album *Abbey Road*. True or False?

3. In 1977 Benson sung the theme song to which bio-pic based upon Muhammad Ali's life. What was the film's title?   A) Ali   B) The Greatest   C) The Fighter

4. Benson made it into the top ten in 1980 with a Rod Temperton song, *Give Me the Night*. Which famous record producer worked with George on the song?
A) Quincy Jones   B) Ted Templeton   C) Phil Spector

5. With which jazz trumpeter did George Benson play in his early career?
A) Louis Armstrong   B) Al Hirt   C) Miles Davis

6. On which album does George sing *On Broadway* with Clifford and the Rhythm Rats?   A) Kermit Unpigged   B) Listen Up   C) Read My Licks

7. The title track of a 1972 Benson album is a cover of which Jefferson Airplane hit, written by Grace Slick and featuring a piano solo by Herbie Hancock?
A) We Built This City   B) White Rabbit   C) Nothing's Gonna Stop Us Now

8. Which Benson song entered the UK Singles Chart on 24 September 1983 and reached a peak position of number 7, his highest UK chart placing?
A) Lady Love Me (One More Time)   B) Love X Love   C) In Your Eyes

9. Benson describes his music as focusing more on love and romance, due to his commitment to his family and devout beliefs - to what religion?

10. George Benson guested on a 1985 album, *Stay Tuned*, a studio album by which famous guitarist?   A) Hank Marvin   B) Chet Atkins   C) Duane Eddy

FIRST LETTER, LAST LETTER

The last letter of answer 1 is the first letter of answer 2 and so on....
1. Electropop duo comprising Andy Bell and Vince Clarke.
2. Rodgers & Hammerstein II song, a No. 2 hit for Vince Hill in 1967.
3. Jerry Lordan wrote 3 instrumental and one vocal hit for The ....?
4. A one hit wonder with Bobby Girl in 1962.
5. Pre-10cc No. 2 hit for Godley, Creme and Stewart in 1970.
6. Neunundneunzig Luftballons in English was a 1984 No.1 for whom.
7. Nicole won Eurovision for Germany in 1982 with this song.

GEORGE BENSON ANSWERS: *1. A) Starship; 2. True; 3. B) The Greatest; 4. A) Quincy Jones; 5. C) Miles Davis; 6. A) Kermit Unpigged; 7. B) White Rabbit; 8. C) In Your Eyes; 9. Jehovah's Witnesses; 10. B) Chet Atkins.*
FIRST LETTER, LAST LETTER ANSWERS: *1. Erasure; 2. Edelweiss; 3. Shadows (Apache, Wonderful Land, Atlantis, I Met a Girl); 4. Susan Maughan; 5. Neanderthal Man (by Hotlegs); 6. Nena (99 Red Balloons); 7. A Little Peace (last letter 'e' completes the circle).*

CHUCK BERRY (October 18, 1926 – March 18, 2017) was an American singer, songwriter and guitarist who pioneered rock and roll. Nicknamed the 'Father of Rock and Roll', he refined and developed rhythm and blues into the major elements that made rock and roll distinctive. Writing lyrics that focused on teen life and consumerism, and developing a music style that included guitar solos and showmanship, Berry was a really major influence on subsequent rock music. Just 11 Top 40 hits including a novelty number one and two more Top 10 hits. Also had 6 Top 20 albums.

1. Chuck's first recorded song, released May 21, 1955, was one of his many rock 'n' roll classics that never charted in the UK. What was it?
A) Roll Over Beethoven   B) Maybelline   C) Thirty Days (To Get Back)

2. True or False? Throughout his life, Berry was jailed twice, given a 6-month suspended prison sentence and was also found guilty of other offences.

3. *Johnny B. Goode* has proved to be a real R&R classic right up until the present day. However the only version to chart in the UK reached No. 35 in 1972. Who had the small hit?   A) Elvis Presley   B) Jerry Lee Lewis   C) Jimi Hendrix Experience

4. Which novelty song was ironically Chuck's biggest hit and a No.1 in the UK in 1972?   A) Speedy Gonzales   B) My Ding-A-Ling   C) Two Little Boys

5. What is the name of the famous on-stage trademark that Berry performed?
A) The duckwalk   B) The moonwalk   C) The electric slide

6. What year was Chuck elected to the Rock and Roll Hall of Fame?
A) 1966   B) 1976   C) 1986

7. The first Rolling Stones' single in 1963 was a remake of which Chuck Berry song?
A) Carol   B) Come On   C) Down the Road Apiece

8. What was Chuck's established nightclub in St. Louis called?
A) The Band   B) Berry's Place   C) Berry's Club Bandstand

9. What Chuck Berry song opens with the lyric - "Runnin' to-and-fro, hard workin' at the mill. Never fail in the mail..."?
A) Too Much Monkey Business   B) Almost Grown   C) No Particular Place To Go

10. Another Berry classic, *Sweet Little Sixteen*, only reached number 16 in the UK in 1958. Which other famous rocker had a small hit with the song four years later?
A) Elvis Presley   B) Little Richard   C) Jerry Lee Lewis

CAN YOU NAME THESE CHUCK BERRY SONGS FROM THE LYRICS?

1. "You could see that Pierre did truly love the mademoiselle".

2. "She's just got to have about half a million framed autographs".

3. "Oh, the engineers would see him sitting in the shade strumming with the rhythm that the drivers made".

4. "I remember the girl next door, We used to play house on the kitchen floor, She would be the queen, I would be the king".

5. "Well, I looked at my watch, it was 9:54 I said, "Rock ballerina, go, go".

CHUCK BERRY ANSWERS: *1. B) Maybelline; 2. True (he had a very chequered history); 3. C) Jimi Hendrix Experience; 4. B) My Ding-A-Ling; 5. A) The duckwalk; 6. C) 1986; 7. B) Come On; 8. C) Berry's Club Bandstand; 9. A) Too Much Monkey Business; 10. C) Jerry Lee Lewis.* **CHUCK BERRY LYRICS ANSWERS:** *1. You Never Can Tell; 2. Sweet Little Sixteen; 3. Johnny B. Goode; 4. My Ding-a-Ling; 5. Reelin' and Rockin'.*

DAVE BERRY *(born 6 February 1941 in Woodhouse, Sheffield, England) is an English rock singer and former teen idol of the 1960s. He performed a mixture of R&B, rock and pop ballads and was popular in Britain, and in Continental Europe, especially Belgium and the Netherlands, but had no commercial success in the US. He often hid behind the upturned collar of his leather jacket, or wrapped himself around, and effectively behind, the microphone lead. He has 7 Top 40 hits (and another got to No. 41), including 3 Top 10 successes. Dave Berry's original hits were recorded with his band, The Cruisers. Berry regularly used session musicians Jimmy Page, John Paul Jones, Big Jim Sullivan and Bobby Graham.*

1. Dave Berry's *Memphis Tennessee* got into the top 20 in 1963. It was a cover version of a song written and sung by which namesake?

2. The flip side of *Memphis Tennessee* was another cover version of an American song which reached number one in 1961 in the US, but failed to chart here. What was the song? A) Tossin' and Turnin' (by Bobby Lewis) B) Pony Time (by Chubby Checker) C) Mother-in-Law (by Ernie K. Doe)

3. His stage act drew on the work of Elvis Presley and Gene Vincent. It proved to be an inspiration for which 1970/80s glam rock singer?
A) Mike Berry B) Alvin Stardust C) Marc Bolan

4. Berry's second single was an Arthur Crudup rhythm and blues song, previously recorded by Elvis Presley. It sneaked into the Top 40. What was it's title?
A) Who's Been Foolin' You B) My Baby Left Me C) Keep Your Arms Around Me

5. Dave reached No. 5 in 1964 with *The Crying Game.* The song went on to be featured as the theme for a 1992 film with the same title. Berry's version did play on the soundtrack, but which singer's version was used as the main theme?

6. In 1965, Berry again reached No. 5 in the UK with Bobby Goldsboro's *Little Things.* The song was used in an advertisement campaign on British TV for which product? A) Cream cakes B) Insurance C) Andrex toilet paper

7. *This Strange Effect* was a minor 1965 hit for Dave. It reached No.1 in the Netherlands and Belgium, but only peaked at No.37 in the UK. Who wrote it?
A) Paul McCartney B) Ray Davies C) Donovan

8. Lyrics: "Who's the one who tied your shoe when you were young, and knew just when to come and see what you had done". The song was a third UK No. 5 for Dave Berry in 1966. What was its title? A) Mama Said B) Mama C) Mama's Song

9. Dave Berry regularly used top session musicians Jimmy Page, John Paul Jones, Big Jim Sullivan and Bobby Graham on his records. True or False?

10. What is Dave Berry's real name?
A) David Holgate Grundy B) Bernard Jewry C) Barry Green

THE CRYING GAME (Written by Geoff Stephens)
I know all there is to know about the crying game
I've had my share of the crying game
First there are kisses
Then there are sighs
And then, before you know where you are
You're sayin' goodbye

One day soon, I'm gonna tell the moon
About the crying game
And if he knows, maybe he'll explain
Why there are heartaches (Heartaches)
Why there are tears (So sad)
Then what to do to stop feeling blue
When love disappears

DAVE BERRY ANSWERS: *1. Chuck Berry; 2. A) Tossin' and Turnin' (by Bobby Lewis); 3. B) Alvin Stardust; 4. B) My Baby Left Me; 5. Boy George; 6. C) Andrex toilet paper; 7. B) Ray Davies (The Kinks); 8. B) Mama; 9. True; 10. A) David Holgate Grundy.*

MIKE BERRY & THE OUTLAWS (Mike Berry (born Michael Hubert Bourne, 24 September 1942) is an English singer and actor. The Outlaws were an English instrumental band that recorded in the early 1960s. Initially the band comprised: Billy Kuy, Bobby Graham, Chas Hodges, Reg Hawkins and others including Ritchie Blackmore, Billy Kuy and Mick Underwood followed. Mike Berry & The Outlaws had 3 Top 40 hits and Mike berry notched up two further Top 40 hits on his own. The Outlaws also had two singles that reached the Top 50 and backed several acts including Gene Vincent, Heinz and John Leyton. Mike also became a familiar face as an actor on TV.

1. Mike Berry and The Outlaws reached No. 24 in the charts with a tribute song, banned by the BBC for being morbid. What was the song's title?
A) Three Stars   B) Tribute To Buddy Holly   C) Tell Laura I Love Her

2. The Outlaws also had two minor hits. The first was a reworking of a classic. What was it called?   A) Swingin' Low   B) Ambush   C) Keep a Knockin'

3. In 1963 Mike Berry had his biggest hit, reaching number six in the charts. What was the title of the song?   A) Don't You Think Its Time   B) Will You Love Me Tomorrow   C) It's Just a Matter of Time

4. The Outlaws bass guitarist Chas Hodges found fame in a duo who had a string of hits in the 1970 and 1980s. Can you name them?

5. 17 years since his last hit, Mike Berry had a Top 10 success in 1980 with a cover version of a romantic song, produced by Chas Hodges. What was the song?
A) Portrait Of My Love   B) Memories   C) Sunshine Of Your Smile

6. The Outlaws were the backing band on which 1961 chart-topper?
A) Shakin' All Over   B) Good Timin'   C) Johnny Remember Me

7. Mike Berry appeared as Mr. Dick Lucas in three series of the BBC sit-com *Are You Being Served*. True or False?

8. Robert Duke wrote many of The Outlaws instrumentals. Who was he?
A) Joe Meek   B) George Meek   C) Norrie Paramor

9. Which Weston-super-Mare born guitarist, prolific in creating guitar riffs and classically influenced solos with Deep Purple, had a spell in the Outlaws?

10. In 1979, Mike Berry was cast as Mr. Peters, along with Jon Pertwee and Una Stubbs, in what popular children's TV show?

NAME THAT GIRL!
COMPLETE THE LYRICS WITH THE MISSING NAME

1. You picked a fine time to leave me ...., four hungry children and a crop in the field. (1977)

2. ...., Picks up the rice in the church where a wedding has been. (1966)

3. .... tries but misunderstands, She's often inclined to borrow somebody's dreams 'til tomorrow (1967)

4. Your voice is soft like summer rain, And I cannot compete with you .... (1976)

5. So before they come to break down the door, Forgive me ...., I just couldn't take anymore (1968)

6. My .... is like the stars that please the night, The sun that makes the day (1968/1986)

7. Hey .... is it cold, In your little corner of the world (1985)

8. .... is not my lover, She's just a girl who claims that I am the one (1983)

9. All I wanna do when I wake up in the morning is see your eyes, ... (1983)

10. 'Cause the life that lived is dead, And the wind screams, ... (1967)

MIKE BERRY & THE OUTLAWS ANSWERS: 1. B) Tribute To Buddy Holly; 2. A) Swingin' Low; 3. A) Don't You Think Its Time; 4. Chas & Dave; 5. C) Sunshine Of Your Smile; 6. C) Johnny Remember Me (John Leyton); 7. False, he was Mr. Bert Spooner who replaced Mr. Lucas (Trevor Bannister); 8. A) Joe Meek (their record producer); 9. Ritchie Blackmore; 10. Worzel Gummidge. **NAME THAT GIRL ANSWERS:** 1. Lucille - Kenny Rogers; 2. Eleanor Rigby - Beatles; 3. Games (Emily) Plays - Pink Floyd; 4. Jolene - Dolly Parton; 5. Delilah - Tom Jones; 6. Barry Ryan / Damned - Eloise; 7. Nikita - Elton John; 8. Billie Jean - Michael Jackson; 9. Rosetta - Toto; 10. The Wind Cries (Mary) - Jimi Hendrix.

BIG COUNTRY are a Scottish rock band formed in Dunfermline, Fife, in 1981. Popularity peaked in the early to mid 1980s, but retain a cult following. Their music incorporated Scottish folk and martial music styles. They engineered their guitar-driven sound to evoke the sound of bagpipes, and other traditional folk instruments. Big Country comprised Stuart Adamson (vocals/guitar/keyboards), Bruce Watson (guitar/mandolin/sitar/vocals), Tony Butler (bass guitar/vocals) and Mark Brzezicki (drums/percussion/vocals). The band had 15 Top 40 hits with 4 songs reaching the Top 10. Also had 9 Top 40 albums including a number one and three other Top 10 hits.

1. What was the name of Big Country's first UK hit, reaching number ten?
A) In a Big Country   B) Chance   C) Fields of Fire (400 Miles)

2. An early line-up of Big Country was five-piece, featuring Peter Wishart (later of Runrig) on keyboards. He became an MP in 2001. What party does he represent?
A) SNP   B) Conservative   C) Green

3. What was the name of Big Country's debut album which got to number three in the UK album charts in 1983?   A) Steeltown   B) The Crossing   C) The Seer

4. Stuart Adamson was previously a member of which Scottish punk rock and new wave band who had some chart success?   A) Skids   B) The Alarm   C) Fear

5. Big Country's highest placed single was number 7 in 1986. What was its title?
A) Chance   B) Wonderland   C) Look Away

6. On what record label did Big Country have their success in the 80's?
A) Vertigo   B) Mercury   C) Cherry Red

7. On the 1986 album title song, *The Seer*, which reached number two, who provided the haunting backing vocals?   A) Kate Bush   B) Lulu   C) Sheena Easton

8. Lyrics: "A score of years this line has run, Above the crests that drown the sun, A mile high the turbines turned, The stokers sweat the monkeys burned". In what number 17 hit from 1984 will you find these words?
A) Wonderland   B) Where the Rose Is Sown   C) East of Eden

9. Known as a Scottish band, how many members of the classic Big Country line up (shown above) were actually born in Scotland?

10. In which US state was Stuart Adamson found dead in a room at the Best Western Plaza Hotel on 16 December 2001?   A) Florida   B) Hawaii   C) California

How many of these TV stars can you name? They had mixed longevity in the music world!

BIG COUNTRY ANSWERS: 1. C) Fields of Fire (400 Miles); 2. A) SNP; 3. B) The Crossing; 4. A) Skids; 5. C) Look Away; 6. B) Mercury; 7. A) Kate Bush; 8. C) East of Eden; 9. None of them - Adamson (Manchester), Watson (Canada), Butler (London), Brzezicki (Slough); 10. B) Hawaii (He had committed suicide by hanging).
SINGING SOAP STARS ANSWERS: A. Will Mellor; B. Nick Berry; C. Adam Rickitt; D. Martine McCutcheon; E. Kylie Minogue; F. Matthew Marsden; G. Anita Dobson; J. Bill Tarmey; K. Natalie Imbruglia; L. Jason Donovan.

MR. ACKER BILK *(Bernard Stanley Bilk, MBE, born Pensford, Somerset on 28 January 1929; died Bath, Somerset on 2 November 2014), known professionally as Acker Bilk, was a British clarinettist and vocalist known for his breathy, vibrato-rich, lower-register style, and distinctive appearance; goatee, bowler hat, striped waistcoat. Had UK's biggest selling single of 1962, 10 Top 40 singles, including 5 Top 10 hits, 6 with Paramount Jazz Band. The second UK artist to have a US No.1. Also, 12 Top 40 albums, including a #1 and five other Top 10 successes.*

1. In 1962, Acker became only the second British artiste to have a number one single in the US. Backed by the Leon Young String Chorale, what was the title of the hit?

2. Bilk got his nickname Acker from Somerset slang for friend or mate. True or False?

3. After National Service, Bilk joined his uncle's business and qualified in what trade?
A) Mechanic B) Blacksmith C) Farmer

4. Acker played with friends on the Bristol jazz circuit, but in 1951 he moved to London to play with whose established jazz band?
A) Kenny Ball B) Chris Barber C) Ken Colyer

5. Bilk's band developed a distinctive style and appearance, complete with striped waistcoats and bowler hats, and became part of the trad jazz boom. Their first hit in 1960 reached No. 5. What was the title, a pun on their home county?

6. In 1961 Acker Bilk and His Paramount Jazz Band appeared on which prestigious televised variety show? A) Royal Variety Performance B) Sunday Night at the London Palladium C) The 6.5 Special

7. Acker had composed a melody and named it after his daughter, but was asked to change it to *Stranger on the Shore* for a TV series of the same name. What was it originally called? A) Gertrude B) Maisie C) Jenny

8. Bilk was only the second British artist to have a No. 1 single in the US. Who was the first? A) Cliff Richard B) Vera Lynn C) Lord Rockingham's XI

9. After 13 years Acker Bilk returned to the singles charts in 1976 with a No. 5 hit . It was again with the Leon String Chorale. What was its title?
A) Aria B) A Taste of Honey C) Lonely

10. Bilk was part of a consortium which took over the Oxford Cheetahs speedway team in 1972. They were re-branded as what after the takeover?
A) Bulldogs B) Strangers C) Rebels

WHAT'S THE NEXT LINE?

FAMOUS LYRICS TO COMPLETE AND NAME THE SONG!

1. You can check out any time you like...

2. I think I'm gonna be sad, I think it's today, yeah...

3. Just one look and I can hear a bell ring ...

4. No April rain, no flowers bloom...

5. I want to be your lover

BJORK (Björk Guðmundsdóttir OTF; Icelandic: born 21 November 1965) is an Icelandic singer, songwriter, composer, record producer, actress and DJ. Over her four-decade career, she has developed an eclectic musical style that draws on influences and genres including electronic, pop, experimental, trip hop, alternative, classical, and avant-garde music. Björk gained international recognition as the lead singer of the alternative rock band the Sugarcubes until 1992. 14 Top 40 hits between 1993-1999, including 3 Top 10 hits. 3 albums between 1993 and 1997 all reached the Top 4.

1. In which city was Bjork born and raised?   A) Akureyri   B) Reykjavik   C) Selfoss

2. Which Massive Attack producer was responsible for producing the majority of the songs on Björk's first album *Debut* in 1993 ?
A) Nellee Hooper   B) Miles Gregory   C) Andrea Larusso

3. At six, Björk was enrolled at Barnamúsíkskóli school, where she studied:
A) Jazz   B) Ballet   C) Classical music

4. In what country did Björk record the album *Homogenic*, a number 4 hit in the UK?
A) England   B) Wales   C) Spain

5. Björk starred in a 1990 Icelandic medieval fantasy drama film based on a Brothers Grimm fairy tale. What was the film's title?   A) The Juniper Tree   B) The Mouse, the Bird, and the Sausage   C) Rapunzel

6. On 12 September 1996, Scotland Yard intercepted a letter bomb sent to Björk's London home by fan Ricardo López before he killed himself. What was packed into the bomb?   A) Ball-bearings   B) Nails   C) Sulphuric acid

7. In 1999, Björk wrote and produced the music score for the a musical drama film, she also played the lead role, Selma, and won the Best Actress Award for her role. What was the title of the film?   A) Alarm Call   B) Dancer in the Dark   C) Selma

8. Björk had her biggest UK hit with a song first recorded by Betty Hutton in 1948. What was the song title?   A) It's Oh So Quiet   B) Hyperballad   C) Isobel

9. According to bjork.com, how did she get the scar on her right palm?
A) Ran into a lamp post   B) Slipped on some ice   C) Was bitten by a dog

10. Bjork's favourite animal is?   A) Killer Whale (Orca)   B) Swan   C) Polar Bear

CLIFF'S FULL CIRCLE

10 QUESTIONS ABOUT CLIFF RICHARD:

LAST LETTER OF Q1 ANSWER IS 1st LETTER OF Q2 ANSWER AND SO ON UNTIL LAST LETTER OF Q10 ANSWER IS 1st LETTER OF Q1 ANSWER.

1. Cliff's debut hit, a No. 2 in 1958, regarded as a Rock 'n' Roll classic. (4,2)

2. HOMEMADE RAFTER (5,3,1,5) is an anagram of a No. 3 hit from 1961.

3. No. 23 theme song for Trainer, a 1991 BBC series about horse racing. (4,2,4)

4. A 1959 film satirising the music industry starred Cliff as Bert Rudge. (8,5)

5. A 1965 No.12 hit recorded in Nashville with The Jordanaires. (2,2,4)

6. A 1981 No.2 song. Cover version of a 1961 Shep & the Limelites song. (6,4)

7. She Means Nothing To Me & All I Have To Do Is Dream. Duets with Phil ......

8. A 1961 British film musical and the No.1 title song, The .... (5,4)

9. Cliff Richard's backing band changed their name from The Drifters to The ....

10. Cliff's No.13 anthem in 1971 featuring Brian Bennett's Orchestra. (4,1,4,2,7)

BJORK ANSWERS: 1. B) Reykjavik; 2. A) Nellee Hooper; 3. C) Classical music; 4. C) Spain; 5. A) The Tree; 6. C) Sulphuric acid; 7. B) Dancer in the Dark; 8. A) It's Oh So Quiet; 9. A) Ran into a lamp post; 10. C) Polar Bear. **CLIFF'S FULL CIRCLE:** 1. Move It; 2. Theme For A Dream; 3. More To Life; 4. Expresso Bongo; 5. On My Word; 6. Daddy's Home; 7. Everly; 8. Young Ones; 9. Shadows; 10. Sing A Song Of Freedom.

CILLA BLACK *(Priscilla Maria Veronica White OBE, 27 May 1943 – 1 August 2015), was an English singer, television presenter, actress, and author. She had 11 top 10 hits, including 2 No. 1's, on the UK Singles Chart between 1963 and 1971, and an additional eight hits that made the top 40. Additionally had 5 Top 30 albums, 3 reaching the Top 10. Brian Epstein managed Cilla, as his only female client, from 1963. Epstein introduced Black to George Martin who signed her to Parlophone Records. Her debut single was written by Lennon & McCartney.*

1. Cilla's first hit only reached a modest No. 35 in the UK charts. Written by her friends, John Lennon and Paul McCartney, what was the song?
A) Love Of The Loved   B) Ain't She Sweet   C) It's For You

2. Black's second single in 1964 was a Burt Bacharach–Hal David composition *Anyone Who Had A Heart*. The song was originally written for which singer?
A) Cher   B) Dionne Warwick   C) Mama Cass

3. Cilla again hit the jackpot with another No.1 in 1964. The original Italian song was titled *Il mio mondo*, what was its English title?
A) What a Wonderful World   B) We Are the World   C) You're My World

4. Lennon & McCartney wrote several songs for Black, but only three were singles. The second of those, *It's For You*, followed Cilla's two number ones. What was its highest chart placing?   A) No. 2   B) No. 5   C) No. 7

5. Cilla reached No. 2 with *You've Lost That Lovin' Feelin'*, but for once she was outdone by a rival version that topped the charts. Who sung the No. 1 version?
A) The Everly Brothers   B) The Righteous Brothers   C) Elvis Presley

6. Cilla Black revealed that she was asked to appear in a 1969 film playing the part of Michael Caine's girlfriend, but negotiations fell through. What was the film?
A) Alfie   B) The Italian Job   C) Get Carter

7. Brian Epstein died in 1967. Who took over as Cilla's manager?

8. In 1968 Black was given her own TV show, *Cilla*. Paul McCartney wrote the theme song which reached number 8 in the singles charts. What was the song?
A) Step Inside Love   B) Blind Date   C) Conversations

9. Black's 1971 single *Something Tells Me (Something's Gonna Happen Tonight)* was used as the soundtrack for which brand of chocolates in 2006?
A) Cadbury's Milk Tray   B) Lindt   C) Ferrero Rocher

10. Cilla Black was honoured with a statue in Liverpool (see above). It is located in which famous street, near the site of the original Cavern Club?

HIT SONGS WITH VOWELS REMOVED  *Complete the five listed song titles*	1. DS YR CHWNG GM LS TS FLVR (N TH BDPST VRNGHT) 2.TH DY THT CRLY BLLY SHT DWN CRZY SM MCGH 3. TSY BTSY TN WN YLLW PLKDT BKN 4. WHT D YU WNT T MK THS YS T M FR 5. D D NYTHNG FR LV (BT WNT D THT)

CILLA BLACK ANSWERS: *1. A) Love Of The Loved; 2. B) Dionne Warwick; 3. C) You're My World; 4. C) No. 7; 5. B) The Righteous Brothers; 6. B) The Italian Job; 7. Bobby Willis; 8. A) Step Inside Love; 9. C) Ferrero Rocher; 10. Mathew Street.* **HIT SONGS WITH VOWELS REMOVED ANSWERS:** *1. Does Your Chewing Gum Lose It's Flavour (On The Bedpost Overnight?)by Lonnie Donegan; 2. The Day That Curly Billy Shot Down Crazy Sam McGhee by The Hollies; 3. Itsy Bitsy Teenie Weenie Yellow Polka Dot Bikini by Brian Hyland (1960) and Bombalurina (1990); 4. What Do You Want To Make Those Eyes At Me For by Emile Ford & Checkmates (1959) and Shakin' Stevens (1987); 5. I'd Do Anything For Love (But I Won't Do That) by Meat Loaf.*

MARY J BLIGE *(born January 11, 1971 in Fordham Hospital in the borough of the Bronx, New York City.) She is an American singer, songwriter and actress. Pursuing a musical career, Blige spent a short time in a Yonkers band named Pride. Her career began in 1991 when she was signed to Uptown Records. Blige is noted for having a tough girl persona and streetwise lyrics. She had 17 UK Top 40 singles (4 of them collaborations) between 1993 and 1999. She also had two Top 10 albums. Blige also made a successful transition to both TV and movies.*

1. In 1988, what song did Mary cover for a demo tape that was passed to the CEO of Uptown Records? A) Chaka Khan - I Feel For You B) Janet Jackson - Let's Wait A While C) Anita Baker - Caught Up In The Rapture

2. What title was bestowed upon her after selling two million copies of *What's The 411?* A) The Queen of Soul B) The Queen of R&B C) The Queen of Hip Hop Soul

3. What job did Mary do before her singing career started?
A) Waitress B) Directory Assistant C) Hair Stylist

4. Mary has her own record label, what is it called?
A) Matron Records B) Matrix Records C) Matriarch Records

5. Blige gained her first two Grammy nominations and won the 1996 Best Rap Performance by a Duo or Group for her collaboration with whom on *I'll Be There for You / You're All I Need to Get By* - a Top 10 UK hit?
A) Method Man B) Jay-Z C) Snoop Dogg

6. *Love Is All We Need*, *Everything* and *Missing You* were all UK hit singles for Mary in 1997. Which of them got highest in the charts?

7. In 1995 Blige recorded a cover version of Aretha Franklin's US smash *(You Make Me Feel Like) A Natural Woman*. The song was only a minor hit for Franklin in the UK, a week after her death 51 years later! Who wrote the song?
A) Carole King and Gerry Goffin B) Aretha Franklin C) Burt Bacharach

8. *Seven Days* was a 1998 hit for Mary, featuring George Benson. The next year she got to No. 4 in the UK with another duet with the song *As*, a Stevie Wonder song. Who sung with her? A) U2 B) George Michael C) Wyclef Jean

9. In 1996 Mary used scenes from the movie *Waiting to Exhale* in her music video for her hit *Not Gon' Cry*. True or False?

10. The 1997 No. 6 hit *Everything* contains a sample of which Hachidai Nakamura song that was a Top 10 hit in 1963 for both Kenny Ball and Kyu Sakamoto?

MATCH THE YEAR WITH THE HIT

1. Too Much - SPICE GIRLS	A. 1990
2. Mr. Blobby - MR. BLOBBY	B. 1991
3. I Have A Dream / Seasons in the Sun - WESTLIFE	C. 1992
4. Stay Another Day - EAST 17	D. 1993
5. Saviours Day - CLIFF RICHARD	E. 1994
6. Goodbye - SPICE GIRLS	F. 1995
7. I Will Always Love You - WHITNEY HOUSTON	G. 1996
8. Bohemian Rhapsody / These Are the Days Of Our Lives - QUEEN	H. 1997
9. Earth Song - MICHAEL JACKSON	J. 1998
10. 2 Become 1 - SPICE GIRLS	K. 1999

1990's Christmas Number Ones

A ROUND OF GENERAL POP MUSIC TRIVIA

1. Johnny Cash's first live album released on Columbia Records on May 6, 1968 was recorded in which prison?

2. What links Oasis, The Hollies and Take That?

3. A copy of which 1964 Frank Sinatra song was played on a Sony TC-50 portable cassette player on the Apollo 10 mission which orbited the Moon?

4. Which Canadian singer won the 1988 Eurovision Song Contest for Switzerland?

5. In which year were Michael Jackson, Prince, Madonna and Belinda Carlisle born?

6. What were Adam and the Ants two number one UK hits in 1981?

7. Which group had their first UK No.1 with the song *Fairground* in 1995?

8. With which band do you associate Irish vocalist Neil Hannon?

9. James Galway had a 1968 hit with *Annie's Song*. What instrument did he play?

10. A) Which band featured a famous model as a mermaid on rocks near South Stack, Anglesey on the cover of their album *Siren*? B) Who was the model?

11. In which year did The Who's unique and eccentric drummer Keith Moon die?

12. Jimi Hendrix got to No. 5 in 1968 with *All Along the Watchtower*. Who wrote it?

13. Which US group were originally called Carl and the Passions?

14. The man who gave The Rolling Stones their name died in the swimming pool at Cotchford Farm, East Sussex the former home of A.A. Milne. Who was he?

15. Who is known as 'The Boss'?

16. Which 1998 Robbie Williams chart-topper had these lyrics?: "We've got stars directing our fate, And we're praying it's not too late"

17. In 1977 *Pearl's a Singer* was Elkie Brooks' first UK hit. Pearl was the nickname of which rock, soul and blues mezzo-soprano singer?

18. What Glam Rock band had 15 consecutive hits between 1973 and 1976, culminating in a cover of Bill Withers' *Lean on Me*?

19. Which 1990s Waterboys song missed out on the charts but was a No. 33 hit 13 years later for Ellie Goulding?

20. Which fashion model had her only chart single, *Love and Tears*, at number 40 for just one week in September 1994?

MUSIC TRIVIA ANSWERS: *1. Folsom; 2. Originated in Manchester; 3. Fly Me To The Moon; 4. Celine Dion; 5. 1968; 6. Stand and Deliver and Prince Charming; 7. Simply Red; 8. The Divine Comedy; 9. Flute; 10. A) Roxy Music; B) Jerry Hall; 11. 1978; 12. Bob Dylan; 13. The Beach Boys; 14. Brian Jones (Rolling Stones); 15. Bruce Springsteen; 16. Millennium; 17. Janis Joplin; 18. Mud; 19. How Long Will I Love You?; 20. Naomi Campbell.*

BLONDIE *is an American rock band co-founded by singer Debbie Harry and guitarist Chris Stein. Pioneers in 1970s US new wave scene. Blondie disbanded in 1982 and Harry pursued a solo career whilst caring for sick partner Stein. Deborah Harry had 4 Top 40 hits, including one Top 10 success and 5 Top 40 albums, including 2 Top 10 hits. Reformed in 1997, with renewed success. Between 1978 and 1999 Blondie had 19 Top 40 singles, including 5 No.1's and 6 other Top 10 hits. Blondie notched up 9 Top 40 albums including two No. 1's and 6 other Top 10 recordings.*

1. Who was the original drummer for Blondie?
A) Billy Murcia   B) Gary Valentine   C) Clem Burke

2. In early 1977, Blondie opened for Iggy Pop and which rock superstar on a tour?
A) David Bowie   B) Elton John   C) Bob Dylan

3. On MTV, what Blondie 1981 No. 5 hit single is often referred to as the first rap video?   A) One Way Or Another   B) Call Me   C) Rapture

4. What was the title of Deborah Harry's debut solo album released before Blondie's last 80's album, *The Hunter*?   A) Kon Kan   B) KooKoo   C) Iko Iko

5. Which Blondie hit was the theme song on the 1980 *American Gigolo* film soundtrack?   A) Call Me   B) The Tide Is High   C) Atomic

6. What life threatening illness did Blondie guitarist Chris Stein contract in 1982?
A) Sickle Cell Anaemia   B) Pemphigus Vulgaris   C) HIV

7. Apart from being a dancer and a secretary at the BBC in New York, Deborah Harry was a waitress at which famous club?
A) Avant Gardner   B) Playboy Club   C) Nowadays

8. Which Blondie single topped the U.K. charts exactly twenty years after *Heart of Glass*?   A) Maria   B) Good Boys   C) Union City Blue

9. Who was Blondie's original bassist?
A) Leigh Fox   B) Gary Valentine   C) Frank Infante

10. Which Blondie songs contains a verse in French? "Hey, j'ai vu ton mec avec une autre fille, Il semblait dans un autre monde, cours te cacher, ……"

FILL IN THE GAPS IN THE TABLE ON THE RIGHT. EITHER THE SONG TITLE, THE ARTISTE OR THE YEAR THE SONG WAS ORIGINALLY A HIT

SONG TITLE	ARTISTE	YEAR
1. Winter Wonderland	…… ……	1958
2. Rock 'n' Roll Winter	Wizzard	…….
3. . ……. ….	David Essex	1982
4. …. ….. .. ……	Bangles	1988
5. A Winter's Tale	…..	1995
6. …………………..	Edgar Winter Group	1973
7. Winter in July	…. … ….	1991
8. …… ….. .. ….	Engelbert Humperdinck	1969
9. Winter	…. ….	1992
10. . …..	Ruby Winters	1977

BLONDIE ANSWERS: *1. C) Clem Burke; 2. A) David Bowie; 3. C) Rapture; 4. B) KooKoo; 5. A) Call Me; 6. B) Pemphigus Vulgaris; 7. B) Playboy Club; 8. A) Maria; 9. B) Gary Valentine; 10. Sunday Girl.* **SONGS OF WINTER ANSWERS:** *1. Johnny Mathis; 2. 1974; 3. A Winters Tale; 4. Hazy Shade of Winter; 5. Queen; 6. Frankenstein; 7. Bomb the Bass; 8. Winter World of Love; 9. Tori Amos; 10. I Will.*

BLUR *are an English rock band. Formed in London in 1988, the group consists of singer Damon Albarn, guitarist Graham Coxon, bassist Alex James and drummer Dave Rowntree. Blur helped popularise the Britpop genre and achieved mass UK popularity, aided by a chart battle with rival band Oasis. The band had 21 Top 40 hits between 1991 and 1999. That included 2 No. 1's and 11 more Top 10 hits. Also 6 Top 20 albums with 4 No. 1's and another reached No. 3. Success continued in to the 21st century.*

1. What were the band called immediately before changing their name to Blur?
A) Circus   B) Seymour   C) Parklife

2. What was Blur's first UK number one record?
A) Girls and Boys   B) Parklife   C) Country House

3. True or False? Blur won four Brit Awards in 1995; Best Album for *Parklife*, Best Single, Best Video for *Parklife* and Best Band.

4. The band claim they wrote their second single, which reached No. 24, in just 15 minutes? What was the song title?   A) Bang   B) Pop Scene   C) For Tomorrow

5. The first Blur UK single in 1992 only reached number 48. What was the song?
A) Chemical World   B) For Tomorrow   C) She's So High

6. Which 1997 No. 5 song contains the lyrics "He said he once was that great game show performer"?   A) Song 2   B) On Your Own   C) MOR

7. What is drummer Dave Rowntree trained as?
A) Racing driver   B) Jockey   C) Pilot

8. For Blur's 1999 No. 11 hit *Coffee & TV*, what animated object was the star?
A) Screwdriver   B) Spoon   C) Milk carton

9. Which 1993 Blur album cover features a painting of the steam locomotive Mallard?
A) Parklife   B) The Great Escape   C) Modern Life Is Rubbish

10. The 1995 'Battle of Britpop' between Blur and Oasis arose as both bands released singles on the same day, the winner would become a media phenomenon.
A) What were the two singles involved, and ..... B) Which band won the 'battle'?

HIT SONG TITLES THAT USE (BRACKETS)

Fill in the missing (words)

1. (. ....) Satisfaction (Rolling Stones 1965)
2. (........... ...) I Do It For You (Bryan Adams 1991)
3. (... .....) Fight For Your Right (.. .....) (Beastie Boys 1987)
4. (.......) The Dock Of The Bay (Otis Redding 1968)
5. Bang A Gong (... .. ..) (T Rex 1971)
6. Ever Fallen In Love (.... ....)? (The Clash 1978)
7. Voodoo Child (...... ......) (Jimi Hendrix Experience 1968)
8. (......... ......) So Strong (Labi Siffre 1987)
9. I Wanna Dance With Somebody (... ....) (Whitney Houston 1987)
10. Sweet Dreams (... ....) (Eurythmics 1983)

BLUR ANSWERS: *1. B) Seymour; 2. C) Country House; 3. True; 4. A) Bang; 5. C) She's So High; 6. B) On Your Own; 7. C) Pilot; 8. C) Milk carton; 9. C) Modern Life Is Rubbish; 10. A) Blur's Country House and Oasis' Roll With It, B) Blur - 274,000 copies, Oasis - 216,000.* **BRACKETS ANSWERS:** *1. I Can't Get No; 2. Everything I Do; 3. You Gotta - To Party; 4. Sittin' On; 5. Get It On; 6. You Shouldn'tve; 7. Slight Return; 8. Something Inside; 9. Who Loves Me; 10. Are Made Of This.*

MICHAEL BOLTON *(Born Michael Bolotin, February 26, 1953), is is an American singer and songwriter. Originally performed in hard rock / heavy metal genres from mid-1970s to mid-1980s, both on his early solo albums and as lead singer with a band. He became better known for his series of pop rock ballads, recorded after a complete style change in the late 1980s. Had 17 Top 40 hits between 1990 and 1999, including 4 Top 10. Also recorded 9 Top 50 albums, including 5 Top 10. Sold more than 75 million records worldwide.*

1. What was the name of the hard rock band fronted by Michael Bolton from 1979 to 1980?   A) Blackjack   B) Aces and Eights   C) Trumps

2. In 1989, Bolton had an international top ten hit with which of his compositions that was originally covered in the US by Laura Branigan?
A) Power of Love   B) How Am I Supposed to Live Without You   C) Gloria

3. Michael Bolton had a No. 8 hit with a cover of which Percy Sledge song in 1991?
A) Warm and Tender Love   B) When a Man Loves a Woman   C) It Tears Me Up

4. In December 1991, Michael Bolton released the song *Missing You Now*. Who is the credited saxophonist on the hit?
A) Raphael Ravenscroft   B) Steve Gregory   C) Kenny G

5. Another hit single from Bolton's 1991 album *Time, Love & Tenderness* was *Steel Bars*. Who co-wrote the song with Michael?
A) Lionel Richie   B) Bob Dylan   C) Elton John

6. In 1992, Michael Bolton released an album of cover songs, *Timeless: The Classics*. Which Bee Gees song got to No.16 in the UK?
A) To Love Somebody   B) Massachusetts   C) Jive Talkin'

7. In 1997, Michael Bolton recorded *Go the Distance*. The song was featured in the end credits of which 1997 Walt Disney film?   A) Mulan   B) A Bug's Life   C) Hercules

8. "Baby, show me what you feel, Come to me, show me somethin' real, I need to know, I need you completely…."   Which Michael Bolton song includes these lyrics?

9. Who filed a lawsuit against Bolton, claiming his 1991 hit song *Love Is a Wonderful Thing* plagiarised their 1966 song of the same name?
A) Bee Gees   B) Isley Brothers   C) Contours

10. Bolton only reached No. 77 in the UK in 1987 with a fabulous cover of which Otis Redding song, that was otherwise a big worldwide hit?
A) (Sittin' On) The Dock of the Bay   B) My Girl   C) Try a Little Tenderness

Use the clues to find the songs that don't include their titles in the lyrics

MISSING TITLES — SONGS THAT DON'T INCLUDE THE TITLE IN THE LYRICS

1. Lyric: "Is this real life?" - A 1975 / 1991 Number One for Queen (8,8)

2. Lyric: "Ground Control to Number 5" - A hit for David Bowie in 1969 (5, 6)

3. Six hit versions of this song - 3 were No.1's, between 1955 & 1995 (8,6)

4. Lyric: "Load up on guns" - A Nirvana No. 7 in 1991 (6,4,4,6)

5. Lyric: "I read the news today, oh boy" - (Sgt. Pepper track) (1,3,2,3,4)

MICHAEL BOLTON ANSWERS: *1. A) Blackjack; 2. B) How Am I Supposed to Live Without You; 3. B) When a Man Loves a Woman; 4. C) Kenny G; 5. B) Bob Dylan; 6. A) To Love Somebody; 7. C) Hercules; 8. Can I Touch You… There; 9. B) Isley Brothers; 10. A) (Sittin' On) The Dock of the Bay.* **MISSING TITLES ANSWERS:** *1. Bohemian Rhapsody; 2. Space Oddity; 3. Unchained Melody; 4. Smells Like Teen Spirit; 5. A Day in the Life*

INSTRUMENTALS *are normally recordings without any vocals, although they may include some inarticulate vocals, such as shouted backup vocals in big band settings. Tracks are sometimes renderings, remixes of a corresponding release that features vocals, but they may also be compositions originally conceived without vocals. Down the years many such recordings have stormed the charts.*

20 INSTRUMENTAL HITS. JUST MATCH THE TITLE WITH THE ARTIST

TITLE	ARTISTES/YEAR
1. TOCCATA	A. RUSS CONWAY - *No. 1 in 1959*
2. STRANGER ON THE SHORE	B. EMERSON, LAKE AND PALMER - No. 2 in 1977
3. TEQUILA	C. ENNIO MORRICONE - *No. 2 in 1981*
4. WIPE OUT	D. PERCY FAITH ORCHESTRA - *No. 2 in 1960*
5. ON THE REBOUND	E. THE SHADOWS - *No. 1 in 1963*
6. GUITAR BOOGIE SHUFFLE	F. THE TORNADOS - *No. 1 in 1962*
7. ROULETTE	G. SIMON PARK ORCHESTRA - *No. 1 in 1973*
8. GREEN ONIONS	H. FLEETWOOD MAC - *No. 1 in 1968*
9. WALK DON'T RUN	J. THE CHAMPS - *No. 5 in 1958*
10. CHI MAI	K. FERRANTE & TEICHER - *No. 6 in 1961*
11. HAVA NAGILA	L. BERT WEEDON - *No. 10 in 1959*
12. TELSTAR	M. THE VENTURES - *No. 8 in 1960*
13. THEME FROM 'A SUMMER PLACE'	N. SKY - *No. 5 in 1980*
14. EXODUS	P. BOOKER T & MG's - *No. 7 in 1979*
15. FOOT TAPPER	Q. FLOYD CRAMER - *No.1 in 1961*
16. WHEELS	R. HAROLD FALTERMEYER - *No. 2 in 1985*
17. EYE LEVEL	S. MR. ACKER BILK - *No. 2 in 1961*
18. ALBATROSS	T. THE STRING-A-LONGS - *No. 8 in 1961*
19. FANFARE FOR THE COMMON MAN	U. THE SURFARIS - No. 5 in 1963
20. AXEL F	V. THE SPOTNICKS - *No. 13 in 1963*

What should appear in the fourth box?

SWEAR IT AGAIN	IF I LET YOU GO	FLYING WITHOUT WINGS	????

*WHAT A LOVELY TUNE! ANSWERS: 1N, 2S, 3J, 4U, 5Q, 6L, 7A, 8P, 9M, 10C, 11V, 12F, 13D, 14K, 15E, 16T, 17G, 18H, 19B, 20R. **FOURTH BOX ANSWER:** I Have A Dream / Seasons In The Sun - The sequence is the first 4 Westlife No.1 UK singles in 1999.*

BON JOVI *is an American rock band formed in 1983 in New Jersey. The original line up was singer Jon Bon Jovi, keyboardist David Bryan, drummer Tico Torres, guitarist Richie Sambora, and bassist Alec John Such. Other significant members are: Hugh McDonald, Dave Sabo and Phil X. Bon Jovi notched up 24 Top 40 singles in the UK, including 11 Top 10 hits. 6 Top 40 albums including 4 number ones and another Top 10 success. Jon Bon Jovi and Richie Sambora also had solo success.*

1. What is Jon Bon Jovi's real surname?   A) Bulsara   B) Bongiovi   C) Hernandez

2. Bon Jovi surprisingly have never had a UK No. 1 hit. What single reached No. 2 in 1994?   A) Please Come Home For Christmas   B) Dry County   C) Always

3. Name the city in which the European leg of the *I'll Sleep When I'm Dead Tour* opened in August 1993.   A) Berlin   B) Milton Keynes   C) Leipzig

4. In what year did Jon act as a painter in a credited role in *Moonlight and Valentino* starring Whoopi Goldberg and Elizabeth Perkins?   A) 1993   B) 1994   C) 1995

5. Jon Bon Jovi's first solo hit was in 1990. It reached No. 13 in the UK charts. Can you name the song?   A) Midnight in Chelsea   B) Blaze of Glory   C) Miracle

6. Why did Bon Jovi name their second, least successful, album *7800 Fahrenheit* ?

7. Bon Jovi like doing covers of songs. Which of these songs have they NOT covered?   A) Imagine   B) Fairytale of New York   C) Africa

8. Which Bon Jovi 1993 hit includes these lyrics: "Sitting here wasted and wounded, At this old piano, Trying hard to capture, The moment this morning I don't know"

9. Richie Sambora is colour blind? What colours does he have problems with? A) Red, blue, black   B) Red, green, brown   C) Green, orange, red

10. The first lineup change since Bon Jovi began happened in 1994. Who left the band?   A) Richie Sambora   B) David Bryan   C) Alec John Such

MATCH THE LEAD SINGER TO THE BAND

1. ALLAN CLARKE	A. AC/DC
2. KELLY JONES	B. STEREOPHONICS
3. RAY ENNIS	C. HOLLIES
4. FRAN HEALY	D. SUEDE
5. JOHN FOGERTY	E. FOREIGNER
6. BRIAN CONNOLLY	F. GEORGIA SATELLITES
7. LOU GRAMM	G. SWEET
8. BON SCOTT	H. TRAVIS
9. DAN BAIRD	J. RED HOT CHILI PEPPERS
10. BRETT ANDERSON	K. SWINGING BLUE JEANS
11. MARTI PELLOW	L. WET WET WET
12. ANTHONY KIEDIS	M. CREEDENCE CLEARWATER REVIVAL

BON JOVI ANSWERS: *1. B) Bongiovi (John Francis Bongiovi Jr.); 2. C) Always; 3. A) Berlin; 4. C) 1995; 5. Blaze of Glory; 6. It is the melting point of most rocks - being a rock band it seemed a cool idea!; 7. C) Africa; 8. Bed of Roses; 9. B) Red, green, brown; 10. C) Alec John Such.* **MATCH THE LEAD SINGER TO THE BAND ANSWERS:** *1C, 2B, 3K, 4H, 5M, 6G, 7E, 8A, 9F, 10D, 11L, 12J.*

BONEY M. *was a Euro-Caribbean vocal group created by Frank Farian in 1976, he was also the group's primary songwriter. Originally based in West Germany, the four original members of the official line-up were Liz Mitchell, Marcia Barrett, Maizie Williams & Bobby Farrell. The group was formed in 1976 and was popular in the disco era of the late 70s. Since the 1980s, various line-ups of the band have performed. 15 Top 40 hits were notched up, including 2 No. 1's and 8 other Top 10 hits. Also 7 Top 40 albums, including 3 No. 1's.*

1. The first Boney M single reached No. 6 in the UK, with founder Frank Farian providing the male voice parts. What was the song?
A) Daddy Cool B) Sunny C) Ma Baker

2. Why were Maizie William's and Liz Mitchelle's voices excluded from their recordings? A) They didn't want to record B) Frank Farian deemed them inadequate for recording C) They were contracted to another label

3. 1981. When the album *Boonoonoonoos* was finally released why was Bobby Farrell fired from the group? A) They didn't like his image) B) They wanted to be an all girl group C) He was unreliable

4. What was the title of the band's first major tour?
A) Daddy Cool Tour B) The Boney M. Tour C) The Black Beauty Circus

5. 1978 was the group's biggest year. A double A-sided single was a No. 1 UK smash. *Rivers of Babylon* was one side what was the other?
A) Painter Man B) Brown Girl in the Ring C) Ma Baker

6. What 1978 album was certified gold a year after its release in the UK?
A) Night Flight to Venus B) Oceans of Fantasy C) The Magic of Boney M.

7. *Hooray! Hooray! It's a Holi-Holiday* was a 1979 No. 3 UK hit. Upon which nursery rhyme was it based?

8. Boney M had a huge hit about a a friend and advisor of Tsar Nicholas II of Russia and his family, during the early 20th century. Who was the friend?
A) Dr. Zhivago B) Rasputin C) Yuri Gagarin

9. Christmas 1978 saw Boney M at No. 1 with a medley of two songs, *Oh My Lord* was a new song mixed with which former Harry Belafonte hit from 1957?
A) Island in the Sun B) Banana Boat Song C) Mary's Boy Child

10. After an 11 year absence from the UK Singles Chart, Boney M got to No. 7 in 1992 with a Megamix. The mix included every one of their Top 10 hits. True or False?

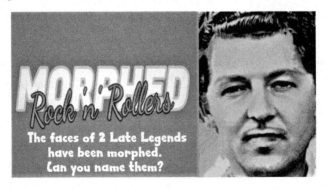

The faces of 2 Late Legends have been morphed. Can you name them?

BONEY M ANSWERS: *1. A) Daddy Cool; 2.B) Frank Farian deemed them inadequate for recording; 3. C) He was unreliable; 4. C) The Black Beauty Circus; 5. B) Brown Girl in the Ring; 6. A) Night Flight to Venus; 7. Polly Wolly Doodle; 8. B) Rasputin; 9. C) Mary's Boy Child; 10. False - does not include Daddy Cool, Belfast, Painter Man and Hooray Hooray It's A Holi-Holiday.* **MORPHED ROCK 'N' ROLLERS ANSWERS:** *Jerry Lee Lewis and Little Richard.*

THE BOOMTOWN RATS *are an Irish rock band originally formed in Dublin in 1975. Between 1977 and 1985, they had a series of Irish and UK hits. The group originally comprised Bob Geldof (vocals), Garry Roberts (lead guitar), Johnnie Fingers (keyboards), Pete Briquette (bass), Gerry Cott (rhythm guitar) and Simon Crowe (drums). The Boomtown Rats broke up in 1986, but reformed in 2013, without Fingers or Cott. Had 11 Top 40 entries including 2 No.1's and 3 other Top 10 hits. Also 6 Top 40 albums, including 4 Top 10 entries. Geldof was granted an honorary knighthood (KBE) in 1986 for charity work in Africa.*

1. The Boomtown Rats took their name from a gang featured in the book *Bound For Glory*. The autobiography of which folk singer?
A) Bob Dylan   B) Woody Guthrie   C) Tom Paxton

2. The Boomtown Rats first single *Looking After No.1* reached No. 11 in 1977. The same year The Rats toured the UK with which American band?
A) The Ramones   B) The Sex Pistols   C) Tom Petty and the Heartbreakers

3. Which band member was rarely seen in conventional clothing, appearing on TV, in videos and promotional pictures in his striped pyjamas!?
A) Simon Crowe   B) Pete Briquette   C) Johnnie Fingers

4. What was the title of The Boomtown Rats first UK number one?
A) Rat Trap   B) Like Clockwork   C) She's So Modern

5. Schoolgirl Brenda Spencer took a gun to her school, killing the principal, the school caretaker and injuring nine students. When asked why she had committed the atrocity, her reply inspired Bob Geldof to write which number one single?
A) Mary of the 4th Form   B) I Don't Like Mondays   C) Looking After Number One

6. In 1980 The Boomtown Rats had their last major hit, a No. 3 success. What was the fruit inspired song?   A) Apple Rocker   B) Raspberry Beret   C) Banana Republic

7. Bob Geldof played the part of Pink in the film adaption of which album?
A) The Wall   B) Give My Regards To Broad Street   C Quadrophenia

8. In 1984, Geldof and Midge Ure founded a charity supergroup to raise money for famine relief in Ethiopia. What was the name of the group of superstars?
A) Rockestra   B) Band Aid   C) Deep End

9. True or False? The Boomtown Rats were the opening act for Live Aid in 1984.

10. Bob Geldof had two solo Top 30 hits in the UK. The highest chart position he reached was No. 15 with the second hit. What was it called?   A) This Is The World Calling   B) The Great Song of Indifference   C) Comfortably Numb

HIT SONGS BRAIN TEASERS

Work out the song and the artistes

A) I ask you to refrain from remaining, on your feet, near myself by body of officers representing the civil authority of government.

B) A sugary infant, belonging to me by firearms & thorny plants.

C) Refrain from halting, the first person, immediately by a female monarch.

D) Hit a timepiece by hot glowing particles struck from a larger mass.

BOOMTOWN RATS ANSWERS: *1. B) Woody Guthrie; 2. C) Tom Petty and the Heartbreakers; 3. C) Johnnie Fingers; 4. A) Rat Trap; 5. B) I Don't Like Mondays; 6. C) Banana Republic; 7. A) The Wall; 8. B) Band Aid; 9. False (it was Status Quo); 10. B) The Great Song of Indifference.*
HIT SONGS BRAIN TEASERS: *A) Don't Stand So Close To Me by Police; 2. Sweet Child 'O Mine by Guns 'N' Roses; C) Don't Stop Me Now by Queen; D) Beat the Clock by Sparks.*
PREVIOUS PAGE MORPH: *Jerry Lee Lewis & Little Richard*

PAT BOONE (Born Patrick Charles Eugene Boone, June 1, 1934) is an American singer, composer, actor, writer, television personality, motivational speaker, and spokesman. Married Shirley Lee Foley when they were both 19, until her death in 2019. A highly successful pop singer during the 1950s and early 1960s, the only performer to rival the chart dominance of Elvis Presley in the US. He sold more than 45 million records, had 26 Top 40 hits, including a number one and 11 other Top 10 hits, ranging from Rock 'n' Roll to Novelty! Also had 4 Top 20 Albums. He appeared in many Hollywood and TV films.

1. Pat's first hit in the UK reached number 7. It was a cover of which song by Fats Domino? A) Blueberry Hill B) Ain't That a Shame C) Blue Monday

2. In 1956 Pat Boone had his only UK number 1 hit, a cover of a song by The Flamingos. What was the song?
A) Remember You're Mine B) Friendly Persuasion C) I'll Be Home

3. In 1957 Pat Boone appeared in a musical film, a remake of *Home in Indiana*, and he also had a UK number 7 hit with the title song. Can you name the film?

4. Pat Boone had a surprise No. 2 hit in 1962. Here are the opening few lines: "It was a moonlit night in old Mexico, I walked alone between some old adobe haciendas, Suddenly, I heard the plaintive cry of a young Mexican girl." Name the song.

5. In 1959, Boone was in a hugely successful science fiction adventure film. He had been reluctant to appear in it, but was given a percentage of the profits. What was the film? A) Journey to the Center of the World B) 20,000 Leagues Under the Sea C) Around the World in 80 Days

6. As a conservative Christian, Boone declined certain songs and movie roles that he felt might compromise his beliefs. Which female film star did he refuse to work with?

7. *Don't Forbid Me, Love Letters in the Sand, A Wonderful Time Up There* and *Speedy Gonzales*. What links these Pat Boone UK hits?

8. Boone played an American encyclopedia salesman Jack Robinson, who arrives at a dilapidated mansion in the English countryside belonging to the Marley family. The basic plot of which 1963 horror film that Boone filed in England?
A) The Horror Of It All B) The Main Attraction C) Never Put It In Writing

9. True or False? Pat Boone played Judas Iscariot in the epic film, *The Greatest Story Ever Told* in 1962.

10. Boone's last chart success was *Moody River* in 1962. What was its peak chart position? A) 2 B) 8 C) 12

1980s GROUPS
Solve the anagrams

1. RED SITARIST (4,7)
2. GABLES THEN (3,7)
3. ERNIE FROG (9)

4. RENEGADE SWOOP (1,1,1,10)
5. FROST SEAFARER (5,3,5)
6. AGHAST KINDLE (7,5)
7. FRED LAPPED (3,7)
8. HATCH LES (3,5)
9. SIX HUNDRED STRINGY MEN (5,8,7)
10. ADJUST SPIRE (5,6)

PAT BOONE ANSWERS: 1. B) Ain't That a Shame; 2. C) I'll Be Home; 3. April Love; 4. Speedy Gonzales; 5. A) Journey to the Center of the World; 6. Marilyn Monroe; 7. All reached number 2 in the UK charts; 8. A) The Horror Of It All; 9. False, he played the Angel at the Tomb; 10. C) 12. **1980s GROUPS ANAGRAMS:** 1. Dire straits; 2. The Bangles; 3. Foreigner; 4. REO Speedwagon; 5. Tears For Fears; 6. Talking Heads; 7. Def Leppard; 8. The Clash; 9. Dexy's Midnight Runners; 10. Judas Priest.

DAVID BOWIE *(Born David Robert Jones. 8 January 1947. Died 10 January 2016). Bowie was an English singer-songwriter and actor. A leading figure in the music industry, he is regarded as a most influential musician of the 20th century. Acclaimed by critics and musicians, particularly for his innovative work in the 1970s. His career was marked by reinvention and visual presentation, and his music and stagecraft had a significant impact on popular music. Had 55 Top 40 hits (including 1 reissue). This included 4 number ones (1 with Mick Jagger) and 19 other Top 10 hits. Had 66 top 40 Albums, 34 of those reached the Top 10, with 11 number ones.*

1. What was the name of the alter ego revealed to the public by David Bowie in 1972? A) Iggy Pop B) Ziggy Stardust C) The Guvnor

2. In 1975, what was the name of Bowie's first UK Number 1 single, a reissue of a 1969 number 5 hit? A) Space Oddity B) The Jean Genie C) Life On Mars

3. Who co-wrote Bowie's 1975 number 17 hit *Fame* with him?
A) Bob Dylan B) Paul McCartney C) John Lennon

4. In which year were David Bowie and Iman Abdulmajid married in Lausanne?
A) 1990 B) 1992 C) 1994

5. Aged 17, of which 'Prevention of Cruelty' Society did Bowie become founder? A) Animals B) Long haired men C) Laughing gnomes

6. When Bowie asked his fans to vote which tracks he should play for his 1990 world tour, what was the most requested?
A) The Jean Genie B) Space Oddity C) The Laughing Gnome

7. Which artist first released a version of the Bowie song *Oh! You Pretty Things*?
A) Mick Jagger B) Bob Dylan C) Peter Noone

8. In Martin Scorsese's 1988 film *The Last Temptation of Christ*, which role did Bowie play? A) Judas Iscariot B) Pontius Pilate C) John the Baptist

9. In 1974, on which folk rock band's album track *To Know Him Is To Love Him* did David Bowie play Alto Sax? A) Steely Dan B) Steeleye Span C) Steel Mill

10. The cover artwork of *Scary Monsters*, features Bowie in the Pierrot costume worn in which of his music videos?
A) Ashes To Ashes B) Fashion C) Up the Hill Backwards

HIT SONGS whose titles include musical instruments. Just fill in the gaps

1. ...... Tango (The Shadows, 1962)
2. Love Is Like A ...... (Ken Dodd, 1960)
3. Sound of ..... (Kula Shaker, 1988)
4. ..... In the Dark (Brenda Russell, 1988)
5. Mr .... Man (The Byrds, 1965)
6. Turn Up the .... (Tyree feat Kool Rock Steady, 1989)
7. 76 .... (The King Brothers, 1961)
8. Duelling ...... (Eric Weissberg, 1972)
9. .... Man (Donovan, 1968)
10. .... in the Moonlight (Perry Como, 1958)

DAVID BOWIE ANSWERS: *1. B) Ziggy Stardust; 2. A) Space Oddity; 3. C) John Lennon; 4. B) 1992; 5. B) Long haired men; 6. C) The Laughing Gnome; 7. C) Peter Noone; 8. B) Pontius Pilate; 9. B) Steeleye Span; 10. A) Ashes to Ashes.* **INSTRUMENTAL TITLES ANSWERS**: *1. Guitar; 2. Violin; 3. Drums; 4. Piano; 5. Tambourine; 6. Bass; 7. Trombones; 8. Banjos; 9. Hurdy Gurdy; 10. Mandolins.*

BOY GEORGE and CULTURE CLUB - *George Alan O'Dowd (born 14 June 1961), known professionally as Boy George, is an English singer, songwriter, DJ, fashion designer, photographer and record producer. He is the lead singer of the new wave pop band Culture Club (Mikey Craig (vocals, bass, keyboards), Roy Hay (guitars, vocals, keyboards), Jon Moss (drums, percussion, vocals). Culture Club had 12 top 40 hits between 1982 and 1999, including 2 No.1's and 7 other Top 10 hits. Boy George had 5 Top 40 hits with a No.1 included. Culture Club also had 7 Top 40 albums, with 5 of them reaching the top 10, and Boy George notched up 3 solo Top 40 albums.*

1. After two 1982 singles reached number 114 and 100 respectively, Culture Club reached number one with their third single of the year. What was the song?
A) White Boy   B) I'm Afraid Of Me   C) Do You Really Want To Hurt Me

2. In which city were Culture Club formed?

3. How many copies did the band's second album, *Colour By Numbers*, sell worldwide?   A) Over 10 million   B) Over 5 million   C) Over 3 million .

4. Who played bass in Culture Club?   A) Roy Hay   B) Mikey Craig   C) Jon Moss

5. What was Culture Club's second No.1, the biggest selling UK single in 1983?
A) Church of the Poison Mind   B) Karma Chameleon   C) Time (Clock of the Heart)

6. True or False? In 1984, Culture Club won Brit Awards for Best British Group, Best British Single, and the Grammy Award for Best New Artist.

7. Which English new wave band, created by manager Malcolm McLaren in 1980, did George O'Dowd briefly join as joint lead singer?
A) Bow Wow Wow   B) New Order   C) Squeeze

8. Why did Culture Club Split up in 1986?   A) Boy George drug problems   B) Boy George & Jon Moss's relationship problems   C) Management disputes

9. Boy George had 5 hits, one reached the top 20, three got into the 20's but *Everything I Own* got to the top spot in 1987. Who had previously got to No.1 in 1974, with David Gates' song?   A) Ken Boothe   B) Bread   C) Olivia Newton-John

10. In which band, featuring a mixture of electronic dance music, Indian classical music and western pop music, was Boy George the lead singer between 1989 and 1992?   A) Bow Down Mister   B) Jesus Loves You   C) Obsession

Who had these 'Animal' hits?

1. RUNNING BEAR (1960)
2. HUNGRY LIKE THE WOLF (1982)
3. ROCK LOBSTER (1979 and 1986)
4. BLACK CAT (1980)
5. EYE OF THE TIGER (1982)
6. CROCODILE ROCK (1973)
7. A HORSE WITH NO NAME (1972)
8. THE LION SLEEPS TONIGHT (1982)
9. BAT OUT OF HELL (1979)
10. SIDEWINDER SLEEPS TONITE (1993)

BOY GEORGE & CULTURE CLUB ANSWERS: 1. C) Do You Really Want To Hurt Me; 2. London; 3. A) Over 10 million; 4. B) Mikey Craig; 5. B) Karma Chameleon; 6. True; 7. A) Bow Wow Wow; 8. B) Boy George & Jon Moss's relationship problems; 9. A) Ken Boothe; 10. B) Jesus Loves You. ANIMAL MAGIC ANSWERS: 1. Johnny Preston; 2. Duran Duran; 3. B-52's; 4. Janet Jackson; 5. Survivor; 6. Elton John; 7. America; 8. Tight Fit; 9. Meat Loaf; 10. REM.

BOYZONE - *were an Irish boy band put together in 1993 by Louis Walsh. The line-up composed of Keith Duffy, Stephen Gately, Mikey Graham, Ronan Keating, and Shane Lynch. Debut single reached No.3 in Ireland. After that Boyzone had 16 hits in the UK, 6 No. 1's, 6 No. 2's, 3 No.3's and a No. 4. All 4 albums between 1995 and 1999 were chart-toppers. Boyzone split in 1999, but made a comeback in 2007. Gately died on 10 October 2009 of natural causes on holiday in Majorca. Keating remained a force in the music industry writing and managing other acts.*

1. Which member of the renowned five, was not in the original line-up and was called in after Richie Rock was released? A) Ronan   B) Mikey   C) Shane

2. Who was the future famed actor who auditioned for the band, but was not selected? A) Aidan Gillen   B) Colin Farrell   C) Cillian Murphy

3. After covering the Four Seasons' *Working My Way Back to You*, Boyzone had a No. 2 hit with *Love Me For a Reason.* Who had sung the original version of that hit?
A) The Osmonds   B) The Jacksons   C) The Commodores

4. The Boyzone debut album reached No.1 in 1995. It included five top 4 songs. What was the album's title?
A) A Different Beat   B) Said and Done   C) Where We Belong

5. Boyzone had their first UK No.1 single in 1986. It was a cover of which Bee Gees hit? A) Words   B) First of May   C) Tomorrow Tomorrow

6. Which 1996 Boyzone No.1 includes these lyrics: "I got a spoonful of sugar, That I think you'd like, No, I don't wanna preach, But I think you might wanna cup"?

7. Katrina and the Waves, representing the UK, were winners of the 1997 Eurovision Song Contest, and Ronan Keating co-presented the show. True or False?

8. What is the name of the 1997 No. 2 Boyzone hit song that appears in the *Mr. Bean* film? A) Picture of You   B) Baby Can I Hold You   C) Isn't It A Wonder

9. The 1998 Record of the Year was *No Matter What.* From which Andrew Lloyd Webber musical was the song taken?
A) Phantom of the Opera   B) Cats   C) Whistle Down the Wind

10. In 1999 Boyzone had two number one hits. *You Needed Me* was one, the other was a cover of which Billy Ocean number one from 13 years earlier?
A) Red Light Spells Danger   B) When the Going Gets Tough   C) Suddenly

---

ACTS FROM IRELAND THAT HIT THE CHARTS
Name the acts that had hits with these songs

1. *Nothing Compares 2U (1990)*	6. *Walk Tall (1964)*
2. *Orinoco Flow (1988)*	7. *What's Another Year (1980)*
3. *Brown Eyed Girl (1967)*	8. *So Young (1998)*
4. *Give a Little Love (1998)*	9. *Don't Go (1988)*
5. *This Is the World Calling (1986)*	10. *McArthur Park (1964)*

Irish CREAM

BOYZONE ANSWERS: *1. B) Mikey; 2. B) Colin Farrell; 3. A) The Osmonds; 4. B) Said and Done; 5. A) Words; 6. A Different Beat; 7. True; 8. A) Picture of You; 9. C) Whistle Down the Wind; 10. B) When the Going Gets Tough.* **IRISH CREAM ANSWERS:** *1. Sinead O'Connor; 2. Enya; 3. Van Morrison; 4. Daniel O'Donnell; 5. Bob Geldof; 6. Val Doonican; 7. Johnny Logan; 8. The Corrs; 9. Hothouse Flowers; 10. Richard Harris.*

ALBUM Covers

The covers of many long players are very famous, some less so, and some absolutely awful. All a matter of opinion really. Below there is a selection of 10 album covers from all eras. So, how many of these album covers can you recognise?

The Hits Of SARAH BRIGHTMAN

Sarah Brightman charted in the Top 40 five times - 4 times in conjunction with another act. Can you fill in the gaps?

A. I Lost My Heart To A Starship Trooper	Sarah Brightman with … ……	1978
B. Pie Jesu	Sarah Brightman with ….. ……..	1985
C. … …….. .. … …..	Sarah Brightman with Steve Harley	1986
D. Wishing You Were Somehow Here Again	Sarah Brightman	….
E. ….. .. … …….. (Con Te Partiro)	Sarah Brightman with Andrea Bocelli	1997

ALBUM COVERS ANSWERS: 1. Bridge Over Troubled Water - Simon & Garfunkel; 2 Rumours - Fleetwood Mac; 3. Revolver - The Beatles; 4. Thriller - Michael Jackson; 5. The Shadows - The Shadows; 6. A Night at the Opera - Queen; 7. Willy and the Poor Boys - Creedence Clearwater Revival; 8. Massive Attack- Protection; 9. Tom Petty - Into the Great Wide Open; 10. Patti Smith - Horses.
THE HITS OF SARAH BRIGHTMAN ANSWERS: A) Hot Gossip; B) Miles Kingston; C) The Phantom of the Opera; D) 1987 E) Time To Say Goodbye.

BROS are an English band formed in 1986 in Camberley, Surrey. The band originally consisted of twin brothers Matt and Luke Goss (born 29 September 1968 in Lewisham, London) and their friend Craig (born 22 April 1969 in Kirkcaldy, Fife, Scotland) who attended Collingwood School in Camberley. The band was managed by former Pet Shop Boys manager Tom Watkins. They achieved chart success and a large teenage fan base in 1988. Early the following year, Logan quit the band and the Goss twins continued as a duo. The first 8 Bros singles reached the top 10, including one No.1, the next three entered the Top 20. Also had 3 Top 10 albums.

1. Who was the youngest brother?

2. The first release by Bros was in 1987. What was the song that reached number 80 in the Top 100?   A) I Owe You Nothing   B) Drop the Boy   C) I Quit

3. The first big hit for Bros was a No. 2 hit in 1988? What was the title?
A) I Owe You Nothing   B) When Will I Be Famous   C) Drop the Boy

4. Bros songs were written by 'The Brothers'. Who were they?
A) Matt and Luke Goss   B) Nicky Graham & Tom Watkins   C) Lennon & McCartney

5. What was the name of their debut album that reached No. 2 in 1988?
A) Pull   B) Push   C) Shove

6. Craig Logan left the band due to illness in 1989. Matt and Luke continued with sold-out world tour which had what title?
A) The Global Push   B) The Big Push   C) In 2 Summer

7. When did Bros first split up?   A) 1992   B) 1991   C) 1990

8. Which brother had 2 Top 40 solo singles in 1995/6?

9. True or False? Luke Goss moved to the US and became a film actor, appearing in numerous films, such as Blade II and Hellboy II: The Golden Army.

10. What bottle tops did Bros famously wear on their shoes?
A) Skol   B) Grolsch   C) Heineken

THE MASKED SINGER 1

Who had Top 40 hits with the following songs:

Pearl's A Singer, Sunshine After The Rain, Lilac Wine Don't Cry Out Loud, Fool If You Think It's Over, Nights In White Satin, No More The Fool

THE MASKED SINGER 2

Who had Top 40 hits with the following songs:

Love Changes Everything, One Step Out of Time, From Here to Eternity, Something Inside (So Strong)

BROS ANSWERS: *1. Matt; 2. A) I Owe You Nothing (re-released the following year and reached No. 1); 3. B) When Will I Be Famous; 4. B) Nicky Graham & Tom Watkins; 5. B) Push; 6. A) The Global Push; 7. A) 1992; 8. Matt; 9. True; 10. B) Grolsch.*
THE MASKED SINGER ANSWERS: *1. Elkie Brooks; 2. Michael Ball.*

1. In which video did Michael Jackson first perform his famous moonwalk in 1983?

2. Which pair make up The Eurythmics?

3. Human League had the Christmas number one in 1981 with what song?

4. What Number One was also known as Stevie Ray Vaughan's 'First Wife'?

5. 'I got sunshine on a cloudy day', is the opening line to which Temptations song?

6. *Welcome to the Pleasuredome* was the debut studio album of which band?

7. Elvis Costello's entire 1985 Live Aid set consisted of which single song, that he called "An old English Northern folk song"?

8. What was Frank Sinatra's middle name?

9. Who was the first woman ever inducted into the Rock and Roll Hall of Fame?

10. Who was the only Spice Girl with a name that was actually a spice?

11. The 1992 film *Wayne's World* gave a revival for which 1975 No.1 song?

12. Who is the only country to win 3 Eurovision Song Contests in a row?

13. In the 1998 film *The Big Lebowski*, 'The Dude' can't stand which band?

14. Which five artists made up the supergroup *The Traveling Wilburys*?

15. What Nabokov book do The Police reference in *Don't Stand So Close to Me*?

16. Which Mama & Papas song starts: "all the leaves are brown and the sky is grey"?

17. On which album cover are band members sitting on an old sofa on a porch, one of them holding a guitar?

18. What was the title of the autobiography Diana Ross published in 1994?

19. Terri Nunn replaced Toni Childs as lead singer in which band who had a number one UK hit with *Take My Breath Away*?

20. What's the name of the Spandau Ballet lead singer?

21. How many instruments could Prince play?   A) 7   B) 17   C) 27

22. Which legendary Country music star formerly sold bibles and vacuum cleaners door-to-door, and became a sales manager for the Encyclopedia Americana?

23. Which US President used Springsteen's *Born in the USA* as his presidential campaign song?

24. Which rock musician played drums for Nirvana and founded the Foo Fighters?

25. Pre being Fatboy Slim, Norman Cook played bass in which 80's indie rock band?

ALLSORTS OF MUSIC TRIVIA ANSWERS: *1. Billie Jean; 2. Annie Lennox & Dave Stewart; 3. Don't You Love Me; 4. His Fender Stratocaster guitar; 5. My Girl; 6. Frankie Goes To Hollywood; 7. All You Need Is Love; 8. Albert; 9. Aretha Franklin; 10. Geri Halliwell (Ginger Spice); 11. Bohemian Rhapsody; 12. Ireland (1992,1993 and 1994); 13. Eagles; 14. George Harrison, Roy Orbison, Jeff Lynne, Tom Petty and Bob Dylan; 15. Lolita; 16. California Dreamin'; 17. Crosby, Stills & Nash; 18. Secrets of a Sparrow; 19. Berlin; 20. Tony Hadley; 21. C) 27; 22. Willie Nelson; 23. Ronald Reagan; 24. Dave Grohl; 25. The Housemartins.*

JAMES BROWN *(James Joseph Brown - May 3, 1933 – December 25, 2006) was an American singer, dancer, musician, record producer, and bandleader. The central progenitor of funk music. A major figure of 20th century music, often referred to by the honorific nicknames 'Godfather of Soul', 'Mr. Dynamite', and 'Soul Brother No. 1'. In a career of over 50 years, he influenced the development of several music genres. Brown was one of the first 10 inductees into the Rock and Roll Hall of Fame at its inaugural induction in New York on January 23, 1986. Had 11 UK Top 40 singles, with only 1 Top 10 success. Four Top 30 Albums (one Top 10).*

1. James Brown's name was meant to have been Joseph James Brown, but his first and middle names were mistakenly reversed on his birth certificate. True or False?

2. When Brown was just four years old, his parents split up, and he went to live with his Aunt Honey in Augusta, Georgia. What type of business did she run?
A) Brothel   B) Hotel   C) Bar

3. What was the name of the first band Brown joined in 1955?
A) Flying Findusters   B) Gospel Starlighters   C) James Brown Trio

4. What was the title of Brown's first UK hit in 1965?
A) Sweet Soul Music   B) Papa's Got a Brand New Bag   C) I Got You

5. What did James Brown do as race riots raged in April 1968?
A) Called for violent protest   B) Ignored the issue   C) Asked for peace

6. In what 1980 film did James Brown make an appearance as a preacher?
A) The Shining   B) The Blues Brothers   C) Caddyshack

7. James Brown's biggest UK hit song, a number 5 in 1985, was featured prominently in *Rocky IV*?   A) Stay With Me   B) Give Me Some Skin   C) Living in America

8. Following a high-speed car chase Brown was convicted of carrying an unlicensed pistol, assaulting a police officer and various drug-related and driving offences. He was sentenced to six years in prison, but was eventually released on parole after serving how many years?   A) 2   B) 3   C) 4

9. How old was James Brown when he picked up his first Grammy for *Papa's Got a Brand New Bag*?   A) 32   B) 35   C) 38

10. James Brown's last Top 40 hit in the UK was in 1998. What was the song?
A) Funk on Ah Roll   B) Can't Get Any Harder   C) I Got You (I Feel Good)

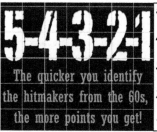

The quicker you identify the hitmakers from the 60s, the more points you get!

5 POINTS - *We had 13 Top 40 hits between 1961 and 1964.*

4 POINTS - *Our first hit in 1961 was a Cole Porter song.*

3 POINTS - *We played at Charles and Di's wedding reception.*

2 POINTS - *Our biggest hit was a No. 2 with a Russian link.*

1 POINT - *We were a trad jazz band led by a trumpet player.*

JAMES BROWN ANSWERS: 1. True; 2. A) Brothel; 3. B) Gospel Starlighters; 4. B) Papa's Got a Brand New Bag; 5. C) Asked for peace; 6. B) The Blues Brothers; 7. C) Living in America; 8. A) 2; 9. C) 38; 10. A) Funk on Ah Roll. **5-4-3-2-1 ANSWER:** *Kenny Ball & His Jazzmen. (Kenny Ball - 22 May 1930 – 7 March 2013).*

JOE BROWN *(James Joseph Roger Brown, MBE - born 13 May 1941 in Swarby, Lincolnshire) is an English entertainer. As a rock and roll singer and guitarist, he performed for more than six decades. He was a stage and TV performer in the late 1950s and has been a UK recording star since the early 1960s. He is highly regarded in the music business as a 'musician's musician' who commands respect and admiration from a wide spectrum of artists. Played lead guitar on numerous tracks for other artistes. Very popular in theatres into the 2010s. Joe had 11 Top 40 singles, three as Joe Brown and the remainder as Joe Brown & The Bruvvers. This included three Top 10 hits. Also had two Top 20 albums.*

1. Joe worked for British Railways at their Plaistow Locomotive works for two years in the late 1950s, becoming a steam locomotive driver. True or False?

2. In 1958, TV producer Jack Good hired Joe as lead guitarist in the orchestra for which new TV series?   A) 6.5 Special   B) Boy Meets Girls   C) Oh Boy

3. Joe was in the backing band for two R 'n' R icons on a UK tour in 1960, which ended prematurely after a car crash at Chippenham when Gene Vincent was injured, and the second star tragically killed. Who died?   A) Eddie Cochran   B) Johnny Kidd   C) Rick Nelson

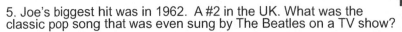

4. Joe played on many tracks as a session guitarist, memorably on which Trevor Peacock / John Barry song, that was an Adam Faith hit, despite being banned by the BBC for 'lewd and salacious lyrics'?
A) Made You   B) Someone Else's Baby   C) The First Time

5. Joe's biggest hit was in 1962. A #2 in the UK. What was the classic pop song that was even sung by The Beatles on a TV show?

6. Brown starred in a hit West End musical with Dame Anna Neagle, between 1965 and 1968. What was the show?   A) Half a Sixpence   B) Charlie Girl   C) Oliver

7. In 1972, he formed another band, which played rock and roll, country and gospel music and featured his wife, Vicki Brown, and Pete Oakman from the Bruvvers. What was the band called?   A) The Browns   B) Brown Sauce   C) Brown's Home Brew

8. Manager Larry Parnes changed Reginald Smith to Marty Wilde; Roy Taylor to Vince Eager and Ron Wycherly to Billy Fury. Joe Brown resisted the new name Parnes had in mind for him, which was?
A) Danny Phantom   B) Dean Prince   C) Elmer Twitch

9. In the 1980s, Brown presented a daytime quiz show called *Square One*. He then recorded a pilot for a prime time game show but eventually lost out to Leslie Crowther. What was the show?
A) The Price is Right   B) Whose Baby   C) Stars in Their Eyes

10. Joe made a brief appearance as Dudley, a crooked club owner, in a 1986 film opposite Bob Hoskins. What was the film that was nominated for multiple awards?
A) Who Framed Roger Rabbit   B) Mona Lisa   C) The Long Good Friday

MAESTROS OF A GOOD FEELING, STEADY PULSE

With which musical acts are these bassists mainly associated?

1. Paul McCartney	5. Sting	9. Peter Hook
2. Jet Harris	6. John Paul Jones	10. Bill Black
3. Jack Bruce	7. John Deacon	11. Flea
4. John Entwistle	8. Bill Wyman	12. Stu Cook

JOE BROWN ANSWERS: *1. False, he was a steam locomotive fireman; 2. B) Boy Meets Girl; 3. A) Eddie Cochran; 4. A) Made You; 5. A Picture of You; 6. B) Charlie Girl; 7. C) Brown's Home Brew; 8. C) Elmer Twitch; 9. A) The Price is Right; 10. B) Mona Lisa.*
BOMB THE BASS ANSWERS: *1. The Beatles; 2. The Shadows; 3. Cream; 4. The Who; 5. The Police; 6. Led Zeppelin; 7. Queen; 8. The Rolling Stones; 9. Joy Division or New Order; 10. Elvis Presley or Bill Black's Combo; 11. Red Hot Chili Peppers; 12. Creedence Clearwater Revival.*

BUCKS FIZZ *are a British pop group that were very successful in the 80s, notably winning the 1981 Eurovision Song Contest. The quartet was formed specifically for the contest and comprised: Bobby G, Cheryl Baker, Mike Nolan and Jay Aston. The group had a successful career around the world (although commercially unsuccessful in the US) They had three No.1 singles and four other Top 10 successes in their 13 Top 40 hits. The group also had four Top 30 albums. The line-up of the group has changed a number of times over the years, most famously when Jay Aston quit the group in 1985 and was replaced by Shelley Preston.*

1. The groups first single was a UK No.1 in 1981, it was also the winning song from the Eurovision Song Contest. What was it called?
A) Save Your Kisses For Me   B) Making Your Mind Up   C) My Camera Never Lies

2. Bucks Fizz won the contest by a margin of just four points.Who did they beat into second place?   A) Ireland   B) Sweden   C) Germany

3. The follow up single, *Piece of the Action*, was a completely different style song. What position did it reach in the UK Singles chart?   A) 12   B) 2   C) 5

4. The fourth Bucks Fizz single produced their second No. 1. It was written by the group's creator Andy Hill, along with former King Crimson member Peter Sinfield. What was its title?   A) My Camera Never Lies   B) The Land of Make Believe   C) Save Your Kisses For Me

5. In March 1982 the band achieved their third No. 1 with another Hill / Martin song. What was the song titled?   A) Now These Days Are Gone   B) My Camera Never Lies   C) Run For Your Life

6. Bucks Fizz were invited to appear before the Queen and Queen Mother in the 1982 Royal Variety Performance, for which musicals were the theme . What song did they perform?   A) You'll Never Walk Alone   B) Edelweiss   C) Somewhere

7. On 11 December 1984 all four members of Bucks Fizz were injured when their coach collided with an articulated lorry on their way home after a sell-out concert. From where were the group returning?   A) Bristol   B) Birmingham   C) Newcastle

8. Following the crash, Cheryl and Mike helped set up a charity for crash victims suffering head injuries. Which charity?   A) Brainwave   B) HeadFirst   C) Headway

9. After Jay left new, a new recording contract was signed with Polydor. The first single brought the group back to prominence. What was the No. 8 hit titled?
A) New Beginning (Mamba Seyra)   B) London Town   C) Golden Days

10. In 1996 Mike Nolan left and was replaced by David Van Day. As half of what duo had Van Day achieved 10 Top 40 hits, five of them Top 10, between 1978 and 1987?
A) Dollar   B) Guys 'n' Dolls   C) The Young Generation.

1. With sales of 1.7m, what Christmas song is the biggest UK single not to reach No. 1?

2. Aaliyah's More Than A Woman was the only posthumous UK number one to be replaced by another - but which single followed it?

3. Which album contained a record of four original UK number one hit singles?

4. What is the only song to have four versions by different artists charting in the Top 20 at the same time (in 1955)?

5. Alex Day's 2012 single Forever Yours entered the chart at No. 4. It had a record drop to which position in the next chart?

BUCKS FIZZ ANSWERS: *1. B) Making Your Mind Up; 2. C) Germany; 3. A) 12; 4. B) The Land of Make Believe; 5. B) My Camera Never Lies; 6. A) You'll Never Walk Alone; 7. C) Newcastle; 8. B) HeadFirst; 9. A) New Beginning (Mamba Seyra); 10. A) Dollar.*
UK SINGLES CHARTS: *1. Last Christmas - Wham; 2. My Sweet Lord - George Harrison; 3. Spice - Spice Girls; 4. Unchained Melody - Al Hibbler, Les Baxter, Jimmy Young and Liberace; 5. 112.*

KATE BUSH *(Catherine Bush CBE, born Bexleyheath, Kent on 30 July 1958) is an English singer, songwriter, musician, dancer and record producer. Her father was an English GP, Robert Bush, and her mother Hannah was an Irish staff nurse. In 1978, aged 19, she topped the UK Singles Chart for the only time with her debut single, becoming the first female artist to achieve a UK number one with a self-written song. She had 23 entries in the singles chart (including an EP). This included 5 Top 10 entries and a further 9 reached the Top 20. Released 8 albums and had 3 No. 1's, with the others hitting the Top 6.*

1. Kate Bush was signed to what record label at the age of 16?
A) EMI   B) RCA   C) Columbia

2. Kate Bush's first recording in 1978 was based upon a novel by which writer?
A) Anne Bronte   B) Emily Bronte   C) Charlotte Bronte

3. Kate Bush sang backing vocals on what Peter Gabriel No. 4 single of 1980?
A) Games Without Frontiers   B) Sledgehammer   C) Don't Give Up

4. What was the first number one album for Kate Bush, a 1980 release?
A) The Kick Inside   B) Lionheart   C) Never For Ever

5. What Kate Bush single hit No. 3 on the UK charts in 1985, her second highest position with a single?   A) Babooshka
B) Cloudbusting   C) Running Up That Hill

6. In 1987 Kate Bush won her only Brit Award in which category?
A) Best British Producer   B) Best British Female   C) Best British Album

7. *This Woman's Work* by Kate Bush was featured in what 1988 John Hughes film?
A) She's Having A Baby   B) Sixteen Candles   C) Pretty In Pink

8. What 1993 Kate Bush No. 2 album was inspired by a 1948 Moira Shearer film?
A) Tales of Hoffman   B) Peeping Tom   C) The Red Shoes

9. Prince, Gary Brooker, Eric Clapton, Nigel Kennedy and Jeff Beck all made appearances on which 1993 Kate Bush album which reached No. 2 in the album charts?   A) The Sensual World   B) The Red Shoes   C) The Hounds Of Love

10. Kate Bush is regarded as the first singer to use what form of technology on her 1979 tour?   A) Pyrotechnics   B) Large projection screens   C) Wireless microphone

Singers Wot Wrote Songs For Others!

Can you match them up?

HIT SONG	SONGWRITER
1. My Girl - Temptations (1992)	A. Michael Bolton
2. Bette Davis Eyes - Kim Carnes (1981)	B. Paul McCartney
3. I Found Someone - Cher (1987)	C. Prince
4. Red Red Wine - UB40 (1983)	D. Michael Jackson
5. Manic Monday - Bangles (1986)	E. Jackie DeShannon
6. Come and Get It - Badfinger (1970)	F. Smokey Robinson
7. Muscles - Diana Ross (1982)	G. George Harrison
8. Bedtime Story - Madonna (1995)	H. Neil Diamond
9. If I Needed Someone - Hollies (1965)	J. John Fogerty
10. Rockin' All Over the World (1977)	K. Bjork

KATE BUSH ANSWERS: *1. A) EMI; 2. B) Emily Bronte (her only novel before her death at just 30); 3. A) Games Without Frontiers (had a duo hit with Gabriel in 1986 with Don't Give Up); 4. C) Never For Ever; 5. C) Running Up That Hill; 6. B) Best British Female; 7. A) She's Having a Baby   8. C) The Red Shoes; 9. B) The Red Shoes; 10. C) Wireless microphone.*
SINGERS WOT WROTE SONGS FOR OTHERS: *1F, 2E, 3A, 4H, 5C, 6B, 7D, 8K, 9G, 10J.*

A PICTURE OF WHO?

Group Names in Picture Form.
Just Name the Hit-Making Bands

THE BYRDS were an American rock band formed in Los Angeles, California in 1964. The band underwent multiple lineup changes throughout its existence, with frontman Roger McGuinn (known as Jim McGuinn until mid-1967) remaining the sole consistent member. In 1991, the Byrds were inducted into the R'n'R Hall of Fame. They had just 5 Top 40 hits in the UK including a No. 1. The Byrds also had 8 Top 40 Albums.

THE BYRDS FIVE UK TOP 40 HITS IN ANAGRAM FORM, CAN YOU SOLVE THEM?

A. INERT MAMBA FORM *(No. 1, 1965)*

B. AARON TOTALLED WILLY *(No. 4, 1965)*

C. RUNT RUNT RUNT *(No. 26, 1965)*

D. GET HIGHISH LIME *(No. 24, 1966)*

E. CHATTER MENUS *(No. 19, 1971)*

GLEN CAMPBELL *(Glen Travis Campbell - April 22, 1936 – August 8, 2017) was an American guitarist, singer, songwriter, actor and TV host. Born in Billstown, Arkansas, Campbell had begun his professional career as a studio musician in Los Angeles, spending several years playing with a famous group of instrumentalists later known as The Wrecking Crew. Glen played guitar on numerous records with many top recording stars. He was better known in the UK for a series of nine Top 40 songs between 1969 and 1977, including five Top 10 hits (one a duet). He also notched up 6 Top 40 albums, including one No. 1 and another Top 10 success.*

1. In 1960 Glen joined which instrumental band who had had a No. 5 hit with *Tequila* two years earlier? A) Champs B) Ventures C) Johnny & The Hurricanes

2. What was Glen's first UK hit, it reached number 7 in 1969?
A) Rhinestone Cowboy B) Honey Come Back C) Wichita Lineman

3. Which instrument did the songwriter Jimmy Webb play on *Wichita Lineman*?
A) Banjo B) Dulcimer C) Hammond Organ

4. In 1969 Campbell played alongside John Wayne in which acclaimed Western?
A) True Grit B) The Sons of Katie Elder C) Rio Lobo

5. In December 1969 Glen duetted with which country star on a revival of the Everly Brothers hit *All I Have To Do is Dream*, his highest UK singles chart position?

6. In 1970 Glen had a No. 4 hit with which song that had already been a big hit for Conway Twitty and Billy Fury?

7. In 1971 Campbell had a No. 39 hit with a cover of which Cindy Walker written song, that was a No. 2 hit for Roy Orbison in 1962?

8. In 1964 and 1965, Glen Campbell was a touring member for what American rock band renowned for their surfing links?

9. Which UK No. 4 hit for Glen Campbell starts with these lyrics, "I've been walkin' these streets so long, Singin' the same old song"?

10. *Glen Campbell's Twenty Golden Greats* was the the title of Glen's 1976 number one album in the UK. True or False?

THERE'S A 1980's NOVELTY

Some people claim that the Eighties were the best music era. How then, do they explain these smash hits! Just name the 10 artists concerned.

1. Shaddap You Face (1981)

2. There's No One Quite Like Grandma (1980)

3. Agadoo (1984)

4. Save Your Love (1982)

5. Rat Rapping (1983)

6. Orville's Song 1982

7. Loadsamoney (Doin' Up The House) (1988)

8. The Chicken Song (1986)

9. 'Ullo John! Gotta New Motor? (1984)

10. Hole In My Shoe (1986)

GLEN CAMPBELL ANSWERS: *1. A) Champs; 2. C) Wichita Lineman; 3. C) Hammond Organ; 4. A) True Grit; 5. Bobbie Gentry; 6. It's Only Make Believe; 7. Dream Baby; 8. Beach Boys; 9. Rhinestone Cowboy; 10. True.*
THERE'S A 1980s NOVELTY: *1. Joe Dolce Music Theatre; 2. St Winifred's School Choir; 3. Black Lace; 4. Renée & Renato; 5. Roland Rat Superstar; 6. Keith Harris and Orville; 7. Harry Enfield; 8. Spitting Image; 9.Alexei Sayle; 10. Neil (Nigel Planer).*

MARIAH CAREY *(born March 27, 1969 in Huntington, New York) is an American singer, songwriter, actress, and record producer. Her parents were Patricia (née Hickey), an Irish former opera singer and vocal coach, and Alfred Roy Carey, an aeronautical engineer of African-American and Afro-Venezuelan lineage. Known for her five-octave vocal range, melismatic singing style, and signature use of the whistle register, she has been called the 'Queen of Christmas'. Had 23 Top 40 singles in the UK, with a No.1 and 14 other Top 10 hits included. Four of them in collaboration with other acts. Also had 9 hit albums in the Top 40 - including 2 number ones and 6 other Top 10 hits. All I Want For Christmas Is You became an annual festive hit.*

1. Which singer handed Mariah Carey's demo tape to the head of Columbia Records Tommy Mottola in 1988?
A) Brenda K. Starr   B) Whitney Houston   C) Dionne Warwick

2. In 1990 Mariah Carey had her first UK hit with which song from her first album titled *Mariah Carey*, that reached No.9 in the singles chart?
A) Love Takes Time   B) Someday   C) Vision of Love

3. Which American music executive, producer and author did Mariah marry in 1993?
A) Tommy Mottola   B) Phil Spector   C) Berry Gordy

4. Carey had a UK No.7 hit in 1993 with a song that she wrote with Walter Afanasieff, originally intended for Gloria Estefan. What is the song?
A) Hero   B) Dreamlover   C) I'll Be There

5. What was the name of the concert tour to support Mariah's fifth studio album that ended on June 23, 1996 at Wembley Stadium London?
A) Sweet Fantasy Tour   B) Daydream World Tour   C) Charmbracelet World Tour

6. Mariah had her first UK No.1 in 1998 with *Without You*. Who wrote the song?
A) Harry Nilsson   B) T.G. Sheppard   C) Pete Ham and Tom Evans

7. With whom did Mariah co-write and co-produce *All I Want For Christmas*?
A) Nile Rodgers   B) Quincy Jones   C) Walter Afanasieff

8. Together with Whitney Houston, Carey had a No. 4 hit at Christmas 1998 with *When You Believe*. On which animated film musical soundtrack is the song featured?
A) The Polar Express   B) The Prince Of Egypt   C) Shrek III

9. "Heartbreaker, you've got the best of me, But I just keep on coming back incessantly" are lyrics from *Heartbreaker*, a No. 5 hit in 1998, sung as a duet with whom?
A) Jay-Z   B) will.i.am   C) Kanye West

10. Mariah paid $600,000 for Marilyn Monroe's white piano. True or False?

HERO written by Mariah Carey / Walter Afanasieff

There's a hero
If you look inside your heart
You don't have to be afraid
Of what you are
There's an answer
If you reach into your soul
And the sorrow that you know
Will melt away.

And then a hero comes along
With the strength to carry on
And you cast your fears aside
And you know you can survive
So when you feel like hope is gone
Look inside you and be strong
And you'll finally see the truth
That a hero lies in you.

It's a long road
When you face the world alone
No one reaches out a hand
For you to hold
You can find love
If you search within yourself
And that emptiness you felt
Will disappear.

MARIAH CAREY ANSWERS: *1. A) Brenda K. Starr; 2. C) Vision of Love; 3. A) Tommy Mottola; 4. A) Hero; 5. B) Daydream World Tour; 6. C) Pete Ham and Tom Evans (from Badfinger); 7. C) Walter Afanasieff; 8. B) The Prince Of Egypt; 9. A) Jay-Z; 10. True.*

MOVIE MUSIC

Hit songs associated with films

Great music and great film go better together than popcorn and butter. This round is all about songs from film soundtracks that have made an impact on the UK charts. Not every film featured here has been critically acclaimed but the music lives on!

1. Which 1977 film about Tony Manero featured *Stayin' Alive* and *Night Fever* by the Bee Gees?

2. *The Exorcist*, a 1973 American supernatural horror film featured which piano music from Mike Oldfield?

3. In *Pulp Fiction* (1994), to what 1964 Chuck Berry song do John Travolta and Uma Thurman dance during the competition at Jack Rabbit Slim's?

4. Which song from *Dirty Dancing* won an Academy Award for Best Original Song?

5. In *Wayne's World* to what song do the main characters sing along with in the car?

6. As the end titles roll in *Robin Hood: Prince of Thieves* which No.1 song is played?

7. R. Kelly's song *I Believe I Can Fly* featured on the soundtrack of which 1996 live-action/animated sports comedy film, winning two Grammy Awards?

8. The title song for which 1983 romantic dance film won an Oscar for Irene Cara?

9. *Hold Me Thrill Me Kiss Me Kill Me* by U2 and *Kiss From a Rose* are two big hits from which 1995 superhero film?

10. True or False? Sylvester Stallone considered *Another One Bites the Dust* by Queen as the theme for Rocky III before settling for *Eye of the Tiger* by Survivor.

11. Albert Hammond and Diane Warren wrote a song for Starship which became a number one in the UK. In what romantic comedy film was the song featured?

12. Aerosmith's 1998 hit *I Don't Want To Miss a Thing* features on the soundtrack of which 1998 disaster film, whose title is GRANDMA ODE as an anagram?

13. Nala sung, "He's holding back, he's hiding, But what, I can't decide, Why won't he be the king I know he is, The king I see inside?". Can you name the song and the film soundtrack on which it appears?

14. Which 1980 Blondie No.1 hit single was used as the theme for *American Gigolo*?

15. B J Thomas sung the Bacharach / David song *Raindrops Keep Fallin' On My Head* in the 1969 film *Butch Cassidy and the Sundance Kid*, but who had a Top 10 hit in the UK with the song?

16. Who sung the Oscar nominated title song for the 1984 musical drama *Footloose*, and achieved his only UK hit with the song?

17. The 1993 Tom Hanks film *Philadelphia*, featured Bruce Springsteen's song *Streets of Philadelphia*. Why was a Springsteen song chosen for this film?

18. What was the title song for the 1977 Bond movie, *The Spy Who Loved Me*?

19. In the animated *Beauty and the Beast* in 1991, which character sung the title song that was to be a massive hit for Celine Dion and Peabo Bryson?

20. What was the first rock song ever used in a 1955 Hollywood film, *The Blackboard Jungle*, a film about teachers in an interracial inner-city school?

MOVIE MUSIC ANSWERS: *1. Saturday Night Fever; 2. Tubular Bells; 3. You Never Can Tell; 4. (I've Had) The Time of my Life; 5. Bohemian Rhapsody by Queen; 6. (Everything I Do) I Do It For You by Bryan Adams; 7. Space Jam; 8. Flashdance…Oh What a Feeling; 9. Batman Forever; 10. True; 11.Mannequin; 12. Armageddon; 13. Can You Feel the Love Tonight in The Lion King; 14. Call Me; 15. Sacha Distel; 16. Kenny Loggins; 17. A mainstream song to raise awareness about AIDS; 18. Nobody Does It Better by Carly Simon; 19. Mrs Potts (Angela Lansbury); 20. Rock Around the Clock by Bill Haley & His Comets.*

BELINDA CARLISLE *(Belinda Jo Carlisle born Hollywood, Los Angeles, August 17, 1958) is an American musician, singer, and author. Carlisle's first venture into music was in 1977 as drummer for the punk rock band the Germs, under the name Dottie Danger. She gained fame as lead singer of the Go-Go's and went on to have a prolific career as a solo artist. She had 19 UK Top 40 hits between 1987 and 1997, including a No.1 and six other Top 10 successes. Carlisle also had 7 Top 20 albums, including a No.1 and four other Top 10 best sellers.*

1. Belinda co-founded the the Misfits. When a new line-up evolved with Charlotte Caffey, Kathy Valentine, and Gina Schock, what were they renamed?
A) Love Unlimited   B) The Emotions   C) The Go-Go's

2. In what year did Belinda Carlisle marry film producer Morgan Mason, son of James?   A) 1985   B) 1986   C) 1987

3. After her first single *Mad About You* failed to make much impact in the UK, her next single in 1987 hit number one, her only chart-topper in the UK. What was the song?
A) Heaven Is a Place on Earth   B) Circle in the Sand   C) Leave a Light On

4. Carlisle embarked on a world tour in 1988, which sold out Wembley Arena. What was the world tour named?
A) World Without You   B) The Good Heavens   C) Leave a Light On

5. Carlisle's second UK album success came in 1989 when it spawned 5 hit singles. What was the album's title?   A) Belinda   B) Heaven on Earth   C) Runaway Horses

6. In 1990 Belinda recorded *Blue Period* with the rock band, The Smithereens. It reached number 29 in the UK charts. True or False?

7. In the late autumn of 1990, the Go-Go's reunited for a tour to support their first best-of album, Greatest. What campaign did the tour promote?
A) Anti-fur   B) Anti-drugs   C) Anti-abortion

8. The Go-Go's reunited in 1994 to support the release of a retrospective double-CD *Return to the Valley of The Go-Go's*. The album included their only UK singles hit. What was the name of the track?
A) The Whole World Lost Its Head   B) Vacation   C) Head Over Heels

9. Belinda Carlisle covered *In Too Deep* for her sixth studio album, *A Woman and a Man* in 1996. It reached No. 6 in the UK, but who sung the original version?
A) Connie Francis   B) Sandie Shaw   C) Jenny Morris

10. In November 1999, Carlisle released her final 20th century album in the UK, a greatest hits album collectively titled *A Place on Earth: The Greatest Hits*. What number did the album reach in the UK charts?   A) 25   B) 15   C) 5

In 1978 two superstars duetted on a No. 5 UK hit single. Their faces are morphed here. Can you name them?

BELINDA CARLISLE ANSWERS: *1. C) The Go-Go's; 2. B) 1986; 3. A) Heaven Is a Place on Earth; 4. B) Good Heavens; 5. C) Runaway Horses; 6. False (it reached number 99); 7. A) Anti-fur; 8. A) The Whole World Lost Its Head; 9. C) Jenny Morris; 10. B) 15.*
DYNAMIC DUO ANSWERS: *Neil Diamond and Barbra Streisand.*

THE CARPENTERS *(officially known as Carpenters) were an American vocal and instrumental duo consisting of siblings Karen (1950–1983) and Richard Carpenter (born 1946). They produced a distinct soft musical style, combining Karen's distinctive three-octave contralto vocal range, with Richard's harmonising, arranging and composition skills. Karen was initially a proficient drummer. The pair formed the Richard Carpenter Trio and Spectrum before becoming Carpenters in 1968. The duo had 16 UK Top 40 hits, including six that reached the Top 10. Their albums were also very successful with 18 Top 40 entries, including 3 No. 1's and 5 other Top 10 recordings.*

1. Richard and Karen Carpenter signed to A&M Records on April 22, 1969. Who was the owner of the label?   A) Phil Spector   B) Herb Alpert   C) George Martin

2. Carpenters debut studio album was originally named *Offering* before being renamed after which Beatles song, that was included on the album?
A) Help   B) Please Please Me   C) Ticket To Ride

3. *(They Long to Be) Close to You* was the first Carpenters hit in the UK. Who penned the song?   A) Burt Bacharach and Hal David   B) Billy Joel   C) Neil Sedaka

4. Which 1969 No. 2 hit, their highest UK chart position, begins with the lyrics: "When I was young, I'd listen to the radio"?

5. Carpenters performed at the White House for which President in 1973?
A) Richard Nixon   B) Jimmy Carter   C) Lyndon B Johnson

6. Who is the main pianist on most, if not all of the songs by the Carpenters?

7. Richard also composed songs, which of these Carpenters hits did he write?
A) End of the World   B) Goodbye To Love   C) Only Yesterday

8. In 1964 Karen persuaded her parents to buy her a Ludwig drum set, similar to which jazz drummer?   A) Buddy Rich   B) Gene Krupa   C) Joe Morello

9. Who was the lyricist for songs composed by Richard Carpenter?
A) Hal Blaine   B) Tony Peluso   C) John Bettis

10. February 4, 1983, Karen died of heart failure brought on by her long, unpublicised struggle with what?   A) Diabetes   B) Anorexia nervosa   C) Obesity

DAVID CASSIDY *(David Bruce Cassidy (Born NYC on April 12, 1950 – Died Fort Lauderdale on November 21, 2017) was an American actor, singer, songwriter, and guitarist. He was best known for his role as Keith Partridge, the son of Shirley Partridge (played by his stepmother, Shirley Jones), in the 1970s musical-sitcom The Partridge Family. This role catapulted Cassidy to teen idol status as a superstar pop singer of the 1970s. Cassidy had 15 hits, either as soloist or as part of the Partridge Family. Of those 2 were #1's and 7 other reached the Top 10. He also had 6 Top 40 albums including a #1 and 3 other Top 10 hits.*

ALL 15 DAVID CASSIDY HITS.
STATE WHETHER THEY WERE SOLO HITS OR AS PART OF THE PARTRIDGE FAMILY

A) I Think I Love You	F) Rock Me Baby	L) If I Didn't Care
B) It's One Of These Nights (Yes love)	G) Looking Through the Eyes Of Love	M) Please Please Me
C) Could It Be Forever / Cherish	H) I'm A Clown / Some Kind Of Summer	N) I Write the Songs / Get It Up For Love
D) Breaking Up Is Hard To Do	J) Walking In the Rain	P) Darlin'
E) How Can I Be Sure	K) Daydreamer / The Puppy Song	Q) The Last Kiss

CARPENTERS ANSWERS: 1. B) Herb Alpert; 2. C) Ticket To Ride; 3. A) Burt Bacharach and Hal David; 4. Yesterday Once More; 5. A) Richard Nixon; 6. Richard Carpenter; 7. All of them A), B) and C); 8. C) Joe Morello (Dave Brubeck's drummer); 9. C) John Bettis; 10. B) Anorexia nervosa. **ALL 15 DAVID CASSIDY HITS ANSWERS**: A) PF; B) PF; C) DC; D) PF; E) DC; F) DC; G) PF; H) DC; J) PF; K) DC; L) DC; M) DC; N) DC; P) DC; Q) DC.

RAY CHARLES *(Ray Charles Robinson Sr. September 23, 1930 – June 10, 2004) was an American singer, songwriter, pianist, and composer. Among friends and fellow musicians he preferred being called 'Brother Ray'. He was often referred to as 'the Genius'. Charles was blinded during childhood, possibly due to glaucoma. Charles pioneered the soul music genre during the 1950s by combining blues, jazz, rhythm and blues, and gospel styles into the music he recorded for Atlantic. He contributed to the integration of country music, rhythm and blues, and pop music during the 1960s with his crossover success on ABC Records. Ray had 12 Top 40 UK hits, including a number one and three other Top 10 hits. Also had 6 Top 40 Albums.*

1. In what 1989 film do Dr. Jeff Weitzman and four mental patients, travelling in a minibus to New York, sing along to Ray's *Hit the Road Jack*, by Buster Poindexter?
A) The Dream Team   B) One Flew Over the Cuckoos Nest   C) Crazy People

2. Ray learned to read and write Braille and to play a number of musical instruments at which Florida school?   A) St. Augustine   B) Miami   C) Tampa

3. Which of these songs was the first to enter the UK Top 40 charts in 1960?
A) What'd I Say   B) Sticks and Stones   C) Georgia on my Mind

4. Ray Charles was a multiple Grammy Award winner during his long musical career. In what year did Ray win his first set of four Grammy Awards?
A) 1959   B) 1961   C) 1963

5. Ray Charles made a cameo appearance in the 1980 film *The Blues Brothers,* singing which song with the help of the Blues Brothers?
A) Gimme Some Lovin'   B) Let the Good Times Roll   C) Shake Your Tailfeather

6. In 1962 Ray reached UK No.1 for two weeks with which Don Gibson song?
A) Sea of Heartbreak   B) I Can't Stop Loving You   C) Oh Lonesome Me

7. Take These Chains from My Heart was another country song that got Ray a Top 10 hit in 1963. Who originally recorded the Fred Rose song in 1952?
A) Hank Williams   B) Marty Robbins   C) George Jones

8. Despite failing to chart for him in the UK, which classic Ray Charles song was sung by virtually every live band in the 1960s and was a Top 10 hit for Jerry Lee Lewis in 1961?   A) What'd I Say   B) Leave My Woman Alone   C) Talkin' 'Bout You

9. In 1985, Charles participated in a charity single recorded by the supergroup USA for Africa. It reached No. 1 in both the US and the UK. What was the song title?
A) Do They Know It's Christmas   B) Love Can Build A Bridge   C) We Are the World

10. Ray's final album was released two months after his death. Consisting of duets with admirers and contemporaries, what is the album's title?
A) Strong Love Affair   B) Genius Loves Company   C) Just Between Us

---

MUSICIANS: Conductor • *Quincy Jones.* **Soloists** *(in order of appearance)* • *Lionel Richie* • *Stevie Wonder* • *Paul Simon* • *Kenny Rogers* • *James Ingram* • *Tina Turner* • *Billy Joel* • *Michael Jackson* • *Diana Ross* • *Dionne Warwick* • *Willie Nelson* • *Al Jarreau* • *Bruce Springsteen* • *Kenny Loggins* • *Steve Perry* • *Daryl Hall* • *Huey Lewis* • *Cyndi Lauper* • *Kim Carnes* • *Bob Dylan* • *Ray Charles.*

Chorus • *Dan Aykroyd* • *Harry Belafonte* • *Lindsey Buckingham* • *Mario Cipollina and Johnny Colla, Bill Gibson, Chris Hayes, Sean Hopper (all Huey Lewis and the News)* • *Sheila E.* • *Bob Geldof* • *Jackie Jackson* • *La Toya Jackson* • *Marlon Jackson* • *Randy Jackson* • *Tito Jackson* • *Waylon Jennings* • *Bette Midler* • *John Oates* • *Jeffrey Osborne* • *Anita June & Ruth Pointer (The Pointer Sisters)* • *Smokey Robinson.*

Instrument players • *John Barnes – keyboards & arrangement* • *David Paich – synthesizers* • *Michael Boddicker, Ian Underwood – synthesizers, programming* • *Paulinho da Costa – percussion* • *Louis Johnson – synth bass* • *Michael Omartian – keyboards* • *Greg Phillinganes – keyboards* • *John Robinson – drums.*

CHUBBY CHECKER: *(Born Ernest Evans; October 3, 1941) is an American rock and roll singer and dancer. He is widely known for popularising many dance styles, including the Twist, the Pony and the Limbo. He had 11 Top 40 hits (including a duet) with three reaching the Top 10. He also had two Top 20 albums.*

1. Checker's 1960 cover of the R&B hit *The Twist* failed to chart in the UK. However a re-issue in 1962 climbed to No.14. Who had written the song and made the original recording of the song?
A) Little Willie John   B) Johnny Otis   C) Hank Ballard

2. In 1961 Checker reached No. 37 with another dance record. It was released 4 months later at Christmas and became his biggest hit. What was the song?
A) Let's Twist Again   B) Do the Hucklebuck   C) The Pony

3. In 1988 Chubby had another No. 2 UK with *The Twist (Yo Twist)*. This was a duet with which hip-hop trio?   A) Beastie Boys   B) The Fat Boys   C) Run-DMC

4. Which Chubby Checker 1962 No.19 hit includes these lyrics? "Cause summertime is party time, And everything's alright, Cause everyone is feelin' fine, And every night is Saturday night yeah."

5. With which other teen idol did Checker combine to have a minor Christmas hit with *Jingle Bell Rock* in 1962?   A) Frankie Avalon   B) Ricky Nelson   C) Bobby Rydell

6. "How low can you go?" is a line from a No. 32 dance hit for Chubby in 1962. Previously recorded by The Champs as an instrumental, what was the title of the hit?
A) Tequila   B)   C) Hoots Mon   C) Limbo Rock

7. Which Beatles track did Checker record in 1969, that reached No.76 in the UK?
A) Back in the USSR   B) Revolution   C) Twist and Shout

CHAS AND DAVE: *(often Chas 'n' Dave) were a British pop rock duo, formed in London by Chas Hodges (Born Edmonton, 28 December 1943 - 22 September 2018) & Dave Peacock (Born Enfield, 24 May 1945) most noted as creators / performers of rockney (a combo of rock and cockney), mixing 'pub singalong, music-hall humour, boogie-woogie piano and pre-Beatles rock 'n' roll'. Drummer Mick Burt, (23 October 1938 - 18 October 2014, completed the trio). Had 8 Top 40 listings (3 with Spurs), including 4 Top 10 hits (2 duets). 8 albums reached the Top 40, including two Top 10.*

1. Dave Peacock used to play in the Rolling Stones. True or False?

2. Chas & Dave were a trio from 1976, with Mick Burt on drums. With what band had he had chart success?   A) Cliff Bennett & the Rebel Rousers   B) Hollies   C) Them

3. Their biggest hit was which ballad which reached No. 2 in 1982?
A) Strummin'   B) Ain't No Pleasing You   C) Gertcha

4. *Rabbit* was a Top 10 chart success. Which product was the song later used to promote in a TV advert?   A) Sainsbury's   B) Waitrose   C) Courage Bitter

5. Chas and Dave linked up with Tottenham Hotspur for the first time in 1981 and had a massive hit with *Ossie's Dream*. Who was Ossie?

6. The boys joined the Matchroom Mob for a No.6 hit in 1986. What was the song?

7. *Margate* was a song that only reached No. 46, but was used instead of the usual theme for which famous Christmas Special of the sit-com *Only Fools and Horses*?

CHUBBY CHECKER ANSWERS: *1. C) Hank Ballard; 2. A) Let's Twist Again; 3. B) The Fat Boys; 4. Dancing Party; 5. C) Bobby Rydell; 6. C) Limbo Rock; 7. A) Back in the USSR.*
CHAS AND DAVE ANSWERS: *1. True (not THE Rolling Stones but another London band); 2. A) Cliff Bennett & the Rebel Rousers; 3. B) Ain't No Pleasing You; 4. C) Courage Bitter; 5. Osvaldo Ardiles (Spurs Argentinian star); 6. Snooker Loopy; 7. The Jolly Boys Outing.*

CHER: *(Born Cherilyn Sarkisian at El Centro, California on 20 May 1946) is an American singer, actress and television personality. She has been described as embodying female autonomy in a male-dominated industry. Cher is known for her distinctive contralto singing voice. Cher has employed various musical styles, including folk rock, pop rock, power ballads, disco, new wave music, rock music, punk rock, arena rock, and hip hop. After having 7 Top 30 singles hits and two Top 20 albums (1 Top 10). with husband Sonny, as Sonny and Cher, she had 24 Top 40 hits including 3 No.1's (1 with multi artists) and a further 8 Top 10 successes plus 9 Top 40 albums including 2 No. 1's and 5 others made the Top 10.*

1. Phil Spector produced Cher's first single, *Ringo, I Love You*, which Cher recorded as Bonnie Jo Mason. True or False?

2. What was Sonny & Cher's first hit in 1965 - a number one for two weeks?
A) Little Man   B) I Got You Babe   C) The Beat Goes On

3. In 1965 Cher had her first solo hit, battling with a rival version by The Byrds. What was the Bob Dylan song that gave both acts a big hit in both the US and UK?
A) Mr. Tambourine Man   B) I Shall Be Released   C) All I Really Want To Do

4. Which Sonny Bono composition took Cher to No. 3 in the UK in 1966?
A) Bang Bang (My Baby Shot Me Down)   B) Needles and Pins   C) Laugh At Me

5. In what year did Cher get divorced from Sonny Bono?
A) 1973   B) 1975   C) 1977

6. As an adult, what condition did Cher discover that she had?
A) Diabetes   B) Dyslexia   C) Arthritis

7. For which film did Cher win the Oscar for Best Actress in 1988?
A) Moonstruck   B) Mask   C) Suspect

8. Cher reached a new commercial peak in 1998 with which upbeat dance-pop song that topped the charts both side of the Atlantic?
A) Gypsies, Tramps and Thieves   B) Strong Enough   C) Believe

9. Who was Cher's role model when she was a young girl?
A) Audrey Hepburn   B) Shirley Bassey   C) Dolly Parton

10. In 1995 Cher, together with Chrissie Hynde, Neneh Cherry and Eric Clapton had a No.1 hit with which *Comic Relief* charity single, that was a former Judds single?

Can you fill in the missing pieces of information?

A

Fleetwood Mac	Shania Twain	Eagles	????
Rumours	Come on Over	Their Greatest Hits	????
1977	1997	1976	1982
27.9	29.6	41.2	49.2

B

PIPES OF PEACE	EBONY AND IVORY	MULL OF KINTYRE	????
1	2	3	????

CHER ANSWERS: *1. True; 2. B) I Got You Babe; 3. C) All I Really Want To Do; 4. A) Bang Bang (My Baby Shot Me Down); 5. B) 1975; 6. B) Dyslexia; 7. A) Moonstruck; 8. C) Believe; 9. A) Audrey Hepburn; 10. Love Will Build A Bridge.*
FILL IN THE GAPS ANSWERS: *A) Michael Jackson and Thriller. Left to right, the top 4 best selling popular music albums in the world. B) Any Beatles number 1. Paul McCartney had a solo No.1 with Pipes of Peace, a No.1 as a duo with Stevie Wonder on Ebony and Ivory, a number one as a trio with Wings with Mull of Kintyre, so any number one in a quartet is OK.*

CHICAGO *is an American rock band formed in 1967 in Chicago, Illinois. They began as a politically charged, experimental, rock band before moving to a predominantly softer sound, generating several hit ballads throughout the 1970s and 1980s, particularly in the US. Chicago are one of the longest-running and most successful rock groups, and one of the world's best-selling groups of all time, having sold more than 100 million records.In the UK the band had 6 Top 20 hits between 1970 and 1985, this included a No. 1 and four other Top 10 hits. 8 albums hit the Top 40 with 4 of them reaching the Top 10.*

1. In 1968 Chicago got exposure to more famous musical artists of the time whilst performing on a regular basis at which nightclub in West Hollywood?
A) Whisky a Go Go   B) Voyeur   C) Boulevard3

2. Chicago first hit the UK charts with *I'm a Man* in 1970. The Steve Winwood song had also been a Top 10 hit for which band, three years earlier?
A) Eagles   B) Spencer Davis Group   C) Hall & Oates

3. Which song was Chicago's first to reach number 1 on the UK singles chart?
A) If You Leave Me Now   B) Hard To Say I'm Sorry   C) Hard Habit To Break

4. Chicago played as support band to which top guitarist, quoted as saying to saxophonist Walter Parazaider, "Jeez, your horn players are like one set of lungs and your guitar player is better than me."
A) Eric Clapton   B) Stevie Ray Vaughan   C) Jimi Hendrix

5. The *Chicago X* album was certified both gold and platinum. In honour of the group's achievement, Columbia Records awarded the group a 25-pound bar of which pure metal produced by Cartier?   A) Gold   B) Silver   C) Platinum

6. Which Chicago founding member died from an unintentional self-inflicted gunshot wound to the head in 1978?   A) Peter Cetera   B) Terry Kath   C) Robert Lamm

7. Who joined the band Chicago in 1981 to sing and to play guitar and keyboards?
A) Bill Champlin   B) Donnie Dacus   C) James Pankow

8. In 1985, who was the son of Elvis Presley's bassist who replaced Peter Cetera on bass and vocals?   A) Jason Scheff   B) DaWayne Bailey   C) Donnie Dacus

9. Drummer Tris Imboden played drums in whose band before joining Chicago?
A) George Benson   B) Stevie Nicks   C) Kenny Loggins

10. After leaving Chicago Peter Cetera had a number three hit in the UK with which song?   A) Hard To Say I'm Sorry   B) Glory of Love   C) The Next Time I Fall

---

THREE'S NOT A CROWD!

Can you name these successful hit making trios?

A

B

C

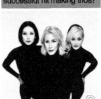
D

E

F

CHICAGO ANSWERS: *1. A) Whisky a Go Go; 2. B) Spencer Davis Group; 3. A) If You Leave Me Now; 4. C) Jimi Hendrix; 5. C) Platinum; 6. B) Terry Kath; 7. A) Bill Champlin; 8. A) Jason Scheff; 9. C) Kenny Loggins; 10. B) Glory of Love.* **THREE'S NOT A CROWD ANSWERS:** *A) Beverley Sisters; B) Supremes; C) Pointer Sisters; D) Bananarama; E) Destiny's Child (just qualified with hits from 1999 !); F) Martha & the Vandellas.*

ERIC CLAPTON CBE (born 30 March 1945 in Ripley, Surrey) is an English rock and blues guitarist, singer, and songwriter, widely regarded as one of the most important and influential guitarists of all time. Clapton joined the Yardbirds but left in 1965 to play with John Mayall & the Bluesbreakers. In 1966, he formed the power trio Cream with drummer Ginger Baker and bassist Jack Bruce, in which Clapton played sustained blues improvisations and 'arty, blues-based psychedelic pop'. He then formed the blues rock band Blind Faith before embarking on a solo career in 1970. As a solo artist he had 12 Top 40 hits, including 2 Top 10. Also had 25 Top 40 albums including a No. 1 and 13 other Top 10 hits.

1. What is Eric Clapton's middle name? A) Hank   B) Patrick   C) Dennis

2. Clapton formed a band in 1968, also comprising Bobby Whitlock, Carl Radle and Jim Gordon. What name did the band accidentally end up being called?

3. The band in question 2 had one massive hit with a rock classic written by Clapton and Jim Gordon. The song reached number 7 in 1972 and, when re-issued a decade later, surpassed that by getting to number four. What was the song?

4. In 1969 Clapton formed Blind Faith with Steve Winwood and Ginger Baker. Which musician, who also played in Family, Traffic and Ginger Baker's Air Force completed the line up on bass? A) Ric Grech   B) Jack Bruce   C) John Paul Jones

5. In 1965 Eric Clapton left The Yardbirds on the same day as the number five single, *For Your Love,* was released. True or False?

6. What was the first single by Cream in 1966, that reached a modest #34 in the UK charts? A) Strange Brew   B) I Feel Free   C) Wrapping paper

7. What is the title of Cream's debut album that was released in 1966 and reached number six in the charts? A) Fresh Cream   B) Sour Cream   C) Clotted Cream

8. In late 1969 Eric made the switch to which model of electric guitar?
A) Fender Telecaster   B) Fender Stratocaster   C) Gibson Firebird

9. Cream had 7 Top 40 hits, the last one of which reached number 18 in 1969. The song was written by Eric and George Harrison. What was it's title?
A) Sunshine of Your Love   B) White Room   C) Badge

10. With whom did Clapton have a number 30 hit, *It's Probably Me*, in 1992?
A) Elton John   B) Sting   C) Paul McCartney

HOW MANY UK ACTS CAN YOU REMEMBER FROM THEIR SONGS?	
1. 1967 - Puppet on a String	7. 1981 - Making Your Mind Up
2. 1969 - Boom-Bang-a-Bang	8. 1988 - Go
3. 1973 - Power To All Our Friends	9. 1992 - One Step Out Of Time
4. 1975 - Let Me Be The One	10. 1993 - Better the Devil You Know
5. 1976 - Save Your Kisses For Me	11. 1997 - Love Shine a Light
6. 1980 - Love Enough For Two	12. 1998 - Where Are You?

EuroVision SONG CONTEST BETTER DAYS!

THE DAVE CLARK FIVE, *often called The DC5, were an English rock and roll band formed in Tottenham in 1958. The classic line up was Dave Clark (Drums), Rick Huxley (Bass), Lenny Davidson (Lead guitar), Denis Payton (Saxophone, harmonica, second guitar), Mike Smith (Keyboards and main vocals). DC5 were a major part of the British Invasion. Achieved 19 UK top 40 hits from 1963 to 1970 (8 Top 10), and briefly were considered serious rivals to the Beatles with their 'Tottenham Sound'. DC5 also had 4 Top 30 albums, 3 of them Top 10. The group disbanded in early 1970.*

1. The DC5 first charted at No. 30 with *Do You Love Me* in 1963. However another version of the song reached No.1. Who were the chart toppers?
A) The Hollies   B) Brian Poole & The Tremeloes   C) The Searchers

2. The band's second single, written by Dave Clark and Mike Smith, produced their only number one in the UK. What was the song with the big 'air hammer' beat?
A) Glad All Over   B) Bits and Pieces   C) You Really Got Me

3. The band employed a famed session drummer on some of their recording to produce the riving beat. What was his name?
A) Clem Cattini   B) Steve White   C) Bobby Graham

4. Which DC5 No. 2 hit includes these lyrics? "Time goes by and goes so slow (Oh yeah), It just doesn't seem true, only just a few days ago, You said you'd love me, never make me blue".

5. The Dave Clark Five starred in a British pop music film in 1965. What was the name of the film for which the title song reached No. 5?

6. The DC5 had two chart hits with the same title. One reached No. 37 in 1965 and the second song reached No. 2 in 1967. What was the title?

7. In 1967 *You Got What It Takes* by The DC5 reached No. 28. It was a cover version of a 1960 No. 7 hit by whom?
A) Johnny Kidd & The Pirates   B) Showaddywaddy   C) Marv Johnson

8. Which No. 7 hit for the DC5 in 1969 was a medley of the songs, *Sweet Little Sixteen, Long Tall Sally, Chantilly Lace, Whole Lotta Shakin' Goin' On*, and *Blue Suede Shoes*?

9.The DC5 made 18 appearances, more than any other British Invasion group, on which major US TV variety show of the time?

10. In 1965 the DC5 had their only US number one hit with a cover of a Bobby Day hit that only reached No. 45 in the UK. What was the song?
A) Over and Over   B) Rockin' Robin   C) Little Bitty Pretty One

TWO into one!

Two faces morphed into one. Can you name the 4 singers who make up the two faces?

THE DAVE CLARK FIVE ANSWERS: *1. B) Brian Poole & The Tremeloes; 2. A) Glad All Over; 3. C) Bobby Graham; 4. Bits and Pieces; 5. Catch Us If You Can; 6. Everybody Knows (1965 song (I Still Love You) added to distinguish it); 7. C) Marv Johnson; 8. Good Old Rock and Roll; 9. Ed Sullivan Show; 10. A) Over and Over.* **TWO INTO ONE ANSWERS:** *A) Dusty Springfield / Sandie Shaw; B) Gary Barlow / Ronan Keating*

PETULA CLARK *(Petula Sally Olwen Clark, CBE (born Ewell, Surrey on 15 November 1932) is a British singer, actress, and composer. Between 1954 and 1988 Pet notched up 21 hits, including two number ones and 10 other Top 10 hits, she also had 6 Top 40 album successes. Petula Clark was also a big star with a string of hits across the Atlantic. Petula has sold more than 70 million records worldwide, making her the best-selling British female vocalist in history. She was awarded the CBE in the 1998 Queen's New Year Honours List for her services to music.*

1. Petula Clark's first hit, in 1954, was based upon the French song, *Le Petit Cordonnier* and was a cover of the Gaylords US version. What was the song?
A) The Little Shoemaker   B) It's a Small World   C) Little Things Mean a Lot

2. Pet had a hit in 1955 with a song all about which Balearic Island?
A) Menorca   B) Majorca   C) Ibiza

3. Petula Clark had a number one record in 1961 with her recording of which song, that was also a Top 10 hit for Anne Shelton?
A) Sailor   B) Lay Down Your Arms   C) Arrivederci Darling

4. Pet had a No. 3 hit in 1961 with a song about which Shakespearean character?
A) Hamlet   B) Macbeth   C) Romeo

5. "Oh, well, I'm sittin' here, la, la, Waiting for my ya ya, Uh huh, uh huh". These lyrics are from which 1962 hit that slotted into the dance craze of the time?

6. A 1964 Tony Hatch song became an international hit for Petula, reaching number two in the UK. What kept the song from being a number one?   A) Yeh Yeh by Georgie Fame   B) Oh, Pretty Woman by Roy Orbison   C) I Feel Fine by The Beatles

7. In 1967 Pet had an unlikely chart battle with Harry Secombe with *This Is My Song*. Secombe reached number two, but Clark hit number one. Who wrote the song?
A) Tony Hatch   B) Charlie Chaplin   C) Dolly Parton

8. Petula Clark starred in several musical films. In 1968 she starred opposite Fred Astaire, and was nominated for the Golden Globe Award for Best Actress for which film?   A) Finian's Rainbow   B) Goodbye Mr. Chips   C) 6.5 Special

9. In 1963, *Je me sens bien auprès de toi* was a No. 5 hit in France. It was a vocal version of which Shadows instrumental?   A) Apache   B) Atlantis   C) Dance On

10. After a 17 year absence from the singles charts, Petula Clark had a Top 10 hit in 1988 with a remix of which of her hits?
A) Don't Sleep in the Subway   B) Downtown   C) I Know a Place

The Coasters are an American rhythm and blues/rock and roll vocal group who had a string of US hits in the late 1950s. The band had just 4 hits in the UK. They appear here in anagram form. Can you work out the song titles?

1. ASH NICER

2. YE KATY KAY

3. BACON WHIRLER

4. I VINO POSY

PETULA CLARK ANSWERS: *1. A) The Little Shoemaker; 2. B) Majorca; 3. A) Sailor; 4. C) Romeo; 5. Ya Ya Twist; 6. C) I Feel Fine by The Beatles (for 3 weeks); 7. B) Charlie Chaplin; 8. A) Finian's Rainbow; 9. C) Dance On; 10. B) Downtown. **ROCK 'N' ROLLER COASTERS ANSWERS**: 1. Searchin'; 2. Yakety Yak; 3. Charlie Brown; 4. Poison Ivy.*

JOE COCKER - *John Robert Cocker OBE (20 May 1944 – 22 December 2014) was an English singer known for his gritty, bluesy voice and dynamic stage performances that featured expressive body movements. Cocker's main musical influences growing up were Ray Charles and Lonnie Donegan. His best known singles were covers of songs by other artists, though he composed a number of his own songs, often in conjunction with songwriting partner Chris Stainton. Cocker had 9 Top 40 hits including one duet. One was a number one, and two more reached the Top 10. He also had 6 Top 40 albums, including 2 Top 10 hits.*

1. Joe Cocker's only UK number one came in 1968 with a soulful version of which Beatles song that had already been a hit for Young Idea and Joe Brown in 1967?
A) With a Little Help From My Friends   B) Here Comes the Sun   C) Something

2. At which festival, on Max Yasgur's dairy farm, did Joe Cocker perform in 1969?
A) Woodstock   B) Newport Jazz Festival   C) Monterey Jazz Festival

3. The title of Joe's first hit album in 1970 was from which Noel Coward song?
A) Mad Dogs & Englishmen   B) I'll See You Again   C) London Pride

4. What kind of lady featured in Joe's 1969 hit, which was a Leon Russell song?
A) Dark   B) Electric   C) Delta

5. In 1970 Cocker covered The Letter, which reached No. 39 in the charts. Which American band had had a big hit with the song in 1967?
A) Lovin' Spoonful   B) Box Tops   C) Paul Revere & The Raiders

6. The theme song to the 1982 film *An Officer and a Gentleman, Up Where We Belong*, was a Top 10 hit for Joe Cocker in a duet with which female singer?
A) Diana Ross   B) Jennifer Warnes   C) Cher

7. Paul McCartney let Cocker use which one of his songs on his second album?   A) She Came In Through the Bathroom Window   B) Lady Madonna   C) In My Life

8. Joe Cocker wrote the overture performed by the then UK Prime Minister Tony Blair, when he famously conducted a live orchestra while in office. True or False?

9. In 1983, Cocker joined Ronnie Lane and a star-studded line-up of British musicians to raise money in aid of which degenerative disease?

10. For which US President did Cocker perform at an inauguration concert in February 1989?   A) Ronald Reagan   B) Bill Clinton   C) George Bush

1.	Freda Payne (No. 1 in 1970)
2.	Four Seasons (No. 3 in 1976)
3.	David Soul (No. 1 in 1977)
4.	Neil Young (No. 10 in 1972)
5.	Sting (No. 16 in 1993)
6.	Hawkwind (No. 3 in 1972)
7.	Jeff Beck (No. 17 in 1967)
8.	Beautiful South (No. 23 in 1994)
9.	Ash (No. 5 in 1996)
10.	David Essex (No. 4 in 1980)

10 hit songs containing the word 'Gold' or 'Silver'. Just name the titles of the hits.

JOE COCKER ANSWERS: *1. A) With a Little Help From My Friends; 2. A) Woodstock; 3. A) Mad Dogs & Englishmen; 4. C) Delta; 5. B) Box Tops; 6. B) Jennifer Warnes; 7. A) She Came In Through the Bathroom Window; 8. False (it was Edward Heath); 9. Multiple Sclerosis (from which Lane was beginning to suffer); 10. C) George Bush.*
GOLD OR SILVER? ANSWERS: *1. Band of Gold; 2. Silver Star; 3. Silver Lady; 4. Heart of Gold; 5. Fields of Gold; 6. Silver Machine; 7. Hi-Ho Silver Lining; 8. Good as Gold; 9. Goldfinger; 10. Silver Dream Machine.*

THE 1950s - *Music of the UK began to develop in the 1950s; from largely insular and derivative forms to become a leading centre of popular music. The significant change of the mid-1950s was the impact of American rock and roll, which provided a new model for performance and recording, based on a youth market. Initially dominated by American acts, but soon British forms appeared, first with skiffle, the uniquely British take on American folk music, then the beginnings of a folk revival placing emphasis on national traditions followed by early attempts to produce British rock and roll.*

30 smash hits from the 1950's. Fill in the blanks. <u>For a bonus point</u> *find the link between all of the tracks*

1. Let's Have a Party	??????	1953
2. That's Amore	??????	1954
3. Cool Water	??????	1955
4. ??????	Mitch Miller	1955
5. Meet Me on the Corner	??????	1955
6. Green Door	??????	1956
7. Walk Hand in Hand	??????	1956
8. Love Letters in the Sand	??????	1957
9. ??????	Russ Hamilton	1957
10. ??????	Debbie Reynolds	1957
11. ??????	Harry Belafonte	1957
12. When I Fall In Love	??????	1957
13. ??????	Four Preps	1958
14. King Creole	??????	1958
15. Bird Dog	??????	1958
16. ??????	Cliff Richard & Drifters	1958
17. A Teenager In Love	??????	1959
18. Baby Face	??????	1959
19. Battle of New Orleans	??????	1959
20. ??????	Johnny Duncan & Bluegrass Boys	1957
21. Ma He's Making Eyes At Me	??????	1957
22. ??????	Mudlarks	1958
23. Be My Girl	??????	1957
24. Tom Hark	??????	1958
25. ??????	Teddy Bears	1958
26. Come Prima	??????	1958
27. Happy Wanderer	??????	1954
28. Swedish Rhapsody	??????	1953
29. Terry's Theme from Limelight	??????	1953
30. Learnin' the Blues	??????	1955

BACK TO THE FIFTIES ANSWERS: *1. Winifred Atwell; 2. Dean Martin; 3. Frankie Laine; 4. Yellow Rose of Texas; 5. Max Bygraves; 6. Frankie Vaughan; 7. Tony Martin; 8. Pat Boone; 9. We Will Make Love; 10. Tammy; 11. Banana Boat Song; 12. Nat 'King' Cole; 13. Big Man; 14. Elvis Presley; 15. Everly Brothers; 16. Move It; 17. Marty Wilde; 18. Little Richard; 19. Lonnie Donegan; 20. Last Train to San Fernando; 21. Johnny Otis Show; 22. Lollipop; 23. Jim Dale; 24. Elias & His Zig Zag Jive Flutes; 25. To Know Him Is To Love Him; 26. Marino Marini; 27. Obemkirchen Children's Choir; 28. Mantovani; 29. Frank Chacksfield; 30. Frank Sinatra. **THE LINK:** All 30 songs reached number two in the UK.*

ALMA COGAN - *Alma Angela Cohen Cogan (19 May 1932 – 26 October 1966) was an English singer of Russian-Romanian Jewish descent. Alma sung traditional pop music in the 1950s and early 1960s. Dubbed the 'Girl with the Giggle in Her Voice', many of her recordings were covers of US hits. Cogan was the highest paid British female entertainer of her era and she topped the annual NME reader's poll as 'Outstanding British Female Singer' four times between 1956 /1960. Cogan had 20 Top 40 hits including a No. 1 and 3 Top 10 hits.*

1. In which area of London was Alma Cogan born?
A) Notting Hill   B) Whitechapel   C) Kensington

2. Her first hit was in 1954 when she got to No. 4 in the charts with a cover of a Teresa Brewer song. What was the song?
A) Bell Bottom Blues   B) Let Me Go, Lover   C) Till I Waltz Again With You

3. Alma Cogan had just one number one hit. What song reached the pinnacle of the charts in 1955?   A) I Can't Tell a Waltz From a Tango   B) Willie Can   C) Dreamboat

4. Also in 1955 what did Alma Cogan say you couldn't do with an eskimo?
A) Get hot   B) Tango   C) Waltz

5. "One looks like Mommy, With a cute little curl on top, And the other ones got, A big bald spot, Exactly like his Pop Pop Pop…..". Lyrics from which Alma Cogan hit?
A) Twenty Tiny Fingers   B) Why Do Fools Fall In Love   C) Little Things Mean a Lot

6. In a 1956 film, the title song was performed by George Goebel and Mitzi Gaynor. Alma Cogan had a No.25 hit with the song in the UK. What was the title of the song?
A) The Birds and Bees   B) Why Do Fools Fall in Love   C) Go On By

7. In 1956 what ran through the middle of the house?
A) The Motorway   B) The Railroad   C) The Footpath

8. Alma covered a traditional Mexican folk song, *Cielito Lindo*, in 1957 and had another hit. What was her version called?
A) Whatever Lola Wants   B) You Me and Us   C) Last Night On the Back Porch

9. Alma was outgunned in the charts in 1958. Her version of Marty Robbins' *The Story Of My Life* reached No. 25, but three other Brits got higher. Gary Miller attained number 14 and Dave King number 20. But who got to No. 1?
A) Vince Eager   B) Tommy Steele   C) Michael Holliday

10. Alma covered The Exciters *Tell Him* in 1963 and was confident it would get her back in the UK charts. However she was pipped by another cover version by which British female singer?   A) Lulu   B) Billie Davis   C) Sandie Shaw

FIVE TRIVIA QUESTIONS. WHAT LINKS THE ANSWERS?

1. Bob Geldof was lead singer with which band?

2. John Phillips, Cass Elliot, Michelle Phillips & Denny Doherty made up which American folk rock vocal group?

3. Which influential band formed in 1980 after the demise of Joy Division, following the suicide of lead singer Ian Curtis?

4. Sisters Vicki Peterson (guitar and vocals) and Debbi Peterson (drums and vocals) were founder members of which band?

5. Which band's lead singer appeared in a Persil soap commercial and made his West End theatrical debut in Tom Brown's Schooldays?

ALMA COGAN ANSWERS: *1. B) Whitechapel; 2. A) Bell Bottom Blues; 3. C) Dreamboat; 4. B) Tango (Never Do a Tango With an Eskimo reached No. 6); 5. A) Twenty Tiny Fingers; 6. A) The Birds and Bees; 7. B) The Railroad; 8. B) You Me and Us; 9. C) Michael Holliday; 10. B) Billie Davis.* **FIND A LINK ANSWERS:** *1. Boomtown Rats; 2. Mamas & Papas; 3. New Order; 4. Bangles; 5. Duran Duran (Simon Le Bon). Link: All had hit songs about Mondays. I Don't Like Mondays; Monday, Monday; Blue Monday; Manic Monday; New Moon on Monday.*

NAT 'KING' COLE - *(Nathaniel Adams Coles, born in Montgomery, Alabama on March 17, 1919. Died February 15, 1965). Cole was an American singer, jazz pianist, and actor. His trio was the model for small jazz ensembles that followed. 33 Top 40 hits (including one duet and one re-issue) between 1952 and 1994. 18 of them reached the Top 10. Cole also acted in films and on television and performed on Broadway. He was the first African-American man to host an American television series. He was the father of singer-songwriter Natalie Cole (1950–2015). Cole consulted with President Kennedy and his successor, Lyndon B. Johnson, on civil rights.*

1. In 1956, what happened during a Nat 'King' Cole concert in Birmingham, Alabama? A) He was attacked on stage by KKK members B) A tornado hit the building while he was performing C) Cole appeared on stage with Elvis

2. True or False? Nat 'King' Cole never had a number one hit in the UK.

3. On which famous record label did Nat 'King' Cole record all his major hits?
A) Parlophone B) Columbia C) Capitol

4. In 1957, Cole became the first African-American to host a network TV variety show in the US. Why did the show finish after just one year? A) White acts refused to appear B) *I Love Lucy* destroyed his ratings C) A lack of national sponsorship

5. Nat's first UK hit reached number three in 1952. What was the song?
A) Somewhere Along the Way B) Because You're Mine C) Pretend

6. In 1965 Nat appeared in the comedy-western film *Cat Ballou*. With whom did he sing the theme song in a memorable opening scene?
A) Frank Sinatra B) Stubby Kaye C) Lee Marvin

7. With which Charlie Chaplin tune, with lyrics added by Geoffrey Parsons, did Nat get to No. 2 in the UK charts in 1954? A) Smile B) Eternally C) Limelight

8. Mona Lisa was amazingly never a hit in the UK for Nat. However a rockabilly version of the song reached number five by which singer in 1959?
A) Carl Mann B) Conway Twitty C) Shakin' Stevens

9. The classic song *Let There Be Love* peaked at number 11 in 1962. With which British jazz pianist did Nat share the credits on the single?
A) Dudley Moore B) Stan Tracey C) George Shearing

10. Nat 'King' Cole had a 1962 Top 5 hit with which Sherman brothers country flavoured singalong song? A) Those Hazy Crazy Days of Summer B) Dear Lonely Hearts C) Ramblin' Rose

11. In response to a Rick Astley version, a Nat 'King' Cole number two hit from 1967 was re-issued, and got him to number four, exactly 25 years after his last chart success. What was the song? A) When I Fall In Love B) Stardust C) Smile

12. In 1991 a Nat 'King' Cole classic hit was back in the Top 20 when modern recording technology was used to reunite Nat and daughter in a duet version of which song? A) Mona Lisa B) Unforgettable C) When I Fall In Love

---

A classic Nat 'King' Cole seasonal song written in 1945 by Robert Wells and Mel Tormé. Known to all by its first line and not its official title, *The Christmas Song (Merry Christmas to You).*

Chestnuts roasting on an open fire
Jack Frost nipping at your nose
Yuletide carols being sung by a choir
And folks dressed up like Eskimos

NAT 'KING' COLE ANSWERS: *1. A) He was attacked on stage by KKK members; 2. True; 3. Capitol; 4. C) A lack of national sponsorship; 5. A) Somewhere Along the Way; 6. B) Stubby Kaye; 7. A) Smile; 8. B) Conway Twitty; 9. C) George Shearing; 10. C) Ramblin' Rose; 11. A) When I Fall in Love; 12. B) Unforgettable.*

PHIL COLLINS - *Philip David Charles Collins LVO (born Chiswick, London on 30 January 1951), is an English drummer, singer, record producer, songwriter, and actor. He is best known as the drummer/singer of the rock band Genesis and for his very successful solo career from 1981. Had 24 solo Top 40 hits between 1981 and 1999, including two duets. Of these three reached number one and another 10 got into the Top 10. Eight hit albums all reached the Top 4, five of them getting to No. 1. Genesis also notched up 21 Top 40 singles hits, 8 of them entering the Top 10 (see Genesis quiz).*

1. The seventh studio album by Genesis featured Phil Collins as lead singer for the first time. What was the title of the album released in February 1976?
A) Wind & Wuthering   B) Selling England by the pound   C) A Trick of the Tail

2. In 1982, Phil Collins had a number one hit with a song, sixteen years after the original song had reached No. 3 by The Supremes. What was the name of the song?
A) You Can't Hurry Love   B) You Keep Me Hangin' On   C) The Happening

3. Phil Collins drummed on which 1983 No. 5 hit for Adam Ant?
A) Stand and Deliver   B) Puss 'N Boots   C) Prince Charming

4. Collins duetted with Earth, Wind & Fire vocalist Philip Bailey on which No.1 hit in 1985?   A) Boogie Wonderland   B) Easy Lover   C) Let's Groove

5. Phil Collins performed at the Live Aid concert in 1985 at Wembley Stadium, London; then flew on Concorde to the US to perform at the concert at JFK Stadium, Philadelphia. True or False?

6. Phil Collins' third solo album was released in January 1985. It won a Grammy Award for Album of the Year in 1986. What was the title of the album?
A) Hello, I Must Be Going   B) Both Sides   C) No Jacket Required

7. Phil Collins starred in the title role of the 1988 film *Buster*. *A Groovy Kind of Love* reached No. 1, but the soundtrack also included which song, specially written for the film by Phil, that reached No. 6 in the UK charts?
A) Two Hearts   B) Another Day in Paradise   C) In the Air Tonight

8. Collins was the subject of the TV show *This Is Your Life* in 1988. At which London location was he surprised by Michael Aspel?
A) Tower of London   B) Covent Garden   C) London Palladium

9. Phil had a cameo role as which character in Steven Spielberg's 1991 film *Hook*?   A) Smee   B) Inspector Good   C) Pockets

10. What is the name of Disney's Broadway musical soundtrack for which Collins wrote the lyrics?   A) Tarzan   B) Toy Story   C) Mulan

1. In the early 60's which brothers from Winchester had 5 Top 40 hits, including Warpaint, and seen as the UK's Everly Brothers?

2. Who are the bespectacled Scottish twins who sang Letter to America?

3. Which Cincinnati brothers reaped a Harvest For the World in 1976?

4. Under what name did Bobby Hatfield and Bill Medley have hits?

5. Which act, claiming to be two brothers, came second in the Eurovision Song Contest for the UK in 1961 with Are You Sure?

PHIL COLLINS ANSWERS: *1. C) A Trick of the Tail; 2. A) You Can't Hurry Love; 3. B) Puss 'N Boots; 4. B) Easy Lover; 5. True; 6. C) No Jacket Required; 7. A) Two Hearts; 8. B) Covent Garden; 9. B) Inspector Good; 10. A) Tarzan.*
BROTHERS IN SONG ANSWERS: *1. The Brook Brothers; 2. The Proclaimers; 3. The Isley Brothers; 4. The Righteous Brothers; 5. The Allisons.*

THE COMMODORES / LIONEL RICHIE - *are an American funk and soul band, which peaked in the late 1970s - mid 1980s. The group met as mostly freshmen at Tuskegee Institute in 1968, and signed with Motown in November 1972. The band featured Lionel Richie, Thomas McClary, William King, Andre Callahan, Michael Gilbert, and Milan Williams. The group were most successful when Lionel Richie was the co-lead singer and had 10 Top 40 singles hits (1 No. 1 + 4 other Top 10) from 1974-1985, plus 7 Top 40 albums (2 Top 10). Lionel Richie had 14 Top 40 singles from including one duet (1 No. 1 and 7 other Top 10). He also had 7 Top 40 albums (inc 2 No. 1's and 3 Top 10).*

1. Which member of the Commodores wrote their first UK hit, *Machine Gun*?
A) Lionel Richie   B) Milan Williams   C) William King

2. What Grammy-winning 1985 song by the Commodores mentioned Marvin Gaye in these lyrics "Marvin, he was a friend of mine, And he could sing his song"?
A) Nightshift   B) Sail On   C) Still

3. In what 1978 Donna Summer film did the Commodores perform the song *Too Hot Ta Trot*?   A) White Knights   B) Endless Love   C) Thank God It's Friday

4. In 1978 the Commodores had their only UK No. 1 hit with which song that topped the charts for five weeks?   A) Three Times a Lady   B) Easy   C) Still

5. By 1984 the Commodores had gradually abandoned its funk roots and moved into the more commercial pop arena. Which former Heatwave singer assumed co-lead vocal duties with drummer Walter Orange?   A) William King   B) James Dean 'J.D.' Nicholas   C) Milan Williams

6. Which 1982 No. 6 hit single was from Lionel Richie's eponymous first solo album?
A) Truly   B) My Love   C) You Are

7. In 1985 Lionel Richie won an Academy Award for *Say You, Say Me* for which film?
A) The Color Purple   B) White Nights   C) Return to Oz

8. Lionel Richie wrote and produced which song for Kenny Rogers, a number twelve hit in 1980?   A) Ruby Don't Take Your Love To Town   B) Lucille   C) Lady

9. "You came in, That's what my little heart was looking for, Laughter in the rain, Feeling like a fool in love again". Lyrics from which Lionel Richie 1992 No. 7 hit?
A) Don't Wanna Lose You   B) Angel   C) My Destiny

10. Lionel Richie had one solo No.1 in the UK. Which song was top for 6 weeks in 1984?   A) Hello   B) All Night Long (All Night)   C) Dancing on the Ceiling

---

1. 'Check out Guitar George, he knows all the chords.' (1978)

2. 'A love like ours will never end, Just touch me and we're there again.' (1989)

3. 'They call her Natasha, When she looks like Elsie' (1978)

4. 'If you can't find a partner use a wooden chair' (1958)

5. 'Bus driver, please look for me, 'Cause I couldn't bear to see ...' (1973)

6. 'Where can you learn to fly, play in sport or skin dive' (1979)

7. 'Night is falling and you just can't see, is this illusion or reality?' (1982)

8. 'You took a mystery and made me want it' (1986)

9. 'Birds sing out of tune, And rain clouds hide the moon (1964)

10. 'Baby hold me tight and let this be' (1990)

Who SUNG That?

In which hits will you find these lyrics?

THE COMMODORES / LIONEL RICHIE ANSWERS: *1. B) Milan Williams; 2. B) Sail On; 3. Thank God It's Friday; 4. A) Three Times a Lady; 5. B) James Dean 'J.D.' Nicholas; 6. A) Truly; 7. B) White Nights; 8. C) Lady; 9. C) My Destiny; 10. A) Hello.*
WHO SUNG THAT? ANSWERS: *1. Sultans of Swing - Dire Straits; 2. Miss You Like Crazy - Natalie Cole; 3. I Don't Wanna Go To (Chelsea) - Elvis Costello & The Attractions; 4. Jailhouse Rock - Elvis Presley; 5. Tie a Yellow Ribbon Round the Old Oak Tree - Dawn feat Tony Orlando; 6. In the Navy - Village People; 7. In the Army Now - Status Quo; 8. Chain Reaction - Diana Ross; 9. A World Without Love - Peter & Gordon; 10. Show Me Heaven - Maria McKee.*

PERRY COMO - *(Pierino Ronald 'Perry' Como; May 18, 1912 – May 12, 2001) was an American singer, actor and TV personality. During a career of more than 50 years, he recorded exclusively for RCA Victor for 44 years, after signing with the label in 1943. He recorded primarily vocal pop and was renowned for recordings in the intimate, easy-listening genre, pioneered by Bing Crosby. Como had 29 Top 40 hits in the UK between 1953 and 1974, of those 14 made the Top 10, with 2 number ones included. He also had 8 Top 40 albums including two number ones and three other Top 10 successes.*

1. Where was Pierino Ronald Como born on May 18th, 1912?
A) Palena, Italy   B) Florence, Italy   C) Canonsburg, Pennsylvania

2. True or False? Perry was the 7th son of a 7th son.

3. Before he became a singer what type of shop did Como run with the aid of two assistants?   A) Sweet   B) Barber   C) Fruit and vegetables

4. Perry's first number one was achieved in 1953. What was the song?
A) Don't Let the Stars Get In Your Eyes   B) Wanted   C) Idle Gossip

5. In 1958 Como hit number one with what Burt Bacharach song?
A) Hot Diggity   B) Magic Moments   C) Delaware

6. In the US the B side of a song that hit number one in the UK in 1958 was the No.1 side. The song includes these lyrics, can you name it? "For love may come and tap you on the shoulder, Some starless night. Just in case you feel you wanna hold her, You'll have a pocket full of starlight."

7. What 1960 No. 3 Perry Como hit has references to 15 states of the United States?
A) Mississippi   B) Alabama   C) Delaware

8. In 1959, Como signed a $25 million deal with which company who sponsored his TV shows?   A) Kraft Foods   B) Budweiser   C) Walmart

9. **IBIS MILESTONES** is an anagram of which song title that surprisingly took Perry back to No. 4 in the UK singles chart in 1971?

10. *And I Love You So* was Perry's last big hit in the UK. Who wrote the song?
A) Don McLean   B) Joni Mitchell   C) Jackson Browne

METEOROLOGY CONNECTIONS!

1. In 1996 and 1998 who appeared on No. 1's with Baddiel & Skinner?

2. Who took Something in the Air to No. 1 with Pete Townshend on bass?

3. Catch the Wind was a 1965 hit for which friend of The Beatles?

4. Which band did Richie Blackmore form after Deep Purple broke up?

5. Rockers Revenge was a studio musical project that had one memorable 1982 hit. What was the Eddy Grant song?

6. Which funk-disco group had a 1977 No. 2 hit with Boogie Nights?

7. Which Elton John tribute song was a hit in 1974, and again in 1997, with re-written lyrics for another woman?

8. Fog On The Tyne (Revisited) was a 1990 Lindisfarne hit with which England international footballer?

9. Which song by the Liverpool Britpop band Cast reached No. 8 in 1995?

10. "Someone left the cake out in the rain" in which 1968 & 1978 hit?

PERRY COMO ANSWERS: 1. C) Canonsburg, Pennsylvania; 2. True; 3. B) Barber; 4. A) Don't Let the Stars Get In Your Eyes; 5. B) Magic Moments; 6. Catch a Falling Star (No. 9 in the UK); 7. C) Delaware; 8. A) Kraft Foods; 9. It's Impossible; 10. A) Don McLean.
WHATEVER THE WEATHER ANSWERS: 1. Lightning Seeds; 2. Thunderclap Newman; 3. Donovan; 4. Rainbow; 5. Walking on Sunshine; 6. Heatwave; 7. Candle in the Wind; 8. Gazza (Paul Gascoigne); 9. Sandstorm; 10. Macarthur Park (Richard Harris (1968) and Donna Summer (1978)

RUSS CONWAY - *(born Trevor Herbert Stanford in Bristol on 2 September 1925 – 16 November 2000) was an English popular music pianist and composer. Awarded the DSM. Conway had 17 piano instrumentals in the UK Singles Chart between 1957 - 1963, including two No. 1 hits and 5 other Top 10 hits. He also had another hit with Dorothy Squires in 1961. He also had 7 Top 30 albums, 6 of them reaching the Top 10.His career was blighted by ill health, including a nervous breakdown and subsequently a stroke, which prevented him from performing between 1968 and 1971.*

RUSS CONWAY'S 18 TOP 40 HITS. MATCH THE HIGHEST CHART POSITIONS TO EACH HIT. (No's 1, 5, 7, and 24 each reached twice with different hits).

1. Party Pops *	A. 1
2. Got A Match	B. 1
3. More Party Pops	C. 5
4. The World Outside	D. 5
5. Side Saddle	E. 7
6. Roulette	F. 7
7. China Tea	G. 10
8. Snow Coach	H. 14
9. More And More Party Pops #	J. 15
10. Royal Event	K. 16
11. Lucky Five	L. 19
12. Passing Breeze	M. 21
13. Even More Party Pops ^	N. 23
14. Pepe	P. 24
15. Say It With Flowers (with Dorothy Squires)	Q. 24
16. Toy Balloons	R. 27
17. Lesson One	S. 30
18. Always You And Me	T. 33

* PARTY POPS: *When You're Smiling (The Whole World Smiles With You); I'm Looking Over A Four Leaf Clover; When You Wore A Tulip And I Wore A Big Red Rose; Row, Row, Row; For Me And My Girl; Shine On Harvest Moon; By The Light Of The Silvery Moon; Side By Side.*

 # MORE PARTY POPS: *Music Music Music (Put Another Nickel In); If You Were The Only Girl In The World; I'm Nobody's Sweetheart Now; Yes Sir That's My Baby; Some Of These Days; The Honeysuckle And The Bee; Hello! Hello! Who's Your Lady Friend?; In A Shanty In Old Shanty Town.*

^ MORE & MORE PARTY POPS: *The Sheik Of Araby; Who Were You With Last Night; Any Old Iron Tiptoe Through The Tulips; If You Were The Only Girl In The World; When I Leave The World Behind.*

RUSS CONWAY ANSWERS: *1. Q or R; 2. S; 3. G; 4. Q or R; 5. A or B; 6. A or B; 7. C or D; 8. E or F; 9. C or D; 10. J; 11. H; 12. K; 13; 13. R; 14. L; 15. N; 16. E or F; 17. M; 18. T.*

SAM COOKE - *(Samuel Cook (Born Mississippi, January 22, 1931 – December 11, 1964), was an American singer, songwriter, and entrepreneur. Considered to be a pioneer and one of the most influential soul artists of all time, Cooke is commonly referred to as the 'King of Soul' for his distinctive vocals, notable contributions to the genre and high significance in popular music. Remarkable then that he had just 9 UK Top 40 hits with 4 Top 10 successes, including a re-issue. Additionally, he had just one Top 10 UK album, a compilation of his music. In the US Cooke had 30 U.S. top 40 hits between 1957 and 1964, plus three more posthumously.*

1. Sam Cooke launched his UK pop career on the London record label. His first hit, self written, was released in 1957 and reached No. 29. What was its title?
A) You Send Me   B) I Love You (For Sentimental Reasons)   C) Blue Moon

2. Cooke next charted in the UK two years after his first hit with another song that he had written. He reached No. 23 with *Only Sixteen*, but which UK singer covered the song and took it to number one?   A) Billy Fury   B) Craig Douglas   C) Al Saxon

3. Which song provided Sam Cooke with his highest chart position (No. 2) in 1986 as a re-release of his 1960 hit, after a cover version was heard in the film *Witness*?
A) Cupid   B) Wonderful World   C) Chain Gang

4. Which 1961 Cooke hit contains these lyrics, "Now I don't mean to bother you but I'm in distress, There's danger of me losing all of my happiness"?

5. Utilising session players, the Wrecking Crew, Sam Cooke had a 1962 hit which capitalised on the Twist dance craze. What song got Sam to No. 6?
A) Twist Twist Senora   B) Peppermint Twist   C) Twistin' the Night Away

6. Yet another Cooke written song charted at No. 23 in 1963. *Another Saturday Night* was then covered in 1974 and reached No. 19. Who had the hit second time around?
A) Cat Stevens   B) Everly Brothers   C) Rod Stewart

7. Sam Cooke's last hit of the 1960s was a cover of which song recorded by over 250 singers, telling of a woman shooting her lover dead?
A) Frankie & Johnny   B) Bonnie & Clyde   C) Bang Bang (My Baby Shot Me Down)

8. Cooke was shot dead, aged 33, on December 11, 1964, at the Hacienda Motel. Where is the motel located?   A) Los Angeles   B) New York   C) Chicago

9. Recorded shortly after he was shot dead, which band reached number 7 with a Sam Cooke song, made as a tribute?
A) The Rolling Stones   B) The Pretty Things   C) The Animals

10. Which other Cooke classic hit from 1960 was he inspired to write with his brother, after a chance meeting with prisoners on a highway, whilst on tour?

A Change Is Gonna Come (Sam Cooke)	It's been a long	Then I go to my brother
I was born by the river, in a little tent	A long time coming	And I say, brother, help me please
Oh, and just like the river	But I know a change gonna come	But he winds up, knockin' me
I've been running ever since	Oh, yes it will	Back down on my knees
It's been a long	I go to the movie	Oh, there been times that I thought
A long time coming	And I go downtown	I couldn't last for long
But I know a change gonna come	Somebody keep telling me	But now I think I'm able, to carry on
Oh, yes it will	Don't hang around	It's been a long
It's been too hard living	It's been a long	A long time coming
But I'm afraid to die	A long time coming	But I know a change gonna come
'Cause I don't know what's up there	But I know, a change gonna come	Oh, yes it will.
Beyond the sky	Oh, yes it will	

SAM COOKE ANSWERS: 1. A) You Send Me; 2. B) Craig Douglas; 3. B) Wonderful World (Herman's Hermits also had a 1965 No. 7 with the song); 4. Cupid; 5. C) Twistin' the Night Away; 6. A) Cat Stevens; 7. A) Frankie & Johnny; 8. A) Los Angeles; 9. C) The Animals (their last single with Alan Price on keyboards); 10. Chain Gang (No. 9 in the UK).

*The artistes initial letter is shown in bold type. A hit song that the artiste had in the 1990s is then shown, together with the year it was a hit. Your task is simply to name all of the artistes. The definitive article **THE** is not used in this round*

(e.g. The Beatles would simply be Beatles)

A. People Everyday (1992)

B. Where Are You Baby (1990)

C. Runaway (1999)

D. When You Tell Me That You Love Me (1991)

E. If You Ever (1996)

F. Vindaloo (1998)

G. Dreams (1993)

H. Mmmbop (1997)

I. Bring Your Daughter… To the Slaughter (1991)

J. Ain't No Doubt (1992)

K. Love Shine a Light (1997)

L. We Have All the Time in the World (1994)

M. Come On You Reds (1994)

N. Big Mistake (1998)

O. Don't Stop (Wiggle Wiggle) (1995)

P. Flava (1996)

Q. Heaven For Everyone (1995)

R. Millennium (1998)

S. Living Next Door To Alice (Who The F**K Is Alice)

T. Babe (1993)

U. Born Slippy (1996)

V. Bitter Sweet Symphony (1997)

W. Your Woman (1997)

X. Move Your Body (Elevation) (1991)

Y. Instant Replay (1990)

Z. Viva Las Vegas (1992)

A-Z 1990S HIT MAKERS ANSWERS: A) Arrested Development; B) Betty Boo; C) Corrs; D) Diane Ross; E) East 17 feat Gabrielle; F) Fat Les; G) Gabrielle; H) Hanson; I) Iron Maiden; J) Jimmy Nail; K) Katrina & The Waves; L) Louis Armstrong; M) Manchester United FC; N) Natalie Imbruglia; O) Outhere Brothers; P) Peter Andre; Q) Queen; R) Robbie Williams; S) Smokie feat Roy 'Chubby' Brown; T) Take That; U) Underworld; V) Verve; W) White Town; X) Xpansions; Y) Yell!; Z) ZZ Top.

ELVIS COSTELLO - (Declan Patrick McManus, OBE (born Paddington 25 August 1954), English singer-songwriter, son of Lilian Alda and Ross MacManus (1927–2011), singer with the Joe Loss Orchestra. Won multiple awards, including Grammy Awards in 1999/2020, twice nominated for Brit Award for Best British Male Artist. Inducted into the Rock & Roll Hall of Fame 2003. In 2004, Rolling Stone ranked Costello No. 80 on a list of 100 Greatest Artists of All Time. Costello had 16 Top 40 singles, 3 reaching the Top 10. 7 of the singles with The Attractions. Costello had 23 Top 40 albums, 13 Top 10 hits.

1. Costello's first broadcast was with his father in a TV commercial which aired in 1974. His father sang and Elvis sang backing vocals for which soft drinks company?
A) Tizer   B) R. White's Lemonade   C) Corona

2. What American West Coast band, based in the UK, backed Elvis Costello on his debut album, *My Aim Is True* in 1977?
A) Clover   B) Huey Lewis & The News   C) Doobie Brothers

3. In 1978 who reached number four in the charts with the Elvis Costello penned song *Girls Talk*?   A) Roy Orbison   B) Johnny Cash   C) Dave Edmunds

4. Which No. 24 Costello hit from 1978, described as one of his best, features a stomping rhythm and the lyrics "I've been on tenterhooks, Ending in dirty looks, Listening to the muzak, Thinking 'bout this and that"?

5. Elvis Costello's highest chart placing came with a 1979 number two hit. What was the song?   A) Oliver's Army   B) I Don't Wanna Go Yo (Chelsea)   C) Radio Radio

6. The single, I Can't Stand Up for Falling Down reached number four in 1980. Which American soul and R&B act originally recorded the song?
A) Wilson Pickett   B) The Miracles C) Sam & Dave

7. Costello's 1981 album, *Almost Blue*, is an album of country music cover songs. Which track was released as a single and climbed to number 6 in the charts?
A) Sweet Dreams   B) Good Year For the Roses   C) Honey Hush

8. 1985 saw Costello appear in a small role as a very bad stage magician in which Alan Bleasdale film?   A) No Surrender   B) The Monocled Mutineer   C) G.B.H.

9. In 1987, he appeared on the HBO special *A Black and White Night*, as one of several 'Friends' who backed which legendary singer?
A) Gene Pitney   B) Del Shannon C) Roy Orbison

10. With whom did Elvis Costello write the song *My Brave Face*, a 1989 No. 18 hit?
A) Paul McCartney   B) Diana Krall   C) David Crosby

Q9

ELVIS COSTELLO ANSWERS: 1. B) R. White's Lemonade; 2. A) Clover; 3. C) Dave Edmunds; 4. Pump it Up; 5. A) Oliver's Army; 6. C) Sam & Dave; 7. B) Good Year For the Roses; 8. A) Surrender; 9. C) Roy Orbison; 10. A) Paul McCartney (who had the hit).

CREEDENCE CLEARWATER REVIVAL *(also known as Creedence or CCR), was an American rock band formed in El Cerrito, California (1959) as the Blue Velvets, then the Golliwogs, evolving into CCR in 1967. The line up: John Fogerty (Lead vocals and guitar, and main songwriter); brother, Tom Fogerty (Rhythm guitar); Stu Cook (Bass); Doug Clifford (Drums). Their songs had the feel of 1950s Rock 'n' Roll. CCR disbanded acrimoniously in late 1972. In the UK they had 9 Top 40 singles including a No. 1 and 3 other Top 10 hits; also 5 Top 40 albums with a No. 1 and 2 other Top 10.*

1. After initially being an instrumental band they evolved into Creedence Clearwater Revival. What prompted the *Clearwater* part of the name? A) Olympia Beer TV commercial   B) A natural swimming pool company   C) Local mineral water spa

2. CCR first hit the UK singles charts with *Proud Mary* in 1969. The song reached number 8. Which other act charted with the song at No. 30 in 1969?
A) Ike & Tina Turner   B) Checkmates Ltd   C) Elvis Presley

3. CCR's only No. 1 contained these lyrics in 1969. What is the song? "Hope you got your things together, Hope you are quite prepared to die, Looks like we're in for nasty weather, One eye is taken for an eye".

4. Another 1970 Top 10 hit from Creedence was later covered by many artistes, including a duet between the writer John Fogerty and Jerry Lee Lewis, on the latter's album *Last Man Standing*. What is the song?
A) Down on the Corner   B) Fortunate Son   C) Travellin' Band

5. True or False? Rejected contenders for the renaming of the band included Muddy Rabbit, Gossamer Wump, and Creedence Nuball and the Ruby.

6. What was the name of the 1970 CCR album that included *Travellin' Band* and *Up Around the Bend,* a No 3 hit in the UK?
A) Cosmo's Factory   B) Willy & The Poor Boys   C) Pendulum

7. Which song was only a minor 1975 hit in the US for John Fogerty, was then adopted by Status Quo in 1977, taken to number 3 in addition to becoming Quo's signature song, with which they opened *Live Aid* in 1985?

8. During a scene in which 1981 film is *Bad Moon Rising* played as David staves off boredom while waiting to transform into a werewolf?

9. CCR do a classic cover version of Marvin Gaye's *I Heard It Through the Grapevine* on the Cosmo's factory album. How long is the track?
A) 7 mins 5 secs   B) 9 mins 10 secs   C) 11 mins 5 secs

10. John Fogerty's third studio album was a minor success in the UK, with the title track entering the lower reaches of the Top 40. What was the title of both the single and the album?   A) Blue Moon Swamp   B) Centrefield   C) Eye of the Zombie

What's in the BOX?

Fill in the missing info in box 4.

   36   *2*   *97*   *?*

CREEDENCE CLEARWATER REVIVAL ANSWERS: 1) A) Olympia Beer TV commercial; 2. B) Checkmates Ltd; 3. Bad Moon Rising; 4. C) Travellin' Band; 5. True; 6. A) Cosmo's Factory; 7. Rockin' All Over the World; 8. An American Werewolf in London; 9. C) 11 mins 5 secs; 10. B) Centrefield. WHAT'S IN THE BOX? ANSWERS: Picture of Alexandra Burke and the number 1. Four versions of the song Hallelujah; Leonard Cohen (who wrote it) got to number 36, Jeff Buckley got to number 2, Rufus Wainwright number 97.

THE CRICKETS were an American rock and roll band from Lubbock, Texas, formed by singer-songwriter Buddy Holly in January 1957. Holly (Lead vocals & Lead guitar), Niki Sullivan (Rhythm guitar) Jerry Allison (Drums), Joe B. Mauldin (Bass). The Crickets helped set template for rock bands with their guitar-bass-rhythm-drums line-up and the talent to write their own material. After Holly's death in 1959 the band continued to tour and record with other band members. They had 12 Top 40 hits including a No. 1 and 3 other Top 10 hits. Also 6 Top 40 albums including 2 No. 1's and 2 other Top 10.

1. What was the title of The Crickets single that topped the charts both sides of the Atlantic in 1957? A) Peggy Sue   B) That'll Be the Day   C) Maybe Baby

2. True or False? The Crickets almost chose the name The Beetles.

3. The second hit for the band only credited Buddy Holly on the label, although The Crickets did all play on the record. What is the song that prominently features Allison playing paradiddles on the drums throughout?
A) Peggy Sue   B) Think It Over   C) Maybe Baby

4. The Crickets had a No. 3 hit in 1957 with a song that reached No.1 for Mud, eighteen years later. What was the song?
A) Tiger Feet   B) The Cat Crept In   C) Oh Boy!

5. *More Than I Can Say* written by Cricket, Sonny Curtis, was a US and UK chart hit for which two artists, one was a No. 4 in 1961, the other a No. 2 in 1980?

6. Who was the singer / guitarist who joined the Crickets for a short while after Buddy Holly's death, who also died in a plane crash, in 1964 aged 21?
A) David Box   B) Earl Sinks   C) Jerry Naylor

7. In 1961 another new lead singer joined the band and they had a 1962 No. 5 hit in the UK with which Gerry Goffin-Carole King song?
A) When You Ask About Love   B) Don't Ever Change   C) Peggy Sue Got Married

8. The Crickets teamed up with a leading singer of the era and together they had a big hit with an album .... *Meets The Crickets* which reached number two. Who was the singer? A) Mike Berry   B) Waylon Jennings   C) Bobby Vee

9. What was the title of the Crickets debut album that reached number 5 in the UK charts in 1958? A) "Chirping" Crickets   B) Cricket Sounds   C) The Crickets

10. The Crickets had their last hit in 1963, a number 17 success with *My Little Girl*. The song opens, "When my little girl goes to the movies". What is the second line?
A) She steals every scene   B) She has such style   C) Nobody looks at the screen

Gerry Goffin & Carole King wrote a string of hits when married to each other. Can you fill in the missing song titles?			
1. ?????	Bobby Vee		Number 1 - 1961
2. ?????	Little Eva / Kylie Minogue		No. 2 - 1962 / No. 2 - 1988
3. ?????	Rockin' Berries	**GOFFIN & KING SONGS**	No. 3 - 1964
4. ?????	Carole King		No. 3 - 1962
5. ?????	Herman's Hermits		No. 1 - 1961
6. ?????	Billy Fury		No. 3 - 1961
7. ?????	Dusty Springfield		No. 10 - 1966
8. ?????	Kenny Lynch / Robson & Jerome		No. 10 - 1962; No. 1 - 1995
9. ?????	The Animals		No. 6 - 1966
10. ?????	Craig Douglas/Jimmy Justice/ The Drifters		No. 9; 9; 31 - 1962

THE CRICKETS ANSWERS: *1. B) That'll Be the Day; 2. True; 3. Peggy Sue; 4. Oh Boy!; 5. A) David Box; 6. A) David Box; 7. B) Don't Ever Change; 8. C) Bobby Vee; 9. A) "Chirping" Crickets; 10. C) "Nobody looks at the screen".*
GOFFIN & KING SONGS ANSWERS: *1. Take Good Care Of My Baby; 2. The Loco-Motion; 3. He's In Town; 4. It Might As Well Rain Until September; 5. I'm Into Something Good; 6. Halfway to Paradise; 7. Going Back; 8. Up On The Roof; 9. Don't Bring Me Down; 10. When My Little Girl Is Smiling.*

SHERYL CROW (born Kennett, Missouri, February 11, 1962) is an American musician, singer, songwriter and actress. The daughter of Bernice (née Cain), a piano teacher, and Wendell Wyatt Crow, a lawyer and trumpet player. Graduated from the University of Missouri and worked as a music teacher at Kellison Elementary School. Teaching during the day gave her the opportunity to sing in bands on the weekends. Sheryl recorded backing vocals for Stevie Wonder, Belinda Carlisle and Don Henley etc. Record producer Jay Oliver helped her by using her in advertising jingles. music incorporates elements of pop, rock, country, jazz and blues. Crow has had 16 Top 40 singles, 4 reached the Top 10 and three Top 10 albums.

1. From 1987 - 1989, Crow toured with which superstar as a backing vocalist during his *Bad* tour? A) Bryan Adams B) Meat Loaf C) Michael Jackson

2. Sheryl found an old poetry book in a used book store in the Los Angeles area, and used a poem as lyrics for which song, that was a No. 4 hit for her in 1994?
A) Strong Enough B) All I Wanna Do C) Can't Cry Anymore

3. At which festival did Crow perform in 1994?
A) Woodstock B) Isle of Wight C) Glastonbury

4. How many UK Top 40 hit singles came from the 1996 album *Sheryl Crow*, produced by Sheryl herself? A) 3 B) 4 C) 5

5. The album was banned from sale at which chain of hypermarkets in the US because in the lyrics to *Love Is a Good Thing*, Crow says the store "sells guns to children". A) Walmart B) Macy's C) Kohl's

6. In 1997, Crow co-wrote and sung the theme song to which James Bond film?
A) Goldeneye B) Tomorrow Never Dies C) The World Is Not Enough

7. Sheryl had a No. 9 hit with *My Favourite Mistake*. Speculation suggested the song was about which famous rock star? A) Prince B) Don Henley C) Eric Clapton

8. In 1999, Crow made her acting debut as an ill-fated drifter in a suspense film which starred her then-boyfriend Owen Wilson as a serial killer. What was the film?
A) 54 B) The Minus Man C) De-Lovely

9. Crow's cover of which Guns N' Roses song was included on the soundtrack of the film *Big Daddy* and reached number 30 in the UK charts?
A) Sweet Child O' Mine B) You Could Be Mine C) Sympathy For the Devil

10. Which Sheryl Crow 1997 No. 8 has these lyrics, "Ten years living in a paper bag, Feedback baby, he's a flipped out cat, He's a platinum canary, drinkin' Falstaff beer"?
A) Strong Enough B) All I Wanna Do C) A Change Would Do You Good

THE CURE are a rock band formed in Crawley, West Sussex in 1978. Through numerous lineup changes, guitarist, lead vocalist, and songwriter Robert Smith is the only constant member. Part of the post-punk and new wave movements, The Cure had 21 Top 40 hits from 1980 - 1996 with 4 Top 10 successes. Also had 16 Top 40 albums with 1 No. 1 and 9 more Top 10 successes. The Cure were inducted into the Rock and Roll Hall of Fame in 2019.

ANAGRAMS OF 9 HIT SONG TITLES FROM THE CURE

1. CATTLE SHOVE (1983)	4. CELT MOOSE (1990)	7. ABSENTEE WINDY (1985)
2. CHARLIE PLATTER (1984)	5. MONDAY VILIFIER (1992)	8. HARDEN NAGGING (1982)
3. BAY LULL (1989)	6. ELK THAW (1983)	9. NO GLOVES (1989)

SHERYL CROW ANSWERS: 1. C) Michael Jackson; 2. B) All I Wanna Do; 3. A) Woodstock; 4. C) 5 - If It Makes You Happy, A Change Would Do You Good, Hard To Make A Stand, Home and Everyday Is a Winding Road; 5. A) Walmart; 6. B) Tomorrow Never Dies; 7. C) Eric Clapton; 8. B) The Minus Man; 9. A) Sweet Child O' Mine; 10. C) A Change Would Do You Good. THE CURE SONG TITLES ANSWERS: 1. The Love Cats; 2. The Caterpillar; 3. Lullaby; 4. Close To Me; 5. Friday I'm In Love; 6. The Walk; 7. In Between Days; 8. Hanging Garden; 10. Lovesong.

BOBBY DARIN (born Walden Robert Cassotto in East Harlem, NYC; May 14, 1936 – December 20, 1973) was an American singer, musician, and actor. By the time he was a teenager, Darin could play several instruments, including piano, drums, and guitar. He later added harmonica and xylophone. He performed jazz, pop, rock and roll, folk, swing, and country music. He started his career as a songwriter for Connie Francis. Darin suffered from poor health his entire life. He died at the age of 37 after a heart operation in Los Angel. Notched up 17 top 40 hits between 1958 and 1966, including 2 No.1's and a further 7 Top 10 hits. He had three Top 40 album hits with one reaching number four.

1. In 1968 Darin discovered that the woman who had raised him was his grandmother, not his mother as he thought. Previously, he thought his birth mother was whom? A) His sister B) His aunt C) His cousin

2. *Splish Splash* was Darin's first hit in 1958, reaching No. 3 in the US but only No. 20 in the UK. Who had the bigger hit in Britain, reaching No. 7?
A) Marty Wilde B) Vince Eager C) Charlie Drake

3. What was Bobby Darin's first UK number one single in 1959?
A) Mack the Knife B) Dream Lover C) Beyond the Sea

4. Bobby joined Rock Hudson and Gina Lollobrigida in a 1960 comedy about housekeepers who turn a villa into a hotel while the owner is away. What was the film's title? A) Come September B) State Fair C) Hell Is for Heroes

5. Which American actress did Bobby Darin marry in 1960?
A) Annette Funicello B) Sandra Dee C) Pamela Tiffin

6. Bobby Darin took a break from performing after Robert Kennedy was assassinated during the 1968 presidential campaign, in which Darin was involved. Which record company did Bobby then start in 1969? A) Colpix B) Clarion C) Direction Records

7. From which song are these lyrics from a 1960 Bobby Darin hit taken, "You know when that shark bites with his teeth, babe, Scarlet billows start to spread, Fancy gloves, oh, wears old MacHeath, babe, So there's never, never a trace of red"?

8. Darin had another UK No. 2 hit in 1962 with which self penned country song, that was covered by several singers, including Robbie Williams on his *Swing when You're Winning* album almost 40 years later? A) Things B) Multiplication C) Lazy River

9. After a three year hiatus, which Tim Hardin folk song put Bobby back in the top ten in 1966; the song also becoming a hit two years later for The Four Tops?

10. Bobby appeared as a racist and anti-Semitic prisoner in a 1962 film, *Pressure Point*, set during World War II. The Nazi sympathiser was treated by a psychiatrist, played by which actor? A) Harry Belafonte B) Sidney Poitier C) Peter Falk

BANDS IN PICTURES

NAME THREE FAMOUS BANDS

A   B   C

BOBBY DARIN ANSWERS: 1. A) His sister; 2. C) Charlie Drake; 3. B) Dream Lover; 4. A) Come September; 5. B) Sandra Dee; 6. C) Direction Records; 7. Mack the Knife; 8. A) Things; 9. If I Were a Carpenter; 10. B) Sidney Poitier (Darin nominated for a Best Actor award but the film lost almost $1m).
BANDS IN PICTURES ANSWERS: A) Radiohead B) T. Rex C) Guns N' Roses.

POP THROUGH THE DECADES

1. Johnny Dankworth's experiments with what animals reached number seven in 1956?

2. What became the first ever single to enter the chart at number one in 1958?

3. What Neil Sedaka co-written song got Connie Francis a No.1 in 1959?

4. "Hello darkness my old friend, I've come to talk with you again" are the opening lines of which 1965 Paul Simon song that The Bachelors took to No. 3?

5. Which band had a 1968 UK number one with *Everlasting Love*?

6. *Everlasting Love* charted 5 more times in the 20thC by Robert Knight, Rex Smith & Rachel Sweet, Worlds Apart and Gloria Estefan. But who reached No. 5 in 1998?

7. In what year was Led Zeppelin's eponymous debut album released?

8. In 1976, what was Elton John's first UK number one single?

9. What kind of roses were a hit for Kaye Sisters (1960) and Marie Osmond (1973)?

10. Which 1970s glam rock band were known for deliberately misspelling song titles?

11. Which 1982 album is the best-selling album of all time, with almost 50m sales?

12. Which song's music video was the first ever to be shown on MTV in 1981?

13. Which singer, who launched her solo career in 1982, went on to become the biggest selling female artist of all time?

14. Whose backup band was called The Revolution?

15. Where have all the good men gone, and where are all the gods" are the opening lines to which 1984 song?

16. In 1993 what became Take That's first UK number one single?

17. Which rapper was shot and killed in Los Angeles in 1997?

18. Fred Durst was lead singer of which American rap rock band formed in 1994?

19. Briana Corrigan, Jacqui Abbott and Alison Wheeler have sung with which band?

20. What number links hit songs by these 5 acts?

NUMBER LINK

POP THROUGH THE DECADES ANSWERS: 1. Mice (Experiments with Mice); 2. Jailhouse Rock by Elvis Presley; 3. Stupid Cupid; 4. The Sound of Silence; 5. Love Affair; 6. The Cast of Casualty (Children in Need charity single, lead vocals by actress Rebecca Wheatley); 7. 1969; 8. Don't Go Breaking My Heart (with Kiki Dee); 9. Paper; 10. Slade; 11. Thriller by Michael Jackson; 12. Video Killed the Radio Star by The Buggles; 13. Madonna; 14. Prince; 15. Holding Out for a Hero by Bonnie Tyler; 16. Pray; 17. The Notorious B.I.G.; 18. Limp Bizkit; 19. Beautiful South; 20. Seven - Queen (Seven Seas of Rhye); Avons (Seven Little Girls Sitting in the Back Seat); Dubliners (Seven Drunken Nights); Goombay Dance Band (Seven Tears); Judge Dread (Big Seven).

CHRIS DE BURGH *(born Christopher John Davison in Venado Tuerto, Argentina, to Colonel Charles John Davison, a British diplomat, and Maeve Emily (née de Burgh), an Irish secretary on 15 October 1948). He is an British-Irish singer-songwriter and instrumentalist. He started out as an art rock performer but subsequently started writing more pop-oriented material. Chris de Burgh signed his first contract with A&M Records in 1974, and supported Supertramp on their Crime of the Century tour, building himself a small fan base. Had just 6 Top 40 singles, including a number one and one other Top 10 hit. His albums are more prolific with 12 Top 40 successes including a No. 1 and 6 other Top 10 hits.*

1. In the 1960s Chris and his family lived in Bargy Castle, a twelfth-century castle. After it was converted into a hotel, young Chris often sang for the guests. Where in Ireland was the castle located? A) Clare B) Wexford C) Limerick

2. De Burgh attended Marlborough College in Wiltshire, before graduating from Trinity College Dublin, with a Master of Arts degree in what subjects? A) Music B) Psychology and Geography C) French, English and History

3. Chris released his first album in 1974. The folk-tinged stab at fantasy in the tradition of the Moody Blues was well received but not a success. What was the albums title? A) Far Beyond These Castle Walls B) Spanish Train and Other Stories C) At the End of a Perfect Day

4. Which song, originally on de Burgh's second album in 1975, was initially released unsuccessfully as a single, did eventually chart in 1986, but has since appeared on many Christmas compilations? A) Don't Pay the Ferryman B) The Snows of New York C) A Spaceman Came Travelling

5. Chris's 6th album finally got him into the Top 30. What was the title of the album that was produced by Rupert Hine? A) Getaway B) Best Moves C) Crusader

6. De Burgh finally hit the jackpot in the singles chart, with a song that hit number one for three weeks. The song tends to divide public opinion and was voted 10th most annoying song of all time. What is the song?

7. A song from Chris's 1975 album, *Spanish Train and Other Stories*, might raise eyebrows in today's world but it still remains a favourite. What is the song that includes these lyrics? "She says God made her a sinner just to keep fat men thinner, As they tumble down in heaps before her feet, They hang around in groups like battle-weary troops, One can often see them queue right down the street"

8. In 1988 de Burgh had an album that entered the chart at number one in the UK. Surprisingly unsuccessful in the US, what was the album's title? A) Into the Light B) Flying Colours C) Man on the Line

9. Which single, taken from de Burgh's 1988 smash hit album, reached number three in the singles chart. What was the title of the song? A) Missing You B) Tender Hands C) This Waiting Heart

10. In 1997 de Burgh composed a song entitled *There's a New Star Up in Heaven Tonight*, the song was released as a 100-copy limited edition as a tribute to whom? A) Mother Teresa B) Diana, Princess of Wales C) Gianni Versace

---

SLOWEST NUMBER ONE HITS

The recordings that took the longest to reach #1 after their first appearance on the chart are:

29 years 42 days. Reet Petite. Jackie Wilson (1957-1986)

25 y 244 days. Stand By Me. Ben E King (61-87)

25 y 83 d. Unchained Melody. Righteous Bros (65-90)

18 y 356 d. He Ain't Heavy He's My Brother. Hollies (69-88)

8 y 284 d. Young At Heart. Bluebells (84-93)

8 y 166 d. Should I Stay Or Should I Go? Clash (82-91)

7 y 327 d. Living On My Own. Freddie Mercury (85-93)

6 y 63 d. Space Oddity. David Bowie (1969-75)

5 y 70 d. Imagine. John Lennon (1975-81)

CHRIS DE BURGH ANSWERS: *1. B) Wexford; 2. C) French, English and History; 3. A) Far Beyond These Castle Walls; 4. C) A Spaceman Came Travelling; 5. A) Getaway; 6. The Lady in Red; 7. Patricia the Stripper; 8. B) Flying Colours; 9. A) Missing You; 10. B) Diana, Princess of Wales.*

DEEP PURPLE - an English rock band formed 1968 in London. Formed as a psychedelic rock and progressive rock band, they shifted to a heavier sound in 1970. There have been several line-up changes and an 8-year hiatus. The most commercially successful line-up consisted of Ian Gillan (vocals), Roger Glover (bass), Jon Lord (keyboards), Ian Paice (drums) and Ritchie Blackmore (guitar). This line-up was active from 1969 to 1973 and was revived from 1984 to 1989 and again from 1992 to 1993. Did notch up 6 Top 40 singles (2 Top 10) and 19 Top 40 albums including 2 No. 1's and 7 more Top 10 recordings.

1. When former Searchers drummer, Chris Curtis, was putting a supergroup together, what was the name prior to Deep Purple? A) Roundabout B) Traffic C) Motorway

2. In May 1968, Deep Purple recorded their debut album, *Shades of Deep Purple*. The album flopped in the UK but was successful in the US where, which single taken from the album, a cover version, was also a big hit? A) Help! B) Hush C) Hello

3. In 1970 *Concerto for Group and Orchestra*, a three-movement epic composed by Lord, got to No. 26 in the album charts. It was a collaboration between Deep Purple and which orchestra conducted by Malcolm Arnold?   A) The Halle Orchestra B) The London Symphony Orchestra C) The Royal Philharmonic Orchestra

4. Deep Purple's first hit single also produced their highest chart placing. Which single got to No. 2? A) Smoke on the Water B) Black Night C) Hallelujah

5. In 1972, DP held the Guinness World Record for 'Globe's Loudest Band' but who broke their record in 1976? A) The Rolling Stones B) Led Zeppelin C) The Who

6. Ian Gillan sang on the original recording of which Andrew Lloyd Webber musical? A) Jesus Christ Superstar B) Phantom of the Opera C) Evita

7. Deep Purple In Rock was a hugely successful album. Which American monument inspired the cover? A) White House B) Mount Rushmore C) Lincoln Memorial

8. In 1971 and 1972 two successive Deep Purple albums topped the charts. What were the titles of the two albums? A) Fireball and Machine Head B) Made in Japan and Burn C) Deepest Purple and Perfect Strangers

9. After Ritchie Blackmore's sudden departure in November 1993, which guitarist substituted for him on lead guitar for the remaining shows? A) Stevie Ray Vaughan B) Eric Clapton C) Joe Satriani

10. Who originally wrote and recorded the song, *Kentucky Woman*, which appeared on the 1968 Deep Purple album *The Book of Taliesyn*? A) Jagger-Richards B) Neil Diamond C) Lennon-McCartney

CHART DEBUTS AT NUMBER ONE

Acts whose singles chart debut went straight to No. 1 (multi-star charity collectives not included)

1969	**1996**	Billie. *Because We Want To*
Beatles with Billy Preston. *Get Back*	Babylon Zoo. *Spaceman*	Spacedust. *Gym And Tonic*
1994	Baddiel & Skinner & Lightning Seeds. *3 Lions*	**1999**
Whigfield. *Saturday Night*	**1997**	Britney Spears. *Baby One More Time*
1995	White Town. *Your Woman EP*	Mr Oizo. *Flat Beat*
Robson & Jerome. *Unchained Melody / The White Cliffs Of Dover*	Hanson. *Mmmbop*	Westlife. *Swear It Again*
	Teletubbies. *Teletubbies Say Eh-Oh!*	Baz Luhrmann. *Everybody's Free (To Wear Sunscreen). The Sunscreen Song*
Dunblane. *Knockin' On Heaven's Door / Throw These Guns Away*	**1998**	S Club 7. *Bring It All Back*
	B*Witched. *C'est la Vie*	

DEEP PURPLE ANSWERS: 1. A) Roundabout; 2. B) Hush; 3. C) The Royal Philharmonic Orchestra; 4. B) Black Night; 5. C) The Who; 6. A) Jesus Christ Superstar (as Jesus); 7. B) Mount Rushmore; 8. A) Fireball and Machine Head; 9. C) Joe Satriani; 10. B) Neil Diamond.

NEIL DIAMOND *(born in Brooklyn, New York as Neil Leslie Diamond, January 24, 1941) is an American singer-songwriter, musician and occasional actor. He has sold more than 100 million records worldwide, making him one of the best-selling musicians of all time. Diamond had 11 Top 40 hits, including 4 Top 10 hits, one as a duet. Neil has been prolific with albums - 26 Top 40 successes, including a number one and seven other Top 10 hits. Compilations of his hits and other songs continued to be popular throughout the later part of the 20th century and it was during this period that he had the No.1 smash hit album with The Greatest Hits 1966-1992.*

1. *I'm a Believer*, and *A Little Bit Me, a Little Bit You* were early Neil Diamond songwriting big hits for which band? A) Turtles B) Partridge Family C) Monkees

2. What was Neil Diamond's first UK hit, a song that reached number 3 in 1970?
A) Shilo B) Cracklin' Rosie C) Holly Holy

3. Which Diamond-penned album track became a small hit for Jimmy James & The Vagabonds in 1968 and a number one for UB40's reggae flavoured version in 1983?
A) Red Red Wine B) I Got You Babe C) Kingston Town

4. Which Neil Diamond 1971 No. 8 has proved to be an enduringly popular classic, possibly inspired by John F Kennedy's 11-year old daughter?
A) Cracklin' Rose B) Sweet Caroline C) Forever in Blue Jeans

5. Apparently, after Neil's sessions with an analyst in Los Angeles, he wrote and recorded which song that reached number 4 both sides of the Atlantic in 1971?
A) I Am... I Said B) Song Sung Blue C) Hello Again

6. Diamond wrote the music for a 1973 film about a young seabird cast out by his flock. The film flopped but Neil's music was a critical and commercial success. What was the film's title? A) The Birds B) Flyaway Home C) Jonathan Livingston Seagull

7. In 1976, Neil was paid $650,000 for four shows to open a new $10m theatre for the performing arts. A 'Who's Who' of stars attended the opening night at which Las Vegas venue? A) Aladdin Hotel B) Rainbow Theatre C) Colosseum at Caesars

8. On 2 July 1977, Diamond performed in front of an audience of 55,000 on the front lawn of which country estate?
A) Longleat House B) Woburn Abbey C) Chatsworth House

9. Neil Diamond had a number 5 hit in the UK in 1978, singing *You Don't Bring Me Flowers*, a duet with which female superstar?
A) Whitney Houston B) Celine Dion C) Barbra Streisand

10. In 1980 which Neil Diamond film, based on a Samson Raphaelson play, includes the songs *Love on the Rocks*, *Hello Again* and *America*?

AMERICA (Neil Diamond)

Far, we've been travelling far
Without a home but not without a star
Free, only want to be free
We huddle close, hang on to a dream

On the boats and on the planes
They're coming to America
Never looking back again
They're coming to America

Home, don't it seem so far away
We're travelling light today

In the eye of the storm
In the eye of the storm

Home, to a new and a shiny place
Make our bed, we'll say our grace
Freedom's light burning warm
Freedom's light burning warm

Everywhere around the world
They're coming to America
Every time that flag's unfurled
They're coming to America

Got a dream to take them there
They're coming to America

Got a dream they've come to share
They're coming to America

They're coming to America
They're coming to America
They're coming to America
They're coming to America today
Today, today, today, today

My country 'tis of thee (today)
Sweet land of liberty (today)
Of thee I sing (today)
Of thee I sing today
Today, today, today
Today, today

NEIL DIAMOND ANSWERS: 1. C) Monkees; 2. B) Cracklin' Rosie; 3. A) Red Red Wine; 4. B) Sweet Caroline; 5. A) I Am... I Said); 6. C) Jonathan Livingston Seagull; 7. A) Aladdin Hotel; 8. B) Woburn Abbey; 9. C) Barbra Streisand; 10. The Jazz Singer.

CELINE DION *(Céline Marie Claudette Dion CC OQ, born in Charlemagne, Quebec on 30 March 1968) is a Canadian singer, noted for powerful and technically skilled vocals. Celine was the youngest of 14 children of French-Canadian parents. Her music has incorporated genres such as pop, rock, R&B, gospel, and classical music. Dion won the 1988 Eurovision Song Contest, singing for Switzerland in Dublin. Dion has had 18 Top 40 singles in the UK, including 2 No. 1's and 10 other Top 10 hits. Also had 7 Top 40 albums including 4 No.1's and one other Top 10.*

1. Dion won the 1988 Eurovision Song Contest, singing for Switzerland. In English the song was *Don't Leave Without Me*. However she sung in French so its title was what? A) Ne Partez Pas Sans Moi B) J'aime La Vie C) Tom Pillibi

2. The theme song for Disney's animated *Beauty and the Beast* took Dion to No. 9 with her first UK hit in 1992. With whom did she duet on the song?
A) R Kelly B) Joe Cocker C) Peabo Bryson

3. Celine's first solo hit in the UK took her to number 4 in 1994 with *The Power of Love* which had topped the charts for which singer nine years earlier?
A) Jennifer Rush B) Whitney Houston C) Vicky Leandros

4. Dion's first UK number one came in 1994 with which song, written by Andy Hill and Peter Sinfield? A) Only One Road B) Think Twice C) Because You Loved Me

5. In 1995 *To Love Me Again* reached No. 7, what French title was shown on the label? A) Hymne a L'amour B) La Vie en Rose C) Tu M'Aimes Encore

6. What song did Celine Dion sing at the Atlanta Olympic Games in 1996?
A) A New Day Has Come B) Power of the Dream C) The Power of Love

7. What was Celine Dion's number one album in 1996 that showed a further progression of her music, complex orchestral sounds, African chanting, and elaborate musical effects that spawned five hit singles including the title track?
A) Falling into You B) The Reason C) Because You Loved Me

8. What Celine Dion number one from 1998 includes these lyrics; "Love can touch us one time, And last for a lifetime, And never let go 'til we're gone"?

9. In 1998 Celine had a Top 5 hit with *Immortality*. The songwriters duetted with her on the single. Who were they? A) Beatles B) Bee Gees C) Eagles

10. Renowned violinist Taro Hakase joined Celine's *Falling Into You Around the World Tour* to perform on which song?
A) River Deep, Mountain High B) Call The Man C) To Love You More

INSERT THE MISSING WORDS

Days Of The Week

A) .... Sunday	Small Faces	1968
B) .... Monday	New Order	1988
C) .... Tuesday	Chairmen of the Board	1971
D) Wednesday	Undertones	1980
E) Thursday's	David Bowie	1999
F) Friday	Easybeats	1966
G) Saturday	Whigfield	1994

CELINE DION ANSWERS: *1. A) Ne Partez Pas Sans Moi; 2. C) Peabo Bryson; 3. A) Jennifer Rush; 4. B) Think Twice; 5. C) Tu M'Aimes Encore; 6. B) Power of the Dream; 7. A) Falling Into You; 8. My Heart Will Go On (Theme from Titanic); 9. B) Bee Gees; 10. C) To Love You More.* **DAYS OF THE WEEK ANSWERS**: *A) Lazy; B) Blue; C) Everything's; D) Week; E) Child; F) On My Mind; G) Night.*

DIRE STRAITS were a British rock band formed in London in 1977 by Mark Knopfler (lead vocals & lead guitar), David Knopfler (rhythm guitar & backing vocals), John Illsley (bass guitar & backing vocals) and Pick Withers (drums & percussion). There were several changes in personnel, with Mark Knopfler and Illsley being the only members throughout the band's existence. They were active from 1977 to 1988 and again from 1991 to 1995. Dire Straits had 12 Top 40 hits (5 Top 10) and 10 top 10 albums including 4 number ones. Mark Knopfler quietly disbanded Dire Straits in 1995 and prepared to work on his first solo album. He had one single that entered the Top 40 before 1999. Also two albums charted, one Top 10.

1. Which of the following albums was released before David Knopfler left the band?
A) Communiqué B) Making Movies C) Brothers in Arms

2. Which of the following films soundtracks did Mark Knopfler work on?
A) Wag the Dog B) Cal C) Local Hero

3. In what venue was *Alchemy Live* recorded by Dire Straits?
A) Bridgewater Hall, Manchester B) Hammersmith Odeon C) Royal Opera House

4. Which Dire Straits hit was written by Mark Knopfler and Sting?
A) Private Investigations B) Money for Nothing C) Tunnel of Love

5. In *Walk of Life*, who is "singing oldies, goldies, *Be-Bop-A-Lula*, baby *What'd I Say*"? A) Chuck B) Buddy C) Johnny

6. *Tunnel of Love* features *The Carousel Waltz* as its intro. Who wrote the waltz from the musical *Carousel*? A) Richard Rodgers & Oscar Hammerstein II B) Andrew Lloyd-Webber & Tim Rice C) Stephen Sondheim

7. Which 1985 Dire Straits album cover features a 1937 14-fret National Style 'O' Resonator guitar? A) Love Over Gold B) Money For Nothing C) Brothers in Arms

8. What country singer, later to be an Eagle, sang backup on Dire Straits' song *The Bug* on the *On Every Street* album? A) Vince Gill B) Dolly Parton C) Kenny Rogers

9. Which 1979 Dire Straits hit song includes the lyrics: "You check out guitar George, he knows-all the chords, Mind, it's strictly rhythm he doesn't want to make it cry or sing"? A) Romeo and Juliet B) Skateaway C) Sultans of Swing

10. Mark Knopfler and Pick Withers had both been part of which pub rock group at different points in and around 1973, before linking up in Dire Straits?
A) Café Racers B) Brewers Droop C) Magna Carta

GIRL SINGER ANAGRAMS
UNRAVEL THE FEMALE SINGERS OF THE 1990s

1. CSEPI RGLSI
2. NE GEUOV
3. SIET'YNSD CILDH
4. ITON XONRTBA
5. IETNYWH THSOONU
6. MARAHI YAERC
7. INELEC ONDI
8. TAJEN KNSACOJ

9. NRETYIB SSRAEP
10. CHTIARSIN ALAUIGRE
11. AAAIHYL
12. IAENDS 'NONRONO
13. ONCMIA
14. RAMY J BGELI
15. ARSHIAK
16. RENIFENJ ZPELO

DIRE STRAITS ANSWERS: 1. A) Communique; 2. B) Cal; 3. B) Hammersmith Odeon;
4. B) Money For Nothing; 5. C) Johnny; 6. A) Richard Rodgers & Oscar Hammerstein II;
7. C) Brothers in Arms; 8. A) Vince Gill; 9. C) Sultans of Swing; 10. B) Brewers Droop.
UNRAVELLED 1990S FEMALE SINGERS: 1. Spice Girls; 2. En Vogue; 3. Destiny's Child;
4. Toni Braxton; 5. Whitney Houston; 6. Mariah Carey; 7. Celine Dion; 8. Janet Jackson; 9.
Britney Spears; 10. Christina Aguilera; 11. Aaliyah; 12. Sinead O'Connor; 13. Monica; 14.
Mary J Blige 15. Shakira; 16. Jennifer Lopez.

FATS DOMINO *(Antoine Dominique Domino Jr. (February 26, 1928 – October 24, 2017), Born in New Orleans, Louisiana. An American pianist and singer-songwriter. A pioneer of rock and roll music, it is estimated that Domino sold over 110 million records. Fats worked with co-writer Dave Bartholomew, contributing his distinctive rolling piano style and had a string of 16 Top 40 hits from 1956. Remarkably with just one Top 10 hit. Inducted into the first Rock and Roll Hall of Fame in 1986. In 1957, he said: "What they call rock 'n' roll now is rhythm and blues. I've been playing it for 15 years in New Orleans"*

1. Which Fats Domino song was his first Top Forty hit in the UK, reaching No. 28?
A) Honey Chile   B) Blue Monday   C) I'm In Love Again

2. Amazingly Fats only had one Top 10 in the UK. What song reached No. 6 in 1956?
A) Ain't That a Shame   B) Blueberry Hill   C) I'm Walkin'

3. Which minor Fats Domino hit in 1957 had previously been a hit for Pat Boone in 1955 and was then to be a hit for the Four Seasons in 1963?
A) Ain't That a Shame   B) Walk Like a Man   C) Valley of Tears

4. What is Fats Domino asking you to do in these song lyrics from a 1959 No. 14 hit; "My, my-oh-my, gee you're so fine, Don't, let me down, I'm the king but you can wear my crown, I'm gonna sing, my band gonna play, I'm gonna make you queen for a day"?   A) Be My Guest   B) Be My Love   C) Be My Girl

5. Fats Domino had a hit about *Walking To .....* where?
A) Happiness   B) New Orleans   C) Memphis

6. Fats Domino's last chart entry in the UK was in 1963 with which song that originally featured in the Broadway production of *Provincetown Follies*, which staged in 1935, and was covered by many artistes including Bing Crosby, Louis Armstrong and The Platters?   A) Red Sails in the Sunset   B) My Prayer   C) Only You

7. Starting off with a very catchy snare drum solo, this Domino No. 32 hit from 1961 is about his 'girl'. What was her name?   A) Carol   B) Margie   C) Josephine

8. In 1956 Fats appeared in two musical comedy films. *Shake, Rattle & Rock!* starred Touch Connors. What was the title of the other film starring Jayne Mansfield?
A) Rock Around the Clock   B)The Girl Can't Help It   C) Anything Goes

9. In 1968 Fats Domino had a final hit in the US charts with a cover of which Beatles song, written by Paul McCartney, that according to some reports he had based upon Fats Domino's style?   A) Lady Madonna   B) Get Back   C) Day Tripper

10. Domino records were released on Imperial Records until 1963. When the label was sold, to which company did he then move?
A) Mercury   B) Reprise   C) ABC-Paramount Records

FATS DOMINO ANSWERS: 1. C) I'm In Love Again; 2. B) Blueberry Hill; 3. A) Ain't That a Shame; 4. A) Be My Guest; 5. B) New Orleans; 6. A) Red Sails in the Sunset; 7. C) Josephine (My Girl Josephine); 8. B) The Girl Can't Help It; 9. A) Lady Madonna; 10. C) ABC-Paramount Records.

LONNIE DONEGAN MBE *(Born Bridgeton, Glasgow as James Donegan 29 April 1931 – 3 November 2002, was an inspirational British skiffle singer, songwriter and musician, referred to as the 'King of Skiffle', who influenced 1960s British pop and rock musicians. Born in Scotland and raised in England, Donegan began his career in the British trad jazz revival playing banjo with both Ken Colyer and Chris Barber. Lonnie transitioned to skiffle in the mid 1950s. Notched up 31 Top 40 hits (inc 3 No. 1's & 14 other Top 10) 1956 & 1962. Donegan had 5 Top 20 albums including 3 Top 3 hits. Ironically Lonnie's last UK hit single coincided with the rise of The Beatles and similar bands to whom he had been a great inspiration.*

1. Lonnie Donegan's first hit in 1956 was written in 1929 by Clarence Wilson and was first recorded by inmates of Arkansas Cummins State Farm prison in 1934. What was the song that told of smuggling pig iron through a toll gate?
A) Rock island Line   B) Stewball   C) Lost John

2. In 1957 Donegan hit No.1 for the first time, and The Vipers No. 10, with an Appalachian folk song that probably dated back to the late 19th century. Which song?
A) Does Your Chewing Gum Lose Its Flavour?   B) Cumberland Gap   C) Stewball

3. Lonnie also reached the top spot with his next single, a double 'A' side single. Gamblin' Man was on one side, what more familiar track was on the other?
A) Don't You Rock Me Daddy-O   B) Jack O' Diamonds   C) Puttin' on the Style

4. "Well, we fired our guns and the British kept a-comin', There wasn't as many as there was a while ago, We fired once more and they began to runnin', On down the Mississippi to the Gulf of Mexico" Lyrics from which Jimmy Driftwood song, a No.1 for Johnny Horton in the US, that Lonnie took to No. 2 in 1959?
A) Battle of New Orleans   B) The Battle's O'er   C) Love is a Battlefield

5. *My Old Man's A Dustman* was a 1960 live recording from the Gaumont Cinema, Doncaster, that got Lonnie to No.1 within 2 weeks of release. The song title was completed with which words that followed in brackets?
A) (A Council Employee's Song)   B) (Ballad Of A Refuse Disposal Officer)
C) (He Wears a Dustman's Hat)

6. Lonnie Donegan's influence led to John Lennon forming which group?
A) The Beatles   B) The Quarrymen   C) The Plastic Ono Band

7. For most of the 60s, into the 70s, Lonnie worked as a record producer for artistes like Justin Hayward. What was the record label?   A) Columbia   B) Decca   C) Pye

8. Which Lonnie Donegan penned song took Tom Jones to No. 2 in 1967 and was also included on an Elvis Presley album?   A) I'll Never Fall In Love Again   B) Green Green Grass of Home   C) I'm Coming Home

9. After quadruple bypass surgery in 1976, Lonnie recorded an album, produced by Adam Faith, of early songs, *Putting On The Style*, in 1978. Which contemporary artist played on the album?   A) Elton John   B) Ringo Starr   C) Brian May   D) All of them

10. In 1984 Lonnie Donegan made his theatrical debut in a revival of which 1920s musical, based on Cinderella, in which the roles reversed; Prince Charming is a successful woman and Cinders a servant?
A) Button Up   B) Mr. Cinders   C) Ugly Brothers

I'll Never Fall In Love Again	*Fall in love, I'm never gonna fall in love*
Written by Lonnie Donegan	*I mean it*
	Fall in love again
I've been in love so many times	*All those things I heard about you*
Thought I knew the score	*I thought they were only lies*
But now you've treated me so wrong	*But when I caught you in his arms*
I can't take anymore	*I just broke down and cried*
And it looks like	*And it looks like*
I'm never gonna fall in love again	*I'm never gonna fall in love again*

LONNIE DONEGAN ANSWERS: 1. A) Rock Island Line; 2. B) Cumberland Gap; 3. C) Puttin' on the Style; 4. A) Battle of New Orleans; 5. B) (Ballad Of A Refuse Disposal Officer); 6. B) The Quarrymen; 7. C) Pye; 8. A) I'll Never Fall In Love Again; 9. D) All of them (plus Rory Gallagher); 10. B) Mr. Cinders.

DONOVAN (Donovan Phillips Leitch born 10 May 1946) is a Scottish singer, songwriter, and guitarist. He developed an eclectic and distinctive style blending folk, jazz, pop, psychedelic rock and world music (notably calypso). Emerging from the British folk scene, Donovan became known in 1965 with live performances on TV series Ready Steady Go! A long and successful collaboration with leading independent record producer Mickie Most was fruitful. A friend of pop and folk musicians including Joan Baez, Brian Jones and the Beatles, Donovan taught John Lennon a finger-picking guitar style that Lennon later employed on recordings. 10 Top 40 hits, including one duet. 7 of them Top 10 hits. Also 7 Top 30 albums (2 Top 10).

1. As a child, Donovan contracted what infectious disease, later to be treated with a vaccine developed by Jonas Salk in the 1950's?   A) Polio   B) Rubella   C) Mumps

2. During Donovan's early years as a recording artist, his style and sound were often compared to what famous American folk and blues singer of the 1960's?
A) Pete Seeger   B) Bob Dylan   C) John Denver

3. In 1965, Donovan had three Top 40 hits, two peaked at No. 4 in the UK Singles Chart. Which of the trio did not get above No. 30?
A) Catch the Wind   B) Colours   C) Turquoise

4. In 1966, Donovan had his biggest UK hit, a number two recording. What was the song?   A) Jennifer Juniper   B) Mellow Yellow   C) Sunshine Superman

5. In mid-1966, Donovan became the first high-profile British pop star to be arrested for possession of what drug?   A) Cannabis   B) Heroin   C) LSD

6. Paul McCartney played bass guitar on portions of *Mellow Yellow*, a 1967 Donovan single that was originally wrongly believed to have been about the hallucinogenic properties of what product?   A) Saffron   B) Lemon peel   C) Banana skins

7. *Hurdy Gurdy Man* was released in May 1968, a harder rock sound than Donovan's usual material. Which guitarist provided the fuzztone guitar solo?
A) Richie Blackmore   B) Alan Parker   C) Jimmy Page

8. *Hurdy Gurdy Man* was included as part of the soundtrack for what popular 1994 film featuring Jim Carrey and Jeff Daniels?
A) Dumb and Dumber   B) Batman Forever   C) The Mask

9. Donovan collaborated with Paul McCartney, on *Postcard*, a 1969 album that he was producing for which Welsh singer?
A) Bonnie Tyler   B) Shirley Bassey   C) Mary Hopkin

10. The last hit song released by Donovan made No.12 in 1969. The Jeff Beck Group were also credited on the label. What was the song?
A) Goo Goo Barabajagal (Love Is Hot)   B) Riki Tiki Tavi   C) Celia of the Seals

SECOND LINES

WE GIVE YOU THE FIRST LINE OF SONGS. YOU ADD THE SECOND!

1. "At first I was afraid, I was petrified"

2. "As I walk through the valley of the shadow of death"

3. "There must be some kinda way out of here"

4. "Come closer, come closer and listen"

5. "You took a mystery and made me want it"

DONOVAN ANSWERS: 1. A) Polio; 2. B) Bob Dylan; 3. C) Turquoise; 4. C) Sunshine Superman; 5. A) Cannabis;; 6. C) Banana skins; 7. B) Alan Parker; 8. A) Dumb and Dumber; 9. C) Mary Hopkin; 10. A) Goo Goo Barabajagal (Love Is Hot). **SECOND LINES ANSWERS:** *1. "Kept thinking I could never live without you by my side" (I Will Survive - Gloria Gaynor); 2. "I take a look at my life and realise there's not much left..." (Gangsta's Paradise - Coolio feat LV); 3. "Said the joker to the thief..." (All Along the Watchtower - Jimi Hendrix Experience); 4. "The beat of my heart keeps on missing" (Boom Bang-a-Bang - Lulu); 5. "You got a pedestal and put me on it" (Chain Reaction - Diana Ross).*

JASON DONOVAN (Jason Sean Donovan (born 1 June 1968) is an Australian actor and singer. He initially achieved fame in the Australian soap Neighbours, playing Scott Robinson, before beginning a career in music in 1988. In the UK he has sold over 3 million records. Signed a recording contract with PWL (Pete Waterman Ltd) in the UK whilst in Neighbours. He has also appeared in several stage musicals, most prominently in the lead role of Joseph and the Amazing Technicolor Dreamcoat in the early 1990s. Jason had 16 Top 40 hits including 4 No. 1's and 6 other Top 10 successes. Also notched up 4 Top 40 albums, including a number one, and 3 others reached the Top 10.

1. In 1986 Jason took over from Darius Perkins in which role in the Australian soap opera *Neighbours*? A) Scott Robinson B) Paul Robinson C) Robbie Robinson

2. Jason's first single released in the UK reached N0. 5 in 1988. What was its title?
A) Too Many Broken Hearts B) Nothing Can Divide Us C) Mission Of Love

3. Also in 1988 Donovan hit number one for the first time with *Especially For You* on which he duetted with which other Australian actor?
A) Natalie Imbruglia B) Holly Valance C) Kylie Minogue

4. The Doin' Fine tour of UK, Ireland, mainland Europe, Australia, Singapore and other parts of South East Asia began in which year? A) 1988 B) 1989 C) 1990

5. Which Cascades No. 5 hit from 1962, was covered by Jason in 1990 and reached No. 9 in the UK? A) Silvery Rain B) Rhythm of the Rain B) Rainbow Valley

6. In 1991, Donovan accepted the lead role in which re-staged London Palladium show, directed by Steven Pimlott? A) Joseph and the Amazing Technicolor Dreamcoat B) The Rocky Horror Show C) Priscilla, Queen of the Desert

7. Which Donovan No.1 hit contains these lyrics; "Far far away, someone was weeping, But the world was sleeping..."?
A) Every Day (I Love You More) B) I'm Doing Fine C) Any Dream Will Do

8. Who previously had a 1962 No. 3 hit with *Sealed With a Kiss*, which became a No. 1 for Jason in 1989? A) Billy Fury B) Brian Hyland C) Bobby Vinton

9. In 1992, Donovan launched a libel action against which publication that had printed allegations that he was homosexual?
A) The Face B) Private Eye C) The Guardian

10. In 1998, what role did Donovan take in the UK touring production of *The Rocky Horror Show*? A) Riff Raff B) Dr. Scott C) Dr. Frank N. Furter

What is a loud music instrument that you have in your ears?

Why did the musician put his head on the piano?

Which kind of phone can make music?

What type of band does not play any music?

Which instrument can't open a door despite having many keys?

JASON DONOVAN ANSWERS: 1. A) Scott Robinson; 2. B) Nothing Can Divide Us;
3. C) Kylie Minogue; 4. C) 1990; 5. B) Rhythm of the Rain; 6. A) Joseph and the Amazing Technicolor Dreamcoat; 7. C) Any Dream Will Do; 8. B) Brian Hyland; 9. A) The Face;
10. C) Dr. Frank N. Furter. **MUSICAL RIDDLES ANSWERS:** A) DRUMS; B) He wanted to play by ear; C) A saxophone; D) A rubber band; E) A piano.

THE DRIFTERS *are a R&B/soul vocal group. Originally formed as a backing group for Clyde McPhatter. A second group of Drifters formed in 1959 led by Ben E. King. After 1965, members drifted in and out of both groups and some formed other groups of Drifters as well. Several groups of Drifters can trace roots back to these original groups, but contain few, if any original members. Owner George Treadwell threatened legal action over naming rights of the UK's Drifters - they became The Shadows! The Drifters inducted into the Rock and Roll Hall of Fame in 1988. The Drifters notched up 20 Top 40 singles, 9 of them Top 10 hits. Also achieved 6 Top 40 album hits (1 Top 10).*

1. The original lead singer of The Drifters, Ben E King, had a UK number one in 1987. What was the song?   A) Treasure of Love   B) Stand By Me   C) Dance With Me

2. The Drifters never had a number one hit in the UK. They did get to #2 in 1960 with which song was written by Doc Pomus & Mort Shuman?
A) Dance With Me   B) When My Little Girl is Smiling   C) Save the Last Dance for Me

3. *Sweets For My Sweet* was a US Top 20 hit for The Drifters in 1961. Which Liverpool group had a UK number one hit with the song in 1963?
A) The Searchers   B) Gerry & The Pacemakers   C) The Swinging Blue Jeans

4. The Drifters had a No. 31 UK hit with *When My Little Girl Is Smiling* in 1962. They were outgunned by two UK cover versions from Craig Douglas and Jimmy Justice. Which chart position did both the British versions reach?   A) 1   B) 5   C) 9

5. Which 1974 No. 2 starts with these lyrics: "Your mama says that through the week, You can't go out with me, But when the weekend comes around, She knows where we will be"   A) Saturday Night at the Movies   B) Kissin' in the Back Row of the Movies   C) There Goes My First Love

6. What colour was the book in the No. 5 hit *You're More Than A Number In My Little ... Book*, written by Roger Greenaway/Tony Macaulay?   A) Black   B) Blue   C) Red

7. Which member of The Drifters is estimated to have sung lead vocals on more of their records than any other member of the group?
A) Clyde McPhatter   B) Ben E. King   C) Johnny Moore *(pictured below L to R)*

8. The Drifters were frequently trumped by UK acts covering their songs. The Goffin-King song *Up On The Roof* was one example. Which UK singer had a Top 10 hit with the song in 1962?   A) Kenny Lynch   B) Julie Grant   C) Ronnie Carroll

9. Robson & Jerome had a triple A-side No.1 hit in the UK in 1996 with *What Becomes Of The Broken Hearted, You'll Never Walk Alone*, and which Drifters hit?
A) Saturday Night At The Movies   B) Under the Boardwalk   C) Like Sister & Brother

10. The Drifters had more Top Ten hits on the UK singles chart than they did on the Billboard Hot 100. True or False?

THE DRIFTERS ANSWERS: 1. B) Stand By Me; 2. C) Save the Last Dance for Me; 3. A) The Searchers; 4. C) 9; 5. B) Kissin' in the Back Row of the Movies . 6. C) Red; 7. C) Johnny Moore; 8. A) Kenny Lynch; 9. A) Saturday Night At The Movies; 10. True (9 UK Top 10, just 5 US Top 10).

DURAN DURAN are an English new wave band formed in Birmingham in 1978. The group was a leading band in the Second British Invasion of the US in the 1980s. The five members featured in the most commercially successful line-up were founders keyboardist Nick Rhodes and bassist John Taylor plus drummer Roger Taylor, guitarist Andy Taylor and lead singer Simon Le Bon. The band had 28 Top 40 singles, including 2 number ones and 11 other Top 10 successes between 1981-1999. Duran Duran also notched up 11 Top 40 albums in the 20th C with 1 No. 1 and 7 other Top 10 placings.

1. Which member of Duran Duran shares his name with a member of the band, Queen? A) Andy Taylor B) Roger Taylor C) John Taylor

2. There were 19 James Bond films released in the 20th century. Duran Duran's *View To A Kill* achieved the highest chart position, reaching number 2. True or False?

3. In 1982, in which country did Duran Duran film videos for *Save a Prayer, Hungry Like the Wolf* and *Lonely in Your Nightmare*? A) Sri Lanka B) Antigua C) Croatia

4. From which film was the band's name, Duran Duran, taken?
A) Flash Gordon B) Barbarella C) Buck Rogers

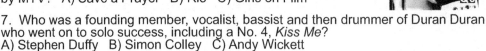

5. In which Birmingham club were Duran Duran the resident band?
A) The Rum Runner B) The Hole in the Wall C) Snobs

6. The video for which Duran Duran No. 5 hit in 1981 was banned by MTV? A) Save a Prayer B) Rio C) Girls on Film

7. Who was a founding member, vocalist, bassist and then drummer of Duran Duran who went on to solo success, including a No. 4, *Kiss Me*?
A) Stephen Duffy B) Simon Colley C) Andy Wickett

8. "Darken the city, night is a wire". The opening lyrics to which 1982 number 5?
A) All She Wants Is B) Hungry Like the Wolf C) Notorious

9. In 1986, who replaced Andy Taylor, becoming a long-term member of Duran Duran until 2001? A) Sterling Campbell B) Warren Cuccurullo C) Alan Curtis

10. Who produced the 1986 album *Notorious*, featuring the top ten single with the same name, which peaked at number 16 in the album charts?
A) Colin Thurston B) Nile Rodgers C) Jonathan Elias

SARAH SONG SUCCESSES *Just fill in the missing surnames!*	
1. SARAH	BROKEN HEARTED MELODY 1959
2. SARAH	& STEVE HARLEY - PHANTOM OF THE OPERA 1986
3. SARAH	I WILL ALWAYS LOVE YOU 1993
4. SARAH	ANYMORE 1996
5. SARAH	ADIA 1998

DURAN DURAN ANSWERS: 1. B) Roger Taylor (both drummers); 2. True; 3. A) Sri Lanka; 4. B) Barbarella (Dr. Durand Durand, Milo O'Shea's character); 5. A) The Rum Runner; 6. C) Girls on Film; 7. A) Stephen 'Tin Tin' Duffy; 8. B) Hungry Like the Wolf; 9. B) Warren Cuccurullo; 10. B) Nile Rodgers. SARAH SONG SUCCESSES ANSWERS: 1. Vaughan; 2. Brightman; 3. Washington; 4. Cracknell; 5. McLachlan.

BOB DYLAN *(Robert Dylan born Robert Allen Zimmerman; May 24, 1941) is an American singer-songwriter, author and visual artist. Often regarded as one of the greatest songwriters of all time, Dylan has been a major figure in popular culture during a career spanning 60 years. Much of his most celebrated work dates from the 1960s. His lyrics during this period incorporated a range of political, social, philosophical, and literary influences, defying pop music conventions and appealing to the burgeoning counterculture. Bob Dylan had 15 UK Top 40 recordings, including six Top 10 and an amazing thirty-nine Top 40 albums with six No. 1's and twenty-one other Top 10 successes.*

1. What musician was a revelation to Dylan, and influenced his early performances?
A) Little Richard   B) Woody Guthrie   C) BB King

2. What was Bob Dylan's first UK Top 10 hit in 1965?
A) The Times They Are A-Changin'   B) Blowin' in the Wind   C) Maggie's Farm

3. At which Rhode Island festival did Dylan often perform?
A) Providence   B) Naragansett   C) Newport

4. Bob Dylan is represented by *"The Jester who plays for the King and Queen"* in the lyrics of which Don McLean number two hit in 1972?
A) American Pie   B) Vincent   C) Crying

5. Complete the lyric from Dylan's 1965 No. 4 hit, *Like a Rolling Stone*: "Like .... in rags, and the language that he used".   A) Wellington   B) Patton   C) Napoleon

6. In 1963 Dylan played at the March on Washington, on the same day and the same stage, and the same microphones, as those used by Martin Luther King Jr. for his famous, *"I Have A Dream"* speech. True or False?

7. Complete the title of the 1966 No. 7 hit; *Rainy Day Women Nos ? and ?*.
A) 6 & 9   B) 12 & 35   C) 12 & 27

8. Between 1968 and 1970 Bob Dylan had four successive No. 1 albums: John Wesley Harding (1968); Nashville Skyline (1969); Self Portrait (1970) - what was the fourth, also in 1970?   A) Before the Flood   B) Planet Waves   C) New Morning

9. Who inspired Bob's change of name from Robert Zimmerman to Bob Dylan?
A) Dylan Thomas   B) 101 Dalmatians character   C) Magic Roundabout character

10. Who took Dylan's song *Mr. Tambourine Man* to UK and US No.1 in 1965?
A) Melanie   B) Glen Campbell   C) The Byrds

Bob Dylan Covered

What Bob Dylan songs were hits for these artistes?

1. Jimi Hendrix (1968)

2. Olivia Newton-John (1971)

3. Johnny Cash (1965)

4. Stevie Wonder (1966)

5. Guns 'N' Roses (1992)

BOB DYLAN ANSWERS: *1. B) Woody Guthrie; 2. A) The Times They Are A-Changin'; 3. C) Newport; 4. A) American Pie; 5. C) Napoleon; 6. True; 7. B) 12 & 35; 8. C) New Morning; 9. A) Dylan Thomas (Welsh poet & writer); 10. C) The Byrds.*
BOB DYLAN COVERED ANSWERS: *1. All Along the Watchtower; 2. If Not For You; 3. It Ain't Me Babe; 4. Blowin' in the Wind; 5. Knockin' on Heaven's Door.*

EAGLES are a US rock band formed in Los Angeles in 1971. Founding members Glenn Frey (guitars, vocals), Don Henley (drums, vocals), Bernie Leadon (guitars, vocals) and Randy Meisner (bass guitar, vocals). Recruited by Linda Ronstadt as her band, some toured with her, all played on her 3rd solo album, before going it alone. Several line up changes along the way with Timothy B. Schmit, Joe Walsh and Don Felder introduced at various stages. The Eagles are one of the world's best-selling bands, with more than 200 million record sales. 7 Top 40 singles in the UK, one Top 10. 10 Top 40 albums with 6 reaching the Top 10.

1. Timothy B. Schmit and Randy Meisner joined the Eagles from the same band. True or False?

2. Don Henley had a solo hit with the co-written *Boys of Summer* in 1985. The song was re-released in 1998. What number did it reach in the charts the second time? A) 4 B)12 C) 36

3. Eagles highest chart placing single in the UK is number 8 in 1977 with *Hotel California*. On what 1998 film soundtrack is the song performed by the Gipsy Kings? A) Enemy of the State B) Lock Stock & Two Smoking Barrels C) The Big Lebowski

4. What was the first UK hit for the Eagles in 1975, which reached a modest number 23 in the charts? A) Peaceful Easy Feeling B) Take It To The Limit C) Lyin' Eyes

5. What is the opening track on the Eagles first Top 40 UK album, *On the Border*, that was sung by Glenn Frey, and has since been regularly performed live by the Eagles? A) Already Gone B) Midnight Flyer C) Desperado

6. The Eagles hit the UK Top 10 albums with *One Of These Nights*. The single of the same name peaked at No.23, as did which other song from the album that has become a real Eagles classic? A) Lyin' Eyes B) Take It To the Limit C) Visions

7. Joe Walsh had a #14 hit in 1978 with a song he wrote that includes these lyrics: "My Maserati does one-eighty-five, I lost my licence, now I don't drive, I have a limo, ride in the back, I lock the doors in case I'm attacked". What was the song? A) Rocky Mountain Way B) Life's Been Good C) Pretty Maids All In A Row

8. In what year were the Eagles inducted into the Rock and Roll Hall of Fame? A) 1978 B) 1988 C) 1998

9. A song lasting over 7 minutes, written by Don Henley and Glenn Frey, originally released on Eagles' 1976 album *Hotel California*, tells how man inevitably destroys the places he finds beautiful. What was the song, later released as the B-side of *Life in the Fast Lane*? A) The Last Resort B) Wasted Time C) Victim of Love

10. After the 1980 break up, Don Henley's recurring statement about any possible reformation of the band, provided a title for the hit 1994 album. What was the album entitled? A) The Long Run B) Hell Freezes Over C) Love Will Keep Us Alive

HOTEL CALIFORNIA (Felder, Henley, Frey,)

On a dark desert highway, cool wind in my hair
Warm smell of colitas, rising up through the air
Up ahead in the distance, I saw shimmering light
My head grew heavy and my sight grew dim
I had to stop for the night
There she stood in the doorway;
I heard the mission bell
And I was thinking to myself,
'This could be Heaven or this could be Hell'
Then she lit up a candle and she showed me the way
There were voices down the corridor,

I thought I heard them say...
Welcome to the Hotel California
Such a lovely place (Such a lovely place)
Such a lovely face
Plenty of room at the Hotel California
Any time of year (Any time of year)
You can find it here
Her mind is Tiffany-twisted, she got the Mercedes Benz
She got a lot of pretty, pretty boys she calls friends
How they dance in the courtyard, sweet summer sweat.
Some dance to remember, some dance to forget
So I called up the Captain,
'Please bring me my wine'..........

EAGLES ANSWERS: 1. True (Poco - 6 years apart!); 2. B) 12; 3. C) The Big Lebowski; 4. B) Take It To The Limit; 5. A) Already Gone; 6. A) Lyin' Eyes; 7. B) Life's Been Good; 8. C) 1998; 9. A) The Last Resort; 10. B) Hell Freezes Over (Henley often said the group would get back together "when hell freezes over").

EARTH WIND & FIRE *(EW&F or EWF) is an American band that has spanned the musical genres of R&B, soul, funk, jazz, disco, pop, dance, Latin, and Afro pop. Described as one of the most innovative and most commercially successful acts in history. Founded in Chicago by Maurice White in 1969, other prominent members of EWF have had many changes in personnel in their history. The band has notched up sales of over 90 million records and they are one of the world's best-selling bands of all time. 10 Top 40 recordings, including 4 Top 10 hits. Also 10 Top 40 albums, including 4 Top 10 successes.*

1. How did Earth, Wind & Fire get the name for their band?
A) A reference to a biblical verse   B) The astrological elements affecting the band leader's zodiac sign   C) A description of the climate of Africa

2. In 1995, Earth, Wind & Fire band leader Maurice White scaled back his involvement with the band. What was the reason for his decision?
A) He had contracted Parkinson's disease   B) He wanted to pursue a solo recording career   C) He had a falling out with Philip Bailey, who took over as leader

3. EW&F's first Top 10 hit in the UK was a 1978 No. 3 hit. What was its title?
A) July   B) August   C) September

4. What EW&F No. 4 hit from 1979 includes these lyrics: "Midnight creeps so slowly into hearts of men, Who need more than they get, Daylight deals a bad hand to a woman, Who has laid too many bets"?   A) Boogie Wonderland   B) Star   C) Fantasy

5. In 1984, Philip Bailey duetted with whom on the number one hit *Easy Lover*?
A) Stevie Wonder   B) Phil Collins   C) Paul McCartney

6. Which 1979 EW&F album reached No. 5 in the album chart and also generated 5 hit singles including *After the Love Has Gone*?   A) I Am   B) Faces   C) Raise!

7. Earth Wind & Fire is from what US city?   A) Boston   B) Indianapolis   C) Chicago

8. What instrument does Earth Wind & Fire member Verdine White play?
A) Bass   B) Saxophone   C) Drums

9. In 1995 Earth Wind & Fire received a star on the Hollywood Walk of Fame. True or False?

10. EW&F appeared in the 1978 feature film *Sgt. Pepper's Lonely Hearts Club Band* where they performed a cover of which Beatles song?
A) Maxwell's Silver Hammer   B)   C) Come Together   C) Got to Get You into My Life

Wet! Wet! Wet!

CAN YOU NAME THE TITLES OF THESE HITS ABOUT WATER!

1. Frankie Laine (1955)	6. Deep Purple (1977)
2. Tommy Steele (1957)	7. Level 42 (1984)
3. P.J. Proby (1965)	8. Julian Lennon (1991)
4. Simon and Garfunkel (1970)	9. TLC (1995)
5. Four Tops (1970)	10. Bee Gees (1997)

EARTH WIND & FIRE ANSWERS: *1. B)The astrological elements affecting the band leader's zodiac sign; 2. A) He had contracted Parkinson's disease; 3. C) September; 4. A) Boogie Wonderland; 5. B) Phil Collins; 6. A) I Am; 7. C) Chicago; 8. A) Bass; 9. True; 10.C) Got to Get You Into My Life.* **WET! WET! WET! ANSWERS:** *1. Cool Water; 2. Water Water; 3. Let the Water Run Down; 4. Bridge Over Troubled Water; 5. Still Water (Love); 6. Smoke On the Water; 7. Hot Water; 8. Saltwater; 9. Waterfalls; 10. Still Waters (Run Deep).*

DUANE EDDY *(Born Corning, New York on April 26, 1938) is an influential American instrumental rock guitarist. Eddy devised a technique of playing lead on his guitar's bass strings to produce a low, reverberating 'twangy' sound. In the late 1950s and early 1960s, he had a string of hit records produced by Lee Hazlewood. His band, The Rebels, included sax players Steve Douglas and Jim Horn and keyboard player Larry Knechtel. He was inducted into the Rock and Roll Hall of Fame in 1994. Duane had 21 Top 10 hits (9 reached the Top 10) and nine Top 20 albums (5 Top 10 included).*

1. *Rebel Rouser*, Duane's first Top 20 UK hit in 1958, was featured on the soundtrack of which multi Oscar winning 1994 American film?
A) Forrest Gump   B) Driving Miss Daisy   C) Braveheart

2. Which atmospheric hit with a stunning opening riff was a No. 6 hit for Eddy in 1959 and a No. 8 hit in 1996 when re-recorded with the Art of Noise?
A) Kommotion   B) Peter Gunn Theme   C) Yep

3. An Eddy 1960 number 4, was covered by The Shadows as the B-side to their 1963 hit single *Geronimo*. What was the title of the song?
A) The Breeze and I   B) This Hammer   C) Shazam!

4. Duane and Lee Hazelwood were in a queue and overheard two men discussing a blind date. One said "OK but she had a face like....". Duane used the rest of the sentence as the title of his 1959 No. 11 hit, which was?
A) Forty Miles of Bad Road   B) The Iguana   C) Thunder of Drums

5. Eddy's biggest hit came with a No. 2 hit in 1960. It was a film theme and featured a string arrangement for the first time. What was the title of the song and film?
A) Pepe   B) Because They're Young   C) Them From Dixie

6. In 1992, Eddy recorded a duet with Hank Marvin for Marvin's album *Into the Light*, The song was a cover version of which Chantays' 1963 hit?
A) Pipeline   B) Walk Don't Run   C) Wipe Out

7. What was Eddy's favoured guitar?   A) Gibson Les Paul Standard   B) 1957 Chet Atkins Gretsch 6120   C) Fender Stratocaster

8. In 1987 Eddy recorded an eponymous album with guest musicians including John Fogerty, George Harrison, James Burton, Steve Cropper and original Rebels, Larry Knechtel and Jim Horn. Who produced tracks on the album?
A) Paul McCartney   B) Jeff Lynne   C) Ry Cooder   D) All of them

9. *Theme For Something Really Important*, written by Jeff Lynne, was featured on the 1987 album. Which UK bass legend covered the track on an album of his own?
A) Paul McCartney   B) Jet Harris   C) John Paul Jones

10. *(Dance With the) Guitar Man* reached #4 in 1962. It was the first Eddy single to credit which vocal group on its label?   A) Eddys   B) Shazams   C) Rebelettes

60s Guitar Instrumentals
Who had these hits?

1. Quite a Party (1961)	6. Love is Blue (1968)
2. Albatross (1968)	7. Perfidia (1960)
3. Scarlett O'Hara (1963)	8. Wipe Out (1963)
4. Riders in the Sky (1961)	9. Hava Nagila (1963)
5. Saturday Nite at the Duckpond (1963)	10. Wheels (1961)

DUANE EDDY ANSWERS: 1. A) Forrest Gump; 2. B) Peter Gunn Theme; 3. C) Shazam!; 4. A) Forty Miles of Bad Road; 5. B) Because They're Young; 6. A) Pipeline; 7. B) 1957 Chet Atkins Gretsch 6120; 8. C) All of them (sadly the album didn't chart); 9. B) Jet Harris; 10. C) Rebelettes. **60s GUITAR INSTRUMENTALS:** 1. Fireballs; 2. Fleetwood Mac; 3. Jet Harris & Tony Meehan; 4. Ramrods; 5. Cougars; 6. Jeff Beck; 7. Ventures; 8. Surfaris; 9. Spotnicks; 10. String-a-Longs.

DAVE EDMUNDS *(David William Edmunds, born 15 April 1944 is a Welsh singer-songwriter, guitarist, and record producer. Although he is mainly associated with pub rock and new wave, having many hits in the 1970s and early 1980s, his natural leaning has always been towards 1950s-style rock and roll and rockabilly. Started in various bands, Love Sculpture was the most successful with Congo Jones (Drums) and John David (Bass). Had a long association with Rockfield Studios, Monmouth. Dave Edmunds had 8 Top 40 singles in the UK (1 No. 1 and 3 more top 10 hits), in addition to a Top 10 hit with Love Sculpture. Also 2 Top 40 albums.*

1. Love Sculpture had a number five hit in 1968 with a speed-crazed rock version of *Sabre Dance* which was a reworking of a classical piece by which composer?
A) Grieg   B) Khachaturian   C) Mozart

2. Edmunds had a UK Christmas Number 1 single in 1970 with a Smiley Lewis cover. What was the song?   A) I Hear You Knocking   B) Blue Monday   C) Down Yonder

3. Dave Edmunds' only acting role was in 1974, he played a band member in which David Essex film?   A) Silver Dream Racer B) That'll Be the Day C) Stardust

4. In 1973, Dave Edmunds had a #8 hit with a song that was a Ronettes No.11 hit in 1963. What was the song? A) Be My Baby   B) Baby I Love You   C) Do I Love You

5. Edmunds had more success with another cover version in 1973, reaching No. 5 with *Born To Be With You*, surpassing a 1956 version by whom that got to No. 8?
A) Chordettes   B) Beverley Sisters   C) Mudlarks

6. Dave Edmunds was musical director for a 1985 TV special starring a rock and roll legend and featuring George Harrison, Eric Clapton and Ringo Starr. Who was the rockabilly star?   A) Jerry Lee Lewis   B) Charlie Gracie   C) Carl Perkins

7. In 1980 Elvis Costello had a self-penned song as the B-side of *I Can't Stand Up For Falling Down*. A year earlier Dave Edmunds had taken the song to #4 in the UK. What was the song?   A) I Knew the Bride B) Almost Saturday Night C) Girls Talk

8. In 1992 Edmunds joined up with whose rock supergroup for tours?
A) Paul McCartney   B) Ringo Starr   C) Jools Holland

9. Edmunds' last appearance in the UK singles chart was in 1981. He teamed up for a #34 hit with which rockabilly band?   A) Rockpile B) The Cramps C) Stray Cats

10. In which of his hits did Dave Edmunds shout out, "Fats Domino, Smiley Lewis, Chuck Berry, Huey Smith!" during a guitar break?
A) I Hear You Knocking   B) Queen of Hearts   C) Singing the Blues

1974, Stardust: Keith Moon, Dave Edmunds, David Essex and Paul Nicholas in action!

DAVE EDMUNDS ANSWERS: *1. B) Khachaturian; 2. A) I Hear You Knocking; 3. C) Stardust; 4. B) Baby I Love You; 5. A) Chordettes; 6. C) Carl Perkins; 7. C) Girls Talk; 8. B) Ringo Starr; 9. C) Stray Cats; 10. A) I Hear You Knocking.*

A ROUND OF GENERAL TRIVIA

1. Who sang the song *Blue (Da Ba Dee)*? A) Eiffel 65 B) Boca 45 C) Front 242

2. "All I wanna do when I wake up in the morning is see your eyes". The opening line of which 1983 #12 from Toto?

3. Which prisons did Johnny Cash famously sing at in 1968 and 1969?

4. Which British rock group has always been fronted by Ray Dorset?

5. Which American new wave band sung the 1990 No. 2 hit song *Love Shack*?

6. Paul 'Bonehead' Arthurs and Paul 'Guigsy' McGuigan were founding members of a Manchester band, the Rain, which evolved into which rock band?

7. Which singer became son-in-law to TV star Leslie Crowther in 1980?

8. *Welcome to the Pleasuredome* was the debut studio album of which band?

9. Which 90s boy band's name was an amalgamation of the initial letters of the 5 members' surnames?

10. Which trio had a 1973 No.1 with *Tie a Yellow Ribbon 'round the Old Oak Tree*?

11. Which disco group had 70s hits with *Get Dancing* and *I Wanna Dance Wit Choo*?

12. Which British musician caused controversy in 1997, when he said taking drugs was 'like having a cup of tea in the morning'?

13. Which Squeeze No. 2 from 1979 begins: "I never thought it would happen, With me and the girl from Clapham"?

14. Brothers Kevin and Jim McGinley were members of which Scottish pop band who had a 1976 UK No.1 hit with *Forever and Ever*?

15. Who won a Grammy for best reggae album in 1995 with *Boombastic*?

16. Gwen Stefani was the lead singer of which group?

Q20

17. Which supergroup included George Harrison, Roy Orbison, Jeff Lynne, Tom Petty and Bob Dylan in their ranks?

18. The daughters of a Beach Boy and two members of the Mamas & The Papas made up which 1990s hit-making duo?

19. Who was Elton John's longtime lyricist?

20. Who is the singer (right), who had two big hits in the 1979s with *Tired of Being Alone* and *Let's Stay Together*?

ALL SORTS ANSWERS: *1. A) Eiffel 65; 2. Rosanna; 3. Folsom and San Quentin; 4. Mungo Jerry; 5. B-52's; 6. Oasis; 7. Phil Lynott; 8. Frankie Goes To Hollywood; 9. NSYNC; 10. Dawn feat Tony Orlando; 11. Disco-Tex and the Sex-O-Lettes; 12. Noel Gallagher; 13. Up the Junction; 14. Slik; 15. Shaggy; 16. No Doubt; 17. Traveling Wilburys; 18. Wilson Phillips (Brian Wilson and John & Michelle Phillips); 19. Bernie Taupin; 20. Al Green.*

ELECTRIC LIGHT ORCHESTRA (ELO) *are an English rock band formed 1970 in Birmingham by songwriting multi-instrumentalists Jeff Lynne and Roy Wood, drummer Bev Bevan, and Richard Tandy on bass (then keyboards). ELO music is typically a fusion of Beatlesque pop, classical arrangements and futuristic iconography. Wood left in 1972 and Lynne became sole leader, arranging and producing every album while writing nearly all of their original material. Numerous personnel changes whilst ELO had 27 Top 40 hits (one No.1 with another artiste, and 14 other Top 10 hits.) Albums also sold well; 13 Top 40 albums, including 2 No. 1's and 6 others reaching the Top 10.*

1. What was the number of the overture in ELO's first ever hit in 1972? A) 40   B) 10538   C) 17

2. Where was ELO's debut concert in April 1972?
A) NEC, Birmingham   B) Greyhound pub, Croydon
C) CBGB's, New York

3. For their second hit, ELO covered Chuck Berry's *Roll Over Beethoven* and took it to #6 in 1973. Before the famous guitar riff, what famous Beethoven symphony was used to open the song?   A) 5th B) 3rd (Eroica)   C) 6th (Pastoral)

Jeff Lynne

4. In 1972, Roy Wood, Bill Hunt and Hugh McDowell left ELO to form which band?
A) The Move   B) The Nightriders   C) Wizzard

5. What was the theme of ELO's album, *El Dorado: A Symphony*, big in the US but a flop in the UK?   A) A boat trip on the canal   B) A day-dreamer   C) A South American chief

6. Which 1978 ELO No. 6, due to its continued popularity and frequent use in multiple TV shows and films, is sometimes described as the band's signature song?   A) Mr. Blue Sky
B) The Diary of Horace Wimp   C) Hold on Tight

Roy Wood

7. In 1980 ELO had their only No.1 hit with the title song of the flop film *Xanadu*. Who shared the billing on the single that was also a No. 1 in several other countries?
A) Olivia Newton-John   B) Dusty Springfield   C) Sheena Easton

8. What 1981 No.1 album used a lot of synthesizers, and whose theme was the future in the year 2095?
A) Discovery   B) Time   C) Secret Messages

9. "Hello, how are you? Have you been alright, Through all those lonely, lonely, lonely, lonely, lonely nights?" are opening lyrics for which 1977 #8, written by Jeff Lynne?

10. Who was drummer, and an founder member, of both The Move and ELO, and founded ELO Part II in 1986?
A) Bobby Elliott   B) Phil Collins   C) Bev Bevan

Richard Tandy

Q10

MR. BLUE SKY (Jeff Lynne)

Sun is shinin' in the sky

There ain't a cloud in sight

It's stopped rainin' everybody's in the play

And don't you know

It's a beautiful new day, hey hey.

ELO ANSWERS: *1. B) 10538; 2. B) Greyhound pub, Croydon; 3. A) 5th; 4. C) Wizzard; 5. B) A day-dreamer; 6. A) Mr. Blue Sky; 7. A) Olivia Newton-John; 8. C) Bev Bevan; 9. B) Time; 10. Telephone Line.*

ERASURE *are an English synth-pop duo formed in London in 1985. Singer songwriter Andy Bell and songwriter, producer and keyboardist Vince Clarke, previously co-founder of Depeche Mode. Erasure established themselves on the UK Singles Chart from mid-1980s to mid-1990s. Erasure also popular within the LGBT community for whom the openly gay singer Andy Bell is an icon in the UK. From 1986 to 1999, the duo achieved 25 consecutive top 40 entries in the UK singles chart (inc 3 EPs - 1 a No.1). Had 8 Top 40 albums, with 5 consecutive number ones and 2 other Top 10 entries.*

1. How did Vince Clarke and Andy Bell meet?   A) Clarke heard Bell sing in London   B) Both in Depeche Mode   C) Bell answered Clarke's Melody Maker advert

2. From which group's hit catalogue did Erasure cover songs for an EP, which went to number one in the UK singles chart in 1992?
A) ABBA   B) The Beatles   C) The Bee Gees

3. Which album was Erasure's first, reaching a disappointing number 71 in the charts?   A) The Circus   B) Wonderland   C) The Innocents

4. Clarke was a founding member of Depeche Mode, when he left the band in late 1981, he forged a similarly notable career as a part of which duo with Alison Moyet?
A) Human League   B) Soft Cell   C) Yazoo

5. Fill in the missing title in the lyrics of the 1990 Erasure hit: "My home is where the heart is, Sweet to surrender to you only, I send my love to you, ... song"

6. Which 1988 No. 1 Erasure album cover features a stained glass image of St. James and Charlemagne?   A) Union Street   B) The Innocents   C) Cowboy

7. The Erasure classic *A Little Respect*, a No. 4 hit in 1988 came from which 1988 album?   A) Wild!   B) The Circus   C) The Innocents

8. Which of these **IS** the title of an Erasure album?
A) Harlequin Love   B) Two Ring Circus   C) Lion Tamer

9. Vince Clarke was a founding member of Depeche Mode. He wrote their first three chart hits. The first, *Dreaming*, reached No. 57, and the third, *Just Can't Get Enough* was a Top 10 hit. What No. 11 song was the second hit?
A) Just Can't Get Enough   B) New Life   C) Get the Balance Right

10. In what year were Erasure voted Best British Group at the Brit Awards?
A) 1989   B) 1988   C) 1987

Heavenly Music

All song titles include heaven. Fill in the missing information.

1. Show Me Heaven	????	1990
2. Three Steps To Heaven	Eddie Cochran	????
3. ????	Tavares	1976
4. Too Much Heaven	????	1978
5. ????	Fiction Factory	1984
6. Heaven Is A Place On Earth	Belinda Carlisle	????
7. ????	Bryan Adams	1992
8. Stairway To Heaven	????	1960
9. ????	Smiths	1984
10. ????	Elgins	1971

ERASURE ANSWERS: 1. C) Bell answered Clarke's Melody Maker advert; 2. A) ABBA; 3. B) Wonderland; 4. C) Yazoo; 5. Blue Savannah; 6. B) The Innocents; 7. C) The Innocents; 8. B) Two Ring Circus; 9. B) New Life; 10. A) 1989.
HEAVENLY MUSIC ANSWERS: 1. Maria McKee; 2. 1960; 3. Heaven Must Be Missing An Angel; 4. Bee Gees; 5. (Feels Like) Heaven; 6. 1987; 7. Thought I'd Died and Gone to Heaven; 8. Neil Sedaka; 9. Heaven Knows I'm Miserable Now; 10. Heaven Must Have Sent You.

DAVID ESSEX OBE *(born Plaistow, Essex as David Albert Cook on 23 July 1947) is an English singer, songwriter, and actor. Starred in the stage musical Godspell in 1971 and in the film That'll Be the Day (1973) and its sequel Stardust a year later. Voted number one British male vocalist in 1974, and was a teen idol for more than a decade. Numerous TV appearances. Spent six years as an ambassador for Voluntary Service Overseas, which earned him an OBE in 1999. Despite his long and successful British career, he remains largely unknown in the United States. He has attained 19 Top 40 singles in the UK (including two number ones and 8 other Top 10) plus 16 Top 40 albums (4 Top 10).*

1. In which live stage show did David play Jesus as a red nose clown?
A) Godspell   B) Jesus Christ Superstar   C) Life of Brian

2. Name the one song with which David had a hit in America, reaching #5 in 1973?
A) Lamplight   B) America   C) Rock On

3. Essex had his first number one in the UK in 1974. With which self-penned song did he hit the top spot?   A) Hold Me Close   B) Gonna Make You a Star   C) Stardust

4. Which Premiership football team does David Essex support?
A) Chelsea   B) Crystal Palace   C) West Ham United

5. In 1975 Essex had another #1 hit. Name the song that includes these lyrics: "And if that road gets weary, Oh I love you, Waiting here if you need me, 'Cause I love the things that you do"?   A) City Lights   B) Hold Me Close   C) Coming Home

6. Essex had a number three hit in 1978 with *Oh What a Circus* taken from the original West End production of Tim Rice and Andrew Lloyd Webber's musical *Evita*. David received top billing in the show, playing which role?
A) Che   B) Juan Peron   C) Agustin Magaldi

7. *Tahiti* was a 1983 number eight hit for Essex. The song was included in a musical that David had written, which ran for 526 performances at the Piccadilly Theatre, London. What was the show?   A) Tommy   B) Mutiny   C) War of the Worlds

8. Which 1988 TV sit-com, starring David Essex, followed the tranquil life of lovable, Cockney, ex-convict Davey Jackson who was lock keeper on the canal near the village of Chumley-on-the-Water?   A) The River   B) The Canal   B) The Broads

9. *Silver Dream Machine* was another Essex hit, reaching number 4 in the UK in 1980. It was a single from which unsuccessful film, also starring David Essex?
A) Silver Dream Racer   B) The Big Bus   C) Smashing Time

10. In 1978, David appeared in which Jeff Wayne musical, playing the Artilleryman?
A) Spartacus   B) Jubilation   C) The War of the Worlds

MATCH THE CORRECT HIT SONG TO THE 1970s ARTISTES

1. **FLEETWOOD MAC:** Before the Next Teardrop Falls / Say You Love Me / Angel

2. **STEVIE WONDER:** Sir Duke / The Air That I Breathe / Ain't No Sunshine

3. **TOM JONES:** She's Gone / The Entertainer / Without Love

4. **DUSTY SPRINGFIELD:** Take Your Mama For a Ride / How Can I Be Sure / Shout

5. **ROD STEWART:** My Marie / Reason to Believe / Rock 'n' Roll Suicide

6. **OLIVIA NEWTON JOHN:** If Not For You / Love and Affection / Wow

---

DAVID ESSEX ANSWERS: *1. A) Godspell; 2. C) Rock On; 3. B) Gonna Make You a Star; 4. C) West Ham United; 5. B) Hold Me Close; 6. A) Che; 7. B) Mutiny; 8. A) The River; 9. A) Silver Dream Racer; 10. C) War of the Worlds.* **HOW MUCH DO YOU KNOW ABOUT THE 70s?:** *Fleetwood Mac - Say You Love Me; Stevie Wonder - Sir Duke; Tom Jones - Without Love; Dusty Springfield - How Can I Be Sure; Rod Stewart - Reason to Believe; Olivia Newton John - If Not For You.*

WORD SEARCH

Find the 20 Bands or Groups hidden horizontally, vertically or diagonally in the puzzle. The prefix 'The' is not used in this instance, so The Dakotas would simply be Dakotas. The names of the acts are listed below the grid.

```
P Z H L T I U C J N C Q P B O Z P M S K C J B K Z
L N N K G U X D Q N K N O K F X O H S H A D O W S
C J T I W H V H Q M N E I E N M A T R E X E M Y V
W S D K Q M T C S T R K N K I V S C N K S A M W X
M S P I C E G I R L S Y T X G V I W N V M G H D T
S T J T Q K W C T Q V L E N N I S G F U A L B T P
C E V P L J P F D O A S R B F C P X T B L E L J B
Z R K I N K S L G X I K S T I V Z M Y Y L S A B S
Q Q C N F F O E F U A E I P H G D J L Q F D A A P
Z J O R B I N E H N R H S B D X T T A Q A U B N S
G Z D V B L U T B K B Y T T J G P H V U C K L A M
K Z W G O K W W V E I D E O H U F N R M E Q O N I
A S K R Y X U O H H A R R Y F R X H C E S X N A T
H S T E Z S D O N U J T S Y T A E N X E E H D R H
V E M R O Q N D M N M Y L U L V L E Q P F C I A S
W A X M N U M M H M Q D P E P R P Q D K O B E M J
B R B C E E V A D U U W L S S R M F V E A W S A T
Y C R F B E F C T Y G O N U E J E Q Q U G M H R B
X H G N P N A M A R J N O P A G E M V P H R R G C
Z E U T R E M E L O E S G X U Q L N E S Z O E N N
C R M F P M X X G R I R Z X C K L D D S V M U E Q
F S E Y V S O B J L A D E A T X V C K D D K A I S
S W K D P P E S P F L L O S A Y D N O D W F V N N
W G M S U L Q L G E O R G I A S A T E L L I T E S
F P V L R A X N X F T R X I R G I V U Z G C U X K
```

Spice Girls	Georgia Satellites	Smiths	Big Three
Eagles	Blondie	Tremeloes	Shadows
Boyzone	Kinks	Bananarama	Fleetwood Mac
Supremes	Oasis	Beatles	Three Degrees
Queen	Searchers	Small Faces	Pointer Sisters

GLORIA ESTEFAN *(born Gloria María Milagrosa Fajardo García Havana, Cuba on 1 September 1957) is a Cuban and American singer, actress, and businesswoman. A contralto, she started her career as the lead singer in the group Miami Latin Boys, which later became known as Miami Sound Machine. Hailed as the 'Queen of Latin Pop' by the media. In addition to her three Grammy Awards, Estefan has received many other awards. She also has a star on the Hollywood Walk of Fame. Billed simply as Gloria Estefan or with the Miami Sound Machine, she amassed 27 Top 40 singles, including 8 Top 10 successes. Gloria also achieved 8 Top 40 albums, including 2 number ones and three more Top 10 successes.*

1. What was Gloria's first hit, together with the Miami Sound Machine, that reached number 10 in 1988? A) Anything For You B) 1-2-3 C) Rhythm Is Gonna Get You

2. Complete the lyrics from a 1989 No. 7 hit: "Don't wanna be just your friend, You keep telling me that you're not in love, You wanna throw it all away, But I can't .....".

3. On 20th March 1990, what incident happened during the *Cuts Both Ways* album tour   A) Terrorist attack B) Tour bus accident C) Gloria lost her voice

4. In which year did Estefan perform at the Super Bowl half-time show for the second time? A) 1997 B) 1998 C) 1999

5. What is the name of the 1994 Gloria Estefan covers album?
A) Hold Me, Thrill Me, Kiss Me B) Breaking Up Is Hard To Do C) Everlasting Love

6. What was the name of Gloria's comeback song after the 1990 incident?
A) Coming Out of the Dark B) Seal Our Fate C) Live For Loving You

7. What 1992 song did Gloria write for the victims of Hurricane Andrew that got to No. 24 in the charts? A) Get On Your Feet B) I See Your Smile C) Always Tomorrow

8. What song did Gloria sing at the Atlanta Olympic Games closing ceremony in 1996? A) Everlasting Love B) Reach C) Here We Are

9. What was the name of the 1999 film in which Gloria appeared as Isabel Vasquez, a teacher, alongside Meryl Streep?
A) Music of the Heart B) Mr Holland's Opus C) Death Becomes Her

10. Gloria married the Miami Sound Machine's band leader, Emilio Estefan, in 1979. True or False?

ANYTHING FOR YOU
(Writer: Gloria Estefan)

Anything for you
Though you're not here
Since you said we're through
It seems like years
Time keeps dragging on and on
And forever's been and gone
Still I can't figure what went wrong
I'd still do anything for you
I'll play your game
You hurt me through and through
But you can have your way
I can pretend each time I see you
That I don't care and I don't need you
And though you'll never see me cryin'
You know inside I feel like dying
And I'd do anything for you
In spite of it all
I've learned so much from you

You made me strong
But don't you ever think that I don't love you
That for one minute I forgot you
But sometimes things don't work out right
And you just have to say goodbye
I hope you find someone to please you
Someone who'll care and never leave you
But if that someone ever hurts you
You just might need a friend to turn to
And I'd do anything for you
I'll give you up
If that's what I should do
To make you happy
I can pretend each time I see you
That I don't care and I don't need you
And though inside I feel like dying
You know you'll never see me cryin'
Don't you ever think that I don't love you
That for one minute I forgot you
But sometimes things don't work out right
And you just have to say goodbye

GLORIA ESTEFAN ANSWERS: *1. A) Anything For You; 2. "... Stay away from you"; 3. B) Tour bus accident (in which Gloria broke her back); 4. C) 1999; 5. A) Hold me, Thrill me, Kiss me; 6. A) Coming Out of the Dark; 7. C) Always Tomorrow; 8. B) Reach; 9. A) Music of the Heart; 10. False (it was 1976).*

ETERNAL were a British R&B girl group formed in 1992. The line up was Easther Bennett, Vernie Bennett, Kéllé Bryan and Louise Nurding (later Louise Redknapp). The group became an international success, selling around 10 million records worldwide. Louise left the group in 1995 and had 8 Top 20 hits before 2000. Kéllé Bryan left the group under undisclosed circumstances in 1998 and had just one Top 20 hit as a soloist. Overall Eternal had 15 Top 20 singles, with one No.1 and 11 other top 10 hits, and also notched up 4 Top 10 albums.

1. Eternal's first hit was in 1993. What song did they take to number 4 in the charts?
A) Stay   B) So Good   C) Crazy

2. What was the title of Eternal's first album which reached No. 2 and yielded 7 chart singles?   A) Before the Rain   B) Power of a Woman   C) Always and Forever

3. Louise left the group in 1995. What was her first solo Top 10 hit?
A) Naked   B) Light of My Life   C) Undivided Love

4. Eternal won 3 Brit Awards in 1995, 1996 and 1998. True or False?

5. Eternal released an album as a trio after Nurding's departure. It entered the UK charts at No. 6 and produced four hit singles. What was its title?
A) Three of a Kind   B) Power of a Woman   C) Before the Rain

6. In 1995 Eternal performed *I Am Blessed* for whom?
A) The Queen   B) President Clinton   C) Pope John Paul II

7. In 1997, Eternal achieved their only UK number one, *I Wanna Be the Only One* was a duet with which US gospel and R&B singer?
A) BeBe Winans   B) Marvin Sapp   C) Kurt Carr

8. What was Eternal's final single as a three-piece, before Kéllé Bryan left the group?
A) What'cha Gonna Do   B) Angel of Mine   C) Don't You Love Me

9. After Kéllé Bryan controversially left the group, she was diagnosed with lupus in 1998. What was her only single to chart at No. 14 in 1999?
A) Higher Than Heaven   B) I Wanna Know   C) Breakfast in Bed

10. Who joined the group for just a few days in 1999, but then left leaving the Bennett sisters to carry on as a duo?   A) Rochelle Humes   B) Mollie King   C) TJ Arlette

NAME THE ACTS THAT HAD THESE NO. 1 HITS
1 - 1960. Starry Eyed
2 - 1961. Blue Moon
3 - 1962. Lovesick Blues
4 - 1963. Bad to Me
5 - 1964. Have I the Right?
6 - 1965. King of the Road
7 - 1966. These Boots Are made For Walkin'
8 - 1967. Let the Heartaches Begin
9 - 1968. Those Were the Days
10 - In the Year 2525 (Exordium & Terminus)

*ETERNAL ANSWERS: 1. A) Stay; 2. C) Always and Forever; 3. B) Light of My Life; 4. False (Had 6 nominations, no wins); 5. B) Power of a Woman; 6. C) Pope John Paul II; 7. A) BeBe Winans; 8. B) Angel of Mine; 9. A) Higher Than Heaven; 10. C) TJ Arlette. **UK NUMBER ONES ANSWERS:** 1. Michael Holliday; 2. The Marcels; 3. Frank Ifield (also had No. 1 with I Remember You in 1962; 4. Billy J Kramer & The Dakotas; 5. The Honeycombs; 6. Roger Miller; 7. Nancy Sinatra; 8. Long John Baldry; 9. Mary Hopkin; 10. Zager & Evans.*

EURYTHMICS *were a British pop duo, Annie Lennox and Dave Stewart. Both were previously in The Tourists. Eurythmics (a pedagogical exercise system) were formed later 1980 in Wagga Wagga, Australia. They had 22 Top 40 hits in the 20th century, with 9 Top 10 hits including a No. 1. Also 11 Top 30 albums including 3 No. 1's and 5 other Top 10 hits. They split in 1990. Stewart became a successful record producer and Lennox had 8 Top 40 hits, and 1 with Al Green, and 2 No.1 albums. Eurythmics reunited to record their 9th album, Peace, in late 1999.*

1. Whilst Dave and Annie were in The Tourists, with which Dusty Springfield cover did the band have a No. 4 hit in 1979?
A) I Only Want to Be with You   B) Goin' Back   B) Son of a Preacher Man

2. Annie Lennox was born on Christmas Day in 1954. True or False?

3. Eurythmics commercial breakthrough came with their 4th single and 2nd album. What was both entitled?   A) In the Garden   B) Sweet Dreams   C) Who's That Girl

4. In the 1970s, Lennox won a place at the Royal Academy of Music in London, where she studied the flute, piano and which other instrument for three years?
A) Violin   B) Harp   C) Harpsichord

5. With which song did Eurythmics get their only UK number 1 in 1985?   A) There Must Be An Angel (Playing With My Heart)   B) Who's That Girl   C) I Need a Man

6. Which 1983 number 6 contains these lyrics: "Comes in like the flood, And it seems like religion, It's noble and it's brutal, It distorts and deranges."?
A) Love Is A Stranger   B) Here Comes the Rain Again   C) Missionary Man

7. In 1992, under the pseudonym Jean Guiot, what Shakespears Sister number one did Dave Stewart co-write with his wife Marcella Detroit and Siobhan Fahey?
A) You're History B) Stay C) I Don't Care

8. When Eurythmics dissolved in 1990, Dave Stewart moved to France and immediately released an album with his new band. What was the name of the band?
A) Longdancer   B) The Spiritual Cowboys   C) Vegas

9. In 1985 Eurythmics joined which 'Queen of Soul' on a Top 10 hit, *Sisters Are Doin' It For Themselves*?

10. To which composer did Eurythmics like to listen in the title of a 1987 hit composed by Stewart/Lennox?   A) Mozart   B) Beethoven   C) Strauss

1. You've Got Your Troubles	??? ????????	1965
2. ? ??? ?????? ????? ??????	Whistling Jack Smith	1967
3. Gasoline Alley Bred	??? ???????	1970
4. Home Lovin' Man	Andy Williams	????
5. ??? ??? ?? ???? ?? ??	Engelbert Humperdinck	1969
6. Like Sister and Brother	??? ????????	1973
7. ????? ????? ????	Cliff Richard	1971
8. Conversations	????? ?????	1969
9. Something's Gotten Hold of my Heart	Gene Pitney	????
10. I'd Like to Teach the World to Sing	??? ??? ???????	1971

SONGS WRITTEN BY THE TWO ROGERS FROM BRISTOL - GREENAWAY & COOK
(Fill in the gaps)

THE EVERLY BROTHERS were an American country rock duo, known for steel-string acoustic guitar playing and close harmony singing. Consisting of Isaac Donald 'Don' Everly (February 1, 1937 – August 21, 2021) and Phillip 'Phil' Everly (January 19, 1939 – January 3, 2014), the duo combined elements of rock and roll, country and pop, big pioneers of country rock. The duo had 29 Top 40 hits, including 4 No.1's and 9 other Top 10 hits. The Everlys also had 10 Top 40 albums including 5 Top 10 hits. The Brothers were in the first 10 artists inducted into the Rock and Roll Hall of Fame in 1986.

1. The Everlys first hit was a #6 in 1957 in the UK. Name the song from these lyrics; "She was my baby 'til he stepped in, Goodbye to romance that might have been".

2. Who were the American husband-and-wife songwriting team who wrote several of the Everly Brothers early hits? A) Gerry Goffin and Carole King B) Boudleaux and Felice Bryant C) Nickolas Ashford and Valerie Simpson

3. The Everly's first UK No.1 was classed as a 'double-A side'. *All I Have To Do Is Dream* and *Claudette*. Who wrote *Claudette*?
A) Del Shannon B) Don Everly C) Roy Orbison

4. The Everly Brothers were backed by The Crickets and Chet Atkins on a 1959 UK #2 hit written by Don Everly. Can you name the title from these lyrics: "You don't realise what you do to me, And I didn't realise what a kiss could be, Mmm ya got a way about ya, Now I can't live without ya"?

5. After three years on Cadence, the Everlys signed with Warner Bros. Records in 1960, What was their first Warner hit, numbered WB1, which was No. 1 for 7 weeks and was their biggest selling hit?

6. What pseudonym did Don use when he recorded a big-band instrumental version of Edward Elgar's first *Pomp and Circumstance* march in 1961?
A) Adrian Kimberly B) Bernard Shakey C) The Nerk Twins

7. Don and Phil were enlisted in the US Army Forces Command in October 1961. True or False?

8. The Everly's had two consecutive UK number ones in 1961. One was another double A-side, *Walk Right Back / Ebony Eyes*. The second was a reverb-heavy production of which old song, written by Nacio Herb Brown and Arthur Freed in the 1930s? A) Singin' in the Rain B) Temptation C) Alone

9. The Everly Brothers recorded an album in 1984 titled *EB 84*. The album contained a moderate hit in the UK, *On the Wings of a Nightingale*. Who penned this song?
A) Paul McCartney B) John Lennon C) Cook-Greenaway

10. In 1998, Don & Phil recorded the song *Cold* for a Andrew Lloyd Webber / Jim Steinman musical. This was the final original recording the Everly Brothers made as a duo. The recording was used in the stage versions of which musical?
A) The Beautiful Game B) Sunset Boulevard C) Whistle Down the Wind

The Everly Brothers Reunion Concert 1983

THE EVERLY BROTHERS ANSWERS: 1. Bye Bye Love; 2. B) Boudleaux and Felice Bryant; 3. C) Roy Orbison; 4.'Til I Kissed You; 5. Cathy's Clown; 6. A) Adrian Kimberly; 7. False. It was the United States Marine Corps Reserve; 8. B) Temptation; 9. A) Paul McCartney; 10. C) Whistle Down the Wind.

ADAM FAITH (Born Acton as Terence Nelhams Wright, (23 June 1940 – 8 March 2003), was an English singer, actor and financial journalist. A teen idol, he was one of the first UK acts to record original songs regularly. Faith also maintained a successful acting career in both films and on TV. By the 1980s, Faith had become an investor and financial adviser, but in June 2002, he was declared bankrupt, owing a reported £32 million. Adam died of a heart attack at 62 in 2003, having had open heart surgery in 1986. Adam Faith notched up 23 Top 40 hits between 1959 and 1965, his first two singles reached No.1, followed by a further 9 Top 10 hits. Faith also had 4 Top 40 albums, one of them reaching the Top 10.

1. Whilst singing in the Worried Men skiffle group in 1957, Adam Faith was noticed by Jack Good whilst appearing on which TV music show?
A) Drumbeat   B) Six-Five Special   C) Oh Boy!

2. With which Les Vandyke song, produced by John Barry, utilising pizzicato strings, did Adam Faith achieve a number one hit in 1959?
A) High School Confidential   B) Ah, Poor Little Baby   C) What Do You Want?

3.Faith appeared as Dave in a 1960 British teen exploitation film which was also John Barry's first film music commission. What was the film title?
A) Mix Me a Person   B) Beat Girl   C) Never Let Go

4. Adam Faith's first number one was still at number two in the UK Singles Chart when his follow up was released. What was the single that also got to No.1?
A) Poor Me   B) Someone Else's Baby   C) How About That

5. Faith had a double A-side which reached number five in 1960. A revival of an American Civil War song, *When Johnny Comes Marching Home*, was on one side and on the other was a BBC banned track, *Made You*, a song written by Trevor Peacock; but who played the intricate lead guitar on the track?
A) Big Jim Sullivan   B) Vic Flick   C) Joe Brown

6. In which TV series, broadcast on ITV between 1971 and 1972, was Adam the eponymous star who was always involved in some hare-brained scheme to make money, usually on the wrong side of the law?   A) Budgie   B) McCloud   C) Minder

7. Between 1963 and 1965, Faith linked up for six Top 40 hits with which backing band, giving him a harder beat group sound that was popular it the time?
A) John Barry Seven   B) The Strangers   C) The Roulettes

8. In 1980 Adam played Bryan, a tour manager for the rock band Angel in the film *Foxes*. Which future American actress starred as his daughter Jeanie?
A) Helen Hunt   B) Jodie Foster   C) Frances McDormand

9. In 1964 Adam had a No. 12 hit with *Message to Martha*, a song written by Burt Bacharach and Hal David. What bracketed words appear on the label after the title?
A) Kentucky Bluebird   B) Bird of Paradise   C) Mocking Bird

10. A track off the 1993 album *Midnight Postcards*, the old Stealers Wheel hit *Stuck in the Middle*, became a minor hit for Adam as a duet with which rock star?
A) Freddie Mercury   B) Roger Daltrey   C) David Essex

LINK THE NAMES	
1. HEATHER (.....) FACES	
2. BOY (......) MICHAEL	
3. JANET (.......) BROWNE	
4. CLIFF (.......) MARX	
5. TODD (.....) JACKS	

GEORGIE FAME *(born in Leigh, Lancashire as Clive Powell on 26 June 1943) is an English R&B and jazz musician and composer. At just 16 years of age he entered into a management agreement with Larry Parnes. Fame played piano for Billy Fury in his backing band, the Blue Flames. When they were all sacked at the end of a 1961 tour they became Georgie Fame & The Blue Flames. Fame had 13 Top 40 hits; he is the only British music act to have achieved three number one hits with his only Top 10 chart entries. In 1997 Georgie was a founding member of Bill Wyman's band, Rhythm Kings. He also had five Top 30 albums, with two reaching the Top 10. He was one of the first white musicians influenced by ska.*

1. Which impresario said to Clive Powell 'If you don't use my name, Georgie Fame, I won't use you in the show'"? A) Mickey Most B) Joe Meek C) Larry Parnes

2. Georgie Fame's fourth single in 1964, was a Latin soul tune that was written as an instrumental, which knocked The Beatles off of #1. What was the song?
A) Yeh,Yeh B) Do the Dog C) Do-Re-Mi

3. In January 1964, Georgie Fame & The Blue Flames debut album was released. A live *Rhythm and Blues at the Flamingo* failed to chart, but in October 1964 the follow-up album reached number 15. What was the album titled?
A) Fame at Last B) Sweet Things C) Sound Venture

4. What song did American GI's play to Georgie at The Flamingo Club in 1962 that influenced him to go out and buy a Hammond organ the next day?
A) Red River Rock by Johnny & The Hurricanes B) Green Onions by Booker T & The MG's C) Happy Organ by Dave 'Baby' Cortez

5. After three moderate hits in 1965; *In the Meantime*, *Like We Used To Be* and *Something*, Fame got to number one in June 1966 with which self-written song?
A) Sunny B) Sitting in the Park C) Get Away

6. In 1972, Fame married Nicolette (née Harrison). As the former wife of a Marquess, she had the title, Marchioness of .....? A) Longleat B) Londonderry C) Lowestoft

7. Georgie Fame's third #1 in 1967, was written by Mitch Murray and Peter Callander. It was a song inspired by a controversial gangster film of the time. What song opened with these lyrics: "...... ... . were pretty lookin' people, But I can tell you people, they were the devil's children"?

8. In 1971 Fame got together with which former Animals keyboard player to have a No. 11 hit with *Rosetta*? A) Gary Brooker B) Alan Price C) Keith Emerson

9. Attended by Princess Margaret, the Royal World Premiere of what film, with music written by Georgie Fame, took place on the 1st of April 1970?
A) The Railway Children B) Cromwell C) Entertaining Mr. Sloane

10. In 1986, a cover of Richie Cole's *New York Afternoon* and a cover of a Gilberto Gil track, *Samba*, were Georgie Fame tracks produced by which songwriting and record producing trio?

What's in the Parentheses? *Complete the song titles*	1. Caribbean Queen (..........) by Billy Ocean (1984)
	2. I'll Be Loving You (..........) by New Kids on the Block (1990)
	3. Love Changes (..........) by Climie Fisher (1988)
	4. I Can't Go For That (..........) by Hall and Oates (1982)
	5. (..........) Fight For Your Right (..........) by Beastie Boys (1987)

*GEORGIE FAME ANSWERS: 1. C) Larry Parnes; 2. A) Yeh,Yeh; 3. A) Fame at Last; 4. B) Green Onions by Booker T & The MG's; 5. C) Get Away; 6. B) Londonderry (tragically she died on 13 August 1993, after jumping off the Clifton Suspension Bridge) ; 7. Ballad of Bonnie and Clyde; 8. A) Alan Price (as Fame & Price Together); 9. C) Entertaining Mr. Sloane; 10. Stock, Aitken & Waterman. **WHAT'S IN THE PARENTHESES? ANSWERS:** 1. No More Love on the Run; 2. Forever; 3. Everything; 4. No Can Do; 5. You Gotta and To Party!.*

BRYAN FERRY & ROXY MUSIC CBE *(born Washington, Co Durham, 26 September 1945) is an English singer and songwriter.* **ROXY MUSIC** *were an English rock band formed 1970 by Bryan Ferry (lead singer) and Graham Simpson (Bass). Long time members Phil Manzanera (guitar), Andy Mackay (sax & oboe), Paul Thompson (drums) also Brian Eno (synthesizer), Eddie Jobson (synthesizer and violin), John Gustafson (bass). Ferry had 16 Top 40 hits (5 Top 10 hits 1973 - 1993. Also 13 Top 40 albums (1 No. 1 & 7 other Top 10). Roxy Music had 17 Top 40 hits (10 Top 10 including 1 No. 1). 15 albums (including 4 No. 1 & 7 Top 10).*

1. In 1976, which supermodel featured in the video for the number 4 hit, *Let's Stick Together*? A) Twiggy   B) Christie Brinkley   C) Jerry Hall

2. Bryan had a Top 10 hit with an extended play record in 1976. What Everly Brothers written song was the first track?
A) The Price of Love   B) Bye Bye Love   C) Cathy's Clown

3. What 1975 #2 single from Roxy Music includes these lyrics: " Aggravated, spare for days, I troll downtown, the red light place, Jump up, bubble up, what's in store"?

4. Roxy Music had a British number one hit with the song *Jealous Guy* in 1981. To whom was the song a tribute?

5. What is the name of the 1982 song and album from Roxy Music that is also a legendary Celtic island?   A) Avalon   B) Atlantis   C) Camelot

6. Bryan Ferry's last UK Top 10 single was *Slave to Love* in 1985. From which album was the single taken?   A) Siren   B) Boys and Girls   C) Flesh and Blood

7. On what Roxy Music album will you find a cover for the 1965 Wilson Pickett hit song, *In the Midnight Hour*?   A) Stranded   B) Manifesto   C) Flesh and Blood

8. In 1970, Bryan Ferry auditioned to be lead vocalist for what British progressive rock band?   A) Yes   B) Emerson, Lake and Palmer   C) King Crimson

9. In November 1970, Bryan Ferry lost his job teaching ceramics at a girls' school for holding impromptu record-listening sessions. True or False?

10. In 1997, which musician from Duran Duran produced a tribute album Dream Home Heartaches... Remaking/Remodelling Roxy Music?
A) John Taylor   B) Roger Taylor   C) Nick Rhodes

15 names to find
Horizontally, vertically or diagonally

```
S H A N I A T W A I N E C Z L L H I U S
G X D K X F B S T I N A T U R N E R E U
L B I T A J O A N J E T T F X M Z Z D Z
O R O T G T S U D O N N A S U M M E R I
R E N O I E E M Q D K P C V O F Z L T Q
I N N N K D Y B Z Z R E X H L N K I J U
A D E I N X L U U L V H L M S I E T U A
E A W B G H U B Z S R I F E F H V T E T
S L A R R H V L J U H H P Q A F E L U R
T E R A X S A N D I E S H A W T D E Q O
E E W X D U S T Y S P R I N G F I E L D
F G I T S J Q O K B Q W F A S K P V M C
A N C O J Q V N C S V Y U P B J X A K H
N T K N P U T A A T I D C S R X Z J D E
L M I G H E L E N S H A P I R O O Q L R
```

BRYAN FERRY & ROXY MUSIC ANSWERS: *1. C) Jerry Hall; 2. A) The Price of Love; 3. Love is the Drug; 4. John Lennon; 5. A) Avalon; 6. B) Boys and Girls; 7. C) Fleas and Blood; 8. C) King Crimson; 9. True; 10. A) John Taylor.* **WORD SEARCH FEMALE SINGERS ANSWERS:** *Dusty Springfield; Shania Twain; Brenda Lee; Little Eva; Gloria Estefan; Tina Turner; Kate Bush; Joan Jett; Dionne Warwick; Donna Summer; Toni Braxton; Cher; Helen Shapiro;Sandie Shaw; Suzi Quatro.*

FLEETWOOD MAC are a British-American rock band, formed in London in 1967 by guitarist Peter Green, drummer Mick Fleetwood and guitarist Jeremy Spencer, bassist John McVie joined the line-up for their self-titled debut album. Danny Kirwan (guitar) was added in 1968 and keyboardist & vocalist Christine Perfect (McVie), joined in 1970. After several more changes, Americans Lindsey Buckingham (guitar) and Stevie Nicks (vocals) were added in 1974. Fleetwood Mac had 17 Top 40 singles successes including one No. 1 and 8 other Top 10 hits. Also 15 Top 40 albums including 4 No.1's and 5 other Top 10 listings. In 1998 FM were inducted into the Rock and Roll Hall of Fame.

1. The first Fleetwood Mac album was released in 1968 and reached number 4, what was the title of the blues rock album?
A) Mr. Wonderful   B) Fleetwood Mac   C) Then Play On

2. Also in 1968, Fleetwood Mac had their only #1 with a hypnotic instrumental that featured Pete Green and Danny Kirwan on guitars. What was it called?
A) Apache   B) Telstar   C) Albatross

3. Who decided to quit Fleetwood Mac after the completion of their European tour in May 1970?   A) Peter Green   B) John McVie   C) Danny Kirwan

4. In 1969, just as she was leaving, with which band did Christine McVie have Top 20 success with the Etta James classic *I'd Rather Go Blind*?
A) Wishbone Ash   B) Frijid Pink   C) Chicken Shack

5. With whom did Stevie Nicks have a secret affair with while part of Fleetwood Mac?
A) John McVie   B) Mick Fleetwood   C) Neil Finn

6. The instrumental section of which song off of the *Rumours* album has been used as the theme tune for the television coverage of Formula One?
A) The Chain   B) Dreams   C) Go Your Own Way

7. Fleetwood Mac's only U.S. chart topping single was in 1977 with which Stevie Nicks penned song?   A) Don't Stop   B) Dreams   C) Big Love

8. Which member of Fleetwood Mac suffered from Epstein-Barr syndrome?
A) Peter Green   B) Christine McVie   C) Stevie Nicks

9. Which 1987 album produced three UK Top 40 singles, *Big Love*, *Little Lies* and *Everywhere*?   A) Behind the Mask   B) Tango in the Night   C) Mirage

10. John McVie played bass on most of Fleetwood Mac's self-titled debut album, but who was the bassist on *Long Grey Mare*, who went on to become a headmaster?
A) Bob Brunning   B) Roger Glover   C) Chris Squire

THE GREEN MANALISHI
(WITH THE TWO PRONG CROWN)
Now, when the day goes to sleep
And the full moon looks
The night is so black that the darkness cooks
Don't you come creepin' around
Makin' me do things I don't wanna do
Can't believe that you need my love so bad
Come sneakin' around tryin' to drive me mad
Bustin' in on my dreams
Makin' me see things I don't wanna see
'Cause you're da Green Manalishi with the two prong crown
All my tryin' is up, all your bringin' is down
Just takin' my love then slippin' away
Leavin' me here just tryin' to keep from followin' you

Songwriter: Peter Green

FLEETWOOD MAC ANSWERS: *1. B) Fleetwood Mac; 2. C) Albatross; 3. A) Peter Green; 4. C) Chicken Shack; 5. B) Mick Fleetwood; 6. A) The Chain; 7. B) Dreams; 8. C) Stevie Nicks; 9. B) Tango in the Night; 10. A) Bob Brunning.*

WHAT DO YOU KNOW ABOUT FILM SOUNDTRACKS?

1. Which American rock band sung the theme for the 1998 film *Armageddon*?

2. During the opening credits for *Apocalypse Now* in 1979 which Doors song was played?

3. What was the number one hit for Whitney Houston from *The Bodyguard* in 1992?

4. The 1992 Elton John hit song *Can You Feel the Love Tonight* from *The Lion King* featured backing vocals by Gary Barlow, Kiki Dee and Rick Astley. True or False?

5. In the 1994 film *Pulp Fiction*, to which 1964 Chuck Berry hit song do Vincent and Mia dance in the competition at Jack Rabbit Slim's?

6. Lyrics from a film title song sung by Queen. "Just a man, with a man's courage, He knows nothing but a man, But he can never fail, No one but the pure in heart may find the golden grail". A) Name the 1980 film   B) Who wrote the song?

7. Which 1973 supernatural thriller, starring Linda Blair, featured the opening piano solo of Mike Oldfield's *Tubular Bells*?

8. In the 1989 film *Say Anything* what Peter Gabriel song does Lloyd play to Diane, on his boombox, whilst he is standing under her open bedroom window?

9. *Don't You (Forget About Me)* by songwriters Steve Schiff and Keith Forsey plays during the opening credits for the John Hughes 1985 film *The Breakfast Club*. Whose hit version of the song is played during the closing credits?

Q10

10. Which 1978 film soundtrack features *Beauty School Dropout* by Frankie Avalon?

11. Which character plays *Johnny B. Goode* during the Enchantment Under the Sea dance in Back to the Future?

12. *Nothing's Gonna Stop Us Now* by Starship was the theme for which 1987 rom-com?

13. In which of the *Batman* film series was *Kiss From a Rose* by Seal featured?

14. Name the band who had a 1998 hit with the the song *Iris* from City of Angels?

15. Which Kim Wilde 1981 hit, written by her father and brother, was covered by The Muffs and is played during the opening titles of the film *Clueless*?

16. Which singer had major UK hits with the title songs from the 1980 teen musical film *Fame* and the 1983 American romantic drama dance film *Flashdance*?

18. Who composed the score for the 1966 Spaghetti Western, *The Good, the Bad and the Ugly*, and took the main theme to number two in the UK charts?

Q20

19. R. Kelly's *I Believe I Can Fly* was No. 1 in 1997 and won two Grammy Awards. On which live-action/animated sports comedy film soundtrack was the song taken?

20. From which film is this picture taken?

ALL ABOUT FILM SOUNDTRACKS ANSWERS: 1. Aerosmith; 2. The End; 3. I Will Always Love You (written by Dolly Parton); 4. True; 5. You Never Can Tell; 6. A) Flash Gordon; B) Brian May; 7. The Exorcist; 8. In Your Eyes; 9. Simple Minds; 10. Grease; 11. Marty McFly; 12. Mannequin; 13. Batman Forever; 14. Goo Goo Dolls; 15. Kids in America; 16. Irene Cara; 17. Ennio Morricone; 19. Space Jam; 20. Expresso Bongo (1959).

THE FOUR SEASONS *(AKA The Four Seasons feat The Sound of Frankie Valli and Frankie Valli & The Four Seasons), are an American rock band, internationally successful in the 1960s and 1970s. The original line up was Frankie Valli (lead singer), Bob Gaudio (keyboards & tenor), Tommy DeVito (lead guitar and baritone), and Nick Massi (electric bass and bass). Sold an estimated 100m records worldwide. Original line-up inducted into Rock and Roll Hall of Fame in 1990. The band had 16 Top 40 hits, including one No. 1 and 6 others reaching the Top 10. Eight albums got into Top 40, 2 entering the Top 10.*

1. Under what name did the group release their first Billboard Hot 100 charting hit?
A) The Varitones   B) The Valleys   C) The Four Lovers

2. When they failed an audition in New Jersey, they took the name of the venue, the Four Seasons, as their new name. What type of establishment was it?
A) Casino   B) Restaurant   C) Bowling alley

3. After releasing a 1961 single called *Bermuda*, which failed to chart, they followed it with a 1962 song that provided their breakthrough. What was the No. 8 UK hit?
A) Sherry   B) Walk Like A Man   C) Big Girls Don't Cry

4. The 'B' side of *Rag Doll*, a No. 2 hit in 1964, was covered by The Tremeloes in 1967 and reached number one in the UK. What was the song?
A) Someone, Someone   B) Silence is Golden   C) Here Comes My Baby

5. What was the group's fifth and final number one hit as a group in the US in 1976, and their only number one success in the UK?   A) December 1963 (Oh, What a Night)   B) My Eyes Adored You   C) Silver Star

6. Frankie Valli's biggest solo hit in the UK was a No. 3 smash in 1978. It was with the title song of which musical film?   A) Dirty Dancing   B) Grease   C) Footloose

7. During the mid-70s why did Frankie Valli relinquish much of the lead singing parts to other members of the group?   A) Otosclerosis (middle ear condition)   B) He was tired of performing   C) He lost the ability to hit the higher notes

8. Which 1975 Four Seasons No. 6 UK hit contains these lyrics: "When tears are in your eyes and you can't find the way, It's hard to make believe you're happy when you're grey"?

9. Drummer Gerry Polci sang lead on the 1976 No. 3 hit *Silver Star*. True or False?

10. The final hit album of the 20th century for the group was a compilation, *The Very Best of Frankie Valli and The Four Seasons*. It reached No. 7 in the UK in 1992. On what label was the album released?   A) Polygram   B) Motown   C) K-Tel

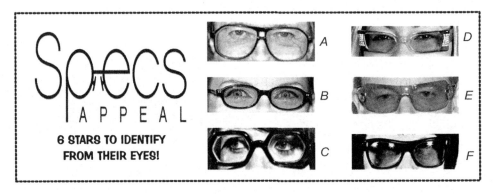

SpeCS APPEAL
6 STARS TO IDENTIFY FROM THEIR EYES!

A

B

C

D

E

F

THE FOUR SEASONS ANSWERS: *1. C) The Four Lovers; 2. C) Bowling alley; 3. A) Sherry; 4. B) Silence is Golden; 5. A) December 1963 (Oh, What a Night); 6. B) Grease; 7. A) Otosclerosis (middle ear condition); 8. Who Loves You; 9. True; 10. A) Polygram.*
SPECS APPEAL ANSWERS: *A) Hank Marvin; B) Annie Lennox; C) Sandie Shaw; D) Anastacia; E) Bono; F) Roy Orbison.*

THE FOUR TOPS *are an American vocal quartet from Detroit who helped define the Motown sound of the 60s. Their repertoire included soul, R&B, disco, adult contemporary, doo-wop, jazz, and show tunes. Lead singer Levi Stubbs, Abdul 'Duke' Fakir, Renaldo 'Obie' Benson and Lawrence Payton remained together for over four decades, from 1953 until 1997 without a personnel change. The group was inducted into the Rock and Roll Hall of Fame in 1990 and into the Vocal Group Hall of Fame in 1999. The Four Tops notched up 30 Top 40 hit singles, including a No. 1 and 10 other Top 10 hits. Also 11 Top 40 albums, including a No. 1 and 4 other Top 10 hits.*

1. All four members of the Four Tops began their careers together while they were high-school students in Detroit. Under what name did they originally perform?
A) Four Aims   B) Ames Brothers   C) Levis Boys

2. The first Four Tops hit was *I Can't help Myself* in 1965. The song was re-issued in 1970 and was a bigger success. What words appear in brackets after the title?

3. The Four Tops only No. 1 UK hit was in 1966. Recorded in just two takes, and initially assumed to be just another album track, what was the song?
A) Standing In The Shadows Of Love   B) Bernadette   C) Reach Out I'll Be There

4. A Tim Hardin folk song by Johnny Cash and June Carter went to #2 on the country chart in 1970. Bobby Darin also had a No.9 hit with the song in 1966 but the Four Tops went two places higher with their version in 1968. What was the song?
A) Reason to Believe   B) If I Were a Carpenter   C) Misty Roses

5. *Seven Rooms Of .....* What is the missing word in the title of this No. 12 hit record by The Four Tops in 1967?   A) Gloom   B) Doom   C) Fun

6. What song links Tommy Edwards (#1-1958), Cliff Richard (#2-1963) and The Four Tops (#5-1970)?

7. *River Deep Mountain High* in 1971 and *You Gotta Have Love In Your Heart* were two Four Tops hits recorded with which female group?
A) Shirelles   B) Supremes   C) Crystals

8. *A Simple Game* was a 1971 Top 5 single for the Four Tops. Mike Pinder wrote the song, which was originally a 'B' side for a single by which band?   A) Searchers   B) Moody Blues   C) Fortunes

9. Which 1981 No. 3 hit from The Four Tops includes these lyrics: "Oh what joy she would bring, Now I've lost everything, She's gone, gone, gone gone, gone!"?
A) Don't Walk Away   B) Sweet Understanding Love   C) When She Was My Girl

10. A 1988 Four Tops hit, *Loco In Acapulco*, featured in the film *Buster*. The song was written by Lamont Dozier and which actor/singer?
A) David Essex   B) Phil Collins   C) Roger Daltrey

On June 20, 1997, 59-year-old Lawrence Payton died as a result of liver cancer, after singing for 44 years with the Four Tops who, unlike many other Motown groups, never had a single lineup change until then.

CONNIE FRANCIS (Born Concetta Rosa Maria Franconero on December 12, 1937 in the Ironbound neighbourhood of Newark, New Jersey). Connie Francis is an American former pop singer, actress, and top-charting female vocalist of the late 1950s and early 1960s. Although her chart success waned in the second half of the 1960s, Francis remained a top concert draw. In the 1960s she appeared in four films. Between 1958 and 1965, Francis had 22 Top 40 hits, including 2 No.1 hits and 8 other Top 10 recordings. In the UK Connie also had four Top 20 album hits, including a number one compilation of her hits.

1. Connie Francis first appeared on TV on Arthur Godfrey's Talent Scouts in 1952 singing *Daddy's Little Girl*. On what instrument did she accompany herself?
A) Piano   B) Guitar   C) Accordion

2. After five flops in the UK, Connie's 6th song hit the jackpot and reached number one in 1957. What question did the song title ask?
A) Who's Sorry Now?   B) What Now My Love?   C) Will You Love Me Tomorrow?

3. After *I'm Sorry I Made You Cry* reached No.11, Francis had another No. 1 with a double 'A' side. *Carolina Moon* was one side, but which singer co-wrote *Stupid Cupid*, on the other side, with Howard Greenfield?
A) Bobby Darin   B) Neil Sedaka   C) Paul Anka

4. Connie had another smash hit in 1959. The No. 3 hit included these lyrics: "When you left me all alone, at the record hop, Told me you were going out, for a soda pop, You were gone for quite a while, half an hour or more, You came back and man oh man, this is what I saw". Name the song.

5. Another 1959 hit, *My Happiness*, credited the orchestra on the label. The bandleader is best known for *The Stripper*. Who is he?
A) Henry Mancini   B) Nelson Riddle   C) David Rose

6. In the 1958 film *The Sheriff of Fractured Jaw*, starring Kenneth More, Connie Francis's singing voice was used for the character Kate. Which actress played Kate?
A) Jayne Mansfield   B) Marilyn Monroe   C) Brigitte Bardot

7. On 3 July 1963 Connie Francis played a Royal Command Performance for Queen Elizabeth II. In which theatre was the show stage?
A) Alhambra Theatre, Glasgow   B) The London Palladium   C) The Liverpool Empire

8. In 1968 Connie Francis recorded a TV political broadcast and recorded a campaign song in support of which successful presidential candidate?
A) Lyndon B Johnson   B) Richard Nixon   C) Gerald Ford

9. On 8 November 1974, what horrendous incident happened to Connie Francis in the Jericho Turnpike Howard Johnson's Lodge, New York?

10. In 1981, which further tragedy struck Francis concerning her brother George Franconero, Jr., with whom she was very close?   A) Murdered by Mafia hit-men B) Killed in a hotel fire   C) Killed in an internal flight to Washington

ASKING THE QUESTIONS!

COMPLETE THESE SONG TITLES THAT ASKED QUESTIONS?
1. Who?   By Ten Pole Tudor (1979)
2. Why?   By Travis (1999)
3. How?   By LeAnn Rimes (1998)
4. What?   By The New Seekers (1970)
5. Where?   By Betty Boo (1990)

CONNIE FRANCIS ANSWERS: 1. C) Accordion; 2. A) Who's Sorry Now?; 3. B) Neil Sedaka; 4. Lipstick On Your Collar; 5. C) David Rose; 6. A) Jayne Mansfield; 7. A) Alhambra Theatre, Glasgow; 8. B) Richard Nixon; 9. She was raped (her rapist was never found, Francis sued the hotel for failing to provide adequate security and reportedly won a $2.5 million judgement); 10.A) Murdered by Mafia hit-men. **ASKING THE QUESTIONS! ANSWERS:** 1. Who Shot Bambi?; 2. Why Does It Always Rain On Me?; 3. How Do I Live?; 4. What Have They Done To My Song Ma?; 5. Where Are You Baby?.

ARETHA FRANKLIN *(March 25, 1942 – August 16, 2018) was an American singer, songwriter and pianist. Referred to as the 'Queen of Soul'. Franklin found acclaim and commercial success once she signed with Atlantic Records in 1966. Aretha received numerous honours throughout her career. In 1987, she became the first female artist to be inducted into the Rock and Roll Hall of Fame. She also was inducted into the UK Music Hall of Fame in 2005. In 2010, Rolling Stone ranked Franklin number one on its list of the '100 Greatest Singers of All Time'. Aretha had 16 Top 40 singles hits, including a number one and three other Top 10 hits. She also had 6 Top 40 albums, including one Top 10 success.*

1. Aretha won her first Grammy Awards for 'Best Rhythm and Blues Recording' and 'Best Female R&B Vocal Performance' in 1968 for which song?
A) Respect   B) (You Make Me Feel Like) A Natural Woman   C) Chain of Fools

2. Who wrote Aretha Franklin's No. 4 hit *I Say a Little Prayer*?   A) Jerry Leiber and Mike Stoller   B) Carole King and Gerry Goffin   C) Burt Bacharach and Hal David

3. At whose funeral in 1968 did Aretha Franklin sing *Precious Lord, Take My Hand*?
A) Sam Cooke   B) Dr. Martin Luther King   C) Robert Kennedy

4. With whom did Aretha duet on the 1987 No. 1 hit, I *Knew You Were Waiting (For Me)*?   A) Marvin Gaye   B) George Michael   C) Elton John

5. Although not a great seller in the UK, Aretha gained her very first 'platinum-certified' album with which of the following titles?
A) Who's Zoomin' Who   B) The First Lady of Soul   C) Through the Storm

6. Which Rolling Stones hit did Aretha cover and take into the lower regions of the charts in 1968?   A) Little Red Rooster   B) Get Off My Cloud   C) Satisfaction7.

7. Which singer was unaccredited on the label, but had a hit singing *It Isn't It Wasn't It Ain't Never Gonna Be*, a duet with Aretha in 1989?
A) Diana Ross   B) Whitney Houston   C) Tina Turner

8. Aretha performed the song *Think* for what film soundtrack?
A) The Shining   B) The Elephant Man   C) The Blues Brothers

9. Who wrote and made the original recording of Aretha Franklin's hit *Respect*?
A) Otis Redding   B) Marvin Gaye   C) Stevie Wonder

10. Who was the leader of Aretha Franklin's backing band, The Kingpins?
A) Booker T. Jones   B) Lonnie Mack   C) King Curtis

FILL IN THE MISSING WORD IN THE LYRICS FROM 1950s HITS

1. COOL WATER - No. 2 for Frankie Laine in 1955. "The nights are cool and I'm a ....".

2. ISLAND IN THE SUN - No. 3 for Harry Belafonte in 1957. "Oh, island in the sun, Willed to me by my father's ....".

3. GOOD GOLLY MISS MOLLY - No. 8 for Little Richard in 1958. "When you're rockin' and a rollin' Can't hear your ..... call".

4. WHOLE LOTTA WOMEN - No. 1 for Marvin Rainwater in 1958. "It take a whole lotta lovin', Just to keep my baby .....".

5. THE MAN FROM LARAMIE - No. 1 for Jimmy Young in 1955. "The man from Laramie, He was a man with a .... turn of mind".

ARETHA FRANKLIN ANSWERS: *1. A) Respect; 2. C) Burt Bacharach and Hal David; 3. B) Dr. Martin Luther King; 4. B) George Michael; 5. A) Who's Zoomin' Who; 6. C) Satisfaction; 7. B) Whitney Houston; 8. C) The Blues Brothers; 9. A) Otis Redding; 10. C) King Curtis.*
1950s SONG LYRICS ANSWERS: *1. Fool; 2. Hand; 3. Momma; 4. Happy; 5. Peaceful.*

BILLY FURY (Born Ronald Wycherley, 17 April 1940 – 28 January 1983), was an English singer, musician, songwriter, and actor. In his early days Fury simultaneously worked full-time on a tugboat and later as a docker. His sexual and provocative stage performances received censure, and he had to tone them down. Fury later concentrated more on mainstream ballads. He had 26 Top 40 hits and spent 332 weeks on the UK chart, but amazingly, he never had a No.1 single or album. Had 11 Top 10 hits. He also had four Top 20 albums, with 2 reaching the Top 10. After many years of heart problems brought on by contracting rheumatic fever in his teens, Fury collapsed from a heart attack at his home in London in 1983, aged 42.

1. Billy Fury's first hit in 1959 contained these lyrics: "I love you baby, I really care, I need your lovin', so hear my prayer." What was the song?
A) Maybe Tomorrow   B) Colette   C) Margot

2. All of the songs on the 1960 album *The Sound of Fury* were written by Billy Fury himself. True or False?

3. Billy's big 1961 No. 3 hit *Halfway To Paradise* was a cover version. Which American singer made the original?
A) Bobby Vinton   B) Brian Hyland   C) Tony Orlando

4. Billy Fury's highest single chart placing was achieved in 1961. With what song did he have a N0. 2 hit?   A) Jealousy   B) Halfway to Paradise   C) A Thousand Stars

5. Billy Fury had a top ten hit in 1964 with a cover of a 1958 UK and US number one hit by Conway Twitty. What was it called?
A) Mona Lisa   B) It's Only Make Believe   C) C'est Si Bon

6. All of Billy Fury's hits from 1959 to 1966 were on one record label. Which record label was it?   A) Decca   B) Columbia   C) Parlophone

7. In 1973 Billy came out of retirement to play which character in the film *That'll Be The Day*?   A) Billy Universe   B) Stormy Tempest   C) Jim Maclaine

8. Where is Billy Fury buried?   A) London   B) Liverpool   C) Brecon Beacons

9. Where in Liverpool is the statue* of Billy Fury, sculpted by Tom Murphy?   A) Outside the Cavern Club   B) Albert Dock   C) Dingle

10. In 1999 advertising agency Saatchi & Saatchi used Billy Fury's 1960 hit, *Wondrous Place*, as the soundtrack for a TV advertisement. What product was being advertised?   A) Sugar Puffs   B) Calvin Klein Obsession   C) Toyota Yaris car

*This statue, made by Liverpool sculptor Tom Murphy in 2003, was commissioned by 'The Sound of Fury' fan club following six years of fundraising and donations from fans. It was very kindly donated to National Museums Liverpool by 'The Sound of Fury' as a lasting tribute to Billy, one of Liverpool's greatest stars. It was originally displayed in the courtyard of the former Museum of Liverpool Life, before moving to its current location in March 2007.

ALBUM COVERS OF THE EIGHTIES

BILLY FURY ANSWERS: 1. A) Maybe Tomorrow; 2. True (6 using pseudonym, Wilber Wilberforce); 3. C) Tony Orlando; 4. A) Jealousy; 5. B) It's Only Make Believe; 6. A) Decca; 7. B) Stormy Tempest; 8. A) London (Mill Hill Cemetery, Paddington); 9. B) Albert Dock; 10. Toyota Yaris car. **80s ALBUM COVERS ANSWERS:** 1) Welcome To the Pleasuredome - Frankie Goes To Hollywood; 2. Respectable - Mel & Kim; 3. Road To Nowhere - Talking Heads; 4. Don't Go - Yazoo.

Can you name the 20 pictured acts who all recorded UK hit singles between 1955 and 1999? A major hit song associated with the act is detailed as a clue.

HIT makers

1. I Want to Know What Love Is (1984)

2. Like I Do (1962)

3. What Do You Want To Make Those Eyes At Me For? (1959)

4. Dreams (1993)

5. 99 Red Balloons (1984)

6. Reasons To Be Cheerful (1979)

7. I Can Help (1974)

8. Buona Sera (1960)

9. Waterloo Sunset (1997)

10. It's Gonna Be a Cold Cold Christmas (1975)

11. Ob-La-Di, Ob-La-Da (1968)

12. Gypsy Woman (La Da Dee (1991)

13. I'm Just a Baby (1962)

14. Only 16 (1959)

15. My Heart (1960)

16. What's Up (1993)

17. All I Wanna Do (1975)

18. Get Out of Your Lazy Bed (1984)

19. Rock Your Baby (1974)

20. All Around My Hat (1975)

HIT MAKERS ANSWERS: 1. Foreigner; 2. Maureen Evans; 3. Emile Ford & The Checkmates; 4. Gabrielle; 5. Nena; 6. Ian Dury & The Blockheads; 7. Billy Swan; 8. Mr. Acker Bilk & His Paramount Jazz Band; 9. Cathy Dennis; 10. Dana; 11. Marmalade; 12. Crystal Waters; 13. Louise Cordet; 14. Craig Douglas; 15. Gene Vincent; 16. 4 Non Blondes; 17. Danii Minogue; 18. Matt Bianco; 19. George McCrae; 20. Steeleye Span.

MARVIN GAYE (born Marvin Pentz Gay Jr. in Washington D.C. on April 2, 1939 – died in Los Angeles, California on April 1, 1984, aged 44). A US singer and songwriter. Helped shape Motown sound in the 60s, as an in-house session player, later as a hit-making solo artist. He was shot and killed by his father, Marvin Gay Sr., at their house after an argument. Marvin Gaye had 16 Top 40 hits, half as duets with other acts, his hits include a #1 and 7 other Top 10 hits. He also had 8 Top 40 albums, with 3 Top 10 successes. Posthumous awards and honours include the Grammy Lifetime Achievement Award. Inducted into the Rhythm and Blues Music Hall of Fame, Songwriters Hall of Fame, and Rock & Roll Hall of Fame.

1. What was Gaye's father's profession? A) Salesman B) Janitor C) Preacher

2. Evolving from a group called The Rainbows, Gaye and his good friend Reese Palmer formed a vocal quartet in 1957. What was the name of the band who backed artistes like Bo Diddley? A) The Marquees B) The Mounties C) The Musicians

3. Marvin Gaye's first UK chart success came in 1967, as part of a duet. *It Takes Two* was the song, who was the female singer?
A) Kim Weston B) Tammi Terrell C) Diana Ross

4. Whist appearing on stage, Marvin Gaye played the piano as his primary instrument, what other instrument did he occasionally play when performing?
A) Guitar B) Drums C) Bass

5. Gaye had his biggest hit in the UK with *I Heard It Through the Grapevine* in 1969. Who had also had a major hit with the song in 1967?
A) Creedence Clearwater Revival B) Barrett Strong C) Gladys Knight & The Pips

6. Which vegetable brought Top 10 chart success to Marvin Gaye, in a fourth duet with Tammi Terrell in 1969? A) Potato B) Onion C) Tomato

7. Gaye married record executive Berry Gordy's sister in June 1963. The couple separated in 1973 and divorced in 1977. What was her name?
A) Anna B) Hazel C) Sherry

8. In October 1967, what happened during a Marvin Gaye and Tammi Terrell stage performance in Farmville, Virginia? A) The two had an argument B) Tammi collapsed in Marvin's arms C) Gaye walked off stage

9. In 1970 Marvin Gaye had a Top 10 hit, *Abraham Martin And John*, about a quartet of famous Americans who had been assassinated. Who were they?

10. These lyrics are from a 1982 No. 4 Marvin Gaye hit: "Whenever blue teardrops are fallin', And my emotional stability is leaving me, There is something I can do I can get on the telephone and call you up, baby". What was the song title?
A) Sexual Healing B) Got To Give It Up C) My Love Is Waiting

Can you name these inductees into the Ohio Rock & Roll Hall of Fame?

The year's shown are
the dates inducted.   A - 1994   B - 1987   C - 1987   D - 1998   E - 2010   F- 2001

MARVIN GAYE ANSWERS: 1. C) Preacher; 2. A) Marquees; 3. A) Kim Weston; 4. B) Drums; 5. C) Gladys Knight & The Pips; 6. B) Onion (The Onion Song); 7. A) Anna; 8. B) Tammi collapsed in Marvin's arms (later diagnosed with a malignant brain tumour and died on 16th March 1970); 9. Abraham Lincoln, John F. Kennedy, Martin Luther-King and Robert Kennedy; 10. A) Sexual Healing.
OHIO ROCK AND ROLL HALL OF FAME ANSWERS: A) Johnny Otis; B) Carl Perkins; C) Jackie Wilson; D) Lloyd Price; E) The Big Bopper; F) Ritchie Valens.

GENESIS *are an English rock band formed at Charterhouse School, Godalming, Surrey. The band's most commercially successful line-up consists of keyboardist Tony Banks, bassist/guitarist Mike Rutherford and drummer/singer Phil Collins. The 1970s line-up featuring singer Peter Gabriel and guitarist Steve Hackett were among the pioneers of progressive rock. Genesis had 21 Top 40 singles, including 8 Top 10 hits. The band notched up an incredible 20 Top 40 albums between 1972 and 1999, with 6 No.1's and 11 more reaching the Top 10.*

1. When did Genesis perform their first ever gig?   A) 1969 B) 1970 C) 1971

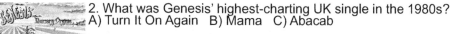

2. What was Genesis' highest-charting UK single in the 1980s?
A) Turn It On Again   B) Mama   C) Abacab

3. Who was Genesis' original drummer?
A) Phil Collins   B) Chris Stewart   C) John Silver

4. According to their first hit in 1974, Genesis knew what they liked, but where did they like it?   A) In Your Pantry   B) In Your Wardrobe   C) In Your Attic

5. A game of what sport is being played by women on the cover picture for the 1974 No. 39 album, *Nursery Cryme*?   A) Cricket   B) Tennis   C) Croquet

6. In 1975, having failed to find a suitable replacement for Peter Gabriel, Phil Collins eventually sung which song from the album *A Trick of the Tail* and persuaded the band they should look no further?   A) Squonk   B) Entangled   C) Ripples…

7. What was the name of the 1977 EP release that collected outtakes from the *Wind & Wuthering* sessions and reached No.14 in the singles chart?
A) Coming Home to Roost   B) Spot the Pigeon   C) Spot the Dog

8. How many consecutive UK No.1 studio albums did Genesis achieve from 1980 to 1991?   A) 6   B) 5   C) 4

9. Complete the following lyric from *I Can't Dance*, a UK Top 10 hit in 1991: "Blue jeans sitting on the beach / Her dog's talking to me…"   A) "But she can't be teached" B) "But she's such a peach"   C) "But she's out of reach"

10. In 1992 a live version of a 1986 Genesis single reached the Top 10. What was the song?   A) In Too Deep   B) Land of Confusion   C) Invisible Touch

GREEN FOR GO

Song Titles including GREEN

1. Jim Lowe, Frankie Vaughan, Glen Mason and Shakin' Stevens all had hits with which song?

2. Name the two singers to have hits with The Green, Green Grass of Home.

3. Who had a No. 7 hit with Green Tambourine in 1968?

4. Which Peter Green song about the evils of money was a hit for Fleetwood Mac in 1970?

5. Who had an instrumental hit with Green Onions in 1979?

GENESIS ANSWERS: *1. A) 1969; 2. B) Mama (Reached No. 4 in 1983); 3. Chris Stewart; 4. B) In Your Wardrobe; 5. C) Croquet; 6. A) Squonk; 7. B) Spot the Pigeon; 8. B) 5 - Duke (1980); Abacab (1981); Genesis (1983); Invisible Touch (1986); We Can't Dance (1991); 9. "But she's out of reach"; 10. C) Invisible Touch.* **GREEN FOR GO ANSWERS:** *1. The Green Door; 2. Engelbert Humperdinck and Elvis Presley; 3. Lemon Pipers; 4. The Green Manalishi (With the Two Pronged Crown); 5. Booker T & The MG's.*

GERRY AND THE PACEMAKERS were a leading British beat group in the 1960s Merseybeat scene. Like The Beatles they were managed by Brian Epstein, and recorded by George Martin. Their early successes helped to popularise the Liverpool sound and launch the wider British beat boom of the mid-60s. Gerry Marsden (vocals/guitar) formed the group in 1956 with his brother Fred (drums), Les Chadwick (bass), and Arthur McMahon (piano - replaced by Les Maguire around 1961). The band had 9 Top 40 hits including 3 No. 1's and 3 other Top 10 hits; also 2 Top 20 albums, one reaching No. 2.

1. Gerry & the Pacemakers first performed under what name before being forced to change it because of objections from a chocolate manufacturer?
A) Gerry & the Kit Kats   B) Gerry & the Crunchies   C) Gerry & the Mars Bars

2. Gerry & the Pacemakers debut single was a Mitch Murray song rejected by Adam Faith and Brian Poole, and reluctantly then recorded by the Beatles. What was the song title?   A) I Like It   B) How Do You Do It?   C) It's Alright

3. Gerry & the Pacemakers became the first act ever to reach number one in the UK Singles Chart with their first three single releases. Which Liverpool group became the second to achieve this feat?   A) Echo & the Bunnymen   B) Frankie Goes to Hollywood
C) Billy J. Kramer with the Dakotas

4. Another Mitch Murray song became the band's second number one. What was the song that included these lyrics: "Do that again, You're driving me insane, Kiss me once more, That's another thing I like you for"?

5. *Hello Little Girl* was to have been the band's third single in 1963, but instead it was released by another Liverpool band, The Fourmost. Who wrote the song?
A) John Lennon   B) Mitch Murray   C) Gerry Marsden

6. Gerry and Co achieved a hat-trick of number ones with *You'll Never Walk Alone*, a song which famously became the signature tune for Liverpool FC. In which musical was the song originally sung?   A) Carousel   B) South Pacific   C) Oklahoma!

7. Which Gerry & the Pacemakers 1964 No 8 hit single was also the title track of a 1965 film starring the band and also Cilla Black, Deryck Guyler and The Fourmost?
A) I'm the One   B) Don't Let the Sun Catch You Crying   C) Ferry Cross the Mersey

8. In 1965 Gerry & the Pacemakers revived a song that was a hit for both Tony Martin and Ronnie Carroll in 1965. What was the song they took to No. 29?
A) Walk Hand in Hand   B) Footsteps   C) Roses Are Red

9. In 1966 Gerry & the Pacemakers recorded a Simon & Garfunkel song, but it didn't make the charts. What was the song?   A) The Big Bright Green Pleasure Machine
B) The Sound of Silence   C) Mrs. Robinson

10. Gerry's song *Ferry Cross the Mersey* was revived as a charity single in 1989. Marsden and Liverpool stars, Paul McCartney, Ringo Starr and Holly Johnson took the song to #1. Proceeds donated to those affected by which disaster?   A) Herald of Free Enterprise ferry   B) Hillsborough stadium   C) The Dunblane Massacre

GERRY & THE PACEMAKERS ANSWERS: 1. C) Gerry & the Mars Bars; 2. B) How Do You Do It; 3. B) Frankie Goes to Hollywood (Relax, Two Tribes, The Power of Love); 4. I Like It; 5. A) John Lennon; 6. A) Carousel; 7. C) Ferry Cross the Mersey; 8. A) Walk Hand in Hand; 9.A) The Big Bright Green Pleasure Machine; 10. B) Hillsborough stadium.

GUNS N' ROSES *are an American hard rock band from Los Angeles, formed 1985. Classic line up: Axl Rose (vocals), Slash (lead guitar), Izzy Stradlin (rhythm guitar), Duff McKagan (bass), Steven Adler (drums). Early hedonism and rebelliousness compared to the young Rolling Stones. The classic lineup, plus Dizzy Reed and Matt Sorum, inducted into Rock and Roll Hall of Fame in 2012. The band had 16 Top 40 singles, (12 Top 10). Also 5 Top 30 albums, including a No. 1 and 2 other Top 10 hits.*

1. Slash grew up in which English city until he was 11 years old?
A) Leicester   B) Stoke-on-Trent   C) Birmingham

2. Guns N' Roses first hit, a No. 24 success in 1988, was remixed and reissued a year later and reached No. 6. What was the song?
A) Welcome to the Jungle   B) Paradise City   C) Sweet Child O' Mine

3. Axl Rose was once a choir boy and Sunday School teacher? True or False?

4. Probably referring to his alcohol problems, who said, "A lot of money would be like instant suicide. I'm scared of the responsibility of having a lot of money."
A) Duff McKagan   B) Izzy Stradlin   C) Steven Adler

5. Which Paul McCartney written James Bond theme, a hit for Wings in 1973, was covered by Guns n' Roses and taken to #5 in the charts in 1991?
A) For Your Eyes Only   B) Live and Let Die   C) Nobody Does It Better

6. *Monsters of Rock* was an annual hard rock and heavy metal music festival held in Castle Donington. In 1988 during a Guns N' Roses set, despite several pleas for the crowd to calm down, how many fans were crushed to death?   A) 3   B) 2   C) 4

7. In 1992, the band performed three songs at the Freddie Mercury Tribute Concert. Who performed *Tie Your Mother Down* with the remaining members of Queen and Def Leppard vocalist Joe Elliott?   A) Axl Rose   B) Slash   C) Duff McKagan

8. In 1992, which Bob Dylan song became the highest placed single in the Guns N' Roses singles discography, reaching No. 2?
A) Mr. Tambourine Man   B) Just Like a Woman   C) Knockin' On Heaven's Door

9. Complete this line from *Sweet Child O' Mine*'s opening lyrics: "She got a smile that it seems to me, reminds me of ..."
A) Childhood memories   B) A calm sea breeze   C) A piece of Cheddar cheese

10. The inclusion of a hidden track in the 1993 *Spaghetti Incident* album caused great controversy, it was a cover of *Look at Your Game, Girl*, which had originally been sung by which notorious criminal?
A) Jeffrey Dahmer   B) Albert DeSalvo   C) Charles Manson

A MORPHED DUO

Name the two singers whose faces have been merged.

BILL HALEY & HIS COMETS *were an American rock and roll band, founded in 1952 and continuing until Haley's death in 1981. Bandleader Bill was a country music performer but changed musical direction to a new sound which became rock and roll. They were at the forefront of R 'n' R in the genre's early years, but more risqué acts such as Elvis Presley led the more clean-cut Haley and Co to decline in popularity by 1957. The band had 14 Top 40 hits, many of those were reissued successfully, including one famous No. 1 and 8 other Top 10 hits. Also 4 Top 40 albums including a No. 1 and 2 Top 10 hits.*

1. The group that later became the Bill Haley & His Comets initially performed between 1949 and 1952 under what name? A) Bill Haley and the Saddlemen B) Bill Haley and the Bobby Dazzlers   C) Bill Haley and the Razzle Dazzlers

2. Bill Haley & His Comets first hit single reached No. 4 in the UK in 1954. What was the song? A) Rock Around the Clock   B) Shake Rattle and Roll   C) Mambo Rock

3. The biggest-selling single of the 1950s was Rock Around the Clock which became Haley's first No. 1 in October 1955. When it was originally released nine months earlier at what chart position did it peak? A) 6   B) 17   C) 25

4. In 1954, Haley and His Comets left the Essex label and joined which New York-based label? A) Decca Records B) RCA C) Columbia

5. Ralph Jones became the first Comets drummer to be featured in a recording session as previous drummers had been replaced by session musicians. On what recording did Jones perform in 1956?
A) Rock-a-Beatin' Boogie B) Rockin' Through the Rye C) See You Later Alligator

6. The huge success of *Rock Around the Cloc*k is attributed to its use in the soundtrack of what 1955 social drama film?
A) Blackboard Jungle B) Rock Around the Clock C) Rebel Without a Cause

7. Haley's mother, Maude Green (1895–1955), was originally from Olveston in Gloucestershire. True or False?

8. What was Bill Haley & the Comets last UK Top 10 hit in 1957?
A) Rock the Joint B) Rip It Up C) Don't Knock the Rock

9. Rock Around the Clock has been covered by many acts. A most unusual version of the song appeared on the album *Great Rock & Roll Swindle*, recorded by which punk rock band? A) The Ramones B) Sex Pistols C) The Clash

10. Bill Haley died at his home in Harlingen, Texas, on February 9, 1981, at the age of 55. Texas. How many people attended his funeral? A) 2,000 B) 350 C) 75

NAME THE SONGS THAT WERE BIG HITS TWICE!

1. ELVIS PRESLEY (1964) & ZZ TOP (1992)

2. BONNIE TYLER (1983) & NICKI FRENCH (1995)

3. ROGER MILLER (1965) & THE PROCLAIMERS (1990)

4. KAYE SISTERS (1960) & MARIE OSMOND (1973)

5. THE MINDBENDERS (1966) & PHIL COLLINS (1988)

6. TOMMY ROE (1969) & VIC REEVES & WONDER STUFF (1991)

BILL HALEY & HIS COMETS ANSWERS: *1. A) Bill Haley and the Saddlemen; 2. B) Shake Rattle and Roll; 3. B) 17; 4. A) Decca Records; 5. C) See You Later Alligator; 6. A) Blackboard Jungle; 7. False (she was from Ulverston, Lancashire); 8. C) Don't Knock the Rock; 9. B) Sex Pistols; 10. C) 75.* **DOUBLE HITS ANSWERS:** *1. Viva Las Vegas; 2. Total Eclipse of the Heart; 3. King of the Road; 4. Paper Roses; 5. Groovy Kind of Love; 6. Dizzy.*

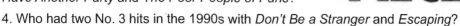

BITS & PIECES

1. David Harman, Trevor Davies, John Dymond, Michael Wilson and Ian Amey were better known as who?

2. *Eye Level* was a No. 1 for the Simon Park Orchestra in 1973. For what TV series was it the theme music?

3. Which pianist had No.1 hits in 1954 and 1956 with *Let's Have Another Party* and *The Poor People of Paris*?

4. Who had two No. 3 hits in the 1990s with *Don't Be a Stranger* and *Escaping*?

5. In what year did The Beatles last top the UK singles chart?

6. Which girl gave Kenny Rogers a No.1 hit in 1977?

7. Cliff Richard and The Shadows entered the Eurovision Song Contest in 1968 and 1975 respectively. Whose song had the highest placing?

8. Which member of the Swedish hit-making Abba machine was actually Norwegian?

9. David Cassidy had 10 Top 20 hits from 1972 and 1985. How many were No.1's?

10. "I see that worried look upon your face", is the opening line of which Roger Cook & Roger Greenaway song that reached number two for The Fortunes in 1965?

11. (*Re-Rewind) The Crowd Say Bo Selecta* was a hit at the very end of the 20th century. With which 'Oliver Twist' character did Craig David perform the duet?

12. What city links The Wurzels, Fred Wedlock, Massive Attack and Russ Conway?

13. Which comic had hits with *Atmosphere* and *All Night Holiday* in the mid 1980s?

14. Name the female singer (below) who had a string of 90s hits, including a #1?

15. Name the female quartet whose first four singles, *C'est La Vie Jun*, *Rollercoaster*, *To You I Belong* and *Blame It On The Weatherman* all hit number one in 1998/1999?

16. Name the Welsh alternative rock band who had a string of hits in the mid-to-late 1990s with Cerys Matthews as their lead singer.

17. Which 1964 Gene Pitney No. 2 was a No.1 when Marc Almond duetted in 1989?

18. *Teardrops* was a 1984 hit for Shakin' Stevens. Who featured on lead guitar?

19. Who performed and co-wrote the 1993 No. 1 *Sleeping Satellite*?

20. Which English singer had two No. 1 hits *The Story of My Life* and *Starry Eyed* in 1958/9 and died at just 38 as a result of a drug overdose?

BITS AND PIECES ANSWERS: 1. Dave Dee, Dozy, Beaky, Mick and Tich; 2. Van Der Valk; 3. Winifred Atwell; 4. Dina Carroll; 5. 1969 (Ballad of John & Yoko); 6. Lucille; 7. Congratulations and Let Me Be the One both finished 2nd; 8. Anna-Frid Lyngstad; 9. 2 (How Can I Be Sure and Daydreamer/The Puppy Song; 10. You've Got Your Troubles; 11. Artful Dodger (garage duo); 12. Bristol; 13. Russ Abbot; 14. Tori Amos; 15. B*Witched; 16. Catatonia; 17. Something's Gotten Hold of my Heart?; 18. Hank Marvin; 19. Tasmin Archer; 20. Michael Holliday.

GEORGE HARRISON MBE *(Born Wavertree, Liverpool on 25 February 1943 – Died Los Angeles on 29 November 2001) was an English musician, singer-songwriter, and music and film producer. Achieved international fame as The Beatles lead guitarist. Harrison embraced Indian culture and helped broaden popular music by incorporating Indian instruments and Hindu spirituality. Harrison released 8 Top 40 singles (1 No.1 and 3 other Top 10 hits) and 7 Top 40 albums (1 No.1 and 2 more Top 10) as a solo performer. Co-founded the supergroup the Traveling Wilburys in 1988.*

1. What type of apprentice was George before he joined The Beatles?
A) Electrician   B) Mechanic   C) Gardener

2. George Harrison's first solo writing credit was for a song on the *With The Beatles* album. What was the song?
A) Think For Yourself   B) I Need You   C) Don't Bother Me

3. What unusual instrument did George play on the *Strawberry Fields Forever*?
A) Zither   B) Swarmandal   C) Sitar

4. George had his first solo hit, a self-written No. 1, *My Sweet Lord* in 1971. He was fined for accidental plagiarism as the melody was similar to which 1963 hit song?

5. In 1974 and 1975 George had two Top 40 hits with *Ding Dong* and *You*. What number did both songs reach in the UK Singles Charts?   A) 18   B) 28   C) 38

6. What was George Harrison's pseudonym on the Traveling Wilburys first album?
A) Spike Wilbury   B) Nelson Wilbury   C) Otis Wilbury

7. In 1981, *All Those Years Ago* reached UK #13. To whom was the song a tribute?
A) John Lennon   B) Elvis Presley   C) Carl Perkins

8. What was the title of George Harrison's autobiography published in 1980?
A) See You In My Dreams   B) I, Me, Mine   C) George

9. George started a new career, in 1978, as a film producer. What was the name of his production company?   A) Apple Films   B) GeorgeH Films   C) HandMade Films

10. In 1999, what very shocking thing happened to George?   A) A crazed person broke into his mansion and stabbed him several times   B) He was involved in a plane crash but survived   C) His yacht capsized and he was stranded on an island

George Harrison (centre) with Eric Idle and John Cleese in The Life of Brian

GEORGE HARRISON ANSWERS: *1. A) Electrician; 2. C) Don't Bother Me; 3. B) Swarmandal; 4. He's So Fine by The Chiffons (a No.16 hit in the UK); 5. C) 38; 6. B) Nelson Wilbury; 7. A) John Lennon; 8. B) I, Me, Mine; 9. C) HandMade Films; 10. A) A crazed person broke into his mansion and stabbed him several times.*

HEART *is an American rock band formed in 1967 in Seattle, Washington, had several name changes and eventually settled upon Heart, in 1973. Original members Roger Fisher (guitar) and Steve Fossen (bass) joined by sisters Ann Wilson (lead vocals/flute), Nancy Wilson (rhythm/vocals), Michael Derosier (drums), and Howard Leese (guitar/keyboards). These core members were included in the band's 2013 induction into the Rock and Roll Hall of Fame. Heart had 8 Top 40 singles in the UK, including 3 Top 10 hits, they also had 7 Top 40 albums with two Top 10 successes.*

1. The band had several name changes before becoming Heart; they were previously called The Army, Hocus Pocus and White Heart. True or False?

2. Heart's first (and biggest) UK hit was a rock ballad composed by Billy Steinberg and Tom Kelly, a number three single in 1987. What was the title of the song?
A) Who Will You Run To   B) Alone   C) Tears of Heaven

3. What was the title of band's debut album, released in 1977?
A) Dreamboat Annie   B) Little Queen   C) Private Audition

4. The cover of their first album was promoted with an ad that upset the band and caused them to break their contract with which record company?
A) Portrait Records   B) Canadian Records   C) Mushroom Records

5. Heart's best charting album was a number 3 in 1990 that included the hit single *All I Wanna Do Is Make Love to You*. What was the album title?
A) Brigade   B) Bad Animals   C) Heart

6. The 1987 hit album's title refers to a situation that the band encountered at a hotel in Charlotte, North Carolina; when Ann's dog was not allowed in the building. What was the name of the album?   A) Bad Animals   B) Hound Dog   C) Black Dog

7. In the autumn of 1991, the *Rock the House Live!* album largely featured tracks from *Brigade*. A single from the album was a version of *You're the Voice*. Which singer had originally charted with the song in 1987?
A) John Parr   B) John Waite   C) John Farnham

8. Who sung the lead vocals on the minor 1987 hit *There's the Girl*?
A) Ann   B) Nancy   C) Roger

9. Nancy Wilson married which famous film director in 1996?
A) Steven Spielberg   B) Cameron Crowe   C) Oliver Stone

10. During the sellout 1987 European tour, what problems did Ann began to have?
A) Panic attacks   B) Memory loss   C) Loss of balance

HEART ANSWERS: *1. True; 2. B) Alone; 3. A) Dreamboat Annie; 4. C) Mushroom Records (Press report suggested the two girls were having a lesbian affair); 5. A) Brigade; 6. A) Bad Animals; 7. C) John Farnham; 8. B) Nancy; 9. B) Cameron Crowe; 10. A) Panic attacks.*

JIMI HENDRIX *(James Marshall Hendrix (born Johnny Allen Hendrix; November 27, 1942 -- September 18, 1970) was an American musician, singer, and songwriter. His mainstream career was only four years, but widely regarded as one of the most celebrated musicians of the 20th century. Hendrix was inspired by American rock and roll and electric blues. He pioneered the use of the instrument as an electronic sound source. He had just 9 Top 40 singles, including a No.1 and four other Top 10 hits. Also notched up 22 Top 40 albums, including ten Top 10 successes.*

1.The authorship of the song that became Jimi's first hit in 1967 has been contested. What was the title of the song, which is about a man who is on the run and planning to head to Mexico after shooting his unfaithful wife?

2. What was the name of Jimi Hendrix's debut album which reached number two in the UK album charts in 1967?
A) Are You Experienced   B) Axis: Bold as Love   C) Electric Ladyland

3. Hendrix had already notched up 4 hits in the UK before he reached the US Top 20 with which song?   A) Hey Joe   B) All Along the Watchtower   C) Purple Haze

4. The last album released whilst Hendrix was alive was *Band Of Gypsys*. On what special date in 1969 was it recorded?
A) New Years' Eve   B) St. Patrick's Day   C) Thanksgiving

5. Where did Hendrix perform his memorable version of *The Star-Spangled Banner* in 1969?   A) Glastonbury   B) Monterey   C) Woodstock

6. What electric guitar did Jimi first play on when he was sixteen?
A) Fender   B) Supro Ozark   C) Gibson

7. In 1966, to which European capital city did Jimi decide to move and recruit members of a band designed to highlight his talents as the Jimi Hendrix Experience?
A) Paris   B) London   C) Berlin

8. What name did Hendrix give to his music?
A) Electric Church   B) Electric Orgasm   C) Cigar Music

9. What jazz player had studio time booked with Hendrix, but which sadly never happened as Hendrix died?   A) Miles Davis   B) Ty Montgomery   C) J.R. Smith

10. Lyrics: Name the Jimi song ".... all in my brain / Lately things they don't seem the same. / Actin' funny, but I don't know why / Excuse me while I kiss the sky."?

NAME THE TV SHOWS FROM THESE HITS
1. I'LL BE THERE FOR YOU - THE REMBRANDTS (1995 & 97)
2. WHOLE LOTTA LOVE - CCS (1970)
3. CROCKETT'S THEME - JAN HAMMER (1987)
4. CHI MAI - ENNIO MORRICONE (1981)
5. I COULD BE SO GOOD FOR YOU - DENNIS WATERMAN (1980)
6. FALLING - JULIE CRUISE)1980)
7. ??????? - VIENNA PHILHARMONIC ORCHESTRA (1971)
8. ??????? - JOHNNY KEATING (1962)
9. ??????? - CLANNAD (1982)
10. ??????? - NICK BERRY (1992)

JIMI HENDRIX ANSWERS: *1. Hey Joe; 2. A) Are You Experienced; 3. B) All Along the Watchtower; 4. A) New Years Eve; 5. C) Woodstock; 6. B) Supro Ozark; 7. B) London; 8. A) Electric Church; 9. A) Miles Davis; 10. Purple Haze.*
THEMES FROM TV SERIES ANSWERS: *1. Friends; 2 Top of the Pops; 3. Miami Vice; 4. The Life and Times of Lloyd George; 5. Minder; 6. Twin Peaks; 7. The Onedin Line; 8. Z Cars; 9. Harry's Game; 10. Heartbeat.*

HERMAN'S HERMITS are an English beat, rock and pop group formed in 1964 in Manchester with a line up of: Peter Noone (lead vocals), Derek Leckenby (lead guitar), Keith Hopwood (rhythm guitar), Karl Green (bass) & Barry Whitwam (drums). Produced by Mickie Most, they were one of the most successful acts in the Beatles-led British Invasion. They appeared in four films, two of them vehicles for the band. From late 1964 - early 1968, Herman's Hermits never failed to reach the US Top 40. In the UK they had 20 Top 40 hits including a number one with nine others reaching the Top 10. They also had 3 Top 40 albums in the UK.

1. Herman's Hermits first single *I'm Into Something Good* was their only UK number one. Who wrote the song?
A) Peter Noone   B) Gerry Goffin & Carole King   C) Burt Bacharach

2. Herman's Hermits had two US No.1 hits with which singles not released in the UK.
A) Can't You Hear My Heartbeat & Silhouettes   B) Mrs. Brown You Have a Lovely Daughter & I'm Henry VIII, I Am   C) No Milk Today & There's a Kind of Hush

3. Who is the only Hermits drummer since their formation in 1964?
A) Barry Whitwam   B) Derek Leckenby   C) Steve Titterington

4. In which British soap opera did Peter Noone appear as a 14 year old?
A) EastEnders   B) Emmerdale Farm   C) Coronation Street

5. In which year were Herman's Hermits the opening act of the Royal Variety Performance from the London Palladium, performing a medley of their hits?
A) 1968   B) 1969   C) 1970

6. Lyrics from a #7 Herman's Hermits hit from 1966: "But all that's left is a place dark and lonely, A terraced house in a mean street back of town". What is the song title?
A) This Door Swings Both Ways   B) No Milk Today   C) A Must To Avoid

7. Peter Noone had a solo UK #12 in 1971 with *Oh! You Pretty Thing*. Who wrote the song?   A) David Bowie   B) Paul McCartney   C) Stevie Wonder

8. Which song was originally sung by The New Vaudeville Band as a 1966 album track and became a 1967 hit for Herman's Hermits, then for The Carpenters in 1976?
A) There's A Kind of Hush   B) Winchester Cathedral   C) Yesterday Once More

9. A 1967 No. 7 hit for Herman's Hermits was previously a hit for Sam Cooke. Unravel this anagram to find the title: ***UNDERWORLD WOLF***

10. In 1966 Herman's Hermits starred in a film and sung nine songs including *Mrs. Brown You've Got a Lovely Daughter* and the title track of the film - which was?
A) When the Boys Meet the Girls   B) Pop Gear   C) Hold On

Peter Noone in a 1961 episode of Coronation Street with William Roache.

HERMAN'S HERMITS ANSWERS: *1. B) Gerry Goffin & Carole King; 2. B) Mrs. Brown You've Got A Lovely Daughter / I'm Henry VIII, I Am; 3. A) Barry Whitwam; 4. C) Coronation Street; 5. C) 1970; 6. B) No Milk Today; 7. A) David Bowie; 8. A) There's A Kind of Hush; 9. Wonderful World; 10. C) Hold On.*

THE HOLLIES *are a UK rock and pop band, formed 1962. A leading UK group 1960s-mid 1970s with distinctive 3-part harmonies. Founded by Allan Clarke and Graham Nash: Line up was Clarke (vocals), Nash (rhythm guitar & vocals), Vic Steele (lead guitar), Eric Haydock (bass) & Don Rathbone (drums). Tony Hicks (lead guitar) & Bobby Elliott (drums) joined in 1963. Ray Stiles (bass/ vocals from 1986 -1990 & 1991-), Ian Parker (keyboards) since 1991. The Hollies had 29 Top 40 hits, including 2 No.1's and 16 other Top 10 hits. Also 12 hit albums, inc 1 No. 1 and 5 Top 10.*

1. The Hollies first chart success was in 1963 with a cover of a Coasters song that was popular with many UK bands of the time. What was the song?
A) Poison Ivy   B) (Ain't That) Just Like Me   C) I'm a Hog For You

2. Which two Hollies smash hits were written by Graham Gouldman of 10cc?
A) On a Carousel & Long Cool Woman in a Black Dress   B) King Midas in Reverse & The Air That I Breathe   C) Bus Stop & Look Through Any Window

3. A Hollies recording of a new George Harrison song only reached No. 20 in 1965, when the Beatles released their own version on the *Rubber Soul* album. What was the song?   A) If I Needed Someone   B) Something   C) Here Comes the Sun

4. *Ain't Heavy, He's My Brother* was twice a hit for The Hollies. Originally a #3 in 1969 it reached No.1 when re-issued. How many years later did it hit the top spot?

5. In the 1967 hit *On a Carousel*, how did the girl win all her presents?   A) Knocking over milk cans   B) Popping balloons with a dart   C) Pulling ducks out of the water

6. During the 1960's, The Hollies had more Top Ten hits on the British pop charts than any other act except Elvis Presley and The Beatles. True or False?

7. When the re-issued *He Ain't Heavy, He's My Brother* reached No.1 it was only the second chart topper that The Hollies recorded. What had been their only other #1 back in 1965?   A) Just One Look   B) Stop, Stop, Stop   C) I'm Alive

8. Who was the new lead vocalist featured on the 1972 Hollies hit, *The Baby*?
A) Peter Howarth   B) Mikael Rickfors   C) Carl Wayne

9. In 1972, *Long Cool Woman In A Black Dress* was a hit. The song was different to other Hollies hits and featured Allan Clarke on lead guitar. The song was influenced by which swamp rock band?
A) Creedence Clearwater Revival   B) Little Feat   C) Delaney & Bonnie

10. The original Hollies reunited in 1983 to make an album and to do a short tour. They also had a minor hit on the US charts with a re-make of which song by Diana Ross & the Supremes?   A) Baby Love   B) Stop in the Name of Love   C) Reflections

NAME THESE HITMAKERS AND FIND A LINK!

A   B   C   D   E

BUDDY HOLLY *(Charles Hardin Holley (Born, Lubbock, Texas on September 7, 1936 – Died, Cerro Gordo County, Iowa on February 3, 1959), was an American singer / songwriter who was a central and pioneering figure of mid-1950s rock and roll. Born in Lubbock, Texas. His style was influenced by gospel music, country music, and rhythm and blues acts, which he performed in Lubbock with his friends from high school. Buddy Holly had 20 Top 40 hits in the UK, this included a #1 and 5 further Top 10 hits. Buddy also had 14 Top 40 albums, including 2 #1's and 7 more Top 10 successes. See The Crickets (page 84).*

1. Recordings credited to the Crickets were released on Brunswick, but recordings under just Buddy Holly's name were released on which subsidiary label?
A) Coral Records   B) London American   C) CBS

2. What familiar Buddy Holly song was on the flipside of his 1957 hit, *Peggy Sue*?
A) Everyday   B) Maybe Baby   C) It's So Easy

3. Which 1955 rhythm and blues song, based on the lullaby *Hush Little Baby*, recorded by Buddy in 1956 became a 1962 No. 4 hit when his recording was backed by over-dubbed Fireballs?   A) Road Runner   B) I'm a Man   C) Bo Diddley

4. Buddy Holly's final studio session became known as "the string sessions". Buddy recorded four songs with the Dick Jacobs Orchestra, an 18-piece ensemble. What posthumous number one was one of the four songs recorded?

5. Shortly after 12:55 am on 3 February, 1959, Buddy Holly, together with Ritchie Valens, J.P. Richardson (the Big Bopper), and 21 year old pilot Roger Peterson, were killed instantly when their Beechcraft Bonanza aircraft crashed into a frozen cornfield five miles northwest of which Iowa city?   A) Mason City   B) Des Moines   C) Ames

6. What Buddy written song, a 1960 hit, contained these lyrics: "Sometimes we'll sigh, Sometimes we'll cry, And we'll know why, Just you and I …"?

7. The 1962 hit *Maria Elena* by Los Indios Tabajaras was a tribute to Buddy Holly's widow. True or False?

8. A 1963 a revival of which Chuck Berry song, reached No. 3 for Buddy in the UK?
A) Sweet Little Sixteen   B) Memphis Tennessee   C) Brown Eyed Handsome Man

9. *The Buddy Holly Story* is a low budget 1978 American biographical film that was successful at the box office. Who played Buddy Holly in the movie, and was nominated for an Oscar?   A) Gary Busey   B) Michael Caine   C) Don Stroud

10. Which Buddy Holly song was used as the title for a 1986 Kathleen Turner film and also played whilst the opening titles were shown?
A) That'll Be the Day   B) Peggy Sue Got Married   C) Rave On

Buddy Holly by Andrew Western

The crash site in Iowa (see question 5)

BUDDY HOLLY ANSWERS: *1. A) Coral Records; 2. A) Everyday; 3. Bo Diddley; 4. It Doesn't Matter Anymore; 5. A) Mason City; 6. True Love Ways; 7. False (tribute to Maria Elena Peraltra, wife of Mexican President Emilio Porter Gil); 8. C) Brown Eyed Handsome Man; 9. A) Gary Busey; 10. B) Peggy Sue Got Married.*

HOT CHOCOLATE *are a British soul band popular during the 1970s and 1980s. Formed in 1968 by Errol Brown and Tony Wilson. The act had at least one hit every year from 1970 to 1984. The initial line-up was: Brown (vocals),Wilson (bass), Franklyn De Allie (guitar), Jim King (soon replaced by Ian King on drums) and Patrick Olive (percussion). Larry Ferguson (keyboards) joined the following year. Hot Chocolate had 26 Top 40 hits (+3 re-issues), including a No.1 and 13 more Top 10 hits. They also had 8 Top 40 albums including 2 No.1's and 2 more Top 10 successes.*

1. In 1969, Hot Chocolate started their recording career with a reggae version of which John Lennon song? A) Imagine   B) Give Peace a Chance   C) Jealous Guy

2. *You Sexy Thing* made the Top 10 in three decades. True or False?

3. Which famous record producer was behind the early Hot Chocolate hits?
A) Mickie Most   B) Tony Hatch   C) George Martin

4. The 1973 No.7 hit, *Brother Louie*, featured a guest spoken vocal from which founding father of British blues? A) John Mayall   B) Cyril Davies   C) Alexis Korner

5. In 1977, after 13 hits, they finally reached Number One with their 14th. Written by Russ Ballard, what was the song?
A) So You Win Again   B) Every 1's a Winner   C) Emma

6. Which 1982 Hot Chocolate No. 5 hit includes these lyrics:
"I remember every little thing, Like fighting in the playground, 'Cause some good looking boys, Had started to hang around"?
A) I'll Put You Together Again   B) It Started With a Kiss   C) Man to Man

7. When Tony Wilson quit the band in 1976, who initially replaced him on bass and sang backing vocals? A) Brian Satterwhite   B) Patrick Olive   C) Harvey Hinsley

8. Which Hot Chocolate hit was used in the 1989 TV advert for *Clearasil* starring Patsy Palmer? A) I'll Put You Together Again   B) Girl Crazy   C) You Sexy Thing

9. Errol Brown quit Hot Chocolate in 1986. When the band reformed in 1992, who took over as lead singer for the rest of the 20th century?
A) Patrick Olive   B) Steve Matthews   C) Greg Bannis

10. Errol Brown had one Top 40 hit as a solo star in 1987. What was the song?
A) Body Rocking   B) Personal Touch   C) Maya

4 LETTER WORDS A-J

1. A - Whose last 20th century hit was Under Attack in 1982?

2. B - The first Deep Purple album to feature David Coverdale on vocals.

3. C - The surname of the Irish family band who had a hit with Runaway.

4. D - Sung Tie a Yellow Ribbon Round the Old Oak Tree with Tony Orlando.

5. E - Who left Clannad to have hits including Orinoco Flow and Anywhere Is?

6. F - Boy Band who hit number one with Keep On Movin' in 1999.

7. G - 1959 title song from a musical romantic comedy film, a hit for Billy Eckstine.

8. H - The title of The Beatles second film.

9. I - Who had a No. 2 hit with Need You Tonight in 1988?

10. J - Name the song that was a hit for Van Halen and also Bus Stop?

HOT CHOCOLATE ANSWERS: 1. B) Give Peace a Chance; 2. True (1975, 1987, 1997); 3. A) Mickie Most; 4. C) Alexis Korner; 5. A) So You Win Again; 6. B) It Started With a Kiss; 7. A) Brian Satterwhite; 8. C) You Sexy Thing; 9. C) Greg Bannis; 10. B) Personal Touch.
***4 LETTER WORDS A-J ANSWERS:** 1. ABBA; 2. Burn; 3. Corr; 4. Dawn; 5. Enya; 6. Five; 7. Gigi; 8. Help!; 9. INXS; 10. Jump.*

WHITNEY HOUSTON *(Whitney Elizabeth Houston - August 9, 1963 – February 11, 2012) was an American singer and actress. Nicknamed 'The Voice', she is certified as the best-selling female R&B artist of the 20th century. Houston has influenced many singers in popular music, she is known for her powerful, soulful vocals and vocal improvisation skills. Whitney notched up 27 Top 40 hits, including 4 No.1's and 10 other Top 10 hits and also five Top 40 albums including a number one and three other Top 10 hits. She starred in The Bodyguard with Kevin Costner, a film that netted over $400 worldwide.*

1. At the age of eleven, Houston began performing as a soloist in the junior gospel choir at the New Hope Baptist Church in Newark, where she also learned to play the piano. What was the first solo that she performed?
A) Guide Me O Thou Great Jehovah   B) Amazing Grace   C) How Great Thou Art

2. For whom did Whitney's mother Cissy provide backing vocals?
A) Elvis Presley   B) Van Morrison   C) Jimi Hendrix   D) All of them

3. What was the title of Whitney's debut album in 1985?
A) Whitney   B) Whitney Houston   C) Houston Calling

4. In which 1986 hit song does Whitney sing these lyrics: "I decided long ago never to walk in anyone's shadows"?
A) How Will I Know   B) The Greatest Love of All   C) Didn't We Almost Have It All

5. Which Houston number one from 1988 opens with these lyrics: "Each day I live, I want to be, A day to give, The best of me, I'm only one, But not alone, My finest day, Is yet unknown"?

6. How many hit singles did the 1992 film *The Bodyguard*, starring Kevin Costner and Whitney, produce in the UK?   A) 5   B) 4   C) 3

7. Where did Whitney meet Bobby Brown, her future husband, in 1989? A) Church social   B) Soul Train music awards
C) A baseball game

8. In 1991, where did Whitney Houston famously perform *The Star-Spangled Banner*?   A) Super Bowl XXV at Tampa Stadium   B) Mandela reception in New York
C) For Ronald Reagan at the White House

9. In 1996, what was the name of the holiday comedy film in which Whitney plays the gospel-singing wife of a pastor played by Denzel Washington?
A) The Bishop's Wife   B) The Preacher's Wife   C) The minister's Wife

10. On the *Magic Johnson Show* in 1998 what did Whitney confess that she liked to do to relax?   A) Gardening   B) Cooking   C) Vacuuming

---

Back to the 70s

NAME THE ARTISTES WHO HAD HITS WITH THESE SONGS

1. Oh Happy Day
2. Rock the Boat
3. Feels Like the First Time
4. Don't You Worry 'Bout a Thing
5. I Get a Little Sentimental Over You
6. Funky Moped / Magic Roundabout

WHITNEY HOUSTON ANSWERS: *1. A) Guide Me O Thou Great Jehovah; 2. D) All of them; 3. B) Whitney Houston; 4. B) The Greatest Love of All; 5. One Moment in Time; 6. A) 5; 7. B) Soul Train music awards; 8. A) Super Bowl XXV at Tampa Stadium; 9. B) The Preacher's Wife; 10. C) Vacuuming.*
BACK TO THE 70s ANSWERS: *1. Edwin Hawkins Singers; 2. Hues Corporation; 3. Foreigner; 4. Incognito; 5. The New Seekers; 6. Jasper Carrott.*

THE HUMAN LEAGUE *are an English synth-pop band formed in Sheffield in 1977. Martyn Ware, Ian Marsh and Philip Oakey, signed to Virgin Records in 1979 and attained much commercial success. The Human League evolved into a successful New Pop band with a line-up now including female vocalists Joanne Catherall and Susan Ann Sulley. Since the mid-1990s, the band has mainly been a trio of Oakey, Catherall and Sulley with various sidemen. The Human League had 17 Top 40 hits, including a No.1 and 7 other Top 10 hits. They also had 10 Top 40 albums including a No.1 and 5 other Top 10 hits.*

1. What Human League single provided the band with their only number one hit on the UK charts in 1981? A) Open Your Heart B) Don't You Want Me C) Love Action

2. What group name had the Human League's Martyn Ware and Ian Marsh once used? A) Dead Daughters B) Oasis C) Heaven 17

3. With which indie label did the Human League first sign?
A) Atom Sounds B) Ninja Tune C) Fast

4. What was the inspiration behind the Human League's name?
A) A John Lennon Song B) A Sci-Fi Board Game C) A Sci-Fi Novel

5. Who produced Human League's 1981 No. 12 hit, *The Sound of the Crowd*?
A) Martin Rushent B) Mick Jones C) Robert Applegate

6. On which Human League album was the 1984 No.11 hit, song *The Lebanon*?
A) Secrets B) Crash C) Hysteria

7. What band did two of the original members of the Human League form after leaving in 1980? A) Heaven 17 B) China Crisis C) Soft Cell

8. Two consecutive Human League singles reached No. 2 in the UK in 1982/3. *Mirror Man* was the first, what was the second?
A) Being Boiled B) Open Your Heart C) (Keep Feeling) Fascination

9. What Human League number three hit from 1981 includes these lyrics: "I've lain alone and cried at night over what love made me do..."?
A) Love Action (I Believe in Love) B) The Sound of the Crowd C) Louise

10. A 1981 Human League album was a No.1 hit on the UK charts. What was the name of the album that included the band's only #1 single?
A) Crash B) Dare C) Hysteria

WHO HAD HITS IN THE UK WITH THESE SONGS?

1. SUKIYAKI (1963 No.6)

2. NORMAN (1962 No.24)

3. LAND OF 1,000 DANCES (1962 No.22)

4. MICHAEL (1961 No.1)

5. LES BICYCLETTES DE BELSIZE (1968 No.5)

6. IN THE BAD BAD OLD DAYS (No. 8 in 1969)

THE HUMAN LEAGUE ANSWERS: 1. B) Don't You Want Me; 2. A) Dead Daughters; 3. C) Fast; 4.B) A Sci-Fi Board Game; 5. A) Martin Rushkent; 6. C) Hysteria; 7. A) Heaven 17; 8. C) (Keep Feeling) Fascination; 9. A) Love Action (I Believe in Love); 10. B) Dare.
***1960s HITS ANSWERS**: 1. Kyu Sakamoto; 2. Carol Deene; 3. Wilson Pickett; 4. The Highwaymen; 5. Engelbert Humperdinck; 6. The Foundations.*

INXS were an Australian rock band, formed 1977 as The Farriss Brothers in Sydney, New South Wales. The founding members were Garry Gary Beers (bass), Andrew Farriss (main composer & keyboards), Jon Farriss (drums), Tim Farriss (guitar), Michael Hutchence (lead singer & main lyricist) and Kirk Pengilly (guitar & saxophone). Initially known for new wave/pop style, INXS later developed a harder pub rock style, including funk and dance elements INXS had 16 Top 40 hits, including just one Top 10 hit. Also 7 Top 40 albums, including a No. 1 and 5 other Top 10 hits.

1. What was the title of the INXS debut album?
A) Kick   B) Underneath the Colours   C) INXS

2. In 1991, INXS teamed up with legendary Australian Rocker Jimmy Barnes with a song that reached No. 18 in the UK charts. What was the song?
A) Good Times   B) Friday on my Mind   C) Hello, How Are You

3. What brand of drums did Jon Farriss use during the INXS peak years?
A) Ludwig   B) Pearl   C) DW

4. In which two cities was the album *Kick* recorded?
A) Sydney / Paris   B) London / Prague   C) Sydney / London

5. In 1988 INXS had their highest chart placing in the UK with which #2 single?
A) Never Tear Us Apart   B) Need You Tonight   C) Mystify

6. In 1983 the first INXS tour was as support to which band?
A) Stray Cats   B) The Kinks   C) Adam and the Ants

7. On 22 November 1997, Michael Hutchence was found dead in a hotel in which city?   A) Sydney   B) Paris   C) London

8. On 12 June 1999, INXS headlined the opening of Stadium Australia in Sydney, with US singer-songwriter Terence Trent D'Arby as a guest vocalist. True or False?

9. The eighth INXS album topped the album charts in the UK in 1992. What was the album's title?   A) Full Moon, Dirty Hearts   B) X   C) Welcome to Wherever You Are

10. How many Farriss brothers were in the INXS line-up?

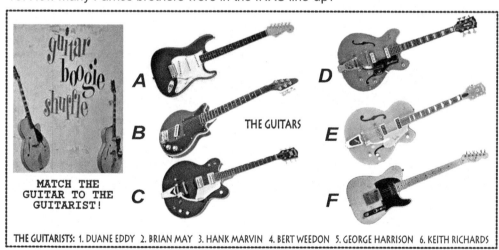

guitar boogie shuffle

A

B

C

THE GUITARS

D

E

F

MATCH THE GUITAR TO THE GUITARIST!

THE GUITARISTS: 1. DUANE EDDY 2. BRIAN MAY 3. HANK MARVIN 4. BERT WEEDON 5. GEORGE HARRISON 6. KEITH RICHARDS

INXS ANSWERS: 1. C) INXS; 2. A) Good Times; 3. B) Pearl; 4. Sydney / Paris; 5. B) Need You Tonight; 6. C) Adam and the Ants; 7. A) Sydney (Ritz-Carlton hotel); 8. True; 9. C) Welcome to Wherever You Are; 10. 3 (Tim, Andrew and Jon).
GUITAR BOOGIE SHUFFLE ANSWERS: 1. A3; 2. B2; 3. C5; 4. D4; 5. E1; 6. F6.

THE JAM were an English mod revival/punk rock band during the 70s/early 80s, formed in 1972 at Sheerwater Secondary School, Woking. Line up: Paul Weller (bass/ lead vocals), Steve Brookes (guitar/vocals) and Rick Buckler (drums).The Jam had 18 consecutive Top 40 singles in the UK, from their debut in 1977 to their break-up in December 1982, including four number one hits. They released 13 albums, one was a #1 and 8 more reached the top 10. When The Jam disbanded their first 15 singles were re-released and all placed within the top 100. See also Style Council / Paul Weller page.

1. Which band did The Jam support on tour in 1977?
A) The Who   B) The Sex Pistols   C) The Clash

2. What was the Jam's first Top 10 hit in the UK?
A) Eton Rifles   B) David Watts   C) All Around the World

3. *A Town Called Malice* was a double A-side with which song, a #1 in 1997?
A) Absolute Beginners   B) Funeral Pyre   C) Precious

4. The photo on the 1977 album cover of *This Is the Modern World* shows which iconic London overpass?
A) Chiswick Flyover   B) The Westway   C) Hammersmith Flyover

5. The 1980 #1 Start, copies a riff from which Beatles song?
A) Day Tripper   B) Get Back   C) Taxman

6. What was the Jam's final tour before the break up?
A) Beat Surrender '82   B) That Was Entertainment   C) Goodbye Jamboree

7. Who manager of The Jam?   A) Eric Hall   B) John Weller   C) Chas Chandler

8. Who duetted with The Jam on the 1982 #2 single *The Bitterest Pill (I Ever Had To Swallow)*?   A) Dee C. Lee   B) Tracie Young   C) Jennie Matthias

9. What 1982 Jam #1 opens with these lyrics: "Some people might say my life is in a rut, I'm quite happy with what I got, People might say that I should strive for more, but I'm so happy I can't see the point"?

10. The sixth and final studio album by The Jam was their only #1 album. What was the title of the album released on 12 March 1982 by Polydor?
A) The Gift   B) Sound Affects   C) Setting Suns

WE ASK THE QUESTIONS!

Identify the hit song titles that were asking a question!

A) WHAT ....? (Jimmy Ruffin 1966)   F) CAN ....? (Jacksons 1981)

B) WHERE ......? (Betty Boo 1990)   G) IS ....? (Bassheads 1991)

C) WHY ....? (Travis 1999)   H) DO ....? (Dionne Warwick 1968)

D) HOW .... ? (Champaign 1981)   J) WILL ....? (Shirelles 1961)

E) ARE ....? (John Inman 1975)   K) WHO ....? (Juicy Lucy 1970)

JANET JACKSON *(Janet Damita Jo Jackson, born May 16, 1966) is an American singer, songwriter, actress, and dancer. She is noted for her innovative, socially conscious and sexually provocative records, as well as elaborate stage shows. Her sound and choreography was a catalyst in MTV growth, as she rose to prominence while breaking gender and racial barriers. Lyrical content focusing on social issues made her a role model for youth. Jackson had 25 Top 40 hits, including 10 Top 10 songs. Also 6 Top 40 albums with one No. 1 and 4 other Top 10 successes.*

1. What was the title of the TV sitcom in which Janet Jackson played Millicent 'Penny' Gordon Woods for two seasons from 1977 to 1979?
A) Diff'rent Strokes   B) Good Times   C) Fame

2. Which singer choreographed the 1986 video for *Nasty* and also made a guest appearance in the video?   A) Ce Ce Peniston   B) Paula Abdul   C) Gloria Estefan

3. Janet is known for her intricate dance choreography. Which 1989 video displays a military style dance choreography?   A) Rhythm Nation   B) Control   C) Nasty

4. On which UK No. 2 single did Jackson duet with Luther Vandross, with special guests BBD & Ralph Tresvant?
A) The Best Things In Life Are Free   B) The Closer I Get To You   C) Endless Love

5. Which punctuation mark finishes the title of the 1993 album *Janet _* ?

6. What Janet Jackson #2 hit from 1993 includes these lyrics: "Like a moth to the flame burned by the fire"?   A) That's the Way Love Goes   B) If   C) Again

7. What was the title of the 1995 duet that she recorded with brother Michael Jackson and had a number three UK hit?
A) Scream   B) Alright   C) The Best Things in Life Are Free

8. What is the title of Janet's 1995 greatest hits album?   A) Number Ones / The Best
B) Icon: Number Ones   C) Design of a Decade: 1986–1996

9. The 1997 song, *Got Til It's Gone*, features a cameo by a multi-talented, poetic singer, perhaps best known for her song, *Big Yellow Taxi*. Who is she?
A) Etta James   B) Joan Baez   C) Joni Mitchell

10. In October 1997 Jackson returned with a dramatic change in image, boasting vibrant red hair, nasal piercings, and tattoos. Her new album primarily centred on the idea that everyone has an intrinsic need to belong. What was the album?
A) The Velvet Rope   B) All for You   C) Damita Jo

How many of these female singing stars can you remember?

JANET JACKSON ANSWERS: *1. B) Good Times; 2. B) Paula Abdul; 3. A) Rhythm Nation; 4. A) The Best Things In Life Are Free; 5. A full stop (the title was Janet.); 6. A) That's the Way Love Goes; 7. A) Scream; 8. C) Design of a Decade: 1986–1996; 9. C) Joni Mitchell; 10. A) The Velvet Rope).* **HERE COME THE GIRLS ANSWERS:** *A) Petula Clark; B) Little Eva; C) Clodagh Rodgers; D) Rosemary Clooney; E) Peggy Lee; F) Susan Maughan; G) Janis Joplin; H) Alannah Myles; J) Joni Mitchell; K) Vera Lynn.*

MICHAEL JACKSON *(August 29, 1958 – June 25, 2009) was an American singer, songwriter, and dancer. The 'King of Pop' is a most significant 20th century figure. For 4 decades, his contributions to music, dance, and fashion, and publicised personal life, made him a global figure in popular culture. He popularised dance moves such as the moonwalk and the robot. The most awarded individual music artist in history. From the late 1980s, he was controversial with a changing appearance, relationships, behaviour, and lifestyle. Jackson notched up 49 Top 40 hits, with 7 No. 1's and only 10 of them not reaching the Top 10. Also 17 Top 40 albums, 6 No. 1's and 3 more Top 10.*

1. In 1972, what was Michael Jackson's first solo UK single, a song that reached number five in the charts? A) Rockin' Robin B) Got To Be There C) Ben

2. What is the opening track on Michael Jackson's 1979 album *Off the Wall*, a song that reached number 3 in the singles charts?
A) Don't Stop 'Til You Get Enough B) Rock With You C) She's Out of My Life

3. Lyrics from the first single release from Michael Jackson's 1987 album *Bad*. Can you name the song? "Each time the wind blows, I hear your voice so I call your name, Whispers at morning, our love is dawning, Heaven's glad you came".
A) I Just Can't Stop Loving You B) Liberian Girl C) Man in the Mirror

4. In which year did Michael Jackson release the No.1 single *Black or White*?
A) 1988 B) 1991 C) 1992

5. Which Michael Jackson 1982 album, stayed in the UK charts for 201 weeks, and is the best-selling album of all time?
A) Dangerous B) Bad C) Thriller

6. What was the name of his pet chimp that Michael would take on tour? A) Ben B) Bubbles C) Albert

7. Who played the guitar solo on the 1983 No. 3 hit, *Beat It*?
A) Eric Clapton B) Eddie Van Halen C) Stevie Ray Vaughan

8. Rod Templeton, the keyboardist and main songwriter for the 1970s funk band Heatwave, wrote three early hits for Michael Jackson, *Off The Wall*, *Rock With You* and *Thriller*. Where was Rod born? A) Cleethorpes B) Stockport C) Kings Lynn

9. Which notable actor recites the closing lyrics to *Thriller*?
A) Peter Cushing B) Christopher Lee C) Boris Karloff

10. What item of white rhinestone clothing was Michael Jackson known for wearing?
A) Hat B) Waistcoat C) Glove

Michael Jackson <u>3</u> duets. Can you name the <u>4</u> hits?

MICHAEL JACKSON ANSWERS: 1. B) Got To Be There; 2. A) Don't Stop 'Til You Get Enough; 3. A) I Just Can't Stop Loving You; 4. B) 1991; 5. C) Thriller; 6. B) Bubbles; 7. B) Eddie Van Halen; 8. A) Cleethorpes; 9. B) Christopher Lee; 10. C) Glove.
MICHAEL JACKSON DUETS ANSWERS: A) With Paul McCartney (twice) - The Girl is Mine & Say Say Say; B) With Stevie Wonder - Get It; C) With Mick Jagger - State of Shock.

THE JACKSON 5 / THE JACKSONS *are an American pop band comprising brothers of the Jackson family. Founded in 1964 in Gary, Indiana, by patriarch Joe Jackson and sons Jackie, Tito, and Jermaine, with Marlon and Michael joining soon after. The group left Motown for Epic Records in early 1976, except Jermaine, who was replaced by youngest brother Randy. The brothers also released solo albums, most successfully Michael. The Jackson 5 had 10 Top 40 hits, 6 reaching the Top 10. The Jacksons had 13 Top 40 hits, including a No.1 and 4 other Top 10 hits. They also had 10 Top 40 albums including a No. 1 and 2 others reaching the Top 10.*

1. In 1968, the Jackson 5 left Steeltown Records and signed with which major label?
A) Motown B) Atlantic C) CBS

2. What was the name of the first Jackson 5 album, released in 1969?
A) ABC B) Diana Ross Presents The Jackson 5 C) Jackson 5 Christmas Album

3. How many brothers did not use their real names - can you name them?

4. Only two brothers played electric instruments, Tito played the guitar, who played the bass? A) Jackie B) Marlon C) Jermaine

5. In 1977, The Jacksons had their only number one success in the UK. What was the title of the hit? A) I'll Be There B) Show You The Way To Go C) ABC

6. In 1968, while negotiations were continuing to get the Jacksons released from Steeltown, the group performed at casinos to make some extra cash. True or False?

7. The first Jackson 5 UK hit was in 1969. The lyrics of which song included: "But someone picked you from the bunch, one glance was all it took, Now it's much too late for me to take a second look"?
A) I Want You Back B) The Love You Save C) ABC

8. The brothers first Top 10 album came as The Jacksons in 1984. What was the title of the album? A) Victory B) Triumph C) Destiny

9. All of the original members of the Jackson 5, not including Randy, were inducted to the Rock and Roll Hall of Fame in what year? A) 1985 B) 1991 C) 1997

10. On October 23rd 1990, a book *My Family, The Jacksons* was published. Who wrote the book? A) Michael Jackson B) Joe Jackson C) Katherine Jackson

The Jackson Family

| Joe b. 1928 | | Katherine b. 1930 |

| Rebbie b. 1950 | Jackie b. 1951 | Tito b. 1953 | Jermaine b. 1954 | La Toya b. 1956 | Marlon b. 1957 | Brandon b./d. 1957 | Michael b. 1958 d. 2009 | Randy b. 1961 | Janet b. 1966 |

JACKSON 5 / THE JACKSONS ANSWERS: 1. A) Motown; 2. B) Diana Ross Presents The Jackson 5; 3. Three - Jackie, real name Sigmund, Tito -Toriano, Randy - Steven; 4. C) Jermaine; 5. B) Show You The Way To Go; 6. False, they played strip clubs like Guys + Dolls; 7. A) I Want You Back; 8. A) Victory; 9. C) 1997; 10. C) Katherine Jackson (the matriarch of the Jackson family).

THE JAM *were an English mod revival/punk rock band formed in 1972 at Sheerwater Secondary School, Woking by Paul Weller and various friends before Bruce Foxton (guitar) and Rick Buckler (drums) became the established line up. The band wore smartly tailored suits reminiscent of 1960s English pop-bands and incorporated mainstream 1960s rock and R&B influences into its sound, particularly from the work of the Who and the Kinks and the music of American Motown. The Jam notched up 19 Top 40 hits, including 4 No.1's and 5 other Top 10 successes. Albums were successful too - 1 No. 1, 8 Top 10 and 4 more Top 40 hits.*

1. The Jam's first eight singles reached the mid to lower reaches of the Top 40. What was the first single that peaked at number 40?
A) All Around the World   B) In The City   C) News of the World

2. The Jam were photographed below a stretch of The Westway for the cover of the *This Is The Modern World* album, but what band name is on Paul Weller's button badge?   A) The Sex Pistols   B) The Who   C) The Beatles

3. Skirmishes between demonstrators on a left-wing Socialist Workers Party *Right to Work* march, and pupils from Eton College, inspired which Jam No. 3 hit in 1979?
A) Town Called Malice   B) Eton Rifles   C) That's Entertainment

4. "You choose your leaders and place your trust, As their lies wash you down ..." Complete the line of lyrics from The Jam's first No. 1, *Going Underground*. A) "and get covered in dust"   B) "as they shower in lust"   C) "and their promises rust"

5. The 1982 single *A Town Called Malice* was a double A-sided #1. The band sung both sides on *Top of the Pops*, an honour only previously given to The Beatles. What was the title of the other track?
A) Just Who Is The 5 O'Clock Hero?   B) Precious   C) Carnation

6. With what type of guitar is Paul Weller generally associated?
A) Fender   B) Gretsch   C) Rickenbacker

7. The string-laden soul ballad *The Bitterest Pill (I Ever Had to Swallow)* peaked at No. 2 in 1982, Who provided the backing vocals on the track?
A) Jennie Matthias   B) Tracie Young   C) Tracey Thorn

8. The bass line, rhythm guitar and guitar solo for The Jam's second No.1 single, *Start!*, is undeniably similarity to which George Harrison written Beatles album track?
A) Taxman   B) Got My Mind Set On You   C) Here Comes the Sun

9. What did The Jam call their final tour?
A) Goodbye Jamboree   B) That Was Entertainment   C) Beat Surrender '82

10. In early 1983, Paul Weller left The Jam and announced the formation of a new band. What was the band's name?
A) Stiff Little Fingers   B) Time UK   C) Style Council

COMPLETE THE LYRICS - AND NAME THE SONGS & ARTISTES!
1. "At first I was afraid I was ...."
2. "When evening falls so hard, I will .... you"
3. "Well we got no class, And we got no ...."
4. "Imagine no ...., I wonder if you can"
5. "Sharing .... that are new to us, Watching the signs along the way"

THE JAM ANSWERS: *1. B) In the City; 2. B) The Who; 3. B) Eton Rifles; 4. C) "and their promises rust"; 5. B) Precious; 6. C) Rickenbacker; 7. A) Jennie Matthias; 8. A) Taxman; 9. C) Beat Surrender '82; 10. C) Style Council (see separate quiz later in this book).*
COMPLETE THE 1970s LYRICS AND NAME THE SONG ANSWERS: *1. Petrified - I Will Survive by Gloria Gaynor; 2. Comfort - Bridge Over Troubled Water by Simon & Garfunkel; 3. Principals - School's Out by Alice Cooper; 4. Possessions - Imagine by John Lennon; 5. Horizons - We've Only Just Begun by The Carpenters.*

JAMES are an English rock band from Whalley Range, Manchester, who were formed in 1982 and remained popular popular throughout the 1990s. The line up was originally Paul Gilbertson (lead guitar), Jim Glennie (bass) and Gavan Whelan (drums). Other musicians drifted rapidly in and out until Tim Booth (vocals) joined. Several notable changes and additions then followed, including the departure of founder Gilbertson in 1985. Live performance continually remained a central part of the band's output. James had eighteen Top 40 hits, four of them reaching the Top 10. They also notched up seven Top 20 albums, including a No. 1, with five others reaching the Top 10.

1. James hit the jackpot with their fourth single. After their first three singles had all reached thirty-something it got to #2 in the UK. What was the memorable single?
A) You're Beautiful   B) It's a Man's Man's Man's World   C) Sit Down

2. One of James' earlier names was Venereal and the Diseases. True or False?

3. Between February and April 1985 who did James support on the *Meat is Murder* tour?   A) Joy Division   B) The Smiths   C) The Clash

4. On the album front, after two low entry chart successes, James had two consecutive number twos in 1990 and 1992. What were the albums?
A) Gold Mother & Seven   B) Laid & Wah Wah   C) Stutter & Strip Mine

5. In November 1988, drummer Whelan had an on-stage fight with Booth and was asked to leave the band. Who replaced him?
A) Ron Yeadon   B) David Baynton-Power   C) Chloe Alper

6. In 1993, James went on an acoustic tour of the US, supporting which musical legend in a series of natural outdoor venues?
A) David Crosby   B) Stephen Stills   C) Neil Young

7. In 1995, James discovered that they owed the Inland Revenue a load of money. How much was the tax bill?   A) £250,000   B) £500,000   C) £750,000

8. In 1998 James achieved their second highest placing in the UK singles charts. The #7 hit was a re-mix of which of their hits?   A) Sit Down   B) Sound   C) Tomorrow

9. The James album,*Whiplash*, released in February 1997 provided James with a successful comeback. Which single from the album also reached the Top 20?
A) Laid   B) She's a Star   C) Waltzing Along

10. On their 1993 hit album *Laid*, the track *Sometimes (...... ......)* contains these lyrics: "On a flat roof, there's a boy, Leaning against a wall of rain, Aerial held high, Calling "Come on thunder, Come on thunder!" What jockey's name is missing from the title?   A) Bob Champion   B) Frankie Dettori   C) Lester Piggott

1. On what did Starship build this city in 1975?

2. Primitives 1988: "Here you go way too fast, Don't slow down, you gonna ....."?

3. In 1989 Bette Midler sang "It must have been cold there in my ....."?

4. "Whenever I hear goodbyes, remind me baby of you" started which 1988 Womack and Womack number three?

5. In the lyrics of the 1983 No. 1, Down Under, Men At Work sing about coming from the land of what?

6. "Say say two thousand zero zero party over, oops, out of time" is from which 1983, 1999 and 2000 Prince hit?   A) Purple Rain   B) 1999   C) Kiss.

JAMES ANSWERS: 1. C) Sit Down; 2. True; 3. B) The Smiths; 4. A) Gold Mother & Seven; 5. B) David Baynton-Power; 6. C) Neil Young; 7. A) £250,000; 8. A) Sit Down; 9. B) She's a Star; 10. C) Lester Piggott. **TOTALLY 80's ANSWERS:** *1. Rock and Roll; 2. Crash; 3. Shadow; 4. Teardrops; 5. Plenty; 6. B) 1999.*

JAMIROQUAI *are an English funk and acid jazz band from London. Formed in 1992 and fronted by vocalist Jay Kay, who loved the native American culture. Jamiroquai is a portmanteau of the words 'jam' and the name of a Native American confederacy, the Iroquois. Jamiroquai were prominent in the London-based funk and acid jazz movement of the 1990s. They built on the sound in their early releases and later drew from rock, disco, electronic and Latin music genres. Kay has remains as the only original member through several line-up changes. Jamiroquai had 16 Top 40 hits, including a No.1, six others reached the Top 10. They also had four very successful albums, 2 No. 1's and 2 No. 2's.*

1. Which one of these was Jamiroquai's first album?
A) A Funk Odyssey   B) Travelling Without Moving   C) Emergency on Planet Earth

2. What is Jay Kay's full name?
A) Jason Luís Cheetham   B) Jason King   C) James Kaye

3. On the *Too Young To Die* debut single the Jamiroquai line up was: Jay Kay (lead vocals), Derrick McKenzie (drums), Toby Smith (keyboards), Stuart Zender (bass), Wallis Buchanan (vibes), Simon Katz (guitar). True or False?

4. Complete the 1994 album title: *Return of the ..... Cowboy.*
A) Midnight   B) Space   C) Urban

5. The *Travelling Without Moving* album cover was a controversial homage to which luxury sports car logo, combined with the band's own Buffalo Man logo?
A) Lamborghini   B) Ferrari   C) Porsche

6. For which single did Jamiroquai win a Grammy in 1996?
A) Cosmic Girl   B) Virtual Insanity   C) Deeper Underground

7. The Jamiroquai single *Canned Heat* was featured in which film?
A) Garden State   B) Zoolander   C) Napoleon Dynamite

8. What is the name of the Jamiroquai album that contains the 1993 No. 3 hit *Virtual Insanity*? A) Travelling Without Moving   B) A Funk Odyssey   C) Synkronized

9. A Jamiroquai performance at what location in January 1997 was aired live on the internet?   A) Hollywood Bowl   B) Los Angeles House Of Blues   C) Forest Hills

10. In the 1990's Jamiroquai signed a deal with Sony BMG to record how many albums?   A) 4   B) 8   C) 10

VIRTUAL INSANITY (Kay, Zender, McKenzie, Katz, Buchanan)
Oh yeah what we're living in let me tell ya
It's a wonder man can eat at all
When things are big that should be small
Who can tell what magic spell we'll be doing for us
And I'm giving all my love to this world
Only to be told I can't see I can' t breathe
No more we will be
And nothing going to change the way we live
'Cos we can always take but never give
And now that things are changing for the worse
See it's a crazy world we're living in
And I just can see that half of us immersed in sin is
All we have to give these
Futures made of virtual insanity
Now always seem to be govern'd by this love we have
For useless twisting our new technology
Oh, now there is no sound for we all live underground
And I'm thinking what a mess we're in,
Hard to know where to begin
If I could slip the sickly ties that earthly man has made,

And now every mother can choose the colour of her child
That's not nature's way
Well that's what they said yesterday
There's nothing left to do but pray
I think it's time I found a new religion
Waoh it's so insane to synthesise another strain
There's something in these future that we have to be told
Futures made of virtual insanity
Now always seem to be govern'd by this love we have
For useless twisting our new technology
Oh, now there is no sound for we all live underground
Now there is no sound for we all live underground
And now it's virtual insanity
Forget your virtual reality
Oh there's nothing so bad I know yeah
Futures made of virtual insanity
Now always seem to be govern'd by this love we have
For useless twisting our new technology
Oh, now there is no sound for we all live underground
Virtual insanity is what we're livin' in
Virtual insanity is what we're livin' in

JAMIROQUAI ANSWERS: 1. C) Emergency On Planet Earth; 2. A) Jason Luís Cheetham; 3. True; 4. B) Space; 5. B) Ferrari; 6. B) Virtual Insanity; 7. C) Napoleon Dynamite; 8. A) Travelling Without Moving; 9. B) Los Angeles House Of Blues; 10. B) 8.

BILLY JOEL *(William Martin Joel - born in the Bronx, New York City 9, 1949) is an American musician, singer-songwriter, and composer. Commonly nicknamed the 'Piano Man' after his first single and signature song of the same name. He has led a commercially successful career as a solo artist since the 1970s. Joel was inducted into the Songwriters Hall of Fame (1992) and the Rock and Roll Hall of Fame (1999). In 1993 he was inducted into the Madison Square Garden Walk of Fame. Joel had 14 Top 40 singles in the UK, including a No.1 and four other Top 10 hits. He also had 11 Top 40 albums, including 6 Top 10 successes.*

1. Joel boxed successfully on the amateur Golden Gloves circuit for a short time, winning 22 bouts. Why did he give up boxing after his 24th boxing match?   A) Had a front tooth knocked out   B) Had his nose broken   C) Tired of being in constant pain

2. Billy Joel's breakthrough came with *The Stranger* album in 1977, produced by Phil Ramone. Which single taken from the album gave Joel his first UK hit single?
A) Just the Way You Are   B) Movin' Out (Anthony's Song)   C) My Life

3. What is described as being wrong with the singer's tie in the lyrics of the 1980 hit, *It's Still Rock and Roll to Me*?   A) Too wide   B) Too narrow   C) Too long

4. Which 1984 Joel hit contains these lyrics: "I had second thoughts at the start, I said to myself, hold on to your heart, now I know the woman that you are, you're wonderful so far, and it's more than I hoped for."   A) Leave a Tender Moment Alone
B) The Longest Time   C) Innocent Man

5. Joel's only No.1, came in 1983. It was a song originally written about which model?   A) Christie Brinkley   B) Twiggy   C) Elle Macpherson

6. In the 1989 No.7 hit, *We Didn't Start the Fire*, a total of how many individuals are mentioned by name?   A) 28   B) 42   C) 56

7. From which album was the 1983 number four hit *Tell Her About It* taken?
A) An Innocent Man   B) The Nylon Curtain   C) The Bridge

8. Joel suffered from depression. In 1970, a career decline and personal tragedies worsened his moods. He left a suicide note, how did he attempt to end his life?
A) By hanging   B) By drinking furniture polish   C) By overdose

9. Billy Joel was convinced to follow a musical career after watching which group on *The Ed Sullivan Show*?   A) The Four Seasons   B) The Beatles   C) The Beach Boys

10. Which 1988 Disney animated film features Joel in a voice acting role as Dodger, a sarcastic Jack Russell who sang the song *Why Should I Worry*?
A) The Black Cauldron   B) Oliver & Company   C) The Land Before Time

BILLY JOEL ANSWERS: *1. B) Had his nose broken; 2. A) Just the Way You Are; 3. A) Too wide; 4. B) The Longest Time; 5. C) Elle Macpherson (later becoming associated with Christie Brinkley, his second wife, too!); 6. C) 56; 7. A) An Innocent Man; 8. B) By drinking furniture polish Later he said, "I drank furniture polish. It looked tastier than bleach" 9. B) The Beatles; 10. B) Oliver & Company.* **PIANO CHART-BUSTERS ANSWERS:** *A) Marvin Hamlisch; B) Russ Conway; C) Liberace; D) Mrs. Mills; E) Joe 'Mr Piano' Henderson; F) Winifred Attwell; G) B. Bumble & The Stingers; H) Vangelis; J) Ferrante & Teicher; K) Floyd Cramer.*

ELTON JOHN *(Sir Elton Hercules John CH CBE - born Reginald Kenneth Dwight in Pinner, Middlesex; 25 March 1947) is an English singer, pianist and composer. The most successful pop artist of the 1970s, he has survived many different pop fads to remain one of Britain's most internationally acclaimed musicians. In the 1970s/80s, he suffered from drug and alcohol addiction and bulimia. He is well known as a campaigner for AIDS research. Including duets, Elton John amassed 62 Top 40 hits between 1971 and 1999. 4 of those were No. 1's and a further 21 reached the Top 10. Elton John albums were also very successful with 32 Top 40 albums, including 5 No. 1's and 17 others getting into the Top 10.*

1. The opening track of Elton John's 1971 eponymous album provided his first UK hit single. What was the song that reached number 7 in the charts?
A) Honky Cat   B) Rocket Man   C) Your Song

2. What reptile provided Elton with a No. 5 hit in 1972?
A) Alligator   B) Crocodile   C) Chameleon

3. Elton had his first UK number one in 1976 as part of a duet with whom?   A) George Michael   B) Kiki Dee   C) RuPaul

4. Which deceased celebrity is the subject of the 1973 No.11 single *Candle in the Wind*?   A) Marilyn Monroe   B) Princess Diana   C) James Dean

5. What 1978 piano instrumental, a No. 4 hit, was a tribute to a Rocket Records motorcycle messenger who was killed in a road accident?
A) Sorry Seems To Be the Hardest Word   B) Bennie & the Jets   C) Song For Guy

6. What was the rocking Elton John anthem that contains the lines "I'm a juvenile product of the working class / Whose best friend floats in the bottom of a glass"?
A) Bennie & the Jets   B) Saturday Night's Alright For Fighting   C) Pinball Wizard

7. In 1995, Elton John and lyricist Tim Rice won an Oscar for Best Original Song for which song from the soundtrack of *The Lion King*?
A) Circle of Life   B) Can You Feel the Love Tonight?   C) I Just Can't Wait To Be King

8. Which song did Elton John and Bernie Taupin rework as a tribute to the late Princess Diana in 1997, a song that he performed at her funeral?
A) Candle in the Wind 97   B) Tiny Dancer   C) Don't Let the Sun Go Down on Me

9. Elton John had a Top 10 hit in 1974 with a Beatles song featuring John Lennon as Dr. Winston O'Boogie . Can you name it?
A) Yesterday   B) Lucy in the Sky With Diamonds   C) Hey Jude

10. In his historic 1980 Central Park concert in New York, Elton John played an encore dressed as which iconic Disney character?
A) Mickey Mouse   B) Simba   C) Donald Duck

CANDLE IN THE WIND '97
(Elton John - Bernie Taupin)
Goodbye England's rose
May you ever grow in our hearts
You were the grace that placed itself
Where lives were torn apart
You called out to our country
And you whispered to those in pain
Now you belong to heaven
And the stars spell out your name

(Chorus) it seems to me you lived your life
Like a candle in the wind
Never fading with the sunset
When the rain set in

And your footsteps will always fall here
Along England's greenest hills
Your candle's burned out long before
Your legend ever will

Loveliness we've lost
These empty days without your smile
This torch we'll always carry
For our nation's golden child
And even though we try
The truth brings us to tears
All our words cannot express
The joy you brought us through the years

(Chorus)........

Goodbye England's rose
May you ever grow in our hearts
You were the grace that placed itself
Where lives were torn apart
Goodbye England's rose
From a country lost without your soul
Who'll miss the wings of your compassion
More than you'll ever know

[Outro] And your footsteps will always fall
Along England's greenest hills
Your candle's burned out long before
Your legend ever will.

ELTON JOHN ANSWERS: *1. C) Your Song; 2. B) Crocodile; 3. B) Kiki Dee; 4. A) Marilyn Monroe; 5. C) Song For Guy; 6. B) Saturday Night's Alright For Fighting; 7. B) Can You Feel the Love Tonight?; 8. A) Candle in the Wind 97; 9. B) Lucy in the Sky With Diamonds; 10. C) Donald Duck*

THE 90's *is a round of general trivia questions about the 1990's popular music scene.*

1. Garbage had a string of hits from the mid to late 90's. Who was their lead singer?

2. With which bass-baritone singer did Tina Turner team up on the 1996 hit *In Your Wildest Dreams*?

3. With which line dancing No.14 hit did Steps make their chart debut in 1997?

4. What were Bran Van 3000 doing in L.A. According to their 1998/9 hit?

5. Which Manchester dance music band had their final chart success with a No.13 hit, *Dreaming*, in 1993?

6. With what 12 letter song title did Meat Loaf have a No. 26 hit in 1994?

7. Name the English DJ, musician, singer and record producer (pictured below), who had a No. 1 with *Killer* in 1990?

8. With whom did Kylie Minogue duet on a 1991 No. 4 hit, *If You Were With Me Now*?

9. With what song did Baddiel & Skinner & the Lightning Seeds have a number one in 1996, and another chart topper in 1998 with a variation of the same song?

10. Which French trio had a No. 2 hit with *Music Sounds Better With You* in 1998?

11. Which Christmas 1993 No.1 included these lyrics: "His philosophy of life will steer him through, And as far as he can see, He's the same as you and me"?

12. Chris Isaak sung about which colour hotel in 1991?

13. *Living On My Own* was the only chart topper for which flamboyant star in 1993?

14. Who was the American jazz singer who had hits like *Broken Hearted Melody*, and died from lung cancer, aged 66 on April 3, 1990?

15. In what year were the following singles all No. 1's - *Things Can Only Get Better* - D:Ream; *Love Is All Around* - Wet Wet Wet and *Saturday Night* - Whigfield?

16. According to the Radiohead 1993 No.32 hit song, what can anyone do?

17. Which film soundtrack features R. Kelly's 1997 No. 1 hit, *I Believe I Can Fly*?

18. Frank Sinatra's final hit before his death in 1998 was a duet with Bono, *I've Got You Under My Skin*. It reached number four, but who wrote the song in 1936?

19. *The Boy is Mine* by Brandy & Monica a 1998 UK No. 2. How many weeks was the song at No.1 in the US?

20. Which boy band lined up with Chris Leng, Giles Kristian, Jamie Browne and Richard Micallef and had 4 Top 30 hits in 1996?

*90's **ANSWERS**: 1. Shirley Manson; 2. Barry White; 3. 5,6,7,8; 4. Drinking; 5. M People; 6. Objects In The Rear View Mirror May Appear Closer Than They Are; 7. Adamski; 8. Keith Washington; 9. 3 Lions (1998 version 3 Lions '98); 10. Stardust; 11. Mr. Blobby; 12. Blue; 13. Freddie Mercury; 14. Sarah Vaughan; 15. 1994; 16. Play guitar; 17. Space Jam; 18. Cole Porter; 19. 13 weeks; 20. Upside Down.*

JOHNNY AND THE HURRICANES were an American instrumental rock band from Toledo, Ohio, US. One of the most distinctive instrumental groups of the '50s and '60s, they specialised in adapting popular traditional melodies into the rock idiom, using organ and saxophone as their featured instruments. The musicians in the band were Johnny Paris (Saxophone); Paul Tesluk (Hammond Chord organ); Dave Yorko (Guitar); Lionel 'Butch' Mattice (Bass) and Bill 'Little Bo' Savich (Drums). The band had seven Top 40 hits in the UK, including four Top 10 hits. They also had two Top 20 albums.

1. Johnny & the Hurricanes were formed in Toledo in 1957. What was their original name? A) The Shadows B) The Ventures C) The Orbits

2. Johnny & the Hurricanes debut single reached number 23 in the US but failed to chart in the UK. What was its title? A) Crossfire B) Lazy C) Buckeye

3. A song written by Jules Verne Allen in the 1890s provided Johnny & the Hurricanes with their breakthrough in 1959, a number five UK hit. What was the title of the hit? A) You Are My Sunshine B) Red River Rock C) The Saints

4. "All right you guys, rise and shine", is the wake up command shouted at the start of which Johnny & the Hurricanes No.14 hit in 1959?

5. In 1960 Johnny & the Hurricanes had their first album hit with a No 18 success in the UK. What was the title of the album?
A) The Hep Canary B) Stormsville C) Juke Box Giants

6. *Jimmy Crack Corn* or *Blue Tail Fly*, a traditional American song got a Johnny & the Hurricanes makeover in 1960. What was the title of their version that reached number eight in the charts? A) The Grass is Greener B) Popcorn C) Beatnik Fly

7. In 1962, Johnny & the Hurricanes played at the Star-Club, Hamburg. Which UK band opened the show for them? A) Searchers B) Beatles C) Big Three

8. How many musicians did Johnny Paris say had played in the band during its fifty-year existence? A) More than 50 B) More than 100 C) More than 300

9. Which 1921 L. Wolfe Gilbert song did Johnny & the Hurricanes take to No. 8 in the UK in 1960? A) Down Yonder B) Ja-Da C) Old Smokie

10. Johnny & the Hurricanes had another No. 3 hit in the UK in 1960, on which Johnny created a memorable sax sound of a bird. What was the hit?
A) Rocking Goose B) Saturday Night at the Duckpond C) Blackbird

No.1's — WITH ONE WORD TITLES SOLVE THE ANAGRAMS!

1. La Rex (1983)
2. Eel vibe (1998)
3. Age mini (1980)
4. Rates (1965)
5. Ban Ewan (1996)
6. Beeps cartel (1987)
7. Nadia (1957)
8. Gail sin (1975)
9. Acne maps (1996)
10. Body finer (1998)

JOHNNY AND THE HURRICANES ANSWERS: 1. C) The Orbits; 2. A) Crossfire; 3. B) Red River Rock; 4. Reveille Rock; 5. B) Stormsville; 6. C) Beatnik Fly; 7. B) Beatles; 8. C) More than 300; 9. A) Down Yonder; 10. A) Rocking Goose. **NO.1's ONE WORD ANAGRAMS ANSWERS:** 1. Relax (Frankie Goes to Hollywood); 2. Believe (Cher); 3. Imagine (John Lennon); 4. Tears (Ken Dodd); 5. Wannabe (Spice Girls); 6. Respectable (Mel & Kim); 7. Diana (Paul Anka); 8. Sailing (Rod Stewart); 9. Spaceman (Babylon Zoo); 10. Boyfriend (Billie).

TOM JONES *(Sir Thomas Jones Woodward OBE - born Pontypridd, 7 June 1940), is a Welsh singer. Jones's voice has been described by AllMusic as a 'full-throated, robust baritone'. His performing range has included pop, R&B, show tunes, country, dance, soul and gospel. Was frontman for Tommy Scott and the Senators in 1963 before getting a recording contract with Decca. Jones has also occasionally dabbled in acting and made numerous TV appearances. Tom Jones had 31 Top 40 hits (1 reissue), including two number ones, 5 number twos and 9 more reached the Top 10. His albums were also successful with 23 Top 40 hits, including 3 No.1's and 10 more Top 10 successes.*

1. Tom's debut *Chills and Fever* failed, but *It's Not Unusual*, written by Les Reed & Gordon Mills got to UK number one in which year? A) 1963 B) 1965 C) 1967

2. Which James Bond theme song did Tom sing, and in what year?

3. Complete these Tom Jones lyrics: "Pussycat, pussycat, you're so thrilling, and I'm so willing to care for you. So go and make up your ...."
A) beautiful kitty eyes B) big little pussycat eyes C) cute little pussycat eyes

4. What 1967 hit song, written by Lonnie Donegan, was the first of three consecutive Tom Jones number two hits?
A) I'll Never Fall In Love Again B) I'm Coming Home C) Delilah

5. What was the name of Tom's ATV variety show which aired for 65 episodes from 1969 to 1971? A) Tom Jones Sings B) Along Came Jones C) This is Tom Jones

6. What country song, sold over a million copies, and gave Tom his second number one in 1966? A) Green, Green Grass of Home B) Detroit City C) Help Yourself

7. In 1988 Tom got together with the Art of Noise to record *Kiss*, a No. 5 hit. Who wrote the song? A) Michael Jackson B) Stevie Wonder C) Prince

8. In which 1996 film is Tom Jones music the only saviour for the human race; as it makes aliens' heads explode? A) Mars Attacks! B) Evolution C) Coneheads

9. Which 1999 Tom Jones duets album reached number one, and also spawned five hit singles with acts like The Stereophonics, Cerys Matthews and Mousse T?
A) Mr. Jones & Friends B) Reload C) The Two of Us

10. Which President invited Tom to sing at the 2000 millennium celebrations in Washington, DC? A) Bill Clinton B) George H.W. Bush C) George W. Bush

---

TILL
(by Carl Sigman & Charles Danvers)

TOM JONES

You are my reason to live
All I own I would give
Just to have you adore me

Till the moon deserts the sky
Till the all the seas run dry
Till then I'll worship you

Till the tropic sun grows cold
Till this young world grows old
My darling, I'll adore you

You are my reason to live
All I own I would give
Just to have you adore me

Till the rivers flow upstream
Till lovers cease to dream
Till then I'm yours, be mine

No. 5 for Tom Jones in 1971

TOM JONES ANSWERS: *1. B) 1965; 2. Thunderball, 1965; 3. B) big little pussycat eyes; 4. A) I'll Never Fall In Love Again; 5. C) This Is Tom Jones; 6. A) Green, Green Grass Of Home; 7. C) Prince; 8. A) Mars Attacks!; 9. B) Reload; 10. A) Bill Clinton.*

KC & THE SUNSHINE BAND *is an American disco and funk band, founded in Hialeah, Florida in 1973. The band took its name from singer Harry Wayne Casey's last name ('KC') and the 'Sunshine Band' from the state of Florida, the Sunshine State. The line up was: Casey (Lead Vocals), Richard Finch (Bass), Jerome Smith (Guitar), Robert Johnson(Drums). The band disbanded in 1985 but reformed in 1991. They had 10 Top 40 UK Singles, including one No.1 and three other Top 10 successes. Also two Top 40 albums, with one entering the Top 10.*

1. The first KC hit was a No. 7 in 1974. Complete the title:
A) Queen of Hearts   B) Queen of Clubs   C) Queen of Spades

2. On which 1974 No.17 hit did the horn section play a prominent role in the band's sound on a party song?
A) Sound Your Funky Horn   B) Get Down Tonight   C) Shake Your Booty

3. Complete the song title of the 1975 #4 hit for KC & The Sunshine Band: "That's the Way (. ....)   A) I Want It   B) I Like It   C) You Do It

4. From which 1976 #31 hit are these lyrics extracted: "Be it early morning late afternoon, Or at midnight it's never too soon, To want to please you…"?
A) Keep It Coming Love   B) I'm Your Boogie Man   C) I Like to Do It

5. The 1974 UK number one *Rock Your Baby* was written by KC. True or False?

6. KC & The Sunshine Band hit the top spot in 1983. Which song was UK No.1, but sometimes credited simply to KC?   A) Only You   B) Too Shy   C) Give It Up

7. The partnership between Richard Finch and KC came to an acrimonious end, in which year?   A) 1979   B) 1981   C) 1983

8. What was the name of KC & The Sunshine Band's 1975 album that included three hit singles; *That's the Way (I Like It)*; *Get Down Tonight* and *Boogie Shoes*?
A) The Sound of Sunshine   B) All In A Night's Work   C) KC & The Sunshine Band

9. For which film did KC receive Grammy Awards for Album of the Year and Producer of the Year in 1978?   A) Grease   B) Staying Alive   C) Saturday Night Fever

10. In 1978, KC & The Sunshine Band recorded a disco-based cover of which Four Tops hit as the lead off single for the band's *Who Do Ya (Love)* album?
A) It's the Same Old Song   B) Reach Out I'll Be There   C) Bernadette

EUROVISION MERGER!

Which two singing groups have been merged?

KC & THE SUNSHINE BAND ANSWERS: *1. B) Queen of Clubs; 2. A) Sound Your Funky Horn; 3. B) I Like It; 4. B) I'm Your Boogie Man; 5. True; 6. C) Give It Up; 7. B) 1981; 8. KC & The Sunshine Band; 9. C) Saturday Night Fever; 10. A) It's the Same Old Song.*
EUROVISION MERGER ANSWERS: *Brotherhood of Man and Bucks Fizz.*

THE KINKS were an English rock band formed in Muswell Hill, north London, in 1963. Original line up was Ray Davies (Rhythm guitar, lead vocals, keyboards), Dave Davies (Lead guitar, vocals), Mick Avory (Drums & percussion) and Pete Quaife (Bass). A really influential 1960s rock band, emerging during the height of British Rhythm and Blues & Merseybeat, briefly part of the UK Invasion of the US until their touring ban in 1965. The Kinks had 21 Top 40 hit singles, including three number ones and 10 more Top 10 hits. They also had 11 Top 40 albums with five of them reaching the Top 10.

1. The Kinks' first single was a cover of which Little Richard song that peaked at number 42 in the UK charts in 1964? A) I Got It B) Long Tall Sally C) Lucille

2. Which top session drummer played on a number of the early Kinks hits?
A) Bobby Graham B) Clem Cattini C) Brian Bennett

3. *You Really Got Me* was the third Kinks single and gave them a number one hit. What is the first word in the lyrics? A) Well B) Yeah C) Girl

4. Ray Davies wrote *Stop Your Sobbing*. Which band had a Top 40 hit with the song in 1979? A) The Pretenders B) Darts C) The Knack

5. At the Capitol Theatre, Cardiff in 1965, after finishing the first song, two Kinks had an on-stage fight, leaving which one unconscious, needing 16 stitches to his head?
A) Ray Davies B) Mick Avory C) Dave Davies

6. "The taxman's taken all my dough, and left me in my stately home...", is the beginning of which 1966 number one hit?
A) Dedicated Follower of Fashion B) Tired of Waiting For You C) Sunny Afternoon

7. Which 1969 concept album, featuring the songs *Victoria* and *Shangri-La* was written as a rock opera? A) Arthur (Or the Decline and Fall of the British Empire) B) The Kinks Are the Village Green Preservation Society C) Percy

8. The 1970 number two hit *Lola* was banned by the BBC because of the use of what brand in the lyrics? A) Coca-Cola B) Durex C) Viagra

9. Which 1965 No.10 hit is seen as the first example of sustained Indian-style drone in rock and the first pop song to evoke an Indian feel?
A) Till the End of the Day B) See My Friends C) Set Me Free

10. In 1966, Pete Quaife was involved in a car accident, and after recovering he decided to leave the band with John Dalton his official replacement. However, Quaife changed his mind and returned whilst Dalton went back to his former job as what?
A) Accountant B) Coalman C) Sound engineer

JOHNNY KIDD AND THE PIRATES recorded one of the best rock and roll songs of all time - Shakin' All Over; a Kidd penned number one hit in 1960. The line up was Johnny Kidd (vocals), Clem Cattini (drums), Alan Caddy (guitar) and Brian Gregg (bass). Joe Moretti played the memorable guitar intro and solo. The band also had five other Top 40 hits - Please Don't Touch; You Got What It Takes; Restless; I'll Never Get Over You and Hungry For Love. Johnny Kidd was tragically killed in a car crash in 1966. A new Pirate trio, Johnny Spence (bass), Frank Farley (drums) and Mick Green (lead guitar), made four albums, but were renowned for their live performances of raw rock and roll throughout the 80s and then the 90s.

THE KINKS ANSWERS: 1. B) Long Tall Sally; 2. A) Bobby Graham; 3. C) Girl; 4. A) The Pretenders; 5. C) Dave Davies (Avory hit him over the head with his hi-hat stand); 6. C) Sunny Afternoon; 7. A) Arthur (Or the Decline and Fall of the British Empire); 8. A) Coca-Cola (a violation of their policy against product placement - re-recorded and replaced by Cherry Cola); 9. B) See My Friends; 10. B) Coalman.

GLADYS KNIGHT AND THE PIPS were an American R&B/soul/funk family music group from Atlanta, Georgia, active on the music charts and performing circuit for over three decades. The line up on their first hits was Gladys Knight, brother Merald 'Bubba' Knight, William Guest and Edward Patten. The group had commercial success after signing with Motown Records in 1966. The group had eighteen Top 40 singles (four Top 10) and Gladys Knight had two further hits to her name, with one Top 10 hit. The group also had six Top 40 albums.

1. What is Gladys Knight's nickname?
A) The Voice   B) Empress of Soul   C) Queen of Soul

2. In what year did Gladys Knight and the Pips join Motown Records?
A) 1962   B) 1964   C) 1966

3. Gladys Knight & The Pips only hit in the 1960s was which No.13 in 1967?
A) Take Me In Your Arms And Love Me   B) Just Walk in My Shoes   C) Look of Love

4. Which 1976 UK Top 10 hit had won the 1974 Grammy Award for Best R&B Vocal Performance by a Duo, Group or Chorus and became Knight's signature song?
A) Midnight Train to Georgia   B) I Heard It Through the Grapevine   C) Look of Love

5. In 1989 Gladys Knight had a UK hit with a Bond theme which peaked at No.6. What was the Bond film?   A) Licence to Kill   B) GoldenEye   C) The Living Daylights

6. Gladys Knight & The Pips twice reached No. 4 in the UK. One hit was *The Way We Were - Try To Remember* in 1975, what was the other in 1977?
A) Part Time Love   B) Midnight Train to Georgia   C) Baby Don't Change Your Mind

7. In 1985 Gladys got together with Dionne Warwick, Elton John and Stevie Wonder to record a No.16 hit, *That's What Friends Are For*. Which charity benefited from the proceeds from the single?   A) Hands Across America   B) The American Foundation for Aids Research   C) Sport Aid

8. From which 1975 No. 7 hit are these lyrics extracted: "If anyone should ever write my life story, For whatever reason there might be, Oh, you'll be there between each line of pain and glory....."?   A) Look of Love   B) Home Is Where The Heart Is   C) Best Thing That Happened To Me

9. In what year were Gladys Knight & The Pips inducted into the Rock and Roll Hall of Fame?   A) 1993   B) 1996   C) 1999

10. In what year did Gladys Knight & The Pips leave Motown and sign with Buddah Records?   A) 1970   B) 1973   C) 1976

1) "Come let me love you, Let me give my life to you", is from whose song?
A) Linda's   B) Annie's   C) Kathy's

2) In 1993, who sang "But that was thirty years ago, when they used to have a show, Now it's a disco, but not for Lola" in a reissued song?

3) "And nobody does it better, Though sometimes I wish someone could"
A) Shania Twain   B) Lulu   C) Carly Simon

4) Who sung: "And you come to me on a summer breeze, Keep me warm in your love"?   A) Queen   B) Bee Gees   C) Bread

5) According to Deep Purple, if there is smoke in the water, what is in the sky?
A) Clouds   B) Lightning   C) Fire

GLADYS KNIGHT & THE PIPS ANSWERS: 1. B) Empress of Soul; 2. C) 1966; 3. A) Take Me In Your Arms And Love Me; 4. A) Midnight Train to Georgia; 5. A) Licence to Kill; 6. C) Baby Don't Change Your Mind; 7. B) The American Foundation for Aids Research; 8. C) Best Thing That Happened To Me; 9. B) 1996; 10. B) 1973.   *1970s LYRICS ANSWERS:* 1) B) Annie's; 2. Barry Manilow (Copacabana); 3.C) Carly Simon (Nobody Does it Better); 4. B) Bee Gees (How Deep Is Your Love); 5. C) Fire (Smoke on the Water).

KOOL & THE GANG *is an American R&B, soul, funk and disco band formed in Jersey City, New Jersey, in 1964 by brothers Robert 'Kool' Bell and Ronald Bell, with Dennis 'Dee Tee' Thomas, Robert 'Spike' Mickens, Charles Smith, George Brown, and Ricky West. They had numerous changes in personnel and explored many musical styles throughout their history, including jazz, soul, funk, disco, rock, and pop music. Kool & The Gang had 18 Top 40 hits, 7 of those reached the Top 10, also 4 Top 40 albums (2 Top 10).*

1. Kool & The Gang's first UK hit came in 1979, 15 years after they formed. What was the title of their No.9 hit? A) Ladies Night B) Too Hot C) Celebration

2. Kool & The Gang's first UK hit album in 1981 produced three hit singles, *Steppin' Out*, *Take My Heart* and *Get Down On It*. What was the title of the album?
A) Good Times B) Wild and Peaceful C) Something Special

3. Kool & the Gang contributed the song *Open Sesame* to which legendary film soundtrack in 1977? A) A Star is Born B) Saturday Night Fever C) Grease

4. In 1980, Kool & the Gang released one of their signature singles. This song is played in many US sporting arenas after a great victory. What is the name of this song? A) Celebration B) Take It To the Top C) Too Hot

5. In 1979, Kool & the Gang changed musical mood, and recorded a soulful ballad about a couple who married too young, and were struggling to maintain the passion in their marriage. What was the name of this song?
A) Too Tired B) Too Hot C) Too Young

6. *Do They Know It's Christmas* was a famous number one at Christmas 1984. Robert 'Kool' Bell was one of the participating artistes. True or False?

7. In 1984 Kool & The Gang performed at Wembley Stadium as part of who's *European Express Tour*? A) Elton John B) Queen C) Rod Stewart

8. George 'Funky' Brown, Robert 'Robbie G' Goble and Timothy Horton have all played which instrument as part of the Kool & The Gang line up?
A) Keyboards B) Guitar C) Drums

9. What role did Kool play in the band? A) Lead vocals B) Bass C) Saxophone

10. "Let's take a walk together near the ocean shore, Hand in hand you and I" begins which Kool & The Gang No. 4 hit from 1985? A) Fresh B) Cherish C) Victory

I KNOW A PLACE

HITS ABOUT LOCATIONS!

A) Which song was written and recorded by American singer Marc Cohn in 1990, but was more successful when covered by Cher in 1995?

B) The 1988 hit Kokomo by The Beach Boys is a fictional island. The song mentions which 5 real islands in the opening lyrics?

C) Which English city is named in the lyrics of Rotterdam by Beautiful South?

D) Which British city is named in the lyrics of ABBA's Super Trouper?

E) Which four cities are mentioned in the lyrics of M's Pop Muzik?

F) Which European capital was in song titles by Kenny Ball & His Jazzmen in 1961 and Michael Jackson in 1996?

*KOOL & THE GANG ANSWERS: 1. A) Ladies Night; 2. C) Something Special; 3. B) Saturday Night Fever; 4. A) Celebration; 5. B) Too Hot; 6. True; 7. A) Elton John; 8. C) Drums; 9. B) Bass; 10. B) Cherish. **I KNOW A PLACE ANSWERS:** A) Walking in Memphis; B) Aruba, Jamaica, Bermuda, Bahama, Key Largo; C) Liverpool; D) Glasgow; E) New York, London, Paris, Munich; F) Moscow (Midnight in Moscow and Stranger in Moscow).*

SO THE LAST SHALL BE FIRST, AND THE FIRST LAST.

Answer question one and the LAST letter of the answer will be the FIRST letter of answer 2 - and so on! Finally, the last letter of answer 20 will be the first letter of answer 1 to complete the circle!

1. Name the seventh letter in the title of Billy Connolly's 1975 number one hit.

2. His first number one was *All Shook Up* in 1957.

3. Name The Bluebells 1984 #8 hit, that became a #1 when it was re-issued in 1993.

4. Duane Eddy was *Deep in the Heart of* which US state in 1962?

5. Name the duo pictured right, who had five Top 15 hits between 1982 and 1990.

6. Name the Bobby Brown 1989 No. 4 hit that was the theme from *Ghostbusters II*.

7. What was the first name of Frank Sinatra's daughter with whom he had a No.1?

8. Who sung with The Plastic Population and told us *The Only Way Is Up* in 1988?

9. Fat Larry's Band had a number two with which song in 1982?

10. Mott The Hoople came *All The Way From* which US city in 1973?

11. What is both Status Quo and Neil Diamond's adjective to describe Caroline?

12. What was the title of Cliff Richard & Hank Marvin's No.7 hit in 1969?

13. In the early 60s, who had 5 Top 10 hits including *Well I Ask You* and *Boys Cry*?

14. What was the song from the Sound of Music that took Vince Hill to No. 2 in 1967?

15. Who was the Small Faces frontman who died in 1991 in a house fire, thought to have been caused by a cigarette?

16. Gene Pitney was only 24 hours from which Oklahoma city in 1963?

17. Who were the Welsh rock band fronted by Andy Fairweather Low?

18. Which Swedish pop rock duo comprised of Marie Fredriksson and Per Gessle?

19. Which Andrew Lloyd Webber & Trevor Nunn song did Elaine Paige take to No. 6?

20. In 1971 James Taylor had his only solo UK hit with which Carole King song?

Who had these hits from the 1970s?

A) Float On (1977)

B) The Night Chicago Died (1974)

C) Keep on Truckin' (1973)

D) Get Up and Boogie (That's Right) (1976)

E) Natural High (1973)

F) Nappy Love / Wild Thing (1975)

G) Wanted (1979)

H) Sorry I'm a Lady (1978)

J) Baker Street (1978)

K) That Same Old Feeling (1970)

SO THE LAST SHALL BE FIRST ANSWERS: 1. E (D.I.V.O.R.C.E); 2. Elvis Presley; 3. Young at Heart; 4. Texas; 5. Yazoo; 6. On Our Own; 7. Nancy; 8. Yazz; 9. Zoom; 10. Memphis; 11. Sweet; 12. Throw Down a Line; 13. Eden Kane; 14. Edelweiss; 15. Steve Marriott; 16. Tulsa; 17. Amen Corner; 18. Roxette; 19. Memory; 20. You've Got a Friend.
***WHO HAD THESE HITS IN THE 1970s? ANSWERS:** A) Floaters; B) Paper Lace; C) Eddie Kendricks; D) Silver Convention; E) Bloodstone; F) Goodies; G) Dooleys; H) Baccara: J) Gerry Rafferty: K) Pickettywitch.*

BILLY J. KRAMER AND THE DAKOTAS - *Liverpool singer Kramer (William Ashton) was paired with a Manchester band (The Dakotas) and had a string of hits under the management of Brian Epstein, including Lennon-McCartney songs. The band lined up with Mike Maxfield (lead guitar); Tony Mansfield, (drums); Ray Jones (bass); Robin MacDonald (rhythm). They had 6 Top 20 hits including 2 No.1's and three other Top 10 hits. They also registered a No. 11 album success. The Dakotas also had a Top 20 hit of their own.*

1. Billy's stage name Kramer was chosen at random from a telephone directory. Who suggested inserting the 'J' to add a "tougher edge" to the name?
A) Brian Epstein   B) George Martin   C) John Lennon

2. Billy J Kramer's first record was a track from The Beatles, *Please Please Me* album. Turned down by Shane Fenton what was the song that got to #2 in the UK?
A) I Saw Her Standing There   B) Do You Want To Know a Secret   C) Misery

3. Dakotas drummer Tony Mansfield (real name Tony Bookbinder) is the brother of Elaine Bookbinder. By what name is she more familiarly known?
A) Elkie Brooks   B) Barbara Dickson   C) Kiki Dee

4. Another Lennon-McCartney song gave Billy his first UK number one in 1963. What was the song that also appeared on The 1963 Beatles Bootleg Recordings?
A) Bad To Me   B) Twist and Shout   C) I Call Your Name

5. The Dakotas had a solo instrumental #18 hit of their own in 1963. What was the title of the hit written by lead guitarist Mike Maxfield?
A) Magic Carpet   B) The Cruel Sea   C) Oyeh

6. The Beatles *She Loves You* and Gerry & The Pacemakers *You'll Never Walk Alone* were the main reasons that Billy's third single in 1963, another Lennon-McCartney song was kept off the top. What was the song?
A) I'll Be On My Way   B) I Know   C) I'll Keep You Satisfied

7. In 1964 Billy got a second number one hit. Against most advisers, Billy turned down another Lennon-McCartney song, and opted for something different. What was the song that included phrases like "give you candy and a quarter"?
A) Twilight Time   B) Little Children   C) It's Gotta Last For Ever

8. A guitarist who played a pivotal role in developing British rock, although never a household name, joined The Dakotas in 1964. Who was the former Pirates guitarist?
A) Dave Gilmour   B) Joe Moretti   C) Mick Green

9. Billy J. Kramer and The Dakotas had a final Top 10 hit in 1964. What was the name of yet another another Lennon-McCartney song, on which Paul can be heard at the very end of the song, harmonising the final word?
A) From a Window   B) It's Gotta Last Forever   C) Big Jim Sullivan

10. Which Burt Bacharach song was turned down by Gene Pitney but was then a hit for both the writer and Billy J. Kramer in 1965 (his last hit!)?
A) The Look of Love   B) Don't Make Me Over   C) Trains and Boats and Planes

LITTLE CHILDREN
(Mort Shuman / J.l. McFarland)

Little children
You better not tell on me.
I'm tellin' you children
You better not tell what you see

And if you're good
I'll give you candy and a quarter
If you're quiet
Like you oughta be
And keep a secret with me......

BILLY J. KRAMER WITH THE DAKOTAS ANSWERS: *1. C) John Lennon; 2. B) Do You Want To Know a Secret; 3. A) Elkie Brooks; 4. A) Bad To Me; 5. B) The Cruel Sea; 6. C) I'll Keep You Satisfied; 7. B) Little Children; 8. C) Mick Green; 9. A) From a Window; 10. C) Trains and Boats and Planes.*

LENNY KRAVITZ *(Leonard Albert Kravitz, born May 26, 1964) is an American singer-songwriter, record producer, multi-instrumentalist, and later as an actor. Lenny is the son of actress Roxie Roker, his music style incorporates elements of rock, blues, soul, R&B, funk, jazz, reggae, hard rock, psychedelic, pop, folk, and ballads. After graduating from high school, Kravitz adopted a musical alter ego whom he called Romeo Blue, before switching to his own name. Lenny Kravitz had just 8 Top 40 singles in the 20th century, including a No.1 and one more Top 10 hit. He also had four Top 20 albums, including a No.1 and 3 more Top 10 hits.*

1. Lenny Kravitz UK breakthrough was in 1990 with a gold selling album. The title track reached #39 in the singles chart. What was the title of both single and album?
A) Let Love Rule   B) I Built This Garden For Us   C) Mr. Cab Driver

2. Actress Lisa Bonet directed Lenny's debut music video. What link did she have with Kravitz?   A) His manager   B) His wife   C) His sister

3. In May 1990, Lenny Kravitz performed which solo song at the John Lennon Memorial concert?   A) Imagine   B) Give Peace a Chance   C) Cold Turkey

4. Lenny Kravitz hit number 11 with his second single, taken from his second studio album *Mama Said* in 1991. What was the title of the track?
A) Fields of Joy   B) Stand By My Woman   C) It Ain't Over 'til It's Over

5. Lenny reached #4 with a hard rocking single that was the lead track of a 1993 #1 Kravitz album. The song was covered in various forms by Metallica, Tom Jones and Robbie Williams, and Mel B. What was the song title?
A) Believe   B) Heaven Help   C) Are You Gonna Go My Way

6. What BRIT International Award did Lenny Kravitz win in 1994?
A) Best male solo artist   B) Best album   C) Best song

7. In 1999 Kravitz had his first UK hit for 4 years - it was also his only No.1 hit. What was the song that featured in a Peugeot TV ad?
A) Rock and Roll is Dead   B) Fly Away   C) Heaven Help

8. On which David Bowie track did Lenny play guitar and get credited on the single which reached number 35 in 1993?
A) The Buddha of Suburbia   B) Dancing in the Street   C) Under Pressure

9. Which 1990 Madonna hit was written by Lenny Kravitz and Ingrid Chavez, with additional lyrics by Madonna?   A) Vogue   B) Hanky Panky   C) Justify My Love

10. Which Kravitz classic opens with these lyrics: "I was born long ago, I am the chosen, I'm the one, I have come to save the day, And I won't leave until I'm done"?

LENNY KRAVITZ ANSWERS: *1. A) Let Love Rule; 2. B) His wife; 3. C) Cold Turkey; 4. C) It Ain't Over 'til It's Over; 5. C) Are You Gonna Go My Way; 6. A) Best male solo artist; 7. B) Fly Away; 8. A) The Buddha of Suburbia; 9. C) Justify My Love; 10. Are You Gonna Go My Way.*

FRANKIE LAINE (born Francesco Paolo LoVecchio; March 30, 1913 – February 6, 2007) was an American singer, songwriter, and actor whose career spanned nearly 75 years. He sang well-known theme songs for many Western film soundtracks. Although his recordings were not charted as a country & western, Laine sang an eclectic variety of song styles and genres, stretching from big band crooning to pop, western-themed songs, gospel, rock, folk, jazz, and blues. Frankie Laine had 24 Top 40 hits between 1952 and 1959, either as a solo artist or with other acts, these included 4 No.1's and 15 other Top 10 hits. He also had two Top 10 albums.

1. Frankie Laine's first UK Top 10 hit in 1957 was *High Noon*. Ironically it was a Western film theme he did not perform on the soundtrack, so who sung the original?
A) Roy Rogers   B) Tex Ritter   C) Gene Autry

2. *Don't Make My Baby Blue* returned Frankie Laine to the US singles chart in 1963 after an absence of 6 years. The song was a hit in the UK, performed by which band, normally associated with instrumentals?   A) Shadows   B) Tornados   C) Fentones

3. Frankie Laine's first number one song was in 1953. It was subsequently covered by many artistes, and became a No. 2 for The Bachelors in 1964, and a No.1 for Robson & Jerome in 1995. What was the song?
A) Unchained Melody   B) You'll Never Walk Alone   C) I Believe

4. In 1953 Frankie Laine had two number ones, becoming the first artiste to have three number ones since charts began in 1952. One chart-topper was *Hey Joe*, what was the other?   A) Answer Me   B) Granada   C) Blowing Wild

5. In which 1955 No. 2 hit do these lyrics appear: "Keep a-movin', Dan, don't you listen to him, Dan, He's a devil, not a man..."?

6. Frankie Laine sang the theme song for the TV series *Champion the Wonder Horse*. True or False?

7. In 1957 Frankie had a double sided hit with *Good Evening Friends / Up Above My Head* ..... It was a duet sung with which other 50s star?
A) Perry Como   B) Tony Bennett   C) Johnnie Ray

8. Frankie played fading funnyman Danny Ross in 1959 in *The Case of the Jaded Joker*. This was an episode of which long-running TV series?
A) Perry Mason   B) Dr. Kildare   C) Dragnet

9. In 1959 Frankie Laine had his last hit single in the UK with the theme song from from which top TV Western series that starred Eric Fleming and Clint Eastwood?
A) Bonanza   B) Rawhide   C) Bronco

10. Which of these film themes did Frankie Laine NOT perform?
A) *True Grit*   B) *Gunfight at the O.K. Corral*   C) *Blazing Saddles*

CYNDI LAUPER *(Cynthia Ann Stephanie Lauper Thornton) (born Brooklyn, New York City on June 22, 1953) is an American singer, songwriter, actress, and activist. Lauper has sold over 50 million records worldwide and is known for her distinctive image, featuring a variety of hair colors and eccentric clothing, and for her powerful and distinctive four-octave singing range.In the early 1970s, Lauper performed as a vocalist with various cover bands. In 1978 saxophone player John Turi and Lauper formed a band named Blue Angel. When the band broke up, Lauper spent time working in retail stores, waitressing and singing in local clubs. Cyndi had 11 UK Top 40 hits, four of them reaching the Top 10 and four Top 40 albums, two of them Top 10 hits.*

1. What was the name of Cyndi Lauper's first album in 1984?
A) It's Not Unusual   B) She's So Unusual   C) Unusual Girl

2. What chart position did Lauper's single *Girls Just Wanna Have Fun* reach in the UK in 1984?   A) 1   B) 2   C) 3

3. Lauper's second single reached number one in the US, but peaked at #3 in the UK. What was the song?   A) Time After Time   B) True Colours   C) She Bop

4. In 1985, Lauper participated in which charity single to raise money for famine-relief?   A) Do They Know It's Christmas   B) We Are the World   C) One Big Family

5. What 1986 #12 hit opens with these lyrics: "You with the sad eyes, Don't be discouraged, Oh I realise, It's hard to take courage, In a world full of people..."?

6. Which Cyndi Lauper Top 10 hit in 1989 had been recorded by Roy Orbison two years earlier, but released posthumously in 1992, and then covered by Celine Dion in 2003?   A) Oh Pretty Woman   B) You Got It   C) I Drove All Night

7. In 1993, Lauper returned to acting, playing a ditsy secretary Geena Briganti, in *Life with Mikey*. Who was her boss in the film?
A) Michael J. Fox   B) Johnny Depp   C) Sean Penn

8. Which jazz legend featured Cyndi's song *Time After Time* on their 1985 album, *You're Under Arrest?*   A) Dizzy Gillespie   B) Ella Fitzgerald   C) Miles Davis

9. Which Marvin Gaye iconic R&B sociopolitical song did Cyndi Lauper cover on her *True Colors* album in 1986?
A) Sexual Healing   B) What's Going On   C) I Heard It Through the Grapevine

10. In 1989 Lauper had a No. 4 hit with a new reggae-tinged arrangement of which of her earlier hits?   A) Girls Just Wanna Have Fun   B) True Colors   C) Time After Time

MORE ONE HIT WONDERS

A) This Time	??????	1961
B) ??????	Ricky Valance	1960
C) Sorry (I Ran All the Way Home)	??????	1959
D) Popcorn	??????	1972
E) ??????	Jerry Keller	1959
F) ??????	B. Bumble & Stingers	1962
G) Ring My Bell	Anita Ward	????
H) Together We Are Beautiful	Fern Kinney	????
J) ??????	Doop	1994
K) I've Never Been To Me	??????	1982

Fill in the missing information!

CYNDI LAUPER ANSWERS: *1. B) She's So Unusual; 2. B) 2; 3. A) Time After Time; 4. B) We Are the World; 5. True Colours; 6. C) I Drove All Night; 7. A) Michael J. Fox; 8. C) Miles Davis; 9. B) What's Going On; 10. A) Girls Just Wanna Have Fun.* **MORE ONE HIT WONDERS ANSWERS:** *A) Troy Shondell; B) Tell Laura I Love Her; C) Impalas; D) Hot Butter; E) Here Comes Summer; F) Nut Rocker; G) 1979; H) 1980; J) Doop; K) Charlene.*

BRENDA LEE *(Brenda Mae Tarpley born Atlanta, Georgia on December 11, 1944), known professionally as Brenda Lee, is an American singer performing rockabilly, pop and country music. Lee achieved her biggest success on the pop charts in the late 1950s through the mid-1960s with rockabilly and rock and roll-styled songs, and she had even more hits with pop-based songs. During the early 1970s, Lee re-established herself as a country music artist. Lee was voted into the Rock and Roll Hall of Fame in 2002. Brenda Lee had 19 Top 40 hits in the UK singles charts, including 7 Top 10 hits. She also had 7 Top 40 albums, with one Top 10 success.*

1. Brenda Lee's first UK hit was a No. 4 in 1960. What was the song composed by Ronnie Self?   A) One Step At A Time   B) Dynamite   C) Sweet Nothin's

2. Brenda Lee's follow up single, *I'm Sorry*, was held back from release as Decca Records were concerned that a 15-year-old girl was not mature enough to sing about unrequited love. True or False?

3. Which Brenda Lee hit from 1959 includes these lyrics: "Goin' to Alabama back from Texarkana, Goin' all round the world..."?
A) Let's Jump the Broomstick   B) I Want To Be Wanted   C) Dum Dum

4. In 1962, while touring West Germany, she appeared at the famous Star-Club, Hamburg. Which band were the opening act?   A) Searchers   B) Beatles   C) Hollies

5. Which rock and roll legend composed a song about Brenda Lee and included it as the opening track on his 1964 *St. Louis to Liverpool* album?
A) Chuck Berry   B) Jerry Lee Lewis   C) Little Richard

6. As Brenda's Pop Chart success dwindled, she became popular on the US Country charts. Which 1974 single was her highest charting single on the Country charts?
A) Big Four Poster Bed   B) Rock On Baby   C) He's My Rock

7. Which 1980 film starring Burt Reynolds and an elephant, featured Brenda Lee in a minor role as Nice Lady?
A) Cannonball Run   B) Smokey and the Bandit   C) Smokey and the Bandit II

8. *Rockin' Around The Christmas Tree* was a No. 6 in the festive season in 1962. Who covered the song 25 years later and reached #3 in the UK charts?
A) Mel & Kim   B) Nancy and Lee   C) Peaches and Herb

9. Brenda's nickname is Little Miss Dynamite. How tall is she?
A) 135 cm   B) 145 cm   C) 155 cm

10. In 1964 Brenda Lee's only hit recorded in the UK reached No.17. Featuring Big Jim Sullivan, Jimmy Page and Bobby Graham and produced by Mickie Most, what was the title of the song?   A) Is It True   B) Think   C) As Usual

60s WORDS — NAME THE HITS

A) "Love was just a glance away, a warm embracing dance away"
B) "I've been havin' a sweet dream, I been dreamin' since I woke up today"
C) "Now if you feel that you can't go on"
D) "Don't know baby what a fool you've made out of me"
E) "High above the dawn is waiting, And my tears are falling rain"
F) "I had no choice but to hear you, You stated your case time and again"
G) "I'm dancing through the fire, Just to catch a flame"
H) "What you do, what you do, what you do to me, You're such a hot temptation!"
J) "So we're different colours and we're different creeds"
K) "Take a look at me, wire to a machine"

BRENDA LEE ANSWERS: *1. C) Sweet Nothin's; 2. True; 3. A) Let's Jump the Broomstick; 4. B) Beatles; 5. A) Chuck Berry; 6. A) Big Four Poster Bed; 7. C) Smokey and the Bandit II; 8. A) Mel and Kim; 9. B) 145 cm (about 4 foot 9 inches); 10. A) Is It True.* **60s WORDS ANSWERS:** *A) Strangers in the Night - Frank Sinatra; B) Daydream - Lovin' Spoonful; C) Reach Out, I'll Be There - Four Tops; D) Restless - Johnny Kidd & Pirates; E) The Carnival is Over - Seekers; F) Head Over feet - Alanis Morissette; G) You Do Something To Me - Paul Weller; H) Ride on Time - Black Box; J) People Are People - Depeche Mode; K) System Addict - Five Star.*

JOHN LENNON *(John Winston Ono Lennon, born Liverpool, John Winston Lennon; 9 October 1940 – 8 December 1980). An English singer, songwriter, musician and peace activist. Renowned globally as founder, co-songwriter, co-lead vocalist, rhythm guitarist of The Beatles. Songwriting partnership with Paul McCartney is the most successful in history. Formed the Quarrymen, which evolved into The Beatles in 1960. Post-Beatles had 16 Top 40 singles, inc 2 No.1's and 8 other Top 10 hits. Also 11 Top 40 albums, inc 3 No.1's and 6 more Top 10 hits. 1997 inducted to Songwriters Hall of Fame & Rock & Roll Hall of Fame twice (The Beatles 1988 & solo 1994). On 8 December 1980, Lennon was shot dead by fan Mark David Chapman outside The Dakota, New York.*

1. During the 1963 Royal Variety Show, Lennon poked fun at the audience. "For our next song, I'd like to ask for your help. For the people in the cheaper seats, clap your hands ... and the rest of you, if you'll just .... Complete the quote.

2. In March 1966, during an interview with *Evening Standard* reporter Maureen Cleave, Lennon caused a furore in the US when he remarked,that the Beatles were more popular than whom?

3. In which 1967 Richard Lester film does Lennon play Gripweed, the batman, to Lieutenant Ernest Goodbody (Michael Crawford)?
A) How I Won the War   B) Oh What a Lovely War   C) The Great Escape

4. At the end of 1968, Lennon participated in The Rolling Stones Rock and Roll Circus, a TV special that was not broadcast. Lennon performed with a supergroup, composed of himself, Eric Clapton, Keith Richards and Mitch Mitchell. What was the name of the supergroup?   A) Odds & Sods   B) The Dirty Mac   C) Silver Beatles

5. Lennon and Ono used their honeymoon as a Bed-In for Peace event that attracted worldwide media ridicule in March 1969. In which city was the Bed-In?
A) Paris   B) Amsterdam   C) London

6. In 1969, Lennon, and his wife Yoko Ono, formed the Plastic Ono Band. Their first single was which song, a #2 in the charts?
A) Cold Turkey   B) Give Peace a Chance   C) Instant Karma

7. Which President's administration tried to have Lennon deported in 1972?   A) Richard Nixon   B) Lyndon B. Johnson
C) Gerald Ford

8. "For the other half of the sky" are the spoken opening lyrics for which John Lennon & The Plastic Ono Band #1 from 1981?
A) Woman   B) (Just Like) Starting Over   C) Imagine

9. What was the final album that John Lennon released during his lifetime?
A) Milk and Honey   B) Rock 'n' Roll   C) Double Fantasy

10. What instrument is John Lennon holding on the cover of *Sgt Pepper's Lonely Hearts Club Band*?   A) Guitar   B) Triangle   C) French Horn

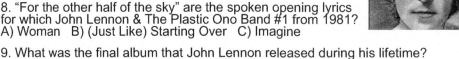

John Lennon's 'Imagine' piano on display at The Beatles Story, Liverpool

LEVEL 42 are an English jazz-funk band formed on the Isle of Wight in 1979. Level 42 were initially a jazz-funk fusion band but crossed over to sophisti-pop and dance-rock. Initial line up: Mark King (Lead vocals/bass, percussion); Mike Lindup (keyboards/falsetto vocals); Phil Gould (drums); Boon Gould (guitar, sax). Numerous personnel changes followed throughout the 80s and 90s. Level 42 had 19 Top 40 hits, including 6 Top 10 successes. They also had 11 Top 40 albums with 7 of them reaching the Top 10.

1. Which book inspired the name Level 42?
A) Dune   B) The Hitchhiker's Guide to the Galaxy   C) The Gutenberg Bible

2. Alongside Mark King, Mike Lindup, Boon Gould and Phil Guild, who was the band's unofficial fifth member, recording synthesizers and co-writing and producing tracks for the band from 1980 to 1994?
A) Wally Badarou   B) Sean Freeman   C) Dan Carpenter

3. Which was the first Level 42 single to reach the UK Top 40 singles chart, reaching #38 in 1981?   A) The Chinese Way   B) Micro Kid C) Love Games

4. Members of which Chicago-based pop, soul, and jazz-fusion band joined Level 42 to help in the recording of *Standing in the Light*, a Top 10 album in 1983?
A) Commodores   B) Ramsey Lewis   C) Earth, Wind & Fire

5. Prior to forming Level 42, Mark King and Phil Gould, (and Wally Badarou) all played with which pop project that had produced a 1979 No. 2 hit with Pop Muzik?
A) Magic Wands   B) M/A/R/R/S   C) M

6. *Lessons in* .... provided Level 42 with their biggest UK hit, a #3 in 1986?   A) Love   B) Life C) Piano

7. After touring with Madonna in 1987, the Gould brothers quit. Gary Husband (drums) and Alan Murphy (guitar) joined. In which band had Murphy previously found fame?
A) China Crisis   B) Go West   C) Living in a Box

8. Phil Gould returned to the band's drum-stool in 1994. Which album marked his return as in 1994?   A) Forever Now   B) True Colours   C) Staring at the Sun

9. **AERATE DUNG** is an anagram of which 1991 Level 43 No.17 hit?

10. Which major Level 42 hit from 1987 opens with these lyrics: "Our dad would send us to our room, He'd be the voice of doom, He said that we would thank him later, All day, he was solid as a rock…"?

TIME MOVES ON

Yesterday's Pop Stars Today!

| A) Come Back and Shake Me | B) Johnny Remember Me | C) Let's Get Together | D) Happy Birthday Sweet Sixteen | E) Puppet On A String |

MORE
BITS AND PIECES

An assortment of questions about all eras of popular music.

1. Who had a number one hit in the US at the age of 13 with the song *Fingertips (Part 2)*?

2. In a popular 1972 No. 2 hit by Dr. Hook, what is the first name of the young woman with the surname Avery?

3. Donna Summer was originally a backing singer with which popular US band, who had hits including *Joy To the World*?

4. Paul Mauriat Orchestra, Jeff Beck and The Dells all had 60s hits with which song?

5. *Bus Stop* by The Hollies, *No Milk Today* by Herman's Hermits and *For Your Love* by the Yardbirds were all hits written by which 10cc member?

6. Which 1965 Petula Clark UK and US No.1 was written by Tony Hatch?

7. Which rock band performed the first ever song on *Top Of The Pops* in 1964?

8. The original lineup of which US new wave band was: Fred Schneider (vocals, percussion), Kate Pierson (vocals, keyboards, synth bass), Cindy Wilson (vocals, percussion), Ricky Wilson (guitar), and Keith Strickland (drums, guitar, keyboards)?

9. What mode of transport did Jasper Carrot consider to be Funky in 1975?

10. "Are the stars out tonight? I don't know if it's cloudy or bright 'cause.....". Complete the line of lyrics from a 1975 Art Garfunkel hit.

11. In 1988, what was Tanita Tikaram's only UK Top 10 hit?

12. Which star of Aussie soap opera *Neighbours* had a No. 2 hit with *Mona* in 1988?

13. *The Goons*, stars of radio comedy, had three UK Top 10 hits. True or False?

14. What river did Pussycat take to number one in 1976?

15. As a singer he had no Top 40 hits. As a parliamentary candidate he holds the record for most seats contested (39). But his stage act was legendary. Who is this?

Q15

16. From which musical does the song *Love Changes Everything* originate?

17. Which was the first album released in 1973 on Richard Branson's Virgin label?

18. Who was the first Spice Girl to have a solo number one hit?

19. Which duo got to No. 2 in 1984 with *Agadoo*?

20. Which 'Queen of Rockabilly' had a hit with Elvis's *Let's Have a Party* in 1960?

MORE BITS AND PIECES ANSWERS: 1. (Little) Stevie Wonder; 2. Sylvia (Sylvia's Mother); 3. Three Dog Night; 4. Love Is Blue; 5. Graham Gouldman; 6. Downtown; 7.The Rolling Stones; 8. The B-52's (Love Shack etc); 9. Moped; 10. I Only Have Eyes For You; 11. Good Tradition; 12. Craig McLachlan; 13. True (I'm Walking Backwards to Christmas/ Bluebottle Blues and Bloodnok's Rock 'N' Roll Call/The Ying Tong Song in 1956 and a reissue of The Ying Tong Song in 1973; 14. Mississippi; 15. Screaming Lord Sutch (David Edward Sutch -10 November 1940 – 16 June 1999) ; 16. Aspects of Love; 17. Tubular Bells by Mike Oldfield; 18. Melanie B (I Want You Back in 1998); 19. Black Lace; 20. Wanda Jackson.

JERRY LEE LEWIS *(Born at Ferriday, Louisiana, September 29, 1935. Died at Nesbit, Mississippi, October 28, 2022) was an American singer, songwriter, and pianist. Nicknamed 'The Killer', he was rock n' roll's first great wild man and one of the most influential pianists of the 20th century. A pioneer of rock and roll and rockabilly music, Lewis made his first records in 1956 at Sun Records, Memphis. Lewis was inducted into the Rock and Roll Hall of Fame in 1986. Jerry Lee, the quintessential rock and roller, did not have the chart success for an artiste of his standing; just nine Top 40 hits, including a number one and three other Top 10 hits. He had only one Top 20 UK album.*

1. Jerry Lee Lewis left home and headed out to find a record company. Which famous producer at Sun Records took a gamble on his brash style of rock and roll?
A) Sam Phillips   B) Ralph Bass   C) Leonard Chess

2. In 1958, 22 year old Lewis's tour of the UK was cancelled after just 3 concerts when facts came to light about his new wife Myra Gale Brown. How old was she?
A) 16   B) 14   C) 13

3. Jerry Lee's first UK hit was with a song first recorded by Big Maybelle. What was the title of the 1957 No. 8 hit that Lewis had radically altered from the original?
A) Breathless   B) High School Confidential   C) Whole Lotta Shakin' Goin' On

4. Jerry Lee Lewis hit No. 1 in the UK at Christmas,1957. The song started with these lyrics: "You shake my nerves and you rattle my brain, Too much love drives a man insane…". What was the classic rock and roll song?
A) Roll Over Beethoven   B) Great Balls of Fire   C) Good Golly Miss Molly

5. In 1972 Jerry Lee Lewis made his final appearance in the UK charts with *Chantilly Lace*. Who wrote the song and had the original hit with it in 1959?
A) The Big Bopper   B) Buddy Holly   C) Ritchie Valens

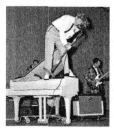

6. In 1976, Jerry Lee Lewis was arrested at the home of a rock and roll legend for being drunk and wielding a gun. At whose home was he trespassing?
A) Elvis Presley   B) Chuck Berry   C) Little Richard

7. In the 1989 biographical movie *Great Balls of Fire* about Lewis's life. Which actor played the role excellently, but mimed to Jerry Lee's vocals?
A) Nick Nolte   B) Dennis Quaid   C) Gary Busey

8. Jerry Lee Lewis has been married eight times, including bigamous marriages and a marriage with his underage cousin. True or False?

9. One major success during the lost years in the sixties was a concert album *Live at the Star Club, Hamburg*, considered one of the greatest live albums ever. With which UK band did Jerry Lee record the album?
A) Nashville Teens   B) Sounds Incorporated   C) The Faces

10. Which Ray Charles written classic, that the blind singer always sung to close his concerts, was covered by Jerry Lee and gave him his final Top 10 hit in 1961?
A) Hit the Road Jack   B) Sticks and Stones   C) What'd I Say

JERRY LEE LEWIS ANSWERS: *1. A) Sam Phillips; 2. C) 13; 3. C) Whole Lotta Shakin' Goin' On; 4. B) Great Balls of Fire; 5. A) The Big Bopper; 6. A) Elvis Presley; 7. B) Dennis Quaid; 8. False (it was 7 times!); 9. A) Nashville Teens; 10. C) What'd I Say.*

LITTLE RICHARD (*Richard Wayne Penniman - December 5, 1932 – May 9, 2020*), *was a US musician, singer, and songwriter. He was an influential figure in popular music and culture for seven decades. The 'Architect of Rock and Roll', his most celebrated work dates from the mid-1950s. His charismatic showmanship, dynamic music, frenetic piano playing, pounding back beat and raspy shouted vocals, laid foundations for R 'n' R. One of the initial inductees into the Rock and Roll Hall of Fame in 1986. Little Richard notched up just 15 Top 40 singles, including 5 Top 10 hits, but he influenced numerous singers and musicians across musical genres from rock to hip hop and shaped rhythm and blues for generations.*

1. What song achieved Little Richard's highest singles chart position in the UK?
A) Long Tall Sally   B) Tutti Frutti   C) Baby Face

2. When Little Richard was young, he loved the Pentecostal church because of their charismatic worship and live music. He sang loudly and earned what nickname?
A) War Hawk   B) Thunder Horse   C) The Screamer

3. What did Little Richard join immediately after leaving school in 1949?
A) The Army   B) Dr. Hudson's Medicine Show, a travelling show   C) The Navy

4. In October 1962, Little Richard played two gigs in the north of England. Who were the supporting band?   A) The Rolling Stones   B) The Beatles   C) The Animals

5. In 1964, Granada Television recorded a Little Richard special TV show that was was a ratings hit, receiving 60,000 fan letters and was rebroadcast twice. What was the show's title?   A) The Little Richard Revue   B) The Little Richard Spectacular C) The Little Richard Extravaganza

6. What No. 8 hit from 1958 contains these lyrics: "I'm going to the corner, Gonna buy a diamond ring, When she hug me and kiss me, Make me ting-a-ling-a-ling…"?

7. Late in 1964, which guitarist joined Richard's Upsetters band as a full member?
A) Stevie Ray Vaughan   B) Eric Clapton   C) Jimi Hendrix

8. What 1986 film featured Little Richard as Orvis Goodnight and featured the Billy Preston / Little Richard penned song *Great Gosh A'Mighty! (It's a Matter of Time)*?
A) Peggy Sue Got Married   B) Crazy People   C) Down and Out in Beverly Hills

9. **BEETHOVEN FLIRTISH MYTHOLOGY** is an anagram of a 1959 hit for Little Richard. Can you work out the title of the No. 17 hit? (2,3,5,2,3,7,4)

10. Little Richard sang a duet on the title song of the film *Twins* starring Arnold Schwarzenegger and Danny DeVito. With whom did he sing the duet?
A) Stevie Wonder   B) Phillip Bailey   C) B.B. King

NUMBER 2 HITS OF THE 1960s

10 hits to peak at No. 2 in the UK in the 1960s. Match the songs to the correct singers

1. Everybody Knows	A) Bobby Darin
2. Oh Well	B) Vikki Carr
3. My Boy Lollipop	C) Bruce Channel
4. It Must Be Him	D) Dave Clark 5
5. Lazy River	E) Millie
6. Hey! Baby	F) Cliff Richard
7. It's All in the Game	G) John Leyton
8. Downtown	H) Billy Fury
9. Wild Wind	J) Fleetwood Mac
10. Jealousy	K) Petula Clark

LITTLE RICHARD ANSWERS: 1. C) Baby Face (No. 2 in 1959); 2. A) War Hawk; 3. B) Dr. Hudson's Medicine Show, a travelling show; 4. B) The Beatles; 5. B) The Little Richard Spectacular; 6. Good Golly Miss Molly; 7. C) Jimi Hendrix; 8. C) Down and Out in Beverly Hills; 9. By the Light of the Silvery Moon; 10. B) Phillip Bailey. **NUMBER 2 HITS OF THE 1960s ANSWERS:** *1D; 2J; 3E; 4B; 5A; 6C; 7F; 8K; 9G; 10H.*

LULU (Lulu Kennedy-Cairns CBE (born Marie McDonald McLaughlin Lawrie in Lennoxtown, Stirlingshire, she grew up in Dennistoun, Glasgow. Lulu is a Scottish singer, actress and TV personality, noted for a powerful singing voice. Backed by The Luvvers from 1964-66, her pop career in the UK thrived. She had several TV series of her own and was internationally known. In 1969, she controversially won the Eurovision Song Contest for the UK. In 1974, she sung the only James Bond title song not to chart. Lulu won the Rear of the Year award in 1983. Including collaborations, she has notched up 18 Top 40 singles, including a number one and nine other Top 10 hits. Before 2000 she had recorded just one Top 20 album.

1. Lulu's fist hit was *Shout*, a No. 6 hit in 1964. The song was written and originally recorded in 1959 by which American vocal group?
A) Isley Brothers   B) Four Seasons   C) Bee Gees

2. Lulu's third Top 10 hit came in 1967 with *The Boat That I Row*. Who wrote the song?   A) Barry Manilow   B) Neil Diamond   C) Billy Joel

3. In 1967, Lulu appeared in a film that dealt with social and racial issues in an inner city school. She also sung the theme for which film which reached No. 1 in the US?
A) Beyond the Blackboard   B) To Sir With Love   C) Angela's Ashes

4. Lulu represented the United Kingdom in the 1969 Eurovision Song Contest singing *Boom Bang-a-Bang*. She was one of four countries who tied for the crown in a remarkable contest. Name the other three countries who shared the victory?

5. In 1974, for which James Bond film did Lulu perform the only title track not to enter the charts in either the UK or the US?
A) Casino Royale   B) The Spy Who Loved Me   C) The Man With the Golden Gun

6. Which Bee Gee did Lulu marry in 1969?
A) Maurice Gibb   B) Barry Gibb   C) Robin Gibb

7. In 1974 she covered a David Bowie song *The Man Who Sold the World*. Bowie and Mick Ronson produced the recordings and Bowie sung backing vocals and played which instrument on the No. 3 hit?   A) Piano   B) Guitar   C) Saxophone

8. Into the eighties, on TV, who did Lulu replace as Adrian Mole's mother in *The Secret Diary of Adrian Aged 13¾*?
A) Victoria Wood   B) Dawn French   C) Julie Walters

9. In 1993, the song *I Don't Wanna Fight*, co-written by Lulu with her brother Billy Lawrie and Steve DuBerry, became an international hit for which singer?
A) Cher   B) Tina Turner   C) Barbra Streisand

10. Also in 1993 Lulu guested on a cover version of the Dan Hartman song *Relight My Fire*. The single reached No.1 in the UK. With which boy band did Lulu have the hit and also guest on their nationwide tour?   A) Take That   B) Westlife   C) 5ive

FIVE CLUES TO NAME A MUSIC LEGEND FROM THE 50s/60s
THE QUICKER YOU IDENTIFY THE MORE POINTS YOU WIN

5 POINTS - *Played with many musical groups like His Harlem Hotshots and Blue Cumberland Rhythm Boys*

4 POINTS - *born in Burges Road, East Ham, London*

3 POINTS - *He was awarded an OBE for his contributions to music*

2 POINTS - *first British guitarist to have a hit in the UK Singles Chart*

1 POINT - *His best-selling tutorial guides, Play in a Day, influenced many leading British guitarists including Eric Clapton*

LULU ANSWERS: *1. A) Isley Brothers; 2. B) Neil Diamond; 3. B) To Sir With Love; 4. Spain, Netherlands, France; 5. C) The Man With the Golden Gun; 6. A) Maurice Gibb; 7. C) Saxophone; 8. C) Julie Walters; 9. B) Tina Turner; 10. A) Take That.*
WHO AM I? ANSWER: *Bert Weedon.*

M PEOPLE is an English dance music band that formed in 1990 and achieved success throughout the 1990s. The name M People is taken from the first initial of band member Mike Pickering, who formed the group. In December 2016. The members of the band from 1990 - present: Heather Small (born London 20 January 1965) – vocals); Mike Pickering (born Manchester 24 February 1958) – keyboards, programming); Paul Heard (born London 5 October 1960 – keyboards, programming); Shovell (born Andrew Lovell, SE London February 1969 – percussion (from 1992). M People had 20 Top 40 hits between 1991 and 1999, 10 of them reaching the Top 10. They also had 5 Top 40 albums, 3 reaching No. 2 and another No.3.

ANAGRAMS OF M PEOPLE HITS

1. No. 29 in 1991 **COLOURMEN VIEW YAHOO**

2. No. 35 in 1992 **COOLLY FUMIER**

3. No. 39 in 1992 **ODES YAM**

4. No. 29 in 1992 **ICED TEX**

5. No. 6 in 1993 **AVON HIGH NINETEEN**

6. No. 2 in 1993 **IMPUGN NOVO**

7. No. 9 in 1993 **ALOOF THORNY TRUNKED**

8. No. 5 in 1994 **ANNIE CARESS**

9. No. 31 in 1994 **CAMERA INELEGANTLY**

10. No. 6 in 1994 **EEYORE GROSS SHIFT**

11. No. 9 in 1995 **PYORRHOEA TUNE**

12. No. 9 in 1995 **FORESHORE HATCHER**

13. No. 32 in 1995 **DEVON LOVER ZEUS**

14. No.11 in 1995 **COCKPIT HOARY**

15. No. 8 in 1996 **AUXOCHROME OMNIVORE WILEY**

16. No. 8 in 1997 **JOYOUS TURF**

17. No. 33 in 1997 **FANTAILS SANDY**

18. No. 8 in 1998 **AGNES LETTER**

19. No.12 in 1998 **FIST YET**

20. No.13 in 1999 **DIM ANGER**

SEARCH FOR THE HERO
(Paul Heard / Mike Pickering)
You've got to search for the hero inside yourself
Search for the secrets you hide
Search for the hero inside yourself
Until you find the key to your life

BONEY M ANSWERS: 1. How Can I Love You More; 2. Colour My Life; 3.Someday; 4.Excited; 5. One Night In Heaven; 6. Moving On Up; 7. Don't Look Any Further; 8. Renaissance; 9. Elegantly American; 10. Sight For Sore Eyes; 11. Open Your Heart; 12. Search For The Hero; 13. Love Rendezvous; 14. Itchycoo Park; 15. How Can I Love You More (remix); 16. Just For You; 17.Fantasy Island; 18. Angel Street; 19.Testify; 20. Dreaming.

PAUL McCARTNEY *(Sir James Paul McCartney CH MBE born Liverpool, 18 June 1942) is an English singer, songwriter, and musician famous initially as co-lead vocalist, co-songwriter, and bassist for the Beatles. One of the most successful composers and performers of all time. Known for his melodic bass-playing, versatile and wide tenor vocal range, and musical eclecticism, exploring styles ranging from pre-rock 'n' roll pop to classical and electronica. His songwriting partnership with John Lennon remains the most successful in history. Post Beatles he had 43 Top 40 singles before 2000, including 4 number ones and 20 other Top 10 hits. He also had 27 Top 40 albums, including 6 No. 1's and 13 more reached the Top 10.*

1. Which of these stars did not feature on the cover of Wings' 1973 album, *Band on the Run*?   A) Christopher Lee B) Sean Connery C) Kenny Lynch C) James Coburn

2. With whom has Paul McCartney not released a hit duet?
A) Stevie Wonder   B) Michael Jackson   C) Elton John

3. On which 1989 No.1 charity song did McCartney appear with the Christians, Holly Johnson, Gerry Marsden and Stock Aitken Waterman?
A) Ferry 'Cross The Mersey   B) Do They Know It's Christmas   C) Help!

4. McCartney duetted with Michael Jackson on the 1982 hit *The Girl is Mine*. What was the title of their hit the following year?
A) Say Say Say   B) Ebony and Ivory   C) We All Stand Together

5. With whom did Paul co-write his 1989 No. 18 hit *My Brave Face*?
A) George Harrison   B) Elvis Costello   C) Billy Joel

6. McCartney's first major foray into classical music came with the release of an album written with conductor Carl Davis and featured the Royal Liverpool Philharmonic Orchestra & Choir in 1991. What was the album?
A) Paul McCartney's Liverpool Oratorio   B) Standing Stone   C) Working Classical

7. A 1999 album *Run Devil Run*, features familiar and obscure 1950s rock and roll songs. Which Deep Purple member was featured together with Mick Green, Dave Gilmour and Pete Wingfield?   A) Ritchie Blackmore   B) Ian Paice   C) Jon Lord

8. In 1971, what was the first single release of McCartney's solo career?
A) Jet   B) Coming Up   C) Another Day

9. What is the subject of the 1973 Wings No. 12 hit, *Helen Wheels*?
A) Paul & Linda's Land Rover   B) Helen Mirren   C) A London Bus

10. Which McCartney 1983 No.1 featured the Pestalozzi Children Choir with Paul singing, playing bass, piano, knee-percussion and drums and writing the orchestra arrangements?   A) Mull of Kintyre   B) Pipes of Peace   C) We All Stand Together

PAUL McCARTNEY ANSWERS: *1. B) Sean Connery; 2. C) Elton John; 3. A) Ferry 'Cross the Mersey; 4. A) Say Say Say; 5. B) Elvis Costello; 6. A) Paul McCartney's Liverpool Oratorio; 7. B) Ian Paice; 8. C) Another Day; 9. A) Paul & Linda's Land Rover; 10. B) Pipes of Peace.*

MADNESS are an English ska band from Camden Town, North London, who formed in 1976. A prominent band in the late 1970s and early 1980s two-tone ska revival. Formed as the North London Invaders. Most familiar line up: Mike Barson (Monsieur Barso) - keyboards / vocals, Chris Foreman (Chrissy Boy) - guitar, Lee Thompson (Kix) - saxophone and vocals, Dan Woodgate (Woody) - drums, Mark Bedford (Bedders) - bass guitar, Graham McPherson (Suggs) - lead vocals. Madness recorded 26 Top 40 hits, including a number one and 16 other Top 10 hits. Madness also had 12 Top 40 albums, including 2 No. 1's and 5 other Top 10 hits.

1. The first Madness hit, *The Prince*, reached No. 16 in 1979. To whom did the song pay homage?   A) Prince Charles   B) Prince Buster   C) Prince Philip

2. The 1984 No. 4 hit *It Must Be Love* was originally a hit for the song's writer, Labi Siffre in 1971. What chart position did Labi Siffre's version reach in the UK?
A) 1   B) 4   C) 14

3. What album title song started a sequence of nine consecutive Top 10 hits for Madness from 1979 to 1981?   A) One Step Beyond   B) My Girl   C) Baggy Trousers

4. Madness made two guest appearances on the BBC comedy *The Young Ones*, performing *House of Fun* in the first season episode *Boring*, and *Our House* in the second season episode *Sick*?   True or False?

5. "Mother has to iron his shirt then she sends the kids to school. Sends them off with a small kiss. She's the one they're going to miss in lots of ways." Lyrics from which 1982 Madness hit?

6. Which film star's name was the title of a No.11 Madness hit from 1984?
A) Grace Kelly   B) Michael Caine   C) Bette Davis

7. In 1978 to what name did Madness briefly change their name?
A) Morris and the Minors   B) The Invaders   C) Sanity

8. What was the name of the weekend festival held at Finsbury Park, London in August 1992, attended by over 75,000 fans that saw Madness reunited?
A) Crunch!   B) The Return Of The Los Palmas Seven   C) Madstock!

9. In 1982, Madness reached #1 in the album charts with their first compilation. What was its title?   A) Complete Madness   B) It's Madness   C) Utter Madness

10. Suggs made his solo debut in the UK charts in 1995 with a double sided hit. *Off On Holiday* was one side, but which song from a Beatles album was on the 'A' side?
A) Tomorrow Never Comes   B) I'm Only Sleeping   C) I Want To Tell You

---

ALL SORTS!

1. Who sang This Time (We'll Get it Right) in 1982?

2. Which Elvis song opens with "Wise men say only fools rush in"?

3. Joy Division, The Hollies and James all come from which UK city?

4. Which Irish band were formerly known as Feedback and The Hype?

5. The biggest-selling single of 1993 was which Meat Loaf No. 1?

6. Which artist designed the 1967 Velvet Underground album cover?

7. In which year were Michael Jackson, Prince and Madonna all born?

8. What do the initials PJ stand for in PJ Harvey's name?

9. Which 1960s US festival was billed as an 'Aquarian Exposition?

10. What is the full title of David Bowie's Ziggy Stardust album?

MADNESS ANSWERS: 1. B) Prince Buster; 2. C) 14; 3. A) One Step Beyond; 4. True; 5. Our House; 6. B) Michael Caine; 7. A) Morris and the Minors; 8. C) Madstock!; 9. A) Complete Madness; 10. B) I'm Only Sleeping. **HODGEPODGE ANSWERS:** *1. England World Cup Squad; 2. Can't Help Falling in Love; 3. Manchester; 4. U2; 5. The biggest-selling single of 1993; 6. Andy Warhol; 7. 1958; 8. Polly Jean; 9. Woodstock; 10. The Rise and Fall of Ziggy Stardust and the Spiders from Mars.*

MADONNA (*Madonna Louise Ciccone; born Bay City, Michigan, August 16, 1958*) *is an American singer-songwriter and actress. Very influential and often referred to as the 'Queen of Pop'. Madonna has continually reinvented herself. Madonna has been versatile in music production, songwriting, and visual presentation, she has pushed the boundaries of artistic expression in mainstream music, while totally controlling every aspect of her career. Her work has incorporated social, political, sexual, and religious themes. She has been controversial and critically acclaimed too. Between 1984 and 1999, Madonna had 52 Top 40 singles, including 8 No. 1's and 40 other Top 10 successes. Madonna also had 12 Top 10 albums including 6 No. 1's.*

1. Madonna won a Golden Globe for Best Actress for her part in which 1996 film?
A) Evita   B) Dick Tracy   C) A League of Their Own

2. Which of the following famous Hollywood names is not included in the lyrics of Madonna's 1990 No. 1 hit *Vogue*?
A) Rita Hayworth   B) Ginger Rogers   C) Joan Crawford

3. For which 1987 music video did Madonna dress as a Geisha Girl?
A) True Blue   B) La Isla Bonita   C) Who's That Girl

4. "It won't be easy, You think it's strange, When I try to explain how I feel". Opening lyrics to which 1996 #3 hit, written by Tim Rice & Andrew Lloyd-Webber?
A) Another Suitcase, Another Hall   B) Don't Cry For Me Argentina   C) Memory

5. Who sang backing vocals on the 1994 hit *Take A Bow*, a rare Madonna track not to make the Top 10 in the UK?   A) Michael Jackson   B) Babyface   C) Prince

6. What song provided Madonna's breakthrough in 1984, reaching number six?
A) Material Girl   B) Like a Virgin   C) Holiday

7. The 1990 No. 2 hit *Justify My Love* was written by Madonna and which rock star?
A) Lenny Kravitz   B) Jon Bon Jovi   C) Prince

8. Which of Madonna's music videos for a 1989 No. 5 hit is animated, and does not feature Madonna in person?   A) Look of Love   B) Dear Jessie   C) Into The Groove

9. A) From what controversial 1993 album was the No. 6 hit single *Fever* taken, and B) Who had sung the song originally?

10. Madonna's Christmas 1998 hit was a double sided success. *The Power Of Good-Bye* was on one side, and the B side was dedicated to her daughter Lourdes. What was the song's title?   A) Little Star   B) Nothing Really Matters   C) Beautiful Stranger

1. RAY DAVIES	A. ARCTIC MONKEYS
2. CHRIS MARTIN	B. SPANDAU BALLET
3. MIKE SMITH	C. MUSE
4. TONY HADLEY	D. SIMPLY RED
5. MICK HUCKNALL	E. JOY DIVISION
6. IAN CURTIS	F. ABC
7. ALEX TURNER	G. KINKS
8. MATTHEW BELLAMY	H. MANIC STREET PREACHERS
9. MARTIN FRY	J. DAVE CLARK FIVE
10. JAMES DEAN BRADFIELD	K. COLDPLAY

MADONNA ANSWERS: *1. A) Evita; 2. C) Joan Crawford; 3. B) La Isla Bonita; 4. B) Don't Cry For Me Argentina; 5. B) Babyface; 6. C) Holiday; 7. A) Lenny Kravitz; 8. B) Dear Jessie; 9. A) Erotica; B) Peggy Lee; 10. A) Little Star.* **MORE LEAD SINGERS ANSWERS:** *1G; 2K; 3J; 4B; 5D; 6E; 7A; 8C; 9F; 10H.*

MANFRED MANN were an English rock band, formed in London and active between 1962 and 1969. Named after their keyboardist Manfred Mann, followed by successful 1970s group Manfred Mann's Earth Band. The band had two different lead vocalists, Paul Jones (1962 -1966) and Mike d'Abo (1966 -1969) and the early line-up was: Mike Hugg (drums); Tom McGuinness (bass); Mike Vickers (guitar). Manfred Mann had 17 Top 40 singles, including 3 No. 1's and 10 more Top 10 hits and Manfred Mann's Earth Band had 3 Top 10 hits. Manfred Mann also had 10 Top 40 albums, four of them making the Top 10.

1. Where was the band founder, Manfred Mann, born?
A) Germany   B) South Africa   C) Scotland

2. Manfred Mann's 1964 hit *5-4-3-2-1* became the theme tune for which ITV pop music show?   A) Ready Steady Go!   B) Oh Boy!   C) Discs-A-Gogo

3. Manfred Mann had three number one records, Paul Jones sung lead vocal on *Do Wah Diddy* and *Pretty Flamingo*, but on which song did Mike d'Abo sing the lead?
A) Semi-Detached Suburban Mr James   B) Ha Ha Said the Clown   C) Mighty Quinn

4. What links these three Manfred Mann hits: *The Mighty Quinn, Just Like a Woman* and *If You Gotta Go, Go Now*?

5. Which former Manfred Mann bassist formed a band who had two hits in the early seventies with *When I'm Dead and Gone* and *Malt and Barley Blues*?

6. Paul Jones converted to Christianity in the mid-1980s as a result of being invited by Cliff Richard to a Luis Palau evangelistic event. True or False?

7. 'She walked through the corn leading down to the river, her hair shone like gold in the hot morning sun. She took all the love that a poor boy could give her, and left me to die like the….. Complete these lyrics with the song title of a 1968 hit.
A) Sweet Pea   B) Ragamuffin Man   C) Fox On the Run

8. The debut album from Manfred Mann in 1964 featured R&B classics like *Smokestack Lightning* and *Got My Mojo Working*. What was the album's title?
A) The Five Faces of Manfred Mann   B) Mann Made   C) Soul of Mann

9. In 1968, the Manfred Mann–Mike Hugg composed the soundtrack to a highly successful UK kitchen sink film. However, the title track was an unsuccessful single for the band. Name the film.   A) Poor Cow   B) Up the Junction   C) A Kind of Loving

10. Of their last UK 11 hit singles, only one failed to hit the Top 10, an instrumental version of which Tommy Roe song?   A) Sheila   B) Dizzy   C) Sweet Pea

I SPY ACTS BEGINNING WITH THE LETTER ....

A   B   C   D

*MANFRED MANN ANSWERS: 1. B) South Africa; 2. Ready Steady Go!; 3. C) Mighty Quinn; 4. All songs were written by Bob Dylan; 5. Tom McGuinness (McGuinness Flint); 6. True; 7. C) Fox On the Run; 8. A) The Five Faces of Mann; 9. B) Up the Junction; 10. C) Sweet Pea. **I SPY ACTS BEGINNING WITH S ANSWERS:** A) The Stargazers; B) Sade C) Shakatak; D) Shakespears Sister.*

172

MANIC STREET PREACHERS *also known simply as the Manics, are a Welsh rock band formed in Blackwood in 1986. The band consists of cousins James Dean Bradfield (lead vocals, lead guitar) and Sean Moore (drums, percussion, soundscapes), Nicky Wire (bass guitar, lyrics). Richey Edwards (Rhythm guitar, lyrics). Edwards disappeared in February 1995 and was legally presumed dead in 2008. The Manic Street Preachers have headlined festivals including Glastonbury, T in the Park, V Festival and Reading. The Manics had 22 Top 40 hit singles between 1991 and 1999, including a No.1 and 6 other Top 10 hits. They also had 5 Top 20 albums with one No. 1 and 3 more Top 10 successes.*

1. In 1992, what is the name of the first album released by the Manics?
A) The Holy Bible   B) Generation Terrorists   C) Know Your Enemy

2. James Dean Bradfield sung which track with Tom Jones on Tom's duets album *Reload* in 1999?   A) Are You Gonna Go My Way   B) Burning Down the House
C) I'm Left, You're Right, She's Gone

3. What was the title of the only 20thC Manic Street Preachers song to reach #1 in the UK?   A) Theme From M.A.S.H. (Suicide Is Painless)   B) If You Tolerate This Your Children Will Be Next   C) A Design For Life

4. Since Richey Edwards went missing in 1995, he has reportedly been seen in a Goa, India, market and on Fuerteventura and Lanzarote islands. True or False?

5. *This Is My Truth Tell Me Yours* was a 1998 number 1 album. The title is a quotation taken from a speech given by which Welsh politician?
A) Aneurin Bevan   B) Neil Kinnock   C) David Lloyd-George

6. From which 1999 Manics' hit are these lyrics extracted: "You have broken through my armour and I don't have an answer. I love you all the same."?
A) You Stole The Sun From My Heart   B) Tsunami   C) The Everlasting

7. Which Pulitzer Prize-winning professional photographer was the subject of a 1996 Manics Top10 hit?   A) Kevin Carter   B) David Bailey   C) August Sander

8. In December 1995, playing their first gig without Richey, who did the Manics support at Wembley Arena?   A) Libertines   B) Charlatans   C) Stone Roses

9. Also in 1995, what song did the Manics cover for *The Help Album*, a charity effort in support of aid efforts in war-torn Bosnia and Herzegovina?
A) Raindrops Keep Fallin' on My Head   B) Help!   C) Come Together

10. Which member of the Manics has played trumpet on a number of their tracks?
A) James Dean Bradfield   B) Sean Moore   C) Nicky Wire

WELSH TOP 10 HITMAKERS

Match the singer to their hit

1. DOROTHY SQUIRES	A. Knock Knock Who's There (1970)
2. RICKY VALANCE	B. Girls Talk (1979)
3. ALED JONES	C. Something (1970)
4. MARY HOPKIN	D. Walking in the Air (1985)
5. DAVE EDMUNDS	E. Like I Do (1962)
6. MAUREEN EVANS	F. Tell Laura I Love Her (1960)
7. BONNIE TYLER	G. A Love Worth Waiting For (1984)
8. HARRY SECOMBE	H. My Way (1970)
9. SHAKIN' STEVENS	J. Holding Out For A Hero (1985)
10. SHIRLEY BASSEY	L. This Is My Song (1967)

MANIC STREET PREACHERS ANSWERS: *1. B) Generation Terrorists; 2. C) I'm Left, You're Right, She's Gone; 3. B) If You Tolerate This Your Children Will Be Next; 4. True; 5. A) Aneurin Bevan; 6. A) You Stole The Sun From My Heart; 7. A) Kevin Carter; 8. C) Stone Roses; 9. A) Raindrops Keep Fallin' On My Head; 10. B) Sean Moore.*
WELSH TOP 10 HITMAKERS ANSWERS: *1H; 2F; 3D; 4A; 5B; 6E; 7J; 8L; 9G; 10C.*

MARILLION are a British rock band, formed in Aylesbury, Bucks, in 1979. They emerged from the post-punk music scene in Britain and existed as a bridge between the styles of punk rock and classic progressive rock, becoming the most commercially successful neo-progressive rock band of the 1980s. Named after J.R.R. Tolkien's book The Silmarillion, shortened in 1981 to avoid copyright complications. There were several early changes in personnel. Marillion had up 19 Top 40 hits between 1983 and 1995, including three Top 10 hits. They also had 14 Top 40 albums, including a number one and seven other Top 10 hits.

1. What is former lead singer Fish's real name?
A) Robert Fripp   B) Dave Cousins   C) Derek Dick

2. In the lyrics of their 1985 #2 hit, who is asked if she remembers dancing in stilettos in the snow?

3. Which of the following has not played the drums with Marillion?
A) Andy Ward   B) Jonathan Mover   C) Jon Moss

4. Which Pink Floyd album cover appears on the sleeve of Marillion album, *Script For a Jester's Tear*?
A) Atom Heart Mother   B) A Saucerful Of Secrets   C) The Dark Side Of The Moon

5. Where was the studio chosen for the recording of Marillion's debut single, *Market Square Heroes* EP, in 1982?
A) Battle, Sussex   B) Rockfield Studios, Wales   C) Marquee Studios, London

6. What is Marillion's third studio album and commercially, their most successful album which reached number one?
A) Fugazi   B) Misplaced Childhood   C) Clutching at Straws

7. Incommunicado was Marillion's last UK Top 10 hit in which year?
A) 1987   B) 1988   C) 1989

8. Marillion are widely considered to have been one of the first mainstream acts to have fully recognised, and tapped, the potential for commercial musicians to interact with their fans via the internet. True or False?

9. Who was the first Marillion drummer to occupy the drum stool from 1979 - 1983?
A) Andy Ward   B) Mick Pointer   C) John 'Martyr' Marter

10. Which 1988 Marillion album shares its title with a Rossini opera?
A) The Thieving Magpie   B) Moses in Egypt   C) William Tell

Match the hit with the artiste

1. ALL KINDS OF EVERYTHING (1970)	A) B*WITCHED
2. WHEN YOU SAY NOTHING AT ALL (1999)	B) JOE DOLAN
3. SEVEN DRUNKEN NIGHTS (1967)	C) ENYA
4. GIVE A LITTLE LOVE (1998)	D) TERRY WOGAN
5. NOTHING COMPARES 2U (1990)	E) DANA
6. ORINOCO FLOW	F) SINEAD O'CONNOR
7. A GOOD HEART	G) DANIEL O'DONNELL
8. FLORAL DANCE	H) DUBLINERS
9. ROLLERCOASTER	J) FEARGAL SHARKEY
10. MAKE ME AN ISLAND (1969)	K) RONAN KEATING

MARILLION ANSWERS: 1. C) Derek Dick; 2. Kayleigh; 3. C) Jon Moss (Culture Club); 4. B) A Saucerful Of Secrets; 5. A) Battle; 6. B) Misplaced Childhood; 7. A) 1987; 8. True (around 1986); 9. B) Mick Pointer; 10. A) The Thieving Magpie.
LUCK O' THE IRISH ANSWERS: 1E; 2K; 3H; 4G; 5F; 6C; 7J; 8D; 9A; 10B.

BOB MARLEY & THE WAILERS *(also known as The Wailing Wailers and The Wailers) were a Jamaican reggae band led by Bob Marley. The band developed from a ska vocal group and the original line-up featured Junior Braithwaite on vocals, Bob Marley on guitar, Peter Tosh on keyboards, Bunny Wailer on percussion, and Cherry Smith & Beverley Kelso on backing vocals. By 1966 Braithwaite, Kelso and Smith had left the band and numerous changes followed. The Band had 15 Top 40 hits between 1975 -1995 before Marley had two further hits with different acts. Of the hits, 8 reached the Top 10. 15 albums reached the Top 40, including a No. 1 and 6 more Top 10.*

1. Where was much of the 1977 No. 8 album, *Exodus*, recorded?
A) Jamaica   B) London   C) New York

2. With which Bob Marley song did Eric Clapton have an international hit in 1974?
A) No Woman No Cry   B) I Shot the Sheriff   C) Redemption Song

3. Bob Marley is the biological father of how many children?
A) 5   B) 8   C) 12

4. In 1976, Bob Marley was shot and wounded in an assassination attempt, his wife Rita and manager Don Taylor, were also seriously injured but also survived. Where did the attack take place?
A) Kingston, Jamaica   B) Miami   C) Delaware

5. In 1980 Bob Marley and the Wailers toured Europe and played in front of their biggest crowd - 100,000. In which city was the open air concert held?   A) Madrid   B) Milan   C) Athens

6. March 1994: When were Bob Wailers and the Wailers inducted into the Rock and Roll Hall of Fame?   A) 1974   B) 1984   C) 1994

7. *Turn Your Lights Down Low* was a Top 20 hit for Bob Marley in 1999, which female rapper is featured on the hit?   A) Lauryn Hill   B) Queen Latifah   C) Nicki Minaj

8. Where was Bob Marley jogging in 1980, when he collapsed as a result of a previously diagnosed cancer that had spread to his brain, lungs and stomach?
A) Hyde Park, London   B) Centennial Park, Sydney   C) Central Park, New York

9. When Bob Marley died, aged 36, he was given a state funeral in Jamaica, then interred in a mausoleum built specifically for his remains. How many people filed past his coffin during the wake?   A) 100,000   B) 50,000   C) 25,000

10. Bob Marley was buried with a Bible turned to Psalm 23, a red Gibson Les Paul guitar and a marijuana bud added by his widow, Rita. True or False?

1. Who was the King of Skiffle, who died on 3 November 2002?
2. Who do the initials E.M.I. Stand for?
3. Jason Donovan and Lee Mead had hits with Any Dream Will Do. From what show is the song taken?
4. Who was the writer of Blue Suede Shoes who died in 1999 aged 65?
5. Which 1973 Elton John hit shares its name with a book from the Bible?
6. Which Alanis Morissette album reached number one in 13 countries?
7. Which stunning Eagles B side tells how man destroys beautiful places?
8. Name the missing character - Native American, US cop, cowboy, GI and biker?
9. What name is given to half a quaver?
10. In what decade did cassette tapes go on sale?

BOB MARLEY & THE WAILERS ANSWERS: *1. B) London; 2. B) I Shot the Sheriff; 3. C) 12; 4. A) Kingston, Jamaica (in his home); 5. B) Milan; 6. C) 1994; 7. A) Lauryn Hill; 8. C) Central Park, New York; 9. A) 100,000; 10. True.* **MUSICAL MISCELLANY ANSWERS:** *1. Lonnie Donegan; 2. Electric and Musical Industries; 3. Joseph and the Amazing Technicolor Dreamcoat; 4. Carl Perkins; 5. Daniel; 6. Jagged Little Pill; 7. The Last Resort; 8. A construction worker (Village People); 9. Semi-quaver; 10. The 1960s.*

MARMALADE *are a Scottish pop rock band originating from Glasgow, formed in 1961 as The Gaylords, later Dean Ford and The Gaylords, recording four singles for Columbia (EMI). In 1966 they renamed The Marmalade on releases with CBS and Decca Records until 1972. The familiar line-up was Graham Knight (vocals, bass); Dean Ford (lead vocals, guitar, harmonica); Patrick Fairley (vocals, six string bass/rhythm guitars); William 'Junior' Campbell (vocals, guitars, keyboards); Alan Whitehead (drums). Marmalade had 11 Top 40 hits, including a No.1 and eight other Top 10 hits.*

1. Marmalade's original name, The Gaylords, was named after homosexual members of the aristocracy. True or False?

2. Which famous record producer signed Dean Ford & The Gaylords to the Columbia label?   A) Norrie Paramor   B) Mickie Most   C) Joe Meek

3. *I See the Rain*, written by Campbell and Ford, was praised by Jimi Hendrix as the "best cut of 1967". Which Hollies member sat in on the recording?
A) Allan Clarke   B) Bobby Elliott   C) Graham Nash

4. While searching for a hit record which song was offered to Marmalade and rejected - and then became a number one for another band?
A) Baby Now That I've Found You   B) Silence is Golden   C) Everlasting Love

5. Marmalade's first hit reached No. 6 in 1968. What was the song that was covered by The Grass Roots and Bobby Rydell?   A) Wild One   B) Lovin' Things   C) Sway

6. Marmalade hit the jackpot with a No.1 smash hit in 1969. With what Beatles song?
A) Ob-La-Di, Ob-La-Da   B) I Am the Walrus   C) The Long and Winding Road

7. *Reflections of My Life* hit No. 3 at the end of 1968 and was followed by another No. 3 early the next year. What was the song title?
A) Rainbow   B) Baby Make It Soon   C) My Little One

8. In 1971 Junior Campbell left the band and was replaced by which singer / guitarist who also went on to write three Marmalade hits, *Cousin Norman*, *Back on the Road* and *Radance*?   A) Hugh Nicholson   B) Dougie Henderson   C) Mike Japp

9. Which 1972 Marmalade hit opens with these lyrics: 'I saw a girl on a Northern dance floor, She looked sixteen, she could have been more, I went to her thinking only of romance'?   A) Dance the Night Away   B) Radancer   C) Cousin Norman

10. *Talking In Your Sleep* was a song co-written by Roger Cook and produced by Roger Greenaway. It failed to chart for Marmalade, but who did have a No.11 hit with the song in 1978?   A) Bucks Fizz   B) Martine McCutcheon   C) Crystal Gayle

Who had these hits with their songs written by Roger Cook & Roger Greenaway?

1. Like Sister and Brother (1973)
2. The Way It Used To Be (1969)
3. Freedom Come, Freedom Go (1971)
4. I Was Kaiser Bill's Batman (1967)
5. Softly Whispering I Love You (1971)
6. Home Lovin' Man (1970)
7. Lovers of the World Unite (1966)
8. Conversations (1969)
9. Melting Pot (1969)
10. (Blame It) On the Pony Express (1970)

MARMALADE ANSWERS: *1. False (named after a notorious post war street gang, Chicago Gaylords); 2. A) Norrie Paramor; 3.C) Graham Nash; 4. C) Everlasting Love (a hit for Love Affair); 5. B) Lovin' Things; 6. A) Ob-La-Di, Ob-La-Da; 7. A) Rainbow; 8. A) Hugh Nicholson; 9. B) Radancer; 10. C) Crystal Gayle.* **BRISTOL'S SONGWRITING ROGERS ANSWERS**: *1. The Drifters; 2. Engelbert Humperdinck; 3. The Fortunes; 4. Whistling Jack Smith; 5. The Congregation; 6. Andy Williams; 7. David & Jonathan; 8. Cilla Black; 9. Blue Mink; 10. Johnny Johnson & The Bandwagon.*

MEAT LOAF *(Michael Lee Aday, born Marvin Lee Aday; Dallas, Texas on September 27, 1947; died Nashville, Tennessee on January 20, 2022), was an American singer and actor. He was noted for his powerful, wide-ranging voice and theatrical live shows. Aday appeared in many films and TV shows, sometimes as himself or as characters resembling his stage persona. Meat Loaf had 15 Top 40 hits, including a No. 1 and 4 other Top 10 hits. His albums were also very successful, notching up 10 Top 40 recordings, including 2 No. 1's and 5 more Top 10 hits.*

1. On the 1985 UK number five, *Dead Ringer For Love*, who provides an unaccredited female lead vocal?   A) Carole King   B) Cher   C) Dusty Springfield

2. In 1993, what was Meat Loaf's only UK number one single?   A) Two Out Of Three Ain't Bad   B) Bat Out Of Hell   C) I'd Do Anything For Love (But I Won't Do That)

3. What is the name of the songwriter who wrote most of Meat Loaf's hits, including *Bat Out of Hell*?   A) Todd Rundgren   B) Jim Steinman   C) Gordon Lightfoot

4. In which of these films did Meat Loaf star?
A) Wayne's World   B) Bill and Ted's Excellent Adventure   C) That'll Be The Day

5. In 1994 meat Loaf had a hit with a song that had a 12 word title: *Objects In The Rear View Mirror May Appear …* complete the title.

6. The 1996 hit single, *Not a Dry Eye In the House* was taken from which album?
A) Bad Attitude   B) Welcome to the Neighbourhood   C) Bat Out of Hell II

7. Which 1978 Meat Loaf hit begins "On a hot summer night, would you offer your throat to the wolf with the red roses"?   A) You Took The Words Right Out Of My Mouth   B) Two Out Of Three Ain't Bad   C) Bat Out Of Hell

8. In 1973, Meat Loaf was cast in the original L.A. Roxy cast of *The Rocky Horror Show*, playing two roles. In the film *The Rocky Horror Picture Show*, what role(s) did he play?   A) Dr. Everett Scott   B) Eddie   C) Dr. Everett Scott & Eddie

9. It is estimated that how many copies of the album *Bat Out of Hell* were sold globally?   A) 23 million   B) 33 million   C) 43 million

10. The title track of the number 8 album in 1984, *Bad Attitude*, featured which lead singer of a top rock band of the time?
A) Roger Daltrey   B) Freddie Mercury   C) Huey Lewis

MEAT LOAF ANSWERS: *1. B) Cher; 2. C) I'd Do Anything For Love (But I Won't Do That); 3. B) Jim Steinman; 4. A) Wayne's World; 5. Closer Than They Are; 6. B) Welcome to the Neighbourhood; 7. A) You Took The Words Right Out Of My Mouth; 8. B) Eddie; 9. C) 43 million; 10. A) Roger Daltrey.*

GEORGE MICHAEL *(born Georgios Kyriacos Panayiotou; 25 June 1963 – 25 December 2016) was an English singer, songwriter and record producer. He is considered one of the most significant cultural figures of the MTV generation and is one of the best-selling music artists of all time, with sales of over 120 million records worldwide. George Michael had 25 Top 40 singles, including five collaborations with other artistes. These included 6 number ones and 12 other Top 10 hits. He also had five hit albums, four reached number one, the other reached number two! He was also very successful with Wham!*

1. In what year did George Michael release his debut album, *Faith*, which reached number one in the UK album charts?   A) 1985   B) 1986   C) 1987

2. The 1987 number two hit *Faith* opens with an instrumental intro taken from which Wham number one single from 1984?
A) Freedom   B) I'm Your Man   C) Wake Me Up Before You Go-Go

3. Also in 1987, with which female soul singer did George Michael have a number one hit with *I Knew You Were Waiting (For Me)*?
A) Gladys Knight   B) Aretha Franklin   C) Dionne Warwick

4. George Michael became infamously known after being arrested following his involvement in a "lewd act" in a public toilet by an undercover police officer. Where was he arrested?   A) Beverly Hills   B) Miami   C) London

5. In which 1996 self-penned No.1 did George Michael sing these lyrics: "And what have I learned from all these tears, I've waited for you all those years Then just when it began he took your love away"?   A) Fast Love   B) Jesus To A Child   C) Spinning the Wheel

6. At the Brit Awards held at the Royal Albert Hall in which year did George Michael receive the first of his two awards for Best British Male Solo Artist?   A) 1986   B) 1987   C) 1988

7. In 1991, Michael published a Penguin Books autobiography, co-written with Tony Parsons. What was its title?   A) Bare   B) Freedom   C) Fast Love

8. What was the title of George Michael's first solo greatest hits collection in 1988?
A) Out of Wham!   B) Ladies & Gentlemen: The Best of George Michael   C) Songs From the Last Century

9. With which female singer did George Michael have a 1999 hit single, *As*, originally written and recorded by whom?
A) Michael Jackson   B) Paul McCartney   C) Stevie Wonder

10. "Throw your arms around the world, at Christmas time" is a line sung by George Michael in Band Aid's *Do They Know It's Christmas* in 1988. True or False?

BY GEORGE!
They've Got
A HIT
Fill in the blanks!

1. Rock Your Baby by George .... (1975)
2. Paloma Blanca by George .... (1975)
3. Shiver by George ...... (1983)
4. What Are We Gonna Get Her Indoors by Dennis Waterman & George .... (1983)
5. Girlie Girlie by ...... George (1985)
6. Bangla Desh by George .... (1971)

GEORGE MICHAEL ANSWERS: 1. C) 1987; 2. A) Freedom; 3. B) Aretha Franklin; 4. A) Beverly Hills; 5. B) Jesus To A Child; 6. C) 1988; 7. A) Bare; 8. B) Ladies & Gentlemen: The Best of George Michael; 9. C) Stevie Wonder; 10. False (Boy George).
BY GEORGE! THEY'VE GOT A HIT ANSWERS: 1. McCrae; 2. Baker Selection; 3. Benson; 4. Cole; 5. Sophia; 6. Harrison.

HODGEPODGE

A MIXTURE OF MUSICAL QUESTIONS!

1. Name the US instrumental group who had hits in the 60s, including *Walk, Don't Run* and *Perfidia*?

2. In which decade did Nancy Sinatra reckon *These Boots are Made For Walking*?

3. In the Freddie Mercury Tribute Concert held on Easter Monday, 20 April 1992 at Wembley Stadium, who sung *Who Wants To Live Forever* with Queen?

4. "She's got electric boots a mohair suit/You know I read it in a magazine". Lyrics from which 1973 hit?

5. Which 1994 Green Day number 13 album included the hit songs *Longview*, *Basket Case*, and *When I Come Around*?

6. In 1963, what famous man produced, co-wrote, and was the husband of Ronettes lead singer Ronnie Bennett who had a big hit with *Be My Baby*?

7. What 1986 hit begins with: "You could have a steam train, If you just lay down your tracks, You could have an aeroplane flying, If you bring your blue skies back"?

8. Otis Redding recorded his biggest UK hit hit just three days before he died in a plane crash on December 10, 1967. What is the name of the song?

9. Which California street was mentioned in the lyrics of Sheryl Crow's 1993-94 single *All I Wanna Do*?

10. Who was the vocalist and founder of Black Sabbath who had a #4 hit with *Paranoid* in 1970?

11. In which decade did Ace of Base take *The Sign* to No. 2 in the UK charts?

12. "Well my temperature's rising and my feet are on the floor, Twenty people knocking 'cause they're wanting some more". Whose hit had these lyrics in 1966?

13. Which 1991 Metallica hit has been widely used as entrance music in sport?

14. In 1977, with whom did Joe Tex say he *Ain't Gonna Bump No More*?

15. Who was featured with Dawn on the 1973 #1, *Tie A Yellow Ribbon Round The Old Oak Tree*?

16. Which South African-born female musician, is best known as the organist in Lord Rockingham's XI who had a 1958 No. 1 hit with *Hoots Mon*?

17. C W McCall took *Convoy* to No. 2 in 1976 and Laurie Lingo & The Dipsticks took *Convoy G.B.* to No. 4 in the same year. Who were Laurie Lingo & The Dipsticks?

18. Which female American rock singer and songwriter had two 1985 hits with *We Belong* and *Love is a Battlefield*?

19. Fill in the year of this #1 from 1969. In The Year …. (Exordium And Terminus).

20. Which country queen had 5 husbands, 25 major operations, was addicted to pain killers, had a 1975 UK No.1 and was abducted whilst shopping in Nashville?

GEORGE MICHAEL ANSWERS: 1. The Ventures; 2. 1960s (1966); 3. Seal; 4. Bennie and the Jets by Elton John; 5. Dookie; 6. Phil Spector; 7. Sledgehammer by Peter Gabriel; 8. (Sittin' On) the Dock Of the Bay; 9. Santa Monica Boulevard; 10. Ozzy Osbourne; 11. 1990s (1994); 12. Spencer Davis Group - Gimme Some Lovin'; 13. Enter Sandman; 14. No Big Fat Woman; 15. Tony Orlando; 16. Cherry Wainer; 17. Radio 1 DJ's Dave Lee Travis and Paul Burnette; 18. Pat Benatar; 19. 2525 (Zager & Evans); 20. Tammy Wynette.

KYLIE MINOGUE *AO OBE; born Kylie Ann Minogue, Melbourne, Australia on 28 May 1968, is a singer, songwriter and actress. The top-selling female Australian artist with over 80m record sales worldwide. Also recognised for reinventing herself in music and fashion and referred to by the European press as the "Princess of Pop" and a style icon. Initially gained recognition for starring in TV soap Neighbours, made a pop star by producers Stock, Aitken & Waterman. Kylie had 26 Top 40 singles between 1988 and 1998, including 4 No.1's and 12 other Top 10 hits. Minogue also had 8 Top 40 albums, including 3 No. 1's and 3 more Top 10 successes.*

1. What character did Kylie play in *Neighbours* from 1986 - 1988?
A) Donna Freed   B) Charlene Robinson   C) Helen Daniels

2. In late 1988, Kylie had a No.1 hit, *Especially For You*. This was a duet with which *Neighbours* co-star?   A) Russell Crowe   B) Guy Pearce   C) Jason Donovan

3. In 1988, Kylie's first UK hit single went to number one. What was its title?
A) I Should Be So Lucky   B) The Loco-Motion   C) Got To Be Certain

4. **AQUARIUS JEEP POISONS** is an anagram of the title of an early Kylie #2 hit. Can you work it out?

5. From what Kylie 1990 #2 song is this lyric taken? "Say you won't leave me no more, I'll take you back again, No more excuses no, no, 'Cos I've heard them all before, A hundred times or more"

6. In 1994 Kylie appeared as herself in the *Community Spirit* episode of which UK sit-com?   A) The Young Ones
B) The Vicar of Dibley   C) Absolutely Fabulous

7. How many of Kylie's first singles reached the top two in the UK?   A) 2   B) 4   C) 7

8. Kylie teamed up with Nick Cave & The Bad Seeds to register a 1995 hit tht just failed to reach the Top 10. What was the song's title?
A) Some Kind of Bliss   B) Where is the Feeling   C) Where The Wild Roses Grow

9. Kylie starred as Sergeant Cammy White in a 1994 action film, alongside Jean-Claude Van Damme and Raul Julia. What was the title of the film?
A) Street Fighter   B) Timecop   C) Double Impact

10. True or false: Kylie performed The Beatles' *Get Back* at the John Lennon tribute concert in 1991.

KYLIE MINOGUE ANSWERS: 1. B) Charlene Robinson; 2. C) Jason Donovan; 3. A) I Should Be So Lucky; 4. Je Ne Sais Pas Pourquoi; 5. Better the Devil You Know; 6. B) The Vicar of Dibley; 7. C) 7; 8. C) Where The Wild Roses Grow. 9. A) Street Fighter; 10. False (she sung Help!). **PICTURE + PICTURE = SONG TITLE ANSWERS:** *A) Hotel California (Eagles); B) Monkey Wrench (Foo Fighters).*

GUY MITCHELL *(born Albert George Cernik; February 22, 1927 – July 1, 1999) was an American pop singer and actor, successful in his homeland, the UK, and Australia. Mitchell was born of Croatian immigrants in Detroit, Michigan. Aged 11, he was signed by Warner Brothers Pictures, to be a child star, and performed on the radio on KFWB in Los Angeles, California. He then worked as a saddle maker, supplementing his income by singing.He sold 44 million records, including six million-selling singles. He had 15 Top 40 hit singles in the UK, including four number ones and 10 other Top 10 hits. Seven of his hits re-entered the charts for a second, or even third time.*

Guy Mitchell had 15 Top 40 hits between 1952 and 1959. Match the highest chart positions to the songs! Some chart positions are replicated, (e.g. 4 No. 1's) and the answers appear in sequence .

1. FEET UP (1952)	A) 25
2. SHE WEARS RED FEATHERS (1953)	B) 1
3. PRETTY LITTLE BLACK EYED SUSIE (1953)	C) 17
4. LOOK AT THAT GIRL (1953)	D) 2
5. CHICKA BOOM (1953/4)	E) 1
6. CLOUD LUCKY SEVEN (1953)	F) 5
7. CUFF OF MY SHIRT (1954)	G) 2
8. SIPPIN' SODA (1954)	H) 11
9. DIME AND A DOLLAR (1954)	J) 2
10. SINGING THE BLUES (1956)	K) 8
11. KNEE DEEP IN THE BLUES (1957)	L) 1
12. ROCK-A-BILLY (1957)	M) 1
13. IN THE MIDDLE OF A DARK DARK NIGHT (1957)	N) 4
14. CALL ROSIE ON THE PHONE (1957)	P) 11
15. HEARTACHES BY THE NUMBER (1959)	Q) 3

THE VERY FIRST CHART PUBLISHED IN THE
NEW MUSICAL EXPRESS ON NOVEMBER 14, 1952

1. Here In My Heart	Al Martino
2. You Belong To Me	Jo Stafford
3. Somewhere Along The Way	Nat King Cole
4. The Isle Of Innisfree	Bing Crosby
5. Feet Up (Pat Him On The Po-Po)	Guy Mitchell
6. Half As Much	Rosemary Clooney
7. High Noon (Do Not Forsake Me)	Frankie Laine
7. Forget Me Not	Vera Lynn
8. Sugarbush	Doris Day and Frankie Laine
8. Blue Tango	Ray Martin
9. The Homing Waltz	Vera Lynn
10. Auf Wiederseh'n Sweetheart	Vera Lynn
11. Cowpuncher's Cantata	Max Bygraves
11. Because You're Mine	Mario Lanza
12. Walkin' My Baby Back Home	Johnnie Ray

GUY MITCHELL ANSWERS: *1D; 2B; 3G; 4E; 5N; 6J; 7H; 8P; 9K; 10L; 11Q; 12M; 13A; 14C; 15F.*

THE MONKEES *were selected specifically to appeal to the youth market as American television's response to the Beatles. Their manufactured personae and carefully produced singles, are seen as a precursor to the modern proliferation of studio and corporation-created bands. But this critical reputation softened, recognising that the band had musical talents. The line-up consisted of American actor/musicians Micky Dolenz, Michael Nesmith and Peter Tork alongside English actor/singer Davy Jones. The Monkees had 9 Top 40 Singles, including a number one and three more Top ten hits. They also had seven Top 40 albums, including two number ones and two more Top ten successes.*

1. In which soap did Davy Jones play Colin Lomax?
A) Emmerdale Farm   B) EastEnders   C) Coronation Street

2. Who sang lead vocals on The Monkees' 1967 No 1, *I'm A Believer*?
A) Micky Dolenz   B) Michael Nesmith   C) Pete Tork

3. Who wrote and originally performed *I'm A Believer*?
A) Neil Diamond   B) Billy Joel   C) Cat Stevens

4. In what year was there a sudden resurgence of interest in The Monkees, followed by a reunion?   A) 1982   B) 1986   C) 1990

5. What did the Monkees wear when they were performing on the first six episodes of the television show?   A) Yellow suits   B) Red suits   C) Green suits

6. Before Micky Dolenz joined The Monkees, in what children's TV series had he starred as a child?   A) Lassie   B) Adventures of Rin Tin Tin   C) Circus Boy

7. Which famous singer changed his name so that he wouldn't be confused with one of The Monkees?   A) Paul Jones   B) Elton John   C) David Bowie

8. What did Michael Nesmith's mother invent that made her rich?
A) Tea bags   B) Liquid paper correction fluid   C) Super glue

9. Which two unusual instruments did Peter Tork play on the original release of the *Headquarters* No. 2 album in 1967?
A) Harpsichord & banjo   B) Harp & recorder   C) Cello & xylophone

10. *Randy Scouse Git* was the original title of The Monkees No. 2 hit in 1967. What was the song re-titled?   A) Alternate Title   B) D. W. Washburn   C) Valleri

THE MONKEES ANSWERS: *1. C) Coronation Street (Ena Sharples' grandson); 2. A) Micky Dolenz; 3. A) Neil Diamond; 4. B) 1986; 5. B) Red suits; 6. C) Circus Boy; 7. C) David Bowie; 8. B) Liquid paper correction fluid; 9. Harpsichord & banjo; 10. Alternate Title.*

YOUR NUMBER'S UP!

Fill in the missing numbers in these hits songs.

1. A .... Pounds of Clay by Craig Douglas (1961)

2. ... by Mansun (1999)

3. Strawberry Letter .. by Brothers Johnson (1977)

4. .....Seas by Echo and the Bunnymen (1984)

5. .... Tons by Tennessee Ernie Ford (1956)

6. ..... Miles of Bad Road by Duane Eddy (1959)

7. ..... Miles High by The Byrds (1966)

8. Disco .... By Pulp (1995)

9. .. Red Balloons by Nena (1984)

10. In the Year .... (Exordium & Terminus) by Zager & Evans (1969)

11. I'm Gonna Be (... Miles) by The Proclaimers (1988)

12. Goody ... Shoes by Adam Ant (1982)

13. .. Ways To Leave Your Lover by Paul Simon (1976)

14. Land of .... Dances by Wilson Pickett (1966)

15. Mambo No. . by Lou Bega

16. .. By Paul Hardcastle (1985)

17. Perfect .. by The Beautiful South (1998)

18. Take .... by Dave Brubeck (1961)

19. .... Trombones by The King Brothers (1961)

20. Mozart Symphony No. .. in G Minor by Waldo De Las Rias (1971)

YOUR NUMBER'S UP! ANSWERS: *1. Hundred; 2. Six; 3. 23; 4. Seven; 5. Sixteen; 6. Forty; 7. Eight; 8. 2,000; 9. 99; 10. 2525; 11. 500; 12. Two; 13. 50; 14. 1,000; 15. 5; 16. 19; 17. 10; 18. Five; 19. Seventy-Six; 20. 40.*

MATT MONRO *(born, Finsbury, North London as Terence Edward Parsons, 1 December 1930 – 7 February 1985) was an English singer. Known as "The Man with the Golden Voice", he performed internationally during his 30-year career. Most of Monro's recordings were produced or overseen by George Martin. He notably recorded several film themes. Monro was a heavy smoker and battled alcoholism from the 1960s until 1981. He died from liver cancer on 7 February 1985 at the Cromwell Hospital, Kensington, London, aged 54. Matt Monro had 11 Top 40 hits, including five Top 10 successes. He also had four Top 40 albums, including one Top 10.*

1. *Portrait of My Love*, written by Norman Newell and Cyril Ornadel, was released by Matt Monro in 1960 and reached number 3 in the UK charts, but who had an international hit with the song?
A) Steve Lawrence   B) Frank Sinatra   C) Dean Martin

2. What Leslie Bricusse song by Matt Monro, reached number five in 1961, and was then covered by Frank Sinatra the following year, reaching number 35?
A) What Kind of Fool Am I?   B) My Kind of Girl   C) Goldfinger

3. Matt Monro was a bus driver on London London Transport, driving Route 77 from Holloway Bus Garage. True or False?

4. What position did Matt finish in the 1964 Eurovision Song Contest, singing *I Love the Little Things*?   A) 2nd B) 3rd C) 4th

5. At Eurovision1964, Matt Monro was impressed by the Austrian entry, performed by songwriter Udo Jürgens, and despite its modest 6th placement. *Warum nur warum?*, then had English words written, and became a number four hit for Matt.What was its English title?   A) My Love and Devotion   B) Walk Away   C) For Mama

6. In 1965, Monro sang the Oscar-winning film title song, which became his signature tune, although it amazingly failed to make the Top 40 in the UK. What was the song?
A) Born Free   B) Wednesday's Child   C) This Way Mary

7. Quincy Jones and Don Black's pop ballad *On Days Like These*, is played prominently in the opening credits of which major 1969 film?
A) Mary, Queen of Scots   B) The Quiller Memorandum   C) The Italian Job

8. For which James Bond film did Matt Monro sing the theme, and take to #20 in the UK charts in 1963?
A) From Russia With Love   B) The Spy Who Loved Me   C) You Only Live Twice

9. Which pianist was an important influence on Terence Parsons' early career, recommending him to Decca Records, and becoming his mentor and providing him with his stage name - Matt Monro?
A) Russ Conway   B) Winifred Atwell   C) Joe 'Mr. Piano' Henderson

10. In 1973, Monro released a vocal version of which popular TV theme, titled *And You Smiled*?   A) Shoestring   B) Maigret   C) Van der Valk

80s MUSICAL FILMS

Name the 5 films   A   B   C   D   E

MATT MONRO ANSWERS: 1. A) Steve Lawrence; 2. B) My Kind of Girl; 3. False - it was a No. 27!); 4. A) 2nd; 5. B) Walk Away; 6. A) Born Free; 7. C) The Italian Job; 8. A) From Russia With Love; 9. B) Winifred Atwell; 10. C) Van der Valk (Instrumental theme was Eye Level, a No. 1 for the Simon Park Orchestra). 80s MUSICAL FILMS ANSWERS: A) Footloose; B) The Blues Brothers; C) Flashdance; D) La Bamba; E) Grease 2.

THE MOODY BLUES *were an English rock band formed in Birmingham in 1964, consisting of Mike Pinder (keyboards), Ray Thomas (multi instruments), Denny Laine (guitar), Graeme Edge (drums) and Clint Warwick (bass). The line up was: Pinder, Thomas, Edge, Justin Hayward (guitar) and John Lodge (bass) until the early 1970s. The Moody Blues took an extended hiatus from 1974 until 1977 and founder Mike Pinder was then replaced by Swiss keyboardist Patrick Moraz in 1978. They had 9 Top 40 hits, including a No.1 with their debut single, and 2 other Top 10 hits. They also had 15 Top 40 albums, including 3 No. 1's with 5 others reaching the Top 10.*

1. The Moody Blues announced their arrival with a No.1 hit, *Go Now!* Who sung lead vocals on the single?   A) Justin Hayward   B) Denny Laine   C) Mike Pinder

2. Founder member Mike Pinder is credited with giving the group its name. What was his explanation upon how how he thought of the name Moody Blues?   A) He heard of a blues band called Muddy Baloos   B) In a TV ad for Moody's blueberry ice cream   C) Playing blues music he was interested how music affected people's moods

3. In 1965, Justin Hayward joined Marty Wilde and his wife Joyce in The Wilde Three. True or False?

4. A 1967 Moody Blues album is considered one of the first successful concept albums and featured The London Festival Orchestra. What is the title of the album? A) Days of Future Passed   B) Octave   C) In Search of the Lost Chord

5. The Moody Blues were inducted into The Rock and Roll Hall of Fame in Cleveland on April 14, 2018. Which female rock singer introduced the band?
A) Ann Wilson   B) Stevie Nicks   C) Christine McVie

6. Complete the next line of lyrics from the 1970 No. 2, *Question*, written by Justin Hayward, "Why do we never get an answer ...."

Drummer Graham Edge - The one constant in the Moody Blues

7. Which Moody Blues single, written by Justin Hayward, reached #19 upon release in 1967, then #9 in 1972 and #14 in 1979 when twice re-released?
A) Go Now   B) Question   C) Nights in White Satin

8. What is the name of the 1969 concept album based around the band's celebration of the first moon landing called?   A) When I Think About The Moon   B) To Our Children's Children's Children   C) To Your Health & For Your Life

9. During the Moody Blues' five-year hiatus. Justin Hayward and John Lodge recorded and released a duo album which reached No. 4 in 1975. What was its title?
A) Blue Jays   B) Nights Winters Years   C) Blue Guitar

10. In 1973 the Moodys had a single that reached #36 in the charts, *I'm Just a Singer* .... Complete the title.

THE MOODY BLUES ANSWERS: *1. B) Denny Laine; 2. C) Playing blues music he was interested how music affected people's moods; 3. True; 4. Days of Future Passed; 5. A) Ann Wilson (Heart); 6. "When we're knocking at the door?"; 7. C) Nights in White Satin; 8. B) To Our Children's Children's Children; 9. A) Blue Jays; 10. In a Rock and Roll Band.*

MUD are an English glam rock band, formed in February 1966 in Carshalton. Their earlier success came in a pop and then glam rock style, while later hits were influenced by 1950s rock and roll. The band was founded by lead guitarist Rob Davis, lead vocalist Les Gray, drummer Dave Mount and bassist Ray Stiles. After years of unsuccessful singles, they were signed to Mickie Most's Rak label. Mud had 15 Top 40 singles, including three number ones and eight more Top 10 hits. Mud also had four Top 40 albums, including two Top 10 successes.

1. Mud's first hit in 1973 shared it's title with a Willie Nelson song, recorded by Patsy Cline in 1961, but not a hit for her until 1990! What was the song title?
A) Always On My Mind   B) On the Road Again   C) Crazy

2. The most successful hits for Mud were written by which songwriting duo?
A) Nicky Chinn & Mike Chapman   B) Roger Cook & Roger Greenaway
C) Doc Pomus and Mort Shuman

3. In 1974 Mud released a cover of *In the Mood*. It was released under the name of Dum (Mud spelt backwards), but failed to chart. True or False?

4. *Tiger Feet* was the biggest-selling single of 1974, and a number one for four weeks for Mud. What did the band wear on their feet on their Top of the Pops appearance?   A) Striped Dr. Marten boots   B) Tiger slippers   C) Nothing

5. *The Cat Crept In*, which reached No. 2 in April 1974, was written to exploit Les Gray's vocal impression of which musical icon?
A) Elvis Presley   B) Little Richard   C) Tom Jones

6. When Mud disbanded, which top band did bass player Ray Stiles join in 1986?
A) Fleetwood Mac   B) The Searchers   C) The Hollies

7. **AUTOTYPE SHEET SKETCHER** is an anagram of the title of which Mud number three hit from 1975?

8. In 1974, Mud had the Christmas number one with which song?
A) Merry Xmas Everybody   B) Lonely This Christmas   C) Merry Christmas Everyone

9. Which Buddy Holly, a number 3 hit for the Crickets in 1957, did Mud take to the top of the charts in 1975?   A) Oh Boy!   B) That'll Be the Day   C) Heartbeat

10. Mud had most of their success on the RAK label. Which music producer owned RAK?   A) Tony Hatch   B) Phil Wainman   C) Mickie Most

WHO IS MISSING FROM THE MIDDLE OF A 1960s TRIO?

MUD ANSWERS: 1. C) Crazy; 2. A) Nicky Chinn & Mike Chapman; 3. True; 4. B) Tiger slippers; 5. A) Elvis Presley; 6. C) The Hollies; 7. The Secrets That You Keep; 8. B) Lonely This Christmas; 9. A) Oh Boy!; 10. C) Mickie Most.
***MISSING FROM THE TRIO ANSWER:** Dusty Springfield (The Springfields —>)*

RICK(Y) NELSON *(Eric Hilliard Ricky Nelson (Born in Teaneck, New Jersey 8, 1940, died December 31, 1985), was an American musician, songwriter and actor. From age eight he starred with his family in a radio and TV series The Adventures of Ozzie and Harriet, and subsequently appeared in a string of TV shows and films. In 1957, he began a long and successful singing career. The expression 'teen idol' was first coined to describe Nelson. He dropped the 'y' from his name in 1961. Nelson died in a plane crash on New Year's Eve 1985, flying from Guntersville, Alabama, to Dallas, Texas, for a concert in a Douglas DC-3, which had a history of mechanical problems. Rick Nelson had 16 UK Top 40 singles, including 4 Top 10 hits between 1958 and 1964.*

1. Which famous jazz label did Ricky Nelson release his first two singles, including the Fats Domino / Dave Bartholomew classic *I'm Walkin'*?
A) Columbia   B) Prestige   C) Verve

2. In 1959, in which western film did Ricky Nelson star alongside John Wayne?
A) Rio Bravo   B) The Sons of Katie Elder   C) North to Alaska

3. Ricky Nelson's first UK Top 10 hit *Poor Little Fool* in 1957, was written by a 17 year old who was later in the taxi with Eddie Cochran which crashed and killed the singer. Who is she?   A) Carole King   B) Ellie Greenwich   C) Sharon Sheeley

4. Ricky Nelson had a double sided hit in 1959. *Never Be Anyone Else But You* reached number 14, but the other side got to number 3. What was the song?
A) It's Late   B) Stood Up   C) Believe What You Say

5. Which influential guitarist, who was made a member of the Rock & Roll Hall of Fame in 2001, played on all of Ricky Nelson's early hits, and was also the leader of Elvis Presley's TCB band?   A) Scotty Moore   B) James Burton   C) Chet Atkins

6. "I've a pretty Senorita waiting for me, Down in old Mexico, If you're ever in Alaska stop and see, My cute little Eskimo". Lyrics from another double sided Rick Nelson No. 2 hit in 1960.   A) What is the song   B) What was on the A side of the record?

7. Rick Nelson's only Grammy Award was a posthumous one. It was for the 1986 Best Spoken Word or Non-musical Album Award for *Interviews From The Class Of '55 - Recording Sessions record*. True or False?

8. One of Rick's later hits, *It's Up To You* in 1963, was originally written for Sam Cooke. The songwriter wrote many songs, including *Young Girl* for Gary Puckett & The Union Gap. Who is he?   A) Neil Sedaka   B) Jerry Fuller   C) Pat Boone

9. What was the name of Ricky Nelson's country-rock band in the early 70s, whose line up included future Eagle, Randy Meisner on bass guitar?
A) The Stone Canyon Band   B) The Country Canyon Band   C) The Travellin' Men

10. Eight years after his last chart single in 1964, Rick Nelson released a song that just failed to get into the UK charts. What is the song that tells of his being booed off of the stage at Madison Square Garden as he had grown long hair and wore modern clothes?   A) You Just Can't Quit   B) Garden Party   C) I Shall Be Released

MUD ANSWERS: 1. C) Verve; 2. A) Rio Bravo; 3. C) Sharon Sheeley; 4. A) It's Late; 5. B) James Burton; 6. A) Travellin' Man; B) Hello Mary Lou; 7. True; 8. B) Jerry Fuller; 9. The Stone Canyon Band; 10. B) Garden Party.

THE NEW SEEKERS are a British pop group, formed in London in 1969 by Keith Potger after the break-up of his highly successful group, The Seekers. The idea was to appeal to the same market as The Seekers, but with pop influence added to the folk music. After some early changes the settled line-up was: Eve Graham, Lyn Paul, Marty Kristian, Peter Doyle, and Paul Layton. The New Seekers had 13 Top 40 hits, including 2 No.1's and 4 other Top 10 hits. They also had 6 Top 40 albums, with just one Top 10 success.

1. What chart position did The New Seekers debut release, a cover of Melanie Safka's *What Have They Done to My Song, Ma* attain? A) 3 B) 19 C) 39

2. Which Roger Cook / Roger Greenaway song began life as a jingle for Coca Cola before becoming a No.1 for the New Seekers in 1971? A) I'd Like To Teach the World to Sing B) Never Ending Song of Love C) Circles

3. The New Seekers were chosen to represent the UK in the 1972 Eurovision Song Contest. What song earned them second place in the contest and also reached # 2 in the charts? A) Beg, Steal or Borrow B) Circles C) The Carnival is Over

4. In July 1971 The New Seekers reached No 2 in the UK charts with *Never Ending Song of Love*, produced by David Mackay. It was a cover of a US hit by which duo? A) Ashford & Simpson B) Delaney & Bonnie C) Captain & Tennille

5. The New Seekers were dropped by the Philips Records label, ironically after having a major hit. To which label did the group sign?
A) Pye Records B) Columbia Records C) Polydor Records

6. The New Seekers had a surprising No.16 in 1973 with a two song medley of which songs originally written and recorded by The Who? A) Pinball Wizard - See Me Feel Me B) My Generation and Substitute C) Happy Jack - Pictures of Lily

7. The New Seekers enjoyed a number of hits in the US. With which major star did they tour the US in 1973? A) Dolly Parton B) Liza Minnelli C) Barbra Streisand

8. Marty Kristian sung lead vocals on a 1972 hit, *Come Softly to Me.*The song was written by Gretchen Christopher, Barbara Ellis, and Gary Troxel who also had the original hit with the song in 1959, performing as which trio?
A) The Platters B) The Del-Vikings C) The Fleetwoods

9. Lyn Paul took the lead for the first time on which song that became a big hit over Christmas and eventually peaked at No.1 in January 1974? A) You Won't Find Another Fool Like Me B) Morningtown Ride C) I Get a Little Sentimental Over You

10. The New Seekers officially disbanded in May 1974 and reformed in 1976 with two personnel changes. Danny Finn replaced Peter Oliver, but who replaced Lyn Paul? A) Donna Jones B) Kathy Ann Rae C) Caitriona Walsh

---

I'D LIKE TO TEACH THE WORLD TO SING by Roger Cook & Roger Greenaway
I'd like to build a world a home
And furnish it with love
Grow apple trees and honey bees
And snow white turtle doves
I'd like to teach the world to sing
In perfect harmony
I'd like to hold it in my arms
And keep it company

THE NEW SEEKERS ANSWERS: *1. C) 39; 2. A) I'd Like To Teach the World to Sing; 3. A) Beg, Steal or Borrow; 4. B) Delaney & Bonnie; 5. C) Polydor; 6. A) Pinball Wizard - See Me Feel Me; 7. B) Liza Minnelli; 8. C) The Fleetwoods; 9. A) You Won't Find Another Fool Like Me; 10. B) Kathy Ann Rae.*

ANTHONY NEWLEY *(24 September 1931 – 14 April 1999) was an English actor, singer, songwriter, and filmmaker. He achieved success as a performer in such diverse fields as rock and roll and stage and screen acting. He was also one of Broadway's leading men from 1959-1962. With Leslie Bricusse, Newley won an Academy Award for the film score of Willy Wonka & the Chocolate Factory (1971). Anthony Newley had 12 Top 40 hits, including two number ones and five other Top 10 hits.Newley also had three Top 20 albums, with two of them reaching the Top 10.*

1. Newley's first hit reached number three in 1959. Lyrics from the song include: "Play me a tune, haunting and blue, Tell me of dreams that never come true, Sing me a lonely song, Till she comes along". What was the song title?   A) If She Should Come To You   B) I've Waited So Long   C) And the Heavens Cried

2. Anthony Newley wrote the lyrics for the title song of the 1964 James Bond film *Goldfinger*, sung by Shirley Bassey. True or False?

3. Anthony Newley was married to his second wife, an actress, from 1963 to 1970, and the couple had two children, Tara and Alexander. Who was his second wife? A) Ann Lynn   B) Diana Dors   C) Joan Collins

4. Anthony Newley took an EP from a film soundtrack into the Top 20 singles in 1959. What was the name of the film in which Newley also starred?
A) Idol on Parade   B) The Lady is a Square   C) Jazz Boat

5. Anthony Newley had a UK No.1 in 1960 with a cover of a Frankie Avalon US No.1, which then became a big hit for Donny Osmond twelve years later. Name the song?
A) Personality   B) Why   C) Puppy Love

6. Name the 1961 musical written by Leslie Bricusse and Anthony Newley with a title allegedly being derived from graffiti?   A) Stop the World I Want To Get Off   B) The Roar of the Greasepaint   C) The Good Old Bad Old Days

7. In 1960 what Newley hit, written by Lionel Bart, became the 100th number 1 single in chart history?   A) Little White Bull   B) Consider Yourself C) Do You Mind

8. Name the folk song that Newley took to No. 3 in 1960, containing these lyrics: "Would you like to pick from my basket!" she said, Singing, singing, butter-cups and Daisies, "My cherries ripe, or my roses red", Fol-de-dee!, You can take a handful, I don't care"   A) Widecombe Fair   B) Strawberry Fair   C) Fairytale of New York

9. Newley also had a hit with which traditional English nursery rhyme in 1961?
A) Pop Goes the Weasel   B) Old King Cole   C) Billy Boy

10. In recognition of his creative skills and body of work, Newley was elected to the Songwriters Hall of Fame in what year?   A)1989   B) 1979   C) 1969

WHAT'S WRONG WITH THIS PICTURE?

ANTHONY NEWLEY ANSWERS: *1. B) I've Waited So Long; 2. True (with Leslie Bricusse); 3. C) Joan Collins; 4. A) Idol on Parade; 5. B) Why; 6. A) Stop the World I Want To Get Off; 7. C) Do You Mind; 8. B) Strawberry Fair; 9. Pop Goes the Weasel; 10. A) 1989.*
WHAT'S WRONG WITH THE PICTURE? ANSWERS: *Herman's Hermits did not have Honey Lantree (The Honeycombs) as their drummer.*

OLIVIA NEWTON-JOHN (*Dame Olivia Newton-John AC DBE, born Cambridge, 26 September 1948, died Santa Ynez Valley, California, US, 8 August 2022). A British-born Australian singer, songwriter, actress, entrepreneur and activist. In 1970, Newton-John was a member of the short-lived group Toomorrow. The next year she had her first two Top 10 UK singles. In 1974, Olivia represented the United Kingdom in the Eurovision Song Contest. Newton-John had 19 Top 40 singles, either as a soloist or in conjunction with other performers, including three No.1's and eight other Top 10 hits (one re-issue). She also had nine Top 40 albums, including just one Top 10 success.*

1. What Bob Dylan song, also recorded by George Harrison, became Olivia Newton-John's first UK hit in 1971?
A) If Not for You   B) Watching the River Flow   C) Don't Think Twice, It's All Right

2. Olivia's second 1971 Top 10 hit includes these lyrics: "I asked my love to take a walk, To take a walk, just a little walk, Down beside where the waters flow…" What is the song's title?   A) Take Me Home Country Roads   B) Banks of the Ohio   C) Sam

3. In 1974, Newton-John represented the United Kingdom in the Eurovision Song Contest with the song *Long Live Love*. Olivia finished fourth at the contest held in Brighton. What was the winning song?   A) Après toi   B) Ding-a-dong   C) Waterloo

4. In 1978 Olivia had two number ones from the soundtrack of *Grease* in partnership with John Travolta. Can you name them?

5. Olivia was appointed United Nations Goodwill Ambassador for the Environment during whose U.S. presidency?   A) Bill Clinton   B) George Bush   C) Jimmy Carter

6. Olivia starred in a 1980 American musical fantasy film. Whilst the film was not a box office success, the title song written by Jeff Lynne, and recorded with E.L.O. reached number one. Name the film.   A) Xanadu   B) Mr. Blue Sky   C) Showdown

7. Olivia had a second hit duet with Cliff Richard in 1995. From which show was the song *Had To Be* taken?   A) Les Miserables   B) Grease   C) Heathcliff

8. After *Grease*, Olivia starred in a romantic fantasy crime comedy film with John Travolta in 1983. What was the film's title?
A) Two Of A Kind   B) Hollywood Nights   C) Stayin' Alive

9. Newton-John's father, Bryn, was an MI5 officer on the Enigma project at Bletchley Park, who took Rudolf Hess into custody during World War II. True or False?

10. The lead single from a 1981 album, produced by John Farrar and written by Steve Kipner and Terry Shaddick, took Newton-John back to the Top 10. Name the song, originally offered to both Rod Stewart and Tina Turner.
A) Landslide   B) Magic   C) Physical

WHAT IS UNUSUAL ABOUT THIS SHOT OF THE SHADOWS PLAYING APACHE?

OLIVIA NEWTON-JOHN ANSWERS: *1. A) If Not for You; 2. B) Banks of the Ohio; 3. Waterloo (by Abba); 4.You're the One That I Want and Summer Nights; 5.B) George Bush; 6. A) Xanadu; 7. C) Heathcliff; 8. A) Two Of A Kind; 9. True; 10. C) Physical.*
SHADOWS APACHE: *Cliff Richard is playing lead guitar instead of Hank on a Cliff TV show!*

GARY NUMAN *(Gary Anthony James Webb, born Hammersmith, London 8 March 1958). Numan became prominent in the 1970s as lead singer, songwriter, and record producer for new wave band Tubeway Army. He faced early hostility from critics and fellow musicians, but became regarded as a pioneer of electronic music. He had a distinctive androgynous voice and had 20 Top 40 entries, this included 2 number ones and five other Top 10 hits. Numan's albums were also successful with three number ones, three other Top 10 successes and 8 other Top 40 hits.*

1. Gary Numan had his first number one fronting a band named Tubeway Army in 1979. What was the title of the chart topper?
A) That's Too Bad   B) Bombers   C) Are Friends Electric?

2. To what Record label was Gary Numan signed in 1978?
A) EMI   B) Beggar's Banquet   C) Island

3. What is the title of Gary Numan's 1997 autobiography?
A) Praying To the Aliens   B) Numan, Nuworld   C) The Godfather Of Electronica

4. On which 1981 Gary Numan album was Queen's Roger Taylor featured on drums and tom-toms?   A) I, Assassin   B) Dance   C) Warriors

5. *She's Got Claws* was a number six hit in 1981 taken from the *Dance* album. Who played fretless bass and saxophone on the track?
A) Chris Payne   B) Cedric Sharpley   C) Mick Karn

6. With what condition was Numan diagnosed at the age of 14?
A) Asperger's Syndrome   B) Diabetes   C) Bulimia

7. Gary Webb picked his stage surname 'Numan' from an advertisement in the Yellow pages for a electrician named 'Neumann'. True or False?

8. *We Are Glass*, *I Die: You Die*, and *This Wreckage* all charted in 1980. All three songs were featured on which number one album?
A) Telekon   B) The Pleasure Principal   C) Berserker

9. In what Gary Numan song, a hit three times, do these lyrics appear? "I feel safest of all, I can lock all my doors, It's the only way to live…"?
A) Are Friends Electric?   B) Cars   C) We Are Glass

10. In November and December 1981, Numan successfully flew around the world in his Piper Navajo with co-pilot Bob Thompson on their second attempt. Why did their first attempt fail?   A) The Cessna crashed   B) Both arrested on suspicion of smuggling and spying   C) Ran out of food and water

What's the song title?

GARY NUMAN ANSWERS: *1. C) Are Friends Electric?; 2. B) Beggar's Banquet; 3. A) Praying To the Aliens; 4. B) Dance; 5. C) Mick Karn; 6. A) Asperger's Syndrome; 7. False, it was a plumber; 8. A) Telekon; 9. B) Cars; 10. B) Both arrested on suspicion of smuggling and spying. **WHAT'S THE SONG TITLE? ANSWERS:** Hey Jude (Hay and Jude Law).*

OASIS *were an English rock band formed in Manchester in 1991. Originally known as the Rain, the group consisted of Liam Gallagher (lead vocals, tambourine), Paul Arthurs (guitar), Paul McGuigan (bass guitar), Tony McCarroll (drums). Noel Gallagher (lead guitar, vocals) later joined to finalise the group's core lineup. They had various lineup changes, with the Gallagher brothers remaining the only staple members. Oasis had 12 Top 40 hits between 1994 and 1998, including four No.1's and 6 other Top 10 hits. Also 6 Top 40 albums, including 3 No. 1's and 1 other Top 10 hit.*

1. The first hit single from Oasis was *Supersonic* in 1994. At what number did it peak in the UK charts?   A) 11   B) 21   C) 31

2. What is Paul Arthurs nickname?   A) Bonehead   B) Slaphead   C) Meathead

3. What was the name of the debut album from Oasis which topped the UK album charts in 1994?   A) Definitely Maybe
B) (What's the Story) Morning Glory?   C) Be Here Now

4. *Shakermaker* reached #11 in 1994. Oasis were sued over its similarity to which song?   A) My Way   B) I'd Like To Teach the World To Sing   C) Michelle

5. Tony McCarroll was replaced by Alan White on the drum stool in 1995. He then sued Oasis, using the same solicitor who had helped Pete Best to sue the Beatles. True or False?

6. Where did Oasis get the name of the band when they changed from The Rain?
A) A packet of sweets   B) A leisure centre   C) A soft drink

7. Which 1995 Oasis No. 2 single includes these lyrics: "And all the roads we have to walk are winding, And all the lights that lead us there are blinding, There are many things that I would like to say to you, but I don't know how"?

8. Which Oasis album won a Brit award for British Album of the Year in 1996?
A) (What's the Story) Morning Glory?   B) Dig Out Your Soul   C) Standing on the Shoulders of Giants

9. What Slade hit did Oasis perform on a 1996 appearance on *Top of the Pops*?
A) Cum On Feel the Noize   B) Coz I Luv You   C) My Friend Stan

10. In April 1995, Oasis bagged their first UK No.1 single, with which song?
A) Shakermaker   B) Some Might Say   C) Cigarettes and Alcohol

NAME THE 1996 SONG TITLE

OASIS ANSWERS: *1. C) 31; 2. A) Bonehead; 3. A) Definitely Maybe; 4. B) I'd Like To Teach the World To Sing; 5. True (Jens Hill got Pete Best £2m, however Tony only got £550,000 - less £250,000 fees); 6. B) A leisure centre (in Swindon); 7. Wonderwall; 8. A) (What's the Story) Morning Glory?; 9. A) Cum On Feel the Noize; 10. B) Some Might Say.* **NAME THE SONG TITLE ANSWER:** *Scooby Snacks by Fun Lovin' Criminals.*

BILLY OCEAN *(Leslie Sebastian Charles, MBE, born 21 January in Fyzabad, Trinidad and Tobago) is a British recording artist who had a string of R&B international pop hits in the 1970s and 1980s. Billy Ocean is the biggest black recording star Britain has ever produced, one who has sold over 30 million records in his lifetime to date. Ocean appeared at Live Aid in 1985. At the 1987 Brit Awards, Ocean was nominated for the Brit Award for Best British Male. Ocean had 12 Top 40 hit singles, including a No. 1, 2 No.2's and a No.3 and two other Top 10 hits. Billy also had five Top 10 hit albums.*

1. *Caribbean Queen (No More Love On The Run)* was a No. 6 UK hit in 1984. Under what other title was it released in other countries?
A) Tanzanian Queen   B) Egyptian Queen   C) African Queen

2. What was the name of Billy Ocean's first hit single in 1976?   A) Love Really Sucks Without You   B) Love Really Hurts Without You   C) Love Is Gone

3. Billy Ocean's *When The Going Gets Tough, The Tough Get Going* is from what film soundtrack?   A) Basic Instinct   B) The Color Of Money   C) Jewel Of The Nile

4. Billy Ocean's 1993 album, *Time To Move On*, had two tracks co-written and produced by which R&B singer?   A) Jay-Z   B) Luther Vandross   C) R. Kelly

5. During his teenage years, Billy sang regularly in London clubs, while also being employed as what?
A) A tailor in Savile Row   B) A porter in Billingsgate   C) A clerk in the Foreign Office

6. Billy Ocean's eponymous debut album contained three 1976 hit singles. On the cover of the album what colour shirt is Billy wearing?   A) Orange   B) Red   C) Blue

7. Billy Ocean's 1984 album *Suddenly* included a cover of what Beatles song?
A) Yesterday   B) The Long and Winding Road   C) Something

8. Which 1985 Billy Ocean dance hit had a music video featuring aliens in a bar?
A) Loverboy   B) There'll Be Sad Songs   C) Love is Forever

9. Billy Ocean's 1986 number one *When the Going Gets Tough the Tough Get Going* became a number one again in 1999. Who sung the cover version?
A) Take That   B) Boyzone   C) Blue

10. From which 1988 No. 3 hit are these lyrics taken: "I'll be the sun shining on you, Hey, Cinderella, step in your shoe, I'll be your non-stop lover, Get it while you can"?

NAME THE HIT AND ARTISTE FROM 1968

BILLY OCEAN ANSWERS: *1. C) African Queen; 2. B) Love Really Hurts Without You; 3. C) Jewel of the Nile; 4. C) R. Kelly; 5. A) A tailor in Savile Row; 6. A) Orange; 7. B) The Long and Winding Road; 8. A) Loverboy; 9. B) Boyzone; 10. Get Outta My Dreams Get Into My Car.* **NAME THE HIT AND ARTISTE FROM 1968 ANSWER:** *White Horses by Jacky.*

ROY ORBISON *(Roy Kelton Orbison (Born Vernon, Texas on April 23, 1936 – December 6, 1988) was an American singer, songwriter, and musician known for his impassioned singing style, complex song structures, and dark, emotional ballads. Described as operatic and nicknamed 'The Caruso of Rock' and 'The Big O'. He sung standing motionless, dressed in black, with dyed black hair and sunglasses, to counter his shyness and stage fright. He notched up 31 Top 40 hits, including three number ones and nine other Top 10 hits. He also had 20 Top 40 albums, with 2 No. 1's and four more Top 10 successes.*

1. In 1957 Roy earned royalties from Sun Records for writing the 'B' side of the Everly Brothers #1 *All I Have To Do Is Dream*. What was the song that he named after the woman who was to become his wife?   A) Lana   B) Claudette   C) Susie

2. What was Orbison's number one in 1960, a song turned down by both the Everly Brothers and Elvis Presley?   A) Blue Angel   B) Only the Lonely   C) Dream Baby

3. 'The Big O' had a 1961 Top 10 hit with a self-written song loosely based on the rhythm of Ravel's *Boléro* and ending with an incredible high 'A' natural note. What was the song?   A) Running Scared   B) The Crowd   C) Borne on the Wind

4. How did Orbison's on-off wife tragically die in 1965?
A) In a motorcycle accident   B) In a house fire   C) Airplane crash

5. In 1988, Orbison joined a British–American supergroup also comprising Bob Dylan, George Harrison, Jeff Lynne, and Tom Petty. What was their name?

6. In 1989 Roy was joined by Bruce Springsteen, Jackson Browne, T Bone Burnett, Elvis Costello, Tom Waits, Bonnie Raitt, Jennifer Warnes, James Burton, and k.d. Lang; for a TV concert, filmed in one take. What was the title of the memorable show, later to be released on DVD and CD?

7. After a 20 year absence from the charts, Roy had a number three UK hit in 1989, a year after his death, with which song, co-written with Jeff Lynne and Tom Petty?
A) Mystery Girl   B) Penny Arcade   C) You Got It

8. In 1991, what Roy Orbison song was famously sung in *Stage Fright,* an episode of *Only Fools and Horses*, featuring the characters Raquel Turner and Tony Angelino?

9. Which 1964 Christmas hit for Roy, written by Willie Nelson, includes these lyrics: "Should you stop, better not, much too busy, You're in a hurry, my how time does fly, In the distance the ringing of laughter, And in the midst of the laughter he cries"?

10. The 'B' side of Orbison's self-penned 1961 hit *Crying* became a #6 hit for Brian Poole and The Tremeloes three years later. What was it's title?
A) Candy Man   B) Do You Love Me   C) Someone Someone

ROY ORBISON ANSWERS: 1. B) Claudette; 2. B) Only the Lonely; 3. A) Running Scared; 4. A) In a motorcycle accident (Claudette); 5. The Traveling Wilburys; 6. Roy Orbison and Friends: A Black and White Night; 7. C) You Got It; 8. Crying (a duo featuring Roy and k.d.lang was a UK hit in 1992); 9. Pretty Paper; 10. A) Candy Man.

ORCHESTRAL MANOUEVRES IN THE DARK (OMD) are an English electronic band formed 1978 in Wirral, Merseyside. The line up was Andy McCluskey (vocals, bass guitar),Paul Humphreys (keyboards, vocals), Martin Cooper (various instruments), Stuart Kershaw (drums); McCluskey the only constant member. Pioneers of electronic music, combining an experimental, minimalist ethos with pop sensibilities, central in late-70s/early-80s emergence of synth-pop. OMD had 17 Top 40 hits, including 7 Top 10 hits. Also 12 Top 40 albums with 6 of those reaching the Top 10.

1. Which German band was a major inspiration to OMD?
A) Kraftwerk   B) Scorpions   C) Tangerine Dream

2. On which synth pop act's debut tour were OMD the support act in 1979?
A) Depeche Mode   B) Erasure   C) Gary Numan

3. A 1979 OMD Top 10 hit was *Enola Gay*. Who or what was Enola Gay?
A) A bomb   B) An aeroplane   C) A submarine

4. Which historical figure was the subject of two OMD Top 5 hits in the early 1980's?
A) Henry VIII   B) Joan of Arc   C) Bonnie Prince Charlie

5. After OMD's split in 1989, Andy McCluskey founded which pop girl group, also serving as their principal songwriter?   A) Sugababes   B) Atomic Kitten   C) All Saints

6. Which 1991 No. 3 hit contains these lyrics: "Sick and tired, I don't know why, Skin and bones, touch the sky, Sex and lies, can't bring me down…"?
A) Souvenir   B) Pandora's Box   C) Sailing on the Seven Seas

7. Which scientist served as the inspiration for a 1984 OMD single title?
A) Thomas Edison   B) Albert Einstein   C) Nikola Tesla

8. What was the first OMD hit single to feature Paul Humphreys on lead vocals?
A) Souvenir   B) Genetic Engineering   C) Locomotion

9. Which Hollywood film features the 1985 OMD hit song *Secret*?
A) St. Elmo's Fire   B) Arthur 2: Arthur On The Rocks   C) The Legend Of Billie Jean

10. Which 1983 OMD No. 5 hit album title refers to a type of warship used in WWI?
A) Liberator   B) Junk Culture   C) Dazzle Ships

OZZY OSBOURNE OR BLACK SABBATH?

All of these songs were hits, just select which of the acts had each one!

A) Bark At the Moon   G) No More Tears

B) Paranoid   H) Neon Knights

C) So tired   J) Perry Mason

D) Never Say Die   K) Turn Up the Night

E) Shot In the Dark   L) TV Crimes

F) Hard Road

ORCHESTRAL MANOUEVRES IN THE DARK ANSWERS: 1. A) Kraftwerk; 2. C) Gary Numan; 3. An aeroplane (that dropped the bomb on Hiroshima in August 1945. The name of the bomb was Little Boy); 4. B) Joan of Arc; 5. B) Atomic Kitten; 6. C) Sailing on the Seven Seas; 7. C) Nikola Tesla; 8. A) Souvenir; 9. B) Arthur 2: Arthur On The Rocks; 10. C) Dazzle Ships. OZZY OR BLACK SABBATH ANSWERS: A) OO; B) BS; C) OO; D) BS; E) OO; F) BS; G) OO; H) BS; J) OO; K) BS; L) BS.

THE OSMONDS were an American family music group who reached the height of their fame in the early to mid-1970s. The Osmond Brothers from Ogden, Utah began as a barbershop quartet consisting of brothers Alan, Wayne, Merrill and Jay. They were later joined by younger siblings Donny and Jimmy, who both had solo hits. The Osmonds also regularly appeared on TV. Their only sister Marie, also occasionally sang with her brothers. They all had a 1980s revival. The Osmonds had 10 Top 40 hit singles in the UK, including a No. 1 and four other Top 10 hits. They also had 7 Top 40 albums, 4 of which reached the Top 10.

1. What were the names of the Osmond's parents?
A) George and Olivia B) George and Olive C) Thomas and Olive

2. From 1962, on which easy-listening crooner's TV show did the Osmond Brothers appear in the early days of their career?
A) Andy Williams B) Perry Como C) Dean Martin

3. In 1987, which Osmond brother was diagnosed with multiple sclerosis, a demyelinating disease which affects the nerve cells in the brain and spinal cord?
A) Merrill B) Jimmy C) Alan

4. Older brothers Virl and Tom could not sing with the group as both had severe hearing impairment from birth. True or False?

5. Who is the the youngest Osmond brother who had three solo hits in the UK, including a number one in 1972? A) Donny B) Jimmy C) Jay

6. What was the Osmonds first UK Top 40 hit?
A) Down By the Lazy River B) Let Me In C) I Can't Stop

7. Name the song, the only hit from the Osmonds to feature Jay Osmond as lead vocalist, which reached number two in 1972? A) Jay B) Donny C) Jimmy

8. Name Donny Osmond's three UK number ones?

9. Which Johnny Bristol song was a No. 1 for the Osmonds and 19 years a No. 2 for Boyzone? A) Words B) No Matter What C) Love Me For a Reason

10. Marie Osmond had four hits with brother Donny, but in 1973 she only had her only UK solo hit, a revival of a 1960 Kaye Sisters hit. What was the song?
A) Come Softly To Me B) Paper Roses C) Who's Sorry Now

GUESS THE SONG TITLES!

A) FOO FIGHTERS (1997)   B) GREEN DAY (1995)   C) THOMPSON TWINS (1984

OSMONDS ANSWERS: 1. B) George and Olive; 2. A) Andy Williams; 3. C) Alan; 4. True (both became the first deaf missionaries from The Church of Jesus Christ of Latter-day Saints); 5. B) Jimmy; 6. A) Down By the Lazy River; 7. A) Jay; 8. Puppy Love, The Twelfth of Never and Young Love; 9. C) Love Me For a Reason; 10. B) Paper Roses.
GUESS THE SONG TITLES! ANSWERS: A) Monkey Wrench; B) Basket Case; C) Doctor Doctor.

GILBERT O'SULLIVAN - *Raymond Edward O'Sullivan was born on 1 December 1946 in Cork Road, Waterford, Ireland. He was one of six children. Gilbert is an Irish singer-songwriter who achieved his most significant success during the early 1970s. O'Sullivan's unique signature look garnered much attention, and often saw him compared to the Bisto Kids. Managed by Gordon Mills prior to a major court case in 1977 about royalties, in which he was awarded £7m in damages. Gilbert had 14 Top 40 hits, including two number ones and five other Top 10 hits. He also had five Top 40 album successes including a number one and three other Top 10 hits.*

1. Gilbert's first band was the Doodles, formed when he attended Swindon Art College. What instrument did Gilbert play?
A) Keyboards   B) Bass Guitar   C) Drums

2. In 1970, which song saw Gilbert enjoy his first top 10 hit in the UK?
A) Underneath the Blanket Go   B) Nothing Rhymed   C) We Will

3. Gilbert's first number one was Clair in 1972. Who provided the inspiration for the song?   A) His manager's sister   B) His daughter   C) His manager's daughter

4. Gilbert's 1993 album *Sounds of the Loop*, features a duet with which legendary singer on the track *Can't Think Straight* ?
A) Peggy Lee   B) Eartha Kitt   C) Bette Midler

5. What Wiltshire landmark, associated with Hovis bread, appears on the cover of the 1989 Gilbert O'Sullivan album, *In the Key of G*?

6. Gilbert released another compilation album in 2004. What soundalike phrase was used in the title of the album?   A) Berry Vest   B) Hig Bits   C) Heatest Grits

7. Which of O'Sullivan's songs did rapper Biz Markie sample, triggering a landmark court case in 1991?   A) Alone Again (Naturally)   B) Clair   C) Get Down

8. When Gilbert first became successful he chose a distinctive dress style of flat cap, pudding basin haircut and shorts. How did the media describe his look?
A) Milky Bar Kid look   B) Bisto Kid look   C) Captain Birdseye look

9. Gilbert had a well-known love of drinking tea, but in which song did he admit that he "drank a little wine" and was "as happy as could be"?
A) Get Down   B) Ooh Baby   C) Ooh-Wakka-Doo-Wakka-Day

10. In 1967, O'Sullivan moved to London in pursuit of a career in music. In which town had he lived for 13 years prior to the move?
A) Bath   B) Swindon   C) Keynsham

GILBERT O'SULLIVAN ANSWERS: *1. C) Drums; 2. B) Nothing Rhymed; 3. C) His manager's daughter; 4. A) Peggy Lee; 5. Gold Hill, Shaftesbury; 6. A) Berry Vest; 7. Alone Again (Naturally); 8. B) Bisto Kid look; 9. A) Get Down; 10. B) Swindon.*

ROBERT PALMER *(Robert Allen Palmer - 19 January 1949 – 26 September 2003) was an English singer-songwriter, musician, and record producer. He was known for his powerful, distinctive, gritty, soulful voice and sartorial elegance, and for combining soul, funk, jazz, rock, pop, reggae, and blues. Palmer's involvement in the music industry began in the 1960s and included a spell with the band Vinegar Joe and with the Power Station. Palmer had 10 Top 40 hit singles, including 5 Top 10 smashes. He also had 2 Top 30 albums, including 4 Top 10 hits. With Power Station he had 2 Top 30 singles and a Top 20 album.*

1. Robert Palmer's first Top 10 hit came, with a self-penned song in1986, that became a regular part of Tina Turner's stage performances. What was the song?
A) Nutbush City Limits   B) Proud Mary   C) Addicted To Love

2. In 1991, Robert Palmer had a Top 10 hit with a medley of which two Marvin Gaye songs?   A) Got to Give It Up & Sexual Healing   B) Mercy Mercy Me (The Ecology) & I Want You   C) You Are Everything & The Onion Song

3. In 1970 Palmer joined a 12-piece jazz-rock fusion band, which featured singer Elkie Brooks and her husband Pete Gage. What was the band called?
A) Vinegar Joe   B) Dada   C) The Alan Bown Set

4. Which 1982 Palmer No.16 hit was originally recorded by The Persuaders in 1973, and was also a No.15 hit for Rod Stewart in 1984?
A) Sailing   B) Handbags and Gladrags   C) Some Guys Have All the Luck

5. Robert got together with Keith Emerson and Greg Lake to record a 1977 number two hit, *Fanfare For the Common Man*. True or False?

6. In 1978, Robert released the album *Double Fun*. Which single from the album, a cover of a Ray Davies song, became Palmer's first top 20 hit on the US Billboard Hot 100?   A) You Really Got Me   B) All Day and All of the Night   C) Waterloo Sunset

7. With whom did Robert Palmer collaborate on the 1990 number 6 hit, *I'll Be Your Baby Tonight*, a Bob Dylan song?   A) Elkie Brooks   B) UB40   C) Andy Taylor

8. Whilst Robert Palmer was in the Power Station, what T. Rex single did the band cover and take to #22 in 1985?   A) Hot Love   B) Jeepster   C) Get It On

9. Which of the following phrases in not used in the lyrics of *Simply Irresistible*, a 1988 hit - #2 in the US and #44 in the UK?   A) She's A Natural Law   B) She's So Completely Kissable   C) She's A Glowing Sun

10. Palmer died from a sudden heart attack in a Paris hotel room on 26 September 2003 at age 54. Where is he buried?
A) Lugano, Switzerland   B) New York City   C) Nassau, Bahamas

ADDICTED TO LOVE by Robert Palmer
Your lights are on, but you're not home
Your mind is not your own
Your heart sweats, your body shakes
Another kiss is what it takes
You can't sleep, you can't eat
There's no doubt, you're in deep
Your throat is tight, you can't breathe
Another kiss is all you need....

***ROBERT PALMER ANSWERS**: 1. C) Addicted To Love; 2. B) Mercy Mercy Me (The Ecology) & I Want You; 3. B) Dada; 4. C) Some Guys Have All the Luck; 5. False (that was drummer, Carl Palmer); 6. A) You Really Got Me; 7. B) UB40; 8. C) Get It On; 9. C) She's a Glowing Sun; 10. A) Lugano, Switzerland.*

THE PET SHOP BOYS - *Neil Tennant (b 19 Jul 1954, Gosforth, Tyne & Wear) & Chris Lowe (4 Oct 1959, Blackpool). 1981 Neil (the primary vocalist) and Chris (keyboards) met in a hi-fi shop on King's Road in Chelsea, London. They discovered that they had a mutual interest in disco and electronic music and began to work together on material. Their band name was taken from friends who worked in a pet shop in Ealing and known as the 'pet shop boys'. The Pet Shop Boys had 32 Top 40 hits between 1985-99, including 4 No.1's and 14 other Top 10 hits. 11 Top 40 albums, including a No.1 and 9 other Top 10 hits. The Pet Shop Boys won 3 Brit Award winners and were 6 times Grammy nominees.*

1. What was Neil Tennant's occupation before he formed the Pet Shop Boys with Chris Lowe? A) Pet Store Owner B) Architect C) Deputy Editor Smash Hits

2. With which female singer did the Pet Shop Boys collaborate on the 1987 No. 2 hit, *What Have I Done To Deserve This* A) Dusty Springfield B) Petula Clark C) Lulu

3. In what year did the Pet Shop Boys debut single *West End Girls* get to No. 1? A) 1983 B) 1984 C) 1985

4. Which former Village People 1978 hit did the Pet Shop Boys take to number two in 1993? A) In the Navy B) Go West C) Can't Stop the Music

5. What 1987 Pet Shop Boys single was about being raised as a Catholic? A) Always On My Mind B) It's a Sin C) Rent

6. The Pet Shop Boys released a single for Comic Relief in 1994 which featured Jennifer Saunders and Joanna Lumley, under another name. True or False?

7. Which singer presented Neil Tennant with the 1987 BPI Best Single award for *West End Girls*? A) Boy George B) Marilyn C) Marc Almond

8. What group did Neil Tennant join with to produce the 1989 hit single *Getting Away With It*? A) Depeche Mode B) The Smiths C) Electronic

9. What was the name of the debut album in 1986 from the Pet Shop Boys? A) Actually B) Very C) Please

10. Their last hit of the 20th century in 1999 was about a boy from where? A) Chicago B) New York C) London

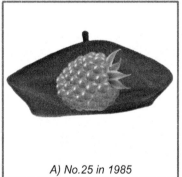

A) No.25 in 1985

B) No.4 in 1989

PET SHOP BOYS ANSWERS: *1. C) Deputy Editor Smash Hits; 2. A) Dusty Springfield; 3. C) 1985; 4. B) Go West; 5. B) It's a Sin; 6. True (Absolutely Fabulous); 7. A) Boy George; 8. C) Electronic (with Bernard Sumner of New Order and ex-Smiths guitarist Johnny Marr); 9. C) Please; 10. B) New York.* **SONG TITLES IN PICTURES ANSWERS:** *A) Raspberry Beret by Prince and the Revolution; B) Donald, Where's Your Troosers by Andy Stewart.*

GENE PITNEY *(Gene Francis Alan Pitney - Born, Hartford, Connecticut on February 17, 1940. Died, Cardiff, Wales on April 5, 2006) was an American singer-songwriter and musician. Pitney's early influences were Clyde McPhatter, country-blues singer Moon Mullican, and doo-wop groups such as The Crows. Pitney wrote hits for others, including Today's Teardrops for Roy Orbison, Rubber Ball for Bobby Vee, Marty Wilde and The Avons; Hello Mary Lou for Ricky Nelson, and He's a Rebel for the Crystals. Gene had 22 Top 40 hits, including a number one collaboration and 10 other Top 10 singles. He also had 10 Top 40 albums with three of them reaching the Top 10.*

1. Gene achieved success as a both a songwriter and as a singer in the early sixties. He had his first hit in 1961. What was the title of the song?
A) Town Without Pity   B) It Hurts To Be In Love   C) (I Wanna) Love My Life Away

2. Pitney's highest chart placing in the UK came with a 1964 #2 smash, a song by Barry Mann and Cynthia Weil, originally recorded by Frankie Laine. What was the song?   A) I'm Gonna Be Strong   B) I Must Be Seeing Things   C) Mecca

3. Gene Pitney reached #7 with the song, *That Girl belongs to Yesterday*, in 1964. Which duo wrote the song?
A) Jagger/Richards   B) Lennon/McCartney   C) Cook/Greenaway

4. Gene Pitney had success with film themes. Which theme written by Dimitri Tiomkin and Ned Washington did he record in 1961 and perform at the Oscar ceremony?
A) Come September   B) Moon River   C) Town Without Pity

5. Pitney had a 1967 No. 5 hit with *Something's Gotten Hold Of My Heart*. 22 years later he re-recorded the song, as part of a duo, and it got to No. 1. With whom did he perform on his only No.1?   A) Mick Jagger   B) Marc Almond   C) David Bowie

Q5

6. Which Bacharach/David song, a 1963 hit, opened with these lyrics: "Dearest darling I had to write to say that I won't be home anymore, Cause something happened to me while I was driving home, And I'm not the same anymore"?

7. A technical error caused Pitney to be involved in a classic, often repeated, gaffe on ITV's *This Morning* in 1989. What happened?
A) He mimed out of sync   B) The wrong song was played   C) Mic fell to pieces

8. In 1965, Pitney recorded two successful albums, *For the First Time! Two Great Stars* and *It's Country Time Again!*. Pitney and his co-star were voted the most promising country-and-western duo of the year. Who was the co-star?
A) Merle Haggard   B) George Jones   C) Glen Campbell

9. **ELBA LUNGE** is an anagram of Gene's last UK Top 40 hit. It's title is the same as a different song that was a hit for Roy Orbison in 1960.

10. *It Hurts to Be in Love* had been recorded by another star, but RCA refused to release it, because it was in violation of that singer's contract. Writers Howard Greenfield and Helen Miller, then presented the song to Pitney who took the song into the charts in 1964. Which singer missed out on a hit?
A) Paul Anka   B) Roy Orbison   C) Neil Sedaka

GENE PITNEY ANSWERS: *1. C) (I Wanna) Love My Life Away; 2. A) I'm Gonna Be Strong; 3. A) Jagger/Richards; 4. C) Town Without Pity; 5. B) Marc Almond; 6. 24 Hours From Tulsa; 7. A) He mimed out of sync; 8. B) George Jones; 9. Blue Angel; 10. C) Neil Sedaka.*

Well known musical act names have been jumbled up. Can you solve these anagrams of acts from the 20th century?

?!?!?!?!?!?!?!?!?!

1. Worst Dater
2. Her Slow Cry
3. Shut It Now, Honey
4. Library Woman
5. Deep Zen Pill
6. Best PR in years
7. Crisis! Get help
8. A pretender
9. Tick Slayer
10. Clarinet cop
11. See sign
12. Dam Oasis!
13. Help Child Properties
14. Felt wise
15. Stands virtual
16. Slick on each jam
17. Six Men Dry Under Things
18. Dyna trollop
19. Terrain nut
20. An upset ballad
21. Marble Boy
22. I like 'em young
23. I spy levelers
24. Splendid first guy
25. Slop exists

MIXED UP STARS ANSWERS: *1. Rod Stewart; 2. Sheryl Crow; 3. Whitney Houston; 4. Barry Manilow; 5. Led Zeppelin; 6. Britney Spears; 7. The Spice Girls; 8. Peter Andre; 9. Rick Astley; 10. Eric Clapton; 11. Genesis; 12. Diana Ross; 13. Red Hot Chilli Peppers; 14. Westlife; 15. Alvin Stardust; 16. Michael Jackson; 17. Dexy's Midnight Runners; 18. Dolly Parton; 19. Tina Turner; 20. Spandau Ballet; 21. Bob Marley; 22. Kylie Minogue; 23. Elvis Presley; 24. Dusty Springfield; 25. Sex Pistols.*

THE POLICE were an English rock band formed in London in 1977. For most of their history the line-up consisted of primary songwriter Sting (lead vocals, bass guitar), Andy Summers (guitar) and Stewart Copeland (drums, percussion). The Police became globally popular in the late 1970s and early 1980s. Emerging in the British new wave scene, they played a style of rock influenced by punk, reggae, and jazz and considered one of the leaders of the Second British Invasion of the US. The Police have sold over 75 million records and had 18 Top 40 singles, including 5 number ones and 5 other Top 10 hits. They also had 9 Top 20 albums, including 6 number ones and 2 other Top 10 successes. (Also see Sting page).

1. Which Police #5 hit from 1980 begins with the lyrics: "Don't think me unkind"?
A) So Lonely   B) De Do Do Do De Da Da Da   C) Invisible Sun

2. The first two Police albums were titled in what language?
A) French   B) English   C) German

3. The content of The Police 1980 number one hit *Don't Stand So Close To Me* is inspired by what novel?   A) Lolita   B) Lady Chatterley's Lover   C) Ada

4. The Police were asked to bleach their hair blonde for their appearance in a commercial ad, which was never aired, for which brand?
A) Coca Cola   B) Wrigley's Spearmint Gum   C) Alberto VO5 Shampoo

5. What song by The Police was a #1 hit in the UK, but surprisingly didn't make the singles chart in the US?
A) Walking on the Moon   B) Message in a Bottle   C) Don't Stand So Close To Me

6. In the 1979 film *Radio On,* a rare example of a British road movie, Sting plays a mechanic who is obsessed with whose music?
A) Queen   B) Elvis Presley   C) Eddie Cochran

7. How many weeks did The Police album, *Outlandos d'Amour,* spend on the British charts?   A) 56   B) 76   C) 96

8. What song on the 1979 album *Reggatta de Blanc* features a rare lead vocal from drummer Stewart Copeland?
A) On Any Other Day   B) The Bed's Too Big Without You   C) Contact

9. In 1983/4, The Police travelled with a crew of how many people during their Synchronicity Tour?   A) 28   B) 58   C) 78

10. For a brief time in 1968, Andy Summers was a member of which band?
A) The Yardbirds   B) Eric Burdon and the Animals   C) Hawkwind

FIND THE LINK
5 HITMAKERS TO NAME, THEN FIND A LINK BETWEEN THE FIVE ACTS!

A) Oldest Swinger in Town (1981)   B) All Mine (1997)   C) Unfinished Sympathy (1991)   D) Jig-A-Jig (1971)   E) Lovers of the World Unite (1966)

THE POLICE ANSWERS: 1. B) De Do Do Do De Da Da Da; 2. A) French (Outlandos d'Amour and Reggatta de Blanc; 3. A) Lolita; 4. B) Wrigley's Spearmint Gum; 5. A) Walking on the Moon; 6. C) Eddie Cochran (he played DJ Just Like Eddie); 7. C) 96; 8. A) On Any Other Day; 9. C) 78; 10. Eric Burdon and the Animals.
FIND THE LINK ANSWERS: A) Fred Wedlock; B) Portishead; C) Massive Attack; D) East of Eden; E) David & Jonathan (Roger Cook & Roger Greenaway).

ELVIS PRESLEY (Elvis Aaron Presley, born at Tupelo, Mississippi, January 8, 1935 – died at Memphis Tennessee, August 16, 1977), was an American singer and actor. The 'King of Rock and Roll' is a major significant cultural figure of the 20th century. Energised interpretations of songs and a sexually provocative style, plus a singularly potent mix of influences across colour lines during a transformative era in race relations, led him to both great success and initial controversy. Presley notched up 124 Top 40 UK singles in the 20th century, this includes seventeen number ones and 61 other Top 10 hits. Elvis also had 83 Top 40 albums, including nine number ones and thirty-four more Top 10 hits.

1. On which record label did Elvis first record under producer Sam Phillips?
A) Sun Records   B) RCA Victor   C) HMV

2. The production costs for the movie *Love Me Tender* were recovered within how many days of its release?   A) 12   B) 7   C) 3

3. How many films did Elvis star in during his lifetime?
A) Over 10   B) Over 20   C) Over 30

4. Elvis was drafted into the US Army at Fort Chaffee, Arkansas in 1958. When he was honourably discharged on March 5 1960, what rank did he hold?   A) Private   B) Corporal   C) Sergeant

5. Elvis allegedly loved eating a *Fool's Gold Loaf*, a hollowed out loaf of bread, filled with peanut butter, jelly, and a pound of steak. True or False?

6. These lyrics are from which 1970 No. 1 Elvis hit: "When no-one else can understand me, When everything I do is wrong, You give me hope and consolation, You give me strength to carry on"?

7. What was the only country outside the US in which Elvis Presley ever performed?
A) Germany   B) Canada   C) England

8. Elvis lived in Memphis, Tennessee for many years, but how old was he when he bought the beautiful Graceland estate?   A) 18   B) 22   C) 26

9. What piece of property, once owned by a US President, did Elvis buy in 1964?
A) Franklin Roosevelt's yacht   B) JFK's plane   C) Theodore Roosevelt's car

10. At the end of his stage act, up to how many encores would Elvis indulge?
A) 4   B) 2   C) He never performed encores

In the 20th Century, Elvis had 17 #1 hits.
Can you name them?

ELVIS PRESLEY ANSWERS: 1. A) Sun Records; 2. C) 3; 3. C) Over 30 (31); 4. C) Sergeant; 5. False (it was a pound of bacon!); 6. The Wonder of You; 7. B) Canada; 8. B) 22; 9. A) Franklin Roosevelt's yacht; 10. C) He Never performed encores.
ELVIS NUMBER ONES ANSWERS: (IN SEQUENCE) - All Shook Up, Jailhouse Rock (1957); One Night / I Got Stung (1958); (Now and Then There's) A Fool Such As I (1959); It's Now or Never, Are You Lonesome Tonight (1960); Surrender, Wooden Heart, (Marie's the Name) His Latest Flame, Can't Help Falling In Love (1961); Good Luck Charm, She's Not You, Return to Sender (1962); (You're the) Devil in Disguise (1963); Crying in the Chapel (1965); The Wonder of You (live) (1970); Way Down (1977).

THE PRETENDERS are an English–American rock band formed in 1978, originally consisting of founder and main songwriter Chrissie Hynde (lead vocals, rhythm guitar), James Honeyman-Scott (lead guitar, backing vocals, keyboards), Pete Farndon (bass guitar, backing vocals), and Martin Chambers (drums, backing vocals, percussion). Following the deaths of Honeyman-Scott in 1982 and Farndon in 1983, the band experienced numerous personnel changes; Hynde has been the band's only consistent member. The Pretenders had 12 Top 40 hits including a number one and five other Top 10 hits. They also had 9 Top 40 albums, including a number one and four other Top 10 successes.

1. The Pretenders first hit the charts in 1979 with a cover of a Ray Davies song, originally featured on the Kinks debut album. What was the song?
A) You Really Got Me   B) Stop Your Sobbing   C) I Go To Sleep

2. The Pretenders' singer, Chrissie Hynde, was born where in the US?
A) Chicago, Illinois   B) Sacramento, California   C) Akron, Ohio

3. The Pretenders had their only UK No.1 hit single in 1979 with a song inspired by a northern English expression for holding money. What was the song title?
A) Brass in Pocket   B) Shortnin' Bread   C) Loadsamoney

4. The Pretenders had a Christmas hit single in 1983, *2000 Miles*. In the accompanying video, in what uniform was Chrissie Hynde dressed?
A) Salvation Army   B) Santa Claus   C) Snowman

Q4

5. These lyrics are from which Pretenders 1981 No.11 hit; "Now look at the people, In the streets, in the bars, We are all of us in the gutter, But some of us are looking at the stars"?   A) Don't Get Me Wrong   B) Talk of the Town   C) Message of Love

6. In addition to fronting The Pretenders, Chrissie Hynde has collaborated with other artists. With whom did she collaborate to record a remake of Sonny and Cher's *I Got You Babe*, a UK No.1 in 1985?   A) UB40   B) Rod Stewart   C) The Kinks

7.Which Pretenders single's video features a couple of the band members manually working in a quarry, whilst Chrissie sings and looks sultry in her denim jacket?
A) Hymn To Her   B) Back on the Chain Gang   C) I Go To Sleep

8. The melody for which Pretenders 1994 hit, originated from Johann Sebastian Bach's *Minuet for Lovers*?
A) Night in my Veins   B) I'll Stand By You   C) Talk of the Town

9. On Tom Jones 1999 *Reload* album, on which Iggy Pop and David Bowie written song did the Pretenders duet with Tom Jones?
A) Lust for Life   B) Sunny Afternoon   C) Baby, It's Cold Outside

10. On 10 April 1999, Hynde led a memorial concert *Here, There and Everywhere – A Concert for Linda* at the Royal Albert Hall, London. Who was being remembered?
A) Linda Ronstadt   B) Linda Lusardi   C) Linda McCartney

THE PRETENDERS ANSWERS: *1. B) Stop Your Sobbing; 2. C) Akron, Ohio; 3. A) Brass in Pocket; 4. A) Salvation Army; 5. C) Message of Love; 6. A) UB40; 7. B) Back on the Chain Gang; 8. B) I'll Stand By You; 9. A) Lust For Life; 10. C) Linda McCartney.*

Let's Get Quizzical
A round of pop trivia

1. What is the first word of Celine Dion's 1998 No. 1, *My Heart Will Go On*?

2. Six songs from Michael Jackson's *Thriller* album charted in the UK, how many of them reached number one?

3. Which song begins with these lyrics: "Sometimes it's hard to be a woman"?

4. Which creature comes next in the classic rock and roll song from Bill Haley: "See you later, alligator…."

5. Shakin' Stevens had a No. 1 in 1981 with *Green Door*. Who reached No. 2 with the song 25 years earlier?

6. Which Scottish rock band, whose lead singer Dan McCafferty died on 8 November 2022, had 7 hits in the 70s, the highest charting ones being Broken Down Angel and Bad Bad Boy?

7. Which single by Sam and Dave got higher in the UK charts, *Soul Man* or *Soul Sister Brown Sugar*?

8. Rudolph, Ronald and O'Kelley were which singing brothers?

9. In 1965 which comic act had a Top 20 hit with *Goodbye-ee*?

10. On which instrument did James Galway perform the 1978 hit *Annie's Song*?

11. As a child, which Spice Girl advertised Milky Way chocolate bars?

12. Kraftwerk had a 1981 No.1 with *The Model*. From which country did they hail?

13. Whose real name is Susan Kay Quatrocchio?

14. Who had a smash hit with the 1995 No.1 album, *Jagged Little Pill*?

15. What song links the four pictures below?

LET'S GET QUIZZICAL ANSWERS: *1. Every; 2. One (Billie Jean); 3. Stand By Your Man by Tammy Wynette; 4. (On the Nile, **Crocodile**); 5. Frankie Vaughan; 6. Nazareth; 7. Soul Sister Brown Sugar 15 (Soul Man reached 24); 8. Isley Brothers; 9. Peter Cook & Dudley Moore; 10. Flute; 11. Emma Bunton; 12. Germany; 13. Suzi Quatro; 14. Alanis Morissette; 15. Penny Lane by The Beatles (lyrics! - look them up).*

PRINCE *(Prince Rogers, born in Nelson, Minneapolis, Minnesota, June 7, 1958 – died in Chanhassen, Minnesota, April 21, 2016, April 21, 2016) was an American singer-songwriter and multi-instrumentalist. Widely regarded as one of the greatest musicians of his generation, known for his flamboyant, androgynous persona and wide vocal range, including far-reaching falsetto and high-pitched screams. Prince had 1 No. 1, 14 Top 10 hits and 23 other Top 40 hits as Prince, Prince & The Revolution, Prince & New Power Generation, The Artist formerly known as Prince and as part of collaborations. He also had 20 Top 40 albums, including 5 No. 1's and 9 other Top 10 hits.*

1. What pseudonym did Prince use as the composer of *Manic Monday*, a hit for The Bangles in 1986? A) Christopher B) Timothy C) Rogers

2. On which Madonna 1989 hit did Prince allegedly play guitar?
A) Material Girl B) Like A Prayer C) Hanky Panky

3. Which Prince song includes the lyrics: "I like 'em fat, I like 'em proud, you've got to have a mother for me..."?
A) Thieves in the Temple B) Gett Off C) Alphabet Street

4. Which song remains Prince's only No.1 single in the UK?
A) The Most Beautiful Girl in the World B) 1999 C) Purple Rain

5. The 1987 No.11 hit song *U Got the Look* features which initially uncredited Scottish singer? A) Billy Connolly B) Lulu C) Sheena Easton

6. Which role as the owner of the Grand Slam Club did Prince play in the 1990 film *Graffiti Bridge*? A) Sundance B) Butch C) The Kid

7. How many different instruments did Prince claim to have played on his debut album *For You* in 1978? A) 7 B) 17 C) 27

8. How tall was Prince? A) 5' (152cm) B) 5'2" (157cm) C) 5'4" (163cm)

9. "Let's look for the purple banana till they put us in the truck." Is this a Real Prince lyric or a Misheard lyric?

10. Prince originally wrote *Nothing Compares 2 U* for his then funk band, the Family. But, who topped the charts with the song in 1990?
A) Sheena Easton B) Sinead O'Connor C) Chaka Khan

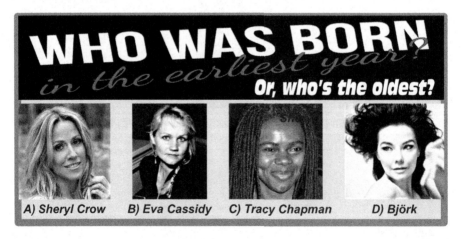

WHO WAS BORN *in the earliest year?* **Or, who's the oldest?**

A) Sheryl Crow   B) Eva Cassidy   C) Tracy Chapman   D) Björk

QUEEN *are a British rock band formed in London in 1970, comprising Freddie Mercury (lead vocals, piano), Brian May (guitar, vocals), Roger Taylor (drums, vocals) and John Deacon (bass). Their earlier works were influenced by progressive rock, hard rock and heavy metal, but gradually venturing into more conventional and radio-friendly works by incorporating arena rock and pop rock. May and Taylor played together in the band Smile. Queen registered 50 Top 40 hits in the 20th century, including 5 No. 1's and 20 other Top 10 hits. They also had 23 Top 40 albums, includin9 No. 1's and 11 other Top 10 successes.*

1. Who designed the Queen crest logo?
A) Freddie Mercury   B) Brian May   C) Roger Taylor   D) John Deacon

2. Which member of Queen became the first to release a solo album?
A) Freddie Mercury   B) Brian May   C) Roger Taylor   D) John Deacon

3. Which keyboard player has been described as the unofficial fifth member of Queen?   A) Morgan Fisher   B) Spike Edney   C) Fred Mandel

4. In 1963, Brian May and his dad Harold built a guitar that Brian would use on many Queen albums and tours. What was it named?
A) Red One   B) Red Special   C) Red Square

5. In 1974 what was the name of Queen's first single that reached #10 in the UK?   A) Seven Seas of Rhye
B) Killer Queen   C) You're My Best Friend

6. A homage is paid to which silent film in the 1984 video which accompanied the #2 hit *Radio Gaga*?
A) Gold Rush   B) The General   C) Metropolis

7. "I'm a shooting star leaping through the sky like a tiger, Defying the laws of gravity, I'm a racing car passing by like Lady Godiva". Lyrics from which 1979 #9 hit?
A) Fat Bottomed Girls   B) Don't Stop Me Now   C) Save Me

8. Which song did Freddie and Brian play acoustically at *Live Aid* in 1985?
A) Love Of My Life   B) One Vision   C) Play the Game

9. Which member of Queen wrote *Another One Bites the Dust*, a #9 hit in 1980?
A) Brian May   B) Freddie Mercury   C) John Deacon   D) Roger Taylor

10. Where did Queen record their 1981 #1 hit with David Bowie?
A) Los Angeles   B) Montreux   C) Munich

DIM FRED LARDS

An anagram of which British folk band, featuring vocalist Cathy Lesurf, who had a 1979 number 3 hit single with *Day Trip to Bangor (Didn't We Have a Lovely Time)*, which reached no. 3 on the UK Singles Chart.

---

*QUEEN ANSWERS: 1. A) Freddie Mercury; 2. C) Roger Taylor; 3. B) Spike Edney; 4. B) Red Special; 5. A) Seven Seas of Rhye; 6. C) Metropolis; 7. B) Don't Stop Me Now; 8. A) Love Of My Life; 9. C) John Deacon; 10. B) Montreux. **ANAGRAM ANSWER:** Fiddler's Dram.*

JIM REEVES *(James Travis Reeves - Born Galloway, Texas on August 20, 1923 – Died Davidson County, Tennessee, July 31, 1964) was an American country and popular music singer-songwriter, well known for the Nashville Sound and prolific during the 1960s. Reeves was known as 'Gentleman Jim'. His songs charted for years after his death in a plane crash when he was piloting a single-engine Beechcraft Debonair aircraft caught up in a violent thunderstorm. Jim is a member of both the Country Music and Texas Country Music Halls of Fame. Reeves had 24 Top 40 hits, including a number one and five other Top 10 hits.He also had 27 Top 40 albums, including two number ones and 12 other Top 10 successes.*

1. What type of singing voice did Jim have?   A) Tenor   B) Baritone   C) Bass

2. Before he became a singer, Jim was a talented sportsman; what sport did he play?
A) Baseball   B) American Football   C) Basketball

3. What became Jim Reeves' first UK Top 10 hit in 1963?
A) He'll Have To Go   B) Mexican Joe   C) Welcome To My World

4. In which year was Jim Reeves elected to the Country Music Hall of Fame?
A) 1967   B) 1963   C) 1959

5. On what record label did Jim Reeves record most of his hits?
A) Decca   B) Pye   C) RCA Victor

6. Jim Reeves had the biggest-selling UK single of 1964 with a Leon Payne song also recorded by Elvis Presley and Johnny Cash. What song took Jim to #5?
A) You're the Only Good Thing   B) I Love You Because   C) Adios Amigo

7. What 1964 #3 hit contains these lyrics: "Though you don't want me now, I'll still love you,Till the breath in my body is gone"?

8. Jim Reeves wore a toupee, which he and his wife Mary Reeves kept a closely guarded secret. True or False?

9. Jim Reeves' only UK #1 was a posthumous hit in 1966. What was the song that remained at #1 for 5 weeks and in the UK Singles Chart for a total of 25 weeks?
A) Bimbo   B) Moonlight and Roses   C) Distant Drums

10. Jim Reeves married Mary White on September 3, 1947. They never had any children, as Jim Reeves was believed to be sterile, due to complications from which condition?   A) Diabetes   B) Mumps   C) Chicken Pox

WHAT NAME LINKS THE SINGERS?

1. PAUL ...... LE BON
2. JIMMY ...... RICHARD
3. DORA ...... ADAMS
4. ELTON ...... PARR
5. RAY ...... AZNAVOUR
6. GEORGE ...... BALL
7. HANK ...... GAYE
8. BRENDA ...... MARVIN
9. KETTY ...... FLATT
10. RUSS ...... Twitty

JIM REEVES ANSWERS: 1. B) Baritone; 2. A) Baseball; 3. C) Welcome To My World; 4. A) 1967; 5. C) RCA Victor; 6. B) I Love You Because; 7. I Won't Forget You; 8. True; 9. C) Distant Drums; 10. B) Mumps. **NAME LINKS ANSWERS:** *1. Simon; 2. Cliff; 3. Bryan; 4. John; 5. Charles; 6. Michael; 7. Marvin; 8. Lee; 9. Lester; 10. Conway.*

CLIFF RICHARD *(Sir Cliff Richard OBE (born Lucknow, India as Harry Rodger Webb; 14 October 1940) is an English singer with British and Barbadian citizenship. The third-top-selling artist in UK Singles Chart history, behind only The Beatles and Elvis Presley. Initially, Richard was originally marketed as a rebellious rock and roll singer in the style of Presley and Little Richard. With his backing group, The Shadows (originally The Drifters), he dominated the British popular music scene pre-Beatles from the late 1950s to early 1960s. Cliff had 118 Top 40 singles between 1958 and 1999, including 14 No.1's and 49 more Top 10. He also had 46 Top 40 albums, including 7 number ones and 27 further Top 10 successes.*

1. What was the name of Cliff's 1958 #2 single that is often described as the first 'authentic UK rock 'n' roll song'?   A) Living Doll   B) C) High Class Baby   C) Move It

2. In 1999 Sir Cliff had a #1 hit with a pop music version of the 'Lord's Prayer'. What was the title of the hit?   A) Millennium Prayer   B) Heaven   C) Saviour's Day

3. Cliff Richard has had many hits duetting with other stars. With which member of a famous American duo did he have a UK #9 in 1983?
A) Paul Simon   B) Phil Everly   C) Cher

4. Who wrote Cliff Richard's 1966 #15 hit *Blue Turns To Grey*?
A) Lennon & McCartney   B) Goffin & King   C) Jagger & Richards

5. Cliff's biggest hit in the US was a #6 hit in 1976. What was the song?
A) We Don't Talk Anymore   B) Devil Woman   C) Miss You Nights

6. In 1979, with whom did Cliff perform a duet at the Royal Albert Hall, to celebrate the London Symphony Orchestra's 75th anniversary?
A) Kate Bush   B) Cilla Black   C) Olivia Newton-John

7. In which film did Cliff try to sell 'Brumburgers', a hamburger originating from the Midlands?   A) Summer Holiday   B) Wonderful Life   C) Take Me High

8. Cliff had two hits with Hank Marvin in 1969 and 1970. *The Joy of Living* reached #25, but what song reached number seven?
A) Throw Down a Line   B) Living Doll   C) Suddenly

9. In his film debut in 1959, Cliff played Curley Thompson. What was the title of the film?   A) Expresso Bongo   B) Serious Charge   C) Some People

10. In 1990 Cliff staged *From a Distance: The Event* show at Wembley Stadium. He had a Top 10 hit from the performance with a former Herman's Hermits #3 hit from 1965. What was the title of the song?
A) No Milk Today   B) Wonderful World   C) Silhouettes

CLIFF HIT DUETS

WITH WHOM DID CLIFF RICHARD SHARE THE BILLING?

1. All I Have To Do Is Dream (1994)
2. Little Town (1982)
3. Living Doll (1986)
4. All I Ask Of You (1986)
5. Whenever God Shines His Light (1989)
6. Had To Be (1995)
7. The Wedding (1996)
8. Suddenly (1980)
9. She Means Nothing To Me (1983)
10. Livin' Lovin' Doll (1959)

CLIFF RICHARD ANSWERS: *1. C) Move It; 2. A) Millennium Prayer; 3. B) Phil Everly; 4. C) Jagger & Richards; 5. B) Devil Woman; 6. A) Kate Bush; 7. C) Take Me High; 8. A) Throw Down a Line; 9. B) Serious Charge; 10. C) Silhouettes.*
CLIFF HIT DUETS ANSWERS: *1. Phil Everly; 2. Tony Rivers & Nigel Perrin; 3. The Young Ones; 4. Sarah Brightman; 5. Van Morrison; 6. Olivia Newton-John; 7. Helen Hobson; 8. Olivia Newton-John; 9. Phil Everly; 10. The Drifters.*

THE ROLLING STONES are an English rock band formed in London in 1962. A most popular and enduring band of the early 1960s rock era. the Pioneers of a gritty, heavier-driven sound that came to define hard rock. The first stable line-up consisted of: Mick Jagger (vocals), Brian Jones (multi instruments), Keith Richards (guitar), Bill Wyman (bass) and Charlie Watts (drums). In their formative years, Jones was the primary leader: he assembled the band, named it, and drove their sound and image. The Rolling Stones had 39 Top 40 hits between 1963 and 1998; this included 8 #1 hits and 13 more Top 10 hits. The Stones also had 38 Top 40 albums, 10 #1, and 22 more Top 10 hits.

1. Brian Jones left the band shortly before he drowned in his swimming pool in 1969. Who had replaced him? A) Mick Taylor   B) Ronnie Wood   C) Ian Stewart

2. Who thought of the idea for the artwork of the 1971 album *Sticky Fingers*?
A) Mick Jagger   B) John Lennon   C) Andy Warhol

3. What was the first Stones album to comprise entirely of Jagger/Richards songs?
A) Aftermath   B) Beggar's Banquet   C) Between the Buttons

4. On which Beatles #1 hit did Brian Jones sing backing vocals?
A) Get Back   B) Yellow Submarine   C) All You Need Is Love

5. When The Stones performed *Let's Spend The Night Together* on The Ed Sullivan Show, they were ordered to change the lyrics to...   A) Let's spend some time together   B) Let's spend less time together   C) Let's spend more time together

6. What was the name of the restaurants Bill Wyman opened in 1989?
A) Beggar's Banquet   B) Little Red Rooster   C) Sticky Fingers

7. What did Mick Jagger release from the stage during their historic 1969 Hyde Park Concert, just days after the death of Brian Jones?
A) Fireworks   B) Thousands of butterflies   C) 12 white doves

8. Which 1966 Stones #2 hit starts with these lyrics: "You're the kind of person you meet at certain dismal, dull affairs, Center of a crowd, talking much too loud, running up and down the stairs"
A) Nineteenth Nervous Breakdown   B) The Last Time   C) Get Off My Cloud

9. In which year did Ronnie Wood became a member of the Rolling Stones, after his years in The Faces and the Jeff Beck Group? A) 1973   B) 1975   C) 1977

10. The Stones performed many Chuck Berry songs. Which one did they cover for their first hit single in 1963? A) Carol   B) Down the Road Apiece   C) Come On

Charlie Watts

THE ROLLING STONES ANSWERS: 1. A) Mick Taylor; 2. C) Andy Warhol; 3. A) Aftermath; 4. B) Yellow Submarine; 5. A) Let's spend some time together; 6. C) Sticky Fingers; 7. B) Thousands of butterflies; 8. A) Nineteenth Nervous Breakdown; 9. B) 1975; 10. C) Come On.

DIANA ROSS *(born Detroit, Michigan on March 26, 1944) is an American singer and actress. She rose to fame as the lead singer of the vocal group The Supremes. In 1970, Ross embarked on a successful solo career in music, television and stage. Diana has also achieved mainstream success and recognition as an actor. After over 20 years with the Motown label, Ross moved to RCA Records for a $20 million, seven-year recording contract. Including collaborations, Diana Ross had 45 Top 40 singles after leaving The Supremes; these included 2 #1's, 16 Top 10 hits and 27 other Top 40 records. Ross also had 2 #1 albums, 9 other Top 10 hit albums and 17 more that reached the Top 40.*

1.Diana Ross is the name on her birth certificate, but her family call her Diana, because a mistake was made on the certificate. True or False?

2. Diana Ross had a successful film career. Particularly receiving much praise for her leading roll in *Lady Sings the Blues*. Which singer's life was the film based upon?
A) Ella Fitzgerald   B) Billie Holiday   C) Etta James

3. In 1981, Diana Ross had a #7 UK hit, *Endless Love*, duetting with which other top Motown singer?   A) Marvin Gaye   B) Smokey Robinson   C) Lionel Richie

4. Which Bee Gees written song did Diana Ross take to number one in 1986?
A) Chain Reaction   B) Islands in the Stream   C) Heartbreaker

5. *Do You Know Where You're Going To* was a #5 in 1976. For what film, starring Diana Ross, was the song the main theme?
A) Mahogany   B) The Wiz   C) Lady Sings the Blues

6. Why did Diana Ross have to stop her 1983 free concert on Central Park's Great Lawn and then rearrange it for the next day?
A) Technical faults B) Illness C) Torrential rain

7. Which Diana Ross 1980 #5 hit contains these lyrics: "His international style, Exudes an air of royalties, His eighty eight key smile, Is so pleasant to see"?
A) Upside Down   B) My Old Piano   C) The Boss

8. In 1981, Diana Ross had a #4 hit with a remake of which Frankie Lymon & The Teenagers #1 UK hit from 1956?
A) Why Do Fools Fall in Love   B) I'm Not a Juvenile Delinquent   C) Goody Goody

9. Diana Ross had two hits singing with Marvin Gaye. *You Are Everything* was a #5 hit in 1974, but what song did the pair chart at #25 later that year?   A) I'm Gonna Make You Love Me   B) Include Me In Your Life   C) Stop Look Listen (To Your Heart)

10. In 1991, at the Victoria Palace Theatre, Ross became one of the few American artists to have headlined which show?
A) Glastonbury B) Royal Variety Show   C) Last Night at the Proms

Every Picture Tells a Story!

Three famous paintings are the clues to the titles of three hit songs. We provide the years - you name the artistes!

A) 1959

B) 1995

C) 1986

DIANA ROSS ANSWERS: 1. True; 2. B) Billie Holiday; 3. C) Lionel Richie; 4. A) Chain Reaction; 5. A) Mahogany; 6. C) Torrential rain; 7. B) My Old Piano; 8. A) Why Do Fool I Love; 9. C) Stop Look Listen (To Your Heart); 10. B) Royal Variety Show.
EVERY PICTURE TELLS A STORY ANSWERS: A) Conway Twitty (Mona Lisa); B) Michael & Janet Jackson (Scream); C) Prince & The Revolution (Kiss).

ROXETTE *were a Swedish pop rock duo, consisting of Marie Fredriksson (30 May 1958 – 9 December 2019 -vocals & keyboards) and Per Gessle (Born 12 January 1959 - vocals and guitar). Formed in 1986, the duo became an international act in the late 1980s. Before becoming a duo, Fredriksson and Gessle were already established artists in Sweden, she having released a number of solo albums. They are Sweden's second-best-selling music act after ABBA. Roxette notched up 19 Top 40 hits, including 6 Top 10 hits. They also had 6 Top 40 albums, five of them reaching the Top 10.*

1. Where does the name Roxette originate?
A) Completely invented   B) A Steve Martin film title   C) Title of a Dr. Feelgood song

2. What is the title of Roxette's first album which reached #4 in the UK?
A) Look Sharp! B) Heartland   C) Pearls of Passion

3. Roxette's first UK hit came in 1989. These are the opening lines of what #7 song: "One, two, three, four walking like a man, Hitting like a hammer, She's a juvenile scam"? A) Listen To Your Heart   B) The Look   C) Dangerous

4. Roxette's highest UK chart position was achieved with their second single, what was the title of the song released in 1990 that reached #3?
A) Dressed For Success   B) Joyride   C) It Must Have Been Love

5. Male lead singer, Per Gessle, was in a successful Swedish band before Roxette. What was their name?   A) Moderna Tider   B) Gyllene Tider   C) Pers Garage

6. What is the title of the 1991 Roxette album which led to the band's first world tour?
A) Joyride   B) Look Sharp!   C) Tourism

7. What major film soundtrack played the Roxette song *It Must Have Been Love* in the background as Julia Roberts travelled in a limo?
A) Hook B) Sleeping With the Enemy   C) Pretty Woman

8. In 1995, what was the title of Roxette's first Greatest Hits album?   A) Don't Ignore Us - Just Adore Us!   B) Don't Bore Us - Get to the Chorus!   C) Greatest

9. After a hiatus of a few years, what was the Roxette album that some people consider to be Roxette's comeback album?
A) Crash! Boom! Bang!   B) Room Service   C) Have a Nice Day

10. Complete the title of the 1992 Roxette that reached #28 - *Queen of ….*
A) Rain B) Hearts C) Puddings

ROXETTE ANSWERS: 1. C) Title of a Dr. Feelgood song; 2. A) Look Sharp!; 3. B) The Look; 4. C) It Must Have Been Love; 5. B) Gyllene Tider; 6. A) Joyride (Join the Joyride Tour); 7. C) Pretty Woman; 8. B) Don't Bore Us - Get to the Chorus!; 9. C) Have a Nice Day; 10. A) Rain.

LEO SAYER (*Gerard Hugh 'Leo' Sayer (born Shoreham-by-Sea in Sussex on May 1948) is an English-Australian singer and songwriter. He was initially discovered by musician David Courtney, who then co-managed and co-produced him with former pop singer turned manager, Adam Faith. After a decade of success, Sayer's career suffered repeated setbacks due to a series of financial and legal problems involving Adam Faith. Leo Sayer had 15 Top 40 hits, including a number one and nine other Top 10 hits (4 of them #2 hits!). He also had 12 Top 40 albums, including a #1 and 5 other Top 10 successes.*

1. Leo Sayer's breakthrough came from songwriting. Which singer launched a solo career with *Giving It All Away*, a #5 hit partly written by Leo?
A) Roger Daltrey   B) Freddie Mercury   C) Mick Jagger

2. Leo's first UK hit, a #2 in 1973, was covered in the US by Three Dog Night. What was the song?   A) Long Tall Glasses   B) One Man Band   C) The Show Must Go On

3. On his 1978 cover of Buddy Holly's *Raining In My Heart*, which peaked at #21, which Fleetwood Mac member performed on the track with Leo?
A) Stevie Nicks   B) Mick Fleetwood   C) Lindsay Buckingham

4. *More Than I Can Say* was a #2 hit for Leo in 1980. Which American singer had taken the song to #4 in the charts in 1961?
A) Bobby Rydell   B) Bobby Vee   C) Bobby Darin

5. A Leo Sayer #22 hit in 1977 was to be a #1 when reworked as a dance remix by Meck in 2006. What was the song that includes these lyrics: "There's a storm ragin' deep in my soul, There's a howlin' wind that I just can't control, There's a fire inside me I can't explain"?   A) Thunder In My Heart   B) How Much Love   C) Orchard Road

6. In his early days, what costume did Leo Sayer wear on TV and stage to promote himself?   A) Pierrot   B) Highwayman   C) Cowboy

7. Leo wrote *Dreamin'* and it became a Top 10 hit for which pop superstar in 1980?
A) Michael Jackson   B) Paul McCartney   C) Cliff Richard

8. Leo Sayer's only solo #1 was attained with *When I Need You* in 1977. Who wrote the song?   A) Albert Hammond/Carole Bayer Sager   B) Gerry Goffin/Carole King
C) Burt Bacharach/Hal David

9. In 1973 Leo made his first TV appearance on which famous BBC2 music programme, commissioned by David Attenborough?
A) Discs-a-Gogo   B) The Old Grey Whistle Test   C) Later ... with Jools Holland

10. Name the other two men in the picture (below) with Leo Sayer at the Long Beach Grand Prix in 1978?

A CROSS SECTION OF POPULAR MUSIC QUESTIONS

1. Which guitarist, killed in a 1990 helicopter crash, played on 3 David Bowie hits in 1983 - *Let's Dance*, *China Girl* and *Modern Love*?

2. Which US instrumental band had Top 10 hits with *Walk, Don't Run* and *Perfidia* in 1960?

3. Who had a #1 hit with *Oh Carolina* in 1993?

4. "To the funny farm, Where life is beautiful all the time", lyrics from what song?

5. Who took *The Most Beautiful Girl* to #2 in 1974?

6. Which regular singer on TV's *Drumbeat*, a Larry Parnes' managed artiste, became cruise director on American luxury cruise ships?

7. What 60s singer, real name Robert Ridarelli, who died on 5 April 2022 aged 79, had hits with *Wild One* and *Sway*?

8. Which made-for-TV act opened with a #1 hit and two #2 hits in 1999 before having 8 more Top 10 hits into the early years of the 21st century?

9. Which one hit wonders had a #1 with *Michael* in 1961?

10. What was the title of Charlene's 1982 number one - her only UK hit?

11. Which artist had the most Top 10 hits in the UK during the 1990s?

12. *The Ugly Duckling* waddled into #10 in 1975. Which comedian/actor took it there?

13. Which Spice Girl advertised Milky Bar Buttons when she was 11 years old?

14. What TV actor, real name David Solberg, had 5 UK hits between 1976/8?

15. Which band did Ritchie Blackmore form upon leaving Deep Purple?

16. Name the five singers below - there is also a link to find!

A   B   C   D   E

17. Which 1920s-style jazz band, known for their surreal performances had four Top 30 hits in 1961?

18. Which heavy rock band tenderly asked *Is This Love* at #9 in 1987?

19. Joe Dolce Music Theatre - *Shaddup You Face*; Aneka - *Japanese Boy* and Julio Iglesias - *Begin The Beguine* were all UK number ones - in what year?

20. In 1991 *Charly* was the first hit for which Essex electronic dance music band?

A CROSS SECTION OF POP MUSIC QUESTIONS ANSWERS: 1. Stevie Ray Vaughan; 2. The Ventures; 3. Shaggy; 4. They're Coming To Take Me Away Ha-Haaa! By Napoleon XIV; 5. Charlie Rich; 6. Vince Eager; 7. Bobby Rydell; 8. S Club 7; 9. The Highwaymen; 10. I've Never Been To Me; 11. Madonna; 12. Mike Reid; 13. Emma Bunton; 14. David Soul; 15. Rainbow; 16. A) Jimmy, B) Paul, C) Tammy, D) Grace & E) Howard JONES (the link); 17. The Temperance Seven; 18. Whitesnake; 19. 1981; 20. The Prodigy.

THE SEARCHERS *are an English Merseybeat group who emerged during the 1960s British Invasion. The band, founded as a skiffle group in Liverpool in 1959, by John McNally (Rhythm) and Mike Pender (Lead guitar) took their name from the 1956 John Ford western film The Searchers. The early quartet was completed by Chris Curtis (Drums) and Tony Jackson (Bass). Frank Allen replaced Jackson on bass in 1964. As musical styles evolved, The Searchers did attempt to move with the times. The Searchers had 12 Top 40 hits, including 3 #1's and 3 other Top 10 hits. The Searchers also had 4 Top 10 albums.*

1. Which Drifters song became the first of The Searchers' singles to top the UK chart in 1963? A) Sweets For My Sweet B) Sweet Nothins' C) Dance With Me

2. The Searchers only had one US top ten hit; what was its title?
A) Farmer John B) Love Potion No. 9 C) Ain't That Just Like Me

3. The Searchers first four albums were UK Top 10 hits. Which album reached the highest position? A) It's the Searchers B) Sugar and Spice C) Meet the Searchers

4. Who sung the lead vocals on *Needles and Pins* in 1964?
A) Mike Pender B) Tony Jackson C) Chris Curtis

5. When Tony Jackson left in 1964, he formed a new band and had one hit, a #38 success. What was the name of Tony's new band? A) The New Searchers
B) Tony Jackson & The Vibrations C) The Jackson Five

6. In 1964 The Searchers reached number three with *When You Walk in the Room*, a song written by which US female singer?
A) Brenda Lee B) Dolly Parton C) Jackie DeShannon

7. The Searchers third and final #1 also came in 1964. What was the title of the song, written by Billy Jackson and Jimmy Wisner?
A) Don't Throw Your Love Away B) Sugar and Spice C) What'd I Say

8. On which record label did all of The Searchers UK chart singles and albums appear? A) Philips B) Pye C) Parlophone

9. The Searchers hit #4 with a ballad that included these lyrics: "And I know that you're not happy at all, Any fool can plainly see, And I know I'm the one you really love, But I can't go on sharing you, sharing you. Name the song.

10. Which band did Frank Allen leave when he replaced Tony Jackson as The Searchers bass guitarist in 1964? A) Johnny Kidd & The Pirates B) Cliff Bennett & The Rebel Rousers C) The Fortunes

Instrumentals In Their Success
NAME THE 1960s BANDS WHO HAD THE HITS

A. 1962
Orange Blossom Special

B. 1962
Telstar

C. 1961
Entry of the Gladiators

D. 1969
Time is Tight

THE SEARCHERS ANSWERS: *1. A) Sweets For My Sweet; 2. B) Love Potion No. 9; 3. C) Meet the Searchers; 4. B) Tony Jackson; 5. B) Tony Jackson & The Vibrations; 6. C) Jackie DeShannon; 7. A) Don't Throw Your Love Away; 8. B) Pye; 9. Goodbye My Love; 10. B) Cliff Bennett & The Rebel Rousers. **INSTRUMENTALS IN THEIR SUCCESS ANSWERS:** A) The Spotnicks; B) The Tornados; C) Nero & The Gladiators; D) Booker T. & MG's.*

NEIL SEDAKA *(Born Brooklyn, New York on March 13, 1939) is an American pop singer and pianist. Since his music career began in 1957 as a founding member of The Tokens. He has sold millions of records as a performer and has written or co-written over 500 songs for himself and others, collaborating mostly with lyricists Howard 'Howie' Greenfield and Phil Cody. His mother had wanted him to become a classical pianist like his contemporary Van Cliburn. He was inducted into the Songwriters Hall of Fame in 1983 and continues to perform. Sedaka achieved a string of 16 Top 40 hit singles over the late 1950s and early 1960s, including 7 Top 10 hits. He also had 7 Top 40 albums, including 2 Top 10 successes.*

1. Neil Sedaka's first UK hit reached 9 in 1959. What was the song, performed in the boogie-woogie style of Jerry Lee Lewis?
A) One Way Ticket   B) I Go Ape   C) Stairway to Heaven

2. *Stupid Cupid*, a Neil Sedaka / Howard Greenfield written song got to number one with *Carolina Moon* on the 'B' side in 1958. Who sung the song?
A) Patsy Cline   B) Carole King   C) Connie Francis

3. Neil Sedaka hit number three in 1959 with *Oh! Carol*. Who was allegedly the subject of the hit?   A) Carole King   B) Carol Deene   C) Carol Burnett

4. What 1961 Neil Sedaka #9 hit contains these lyrics: "You start the year off fine, (February) You're my little Valentine, (March) I'm gonna march you down the aisle, (April) You're the Easter Bunny when you smile"?

5. Neil Sedaka's piano playing is heard on *Dream Lover*, Bobby Darin's 1959 #1 hit. True or False?

6. *Tu non lo sai* is an Italian version of which of Sedaka's biggest hits?
A) Little Devil   B) Stairway to Heaven   C) Breaking Up Is Hard To Do

7. In 1973, Andy Williams had a big hit with a Sedaka / Phil Cody written song, which was also a smaller hit for The Carpenters two years later. What was the song?
A) Solitaire   B) Can't Take My Eyes Off You   C) Top of the World

8. Neil Sedaka joined Phil Cody in writing English lyrics for the title track of ABBA's 1973 debut album. What was the song?
A) Waterloo   B) Mamma Mia   C) Ring Ring

9. In the seventies, Sedaka released three albums on Rocket Records. Who owned the company?   A) Billy Joel   B) Elton John   C) Paul Anka

10. Which Neil Sedaka song failed to chart in the UK for him, was a #18 for Tony Christie in 1971, and was to be a huge #1 hit in the 20th century as a charity song?

SONGS GIVEN THE *GREEN* LIGHT
Who had the hits as indicated?

1. Green Door (1981)

2. Green Onions (1979)

3. Green Tambourine (1968)

4. Ballad of the Green Berets (1966)

5. Green River (1969)

6. Green Fields (1960)

7. The Green Leaves of Summer (1962)

8. Green Green Grass of Home (1975)

9. Little Green Apples (1968)

10. Rhythm and Greens (1964)

NEIL SEDAKA ANSWERS: *1. B) I Go Ape; 2. C) Connie Francis; 3. A) Carole King; 4. Calendar Girl; 5. True; 6. C) Breaking Up Is Hard To Do; 7. A) Solitaire; 8. C) Ring Ring; 9. B) Elton John; 10. Is This the Way To (Amarillo).* **SONGS GIVEN THE GREEN LIGHT ANSWERS:** *1. Shakin' Stevens; 2. Booker T. & The MG's; 3. Lemon Pipers; 4. Staff Sergeant Barry Sadler; 5. Creedence Clearwater Revival; 6. Beverley Sisters; 7. Kenny Ball & His Jazzmen; 8. Elvis Presley (Tom Jones was 1966); 9. Roger Miller; 10. The Shadows.*

THE SEEKERS *were an Australian folk-influenced pop quartet, formed in Melbourne in 1962. They were the first Australian pop music group to achieve major chart and sales success in the UK and the US. They were especially popular during the 1960s with their best-known configuration of Judith Durham on vocals, piano and tambourine; Athol Guy on double bass and vocals; Keith Potger on twelve-string guitar, banjo and vocals; and Bruce Woodley on guitar, mandolin, banjo and vocals. The Seekers had 8 Top 40 singles including two number ones and 4 other Top 10 hits (the other two reaching #11). The Seekers also had 7 Top 20 albums, including a #1 and 4 other Top 10 successes.*

1. What was the traditional song that was issued as The Seekers debut single and failed to chart? A) Pub With No Beer B) Waltzing Matilda C) Sun Arise

2. In 1964 The Seekers travelled to the UK intending to stay just ten weeks, but they were offered work by the Grade Organisation and stayed. Their first hit in the UK was which #1 hit, written by Tom Springfield (of Springfields fame)?
A) A World Of Our Own B) I'll Never Find Another You C) Beg, Steal or Borrow

3. The Seekers provided the title track for which 1966 film, starring James Mason and Lynn Redgrave? A) Alfie B) The Trap C) Georgy Girl

4. Judith Durham performed one of her own creations, *Australia, Land of Today*, at which major 1992 event? A) World Cup cricket final B) State Opening of Parliament C) 60th anniversary of Sydney Harbour Bridge

5. *Someday One Day* reached #11 in 1966. Who wrote the song?
A) Burt Bacharach B) Paul Simon C) Bob Dylan

6. Why did Judith Durham have to temporarily leave the group and be replaced for a few months in 1965 by Ellen Wade?
A) Emergency nasal surgery B) She was homesick C) She had a baby

7. Durham returned to the group and their next single reached number one. The melody is based on a Russian folk song, with lyrics written by Tom Springfield. What was the title of the song?
A) Walk With Me B) I'd Like To Teach the World to Sing C) The Carnival Is Over

8. In which year did The Seekers reunite with the classic line-up of Durham, Guy, Potger and Woodley and perform a reunion concert, which led to a 102-date tour?
A) 1972 B) 1982 C) 1992

9. In 1966 The Seekers performed in the pantomime *Humpty Dumpty* with comic Ted Rogers. What was the venue for the pantomime?
A) London Palladium B) Bristol Hippodrome C) Liverpool Empire

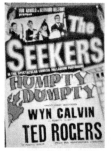

10. During the Panto season The Seekers hit #2 with which song that opened with these words: "Train whistle blowing makes a sleepy noise, Underneath their blankets go all the girls and boys"?
A) Starlight Express B) Runaway Train C) Morningtown Ride

THE SEEKERS ANSWERS: *1. B) Waltzing Matilda; 2. B) I'll Never Find Another You; 3. C) Georgy Girl; 4. A) World Cup cricket final; 5. B) Paul Simon; 6. A) Emergency nasal treatment; 7. C) The Carnival is Over; 8. C) 1992; 9. B) Bristol Hippodrome; 10. C) Morningtown Ride.*

THE SHADOWS *(originally The Drifters) were an English instrumental / vocal rock group, who dominated British pop music charts in the late 1950s / early 1960s, pre-Beatles era. They were the backing band for Cliff Richard from 1958 to 1968, the first backing band to emerge as stars. Pioneers of the four-member instrumental format, the band consisted of lead guitar, rhythm guitar, bass guitar and drums. A few line up changes during their long career. The Shadows had 29 solo Top 40 hits, this included 5 #1 hits and 11 other Top 10 hits. The Shads also had 26 solo Top 40 albums, including 4 #1 and a further 8 Top 10 hits. Of course they also appeared on many Cliff Richard hits.*

1. The Shadows were originally known by which different name, before an established American group threatened legal action over naming rights.
A) Drifters   B) Silhouettes   C) Shades

2. Jerry Lordan's *Apache* provided the Shadows breakthrough, reaching #1 for 5 weeks in 1960. What Thor Heyerdahl craft provided the title for their second #1 in 1961?   A) Titanic   B) Kon Tiki   C) Cutty Sark

3. In 1963 The Shadows 13th single became their first record not to reach the Top 10. The title was the name of which Native American chief?
A) Sitting Bull   B) Crazy Horse   C) Geronimo

4. Jet Harris (Bass) and Tony Meehan (Drums) left The Shadows in 1961/2 and had a #1 hit in 1963 as a duo. What was the title of the Jerry Lordan composition?
A) Scarlett O'Hara   B) Diamonds   C) Besame Mucho

5. Brian Bennett and Brian 'Licorice' Locking replaced Harris and Meehan in The Shadows, in whose backing band did the pair previously play?
A) Tommy Steele   B) Vince Taylor   C) Marty Wilde

6. The Marvin, Welch, Locking & Bennett line-up had 7 hits including which 2 #1's?
A) Guitar Tango & Dance On   B) Foot Tapper & Dance On   C) Atlantis & Shindig

7. When John Rostill replaced Locking, who left to spend more time as a Jehovah's Witness, The Shadows had 10 more hits, the biggest being a #5, *The Rise and Fall of ....* Complete the title.   A) Adolf Hitler   B) The British Empire   C) Flingel Bunt

8. The Shadows had their first vocal hit in 1965, which #17 had these opening lyrics: "Everyday now seems endless, How slow the moments go but how fast they'll fly"?
A) Mary Anne   B) Don't Make My Baby Blue   C) I Met a Girl

9. The Shadows represented the UK in 1975 at the Eurovison Song Contest in Stockholm, Sweden and came second to the Dutch entry, Teach-In's *Ding-A-Dong*. What was The Shadows song?
A) Let Me Be the One   B) That's What Friends Are For   C) Stand Up Like a Man

10. The Shadows returned to the charts in 1978, reaching #5 with an instrumental version of which song from a top Lloyd-Webber/Rice musical?
A) Memory   B) Love Changes Everything   C) Don't Cry For Me Argentina

The Shadows at Eurovision 1975. Strangely Bruce Welch 'played' bass on the night. Not so! The only live element of the performance was Bruce singing the lead vocals. (L to R) John Farrar, Brian Bennett, Bruce, Alan Tarney (on piano, but who really played the bass part), and Hank B Marvin.

THE SHADOWS ANSWERS: *1. A) Drifters; 2. B) Kon Tiki; 3. C) Geronimo; 4. B) Diamonds; 5. C) Marty Wilde (in The Wild Cats - changed to The Krew Kats with some success); 6. B) Foot Tapper & Dance On; 7. Flingel Bunt; 8. A) Mary Anne; 9. A) Let Me Be the One; 10. C) Don't Cry For Me Argentina.*

DEL SHANNON *(Charles Weedon Westover - December 30, 1934 – February 8, 1990), was an American musician, singer and songwriter, he also had minor acting roles. In early 1959 he added the keyboardist Max Crook to his band The Moonlight Ramblers, he played a Musitron (an early synthesizer he invented based upon the commercially released Clavioline. In 1999, Del was inducted into the Rock and Roll Hall of Fame. Shannon committed suicide, shooting himself at his home in Santa Clarita, California, on February 8, 1990. Del Shannon had 14 Top 40 hit singles, including a #1 and 7 other Top 10 hits. He had just two charting UK albums reaching #9 and #15 respectively.*

1. What was the original title of Del's classic 1961 #1 hit *Runaway*, the biggest hit single of the year in the UK?   A) Little Runaway   B) Walk Along   C) I Wonder

2. In 1963, Del Shannon became the first American artist to record a Lennon-McCartney song. It actually charted before the Beatles version, but only peaked at #77 in the US. What was the song?
A) She Loves You   B) From Me To You   C) I Want To Hold Your Hand

3. The follow up to *Runaway* reached #6 in the UK, and was another Shannon penned song. What was the title?
A) Hey Little Girl   B) Hats Off To Larry   C) So Long Baby

4. Which 1960 #3 Jimmy Jones hit, was covered as a single by Del Shannon in 1975, reaching #36 in the UK charts?   A) Good Timin'   B) I Told You So   C) Handy Man

5. What Del Shannon #2 from 1962 includes these lyrics: "Some day papa said, Some day we'll go, Down to the village in the valley, Then you'll meet a nice young man, Ask for your hand, Then you'll be happy"?

6. Which member of the Traveling Wilburys co-produced the posthumous Shannon album *Rock On!* In 1991?   A) George Harrison   B) Jeff Lynne   C) Tom Petty

7. In 1962 which British musical film did Del Shannon appear with Helen Shapiro and Craig Douglas?   A) The Girl Can't Help It   B) Follow a Star   C) It's Trad Dad

8. Which Shannon penned song was a US #9 hit for Peter and Gordon, but failed to chart in the UK?   A) I Go To Pieces   B) Lady Godiva   C) Nobody I Know

9. *So Long, Baby* was a #10 hit for Del Shannon in 1961 but the 'B' side remains more popular in the UK. What is the song's title?
A) Ginny In the Mirror   B) The Answer To Everything   C) Don't Gild the Lily, Lily

10. Which Peter Phillips song, a #3 UK hit for Marty Wilde in 1959, was covered by Del Shannon in 1981?   A) Bad Boy   B) A Teenager In Love   C) Sea Of Love

THE TRAVELING WILBURYS
BOB DYLAN (LUCKY)
JEFF LYNNE (OTIS)
TOM PETTY (CHARLIE T. JR)
GEORGE HARRISON (NELSON)
ROY ORBISON (LEFTY)

DEL SHANNON ANSWERS: *1. A) Little Runaway; 2. B) From Me To You (Beatles reached #41); 3. B) Hats Off To Larry; 4. C) Handy Man; 5. Swiss Maid; 6. B) Jeff Lynne; 7. C) It's Trad Dad; 8. A) I Go To Pieces; 9. B) The Answer To Everything; 10. C) Sea of Love.*

SANDIE SHAW MBE (born Dagenham, Essex as Sandra Ann Goodrich; 26 February 1947) is an English singer. One of the most successful British female singers of the 1960s. On leaving school, she worked at the Ford Dagenham factory, did some part-time modelling and then came 2nd in a local talent contest and appeared at a concert in London, where she was spotted by Adam Faith. She was given a contract with Pye Records in 1964 as Sandie Shaw. In 1967 she won the 1967 Eurovision Song Contest for the UK in Vienna. Shaw went on to have 16 Top 40 hits, including 3 #1's and a further 5 Top 10 hits. Sandie also recorded one Top 10 album.

1. In 1964, Sandie Shaw's first single on Pye was *As Long as You're Happy Baby*. True or False?

2. Which Burt Bacharach / Hal David song did Sandie Shaw sing on TV pop show, *Ready Steady Go* in 1964, and see the song go to number one for three weeks?
A) Girl Don't Come   B) (There's) Always Something There to Remind Me   C) Run

3. Which English singer / songwriter wrote 11 of Sandie Shaw's Top 40 songs?
A) Adam Faith   B) Marty Wilde   C) Chris Andrews

4. Sandie Shaw published a best-selling autobiography. What was the title of the book?   A) It's a Puppet   B) The World At My Feet   C) Shaw Thing

5. Which Sandie Shaw #1 from 1965 opens with these words: "Venus must have heard my plea, She has sent someone along for me"?

6. Which of her major hits did Sandie Shaw refuse to include in her cabaret act?
A) Message Understood   B) Puppet On A String   C) I'll Stop At Nothing

7. Sandie Shaw's last album of the 60s was a set of songs originally performed by the likes of Bob Dylan, the Rolling Stones, Led Zeppelin and Donovan. The title track however, was which song from the musical *Oliver*?
A) Reviewing the Situation   B) As Long As He Needs Me   C) Consider Yourself

8. Which Les Reed & Gordon Mills's song was originally written for Sandie Shaw but eventually became a #1 for which singer who had recorded the original demo disc?
A) It's Not Unusual   B) I Pretend   C) Tell Me When

9. Sandie Shaw's last Top 10 hit came in 1969. What was the title of the song?
A) Monsieur Poirot   B) Monsieur Dupont   C) Monsieur De Gaulle

10. In 1992, Sandie Shaw began studying at Oxford and the University of London and qualified in 1994 as a what?   A) Psychotherapist   B) Pathologist   C) Physiotherapist

1960s GIRLS
Name the song titles that include 'GIRL'

A) The Bruisers (1963)	F) The Seekers (1967)
B) Matt Monro (1961)	G) Herman's Hermits (1968)
C) Neil Sedaka (1961)	H) Gary Puckett & Union Gap (1968)
D) Susan Maughan (1962)	J) Marty Wilde (1960)
E) Sandie Shaw (1964)	K) Jess Conrad (1961)

SANDIE SHAW ANSWERS: 1. True; 2. B) (There's) Always Something There to Remind Me; 3. C) Chris Andrews; 4. B) The World At My Feet; 5. Long Live Love; 6. B) Puppet On A String; 7. A) Reviewing the Situation; 8. A) It's Not Unusual (Tom Jones did the demo disc!); 9. B) Monsieur Dupont; 10. A) Psychotherapist. **1960s GIRLS ANSWERS:** A) Blue Girl; B) My Kind of Girl; C) Calendar Girl; D) Bobby's Girl; E) Girl Don't Come; F) Georgy Girl; G) Sunshine Girl: H) Young Girl; J) Little Girl; K) Mystery Girl.

SHOWADDYWADDY are a R 'n' R band from Leicester. They specialise in revivals of 1950s and early 1960s songs, as well as original material. Unusual 8 man line-up with 'doubled up' instruments. Originally Malcolm "Duke" Allured (drums); Dave Bartram (vocals); Russ Field (guitar); Buddy Gask (vocals); Al James (bass / vocals); Trevor Oakes (guitar); Rod Deas (bass); Romeo Challenger (drums). They had 23 Top 40 hits, including a #1 and 9 other Top 10 hits. They also had 7 Top 40 albums, including a #1 and 4 more Top 10 successes.

SHOWADDYWADDY TOP 10 HITS
Name the hits from the clues supplied

1. The first hit was a #2 in 1974 written by the band containing the lyrics "Standing on the corner in my new blue jeans, Dreamin' 'bout the girl in my limousine".

2. Another #2 followed in 1975, a revival of a posthumous Eddie Cochran chart topper from 1960.

3. A Buddy Holly written song, a hit for the great rock and roller in 1958, reached #7 by Showaddywaddy in 1975. Nick Berry and Steps also had 1990s hits with the song.

4. The only Showaddywaddy UK #1 revived of a minor 1961 US hit by Curtis Lee.

5. The Kalin Twins were one hit wonders in the UK. Their only hit was a #1 in 1958 that stayed top for 5 weeks. Showaddywaddy took the song to #3 in 1977.

6. A #25 for Johnny Kidd & The Pirates in 1960, A #7 for Marv Johnson also in 1960 and a #28 for the Dave Clark Five in 1967 Showaddywaddy took it to #2 in 1977.

7. Chubby Checker got the Showaddywaddy treatment next, his #19 from 1962 provided the band with a #4 in 1977.

8. A Dion & The Belmonts US hit from 1958, a cover of which was sung by Nicolas Cage in the film *Peggy Sue Got Married* gave Showaddywaddy a #2 in 1978.

9. A bluesy soul US hit by the Jarmels in 1961 was covered by Showaddywaddy in 1978 and became the only version to reach the UK charts, #5 in 1978.

10. Another Curtis Lee song, a minor success in the UK, became Showaddywaddy's last UK Top 10 in 1978, reaching #5.

SHOWADDYWADDY ANSWERS: *1. Hey Rock and Roll; 2. Three Steps To Heaven; 3. Heartbeat; 4. Under the Moon of Love; 5. When; 6. You Got What It Takes; 7. Dancin' Party; 8. I Wonder Why; 9. A Little Bit of Soap; 10. Pretty Little Angel Eyes.*

1. In which decade was Frank Sinatra born?

2. Which band recorded the 1990s albums, *The Bends* and *OK Computer*?

3. In 1976 Chicago had their only UK number one. What was its title?

4. Which American R&B singer had a #1 in 1998 with *You Make Me Wanna*?

5. Which band released the albums *The Piper at the Gates of Dawn* in 1967 and *The Division Bell* in 1994?

6. Fifth Dimension had a medley of *Aquarius / Let The Sun Shine In (The Flesh Failures)* at #11 in 1969. In which musical were the songs featured?

7. Dutch brothers, lead guitarist Eddie and drummer Alex used their surname as the name for which American hard rock band?

8. Who was the frontman of The Shondells, who had a #1 in 1968 with *Mony Mony*?

9. Which Michael was the frontman of R.E.M.?

10. Billie Jo Spears had just two Top 10 hits in the UK, *Blanket On The Ground* in 1975 and *What I've Got In Mind*. Which of them got highest in the charts?

11. Which American TV criminal defence lawyer was the subject of a #23 hit for Ozzy Osbourne in 1995?

12. Which American girl group whose UK hits in the1990s included *Waterfalls*, comprised of T Boz, Left Eye and Chilli?

13. What was The first Beatles single to top the US charts?

14. In the lyrics of the 1974 #1 *Annie's Song* by John Denver, how many times is Annie's name mentioned in the lyrics?

15. Anita, Bonnie, June and Ruth make up which American singing group?

16. Alanis Morissette followed up her *Jagged Little Pill* #1 album in 1995 with which #3 album, three years later?

17. In the 1960s which singer was the first British born artist to have three consecutive number one hits?

18. Name Billie's two 1998 UK number ones?

19. What was Michael Jackson's last #1 in the 20th century?
A) Blood on the Dancefloor   B) Earth Song   C) You Are Not Alone

20. James Michael Aloysious Bradford had seven Top 10 hits in the 1980s & 1990s, including the #1 *Ain't No Doubt*. How was the actor / singer better known?

YET MORE POP TRIVIA ANSWERS: 1. 1910s (12 December 1915); 2. Radiohead; 3. If You Leave Me Now; 4. Usher; 5. Pink Floyd; 6. Hair; 7. Van Halen; 8. Tommy James; 9. Stipe; 10. What I've Got In Mind reached 4 (Blanket On The Ground #6); 11. Perry Mason; 12. TLC; 13. I Want To Hold Your Hand; 14. Never; 15. The Pointer Sisters; 16. Supposed Former Infatuation Junkie; 17. Frank Ifield; 18. Because We Want To and Girlfriend; 19. A) Blood on the Dancefloor; 20. Jimmy Nail.

SIMON & GARFUNKEL *were an American folk rock duo consisting of singer-songwriter Paul Simon (born October 13, 1941) and singer Art Garfunkel (born November 5, 1941). They were brought up in Kew Gardens Hills, Queens, New York. Simon & Garfunkel had 8 UK Top 40 hits, including a #1 and 4 more Top 10 hits. S&G also had 10 Top 40 albums, including 2 #1 and 5 more Top 10 hits. Paul Simon had 10 Top 40 solo hits, including 3 Top 10 successes. He also had 9 Top 40 albums, including 2 #1 and 5 more Top 10 hits. Art Garfunkel had just 3 Top 40 singles, including 2 number ones! He also had 6 Top 40 albums, including 2 Top 10 successes.*

1. By what name were Simon & Garfunkel previously known?
A) Tom and Jerry   B) Fred & Barney   C) Rolls & Royce

2. Simon & Garfunkel had a #1 in the US with *The Sound of Silence*, who had a #3 UK hit with a cover version?   A) King Brothers   B) The Bachelors   C) The Byrds

3. "I am just a poor boy. Though my story's seldom told." are the opening lyrics to which 1969, #6 hit for Simon & Garfunkel?

4. Simon and Garfunkel's 1991 hit *A Hazy Shade of Winter* had been covered three years earlier and was a #11 hit, by which US band?
A) The Bangles   B) Wilson Phillips   C) Buffalo Springfield

5. What Simon & Garfunkel song, initially titled *Eleanor Roosevelt* became a big hit in 1968 after appearing on the soundtrack of the film *The Graduate*?
A) Mrs Flintstone   B) Mrs Jones   C) Mrs Robinson

6. What was Art Garfunkel's first solo #1 hit in 1975?
A) Bright Eyes   B) I Only Have Eyes For You   C) All I Know

7. And which song gave Paul Simon his highest position in the UK Singles chart?
A) Mother and Child Reunion   B) You Can Call Me Al   C) The Obvious Child

8. *Bridge Over Troubled Water* was Simon & Garfunkel's only UK #1. Who also had an up-tempo disco version of the song in the UK Top 40, nine years later?
A) Linda Clifford   B) Brenda Lee   C) Eva Cassidy

9. In what year were Simon & Garfunkel inducted into the Rock & Roll Hall of Fame?
A) 1970   B) 1980   C) 1990

10. On what label were all of the Simon & Garfunkel hits recorded?
A) Decca   B) Columbia   C) RCA

ANDREW WESTERN GALLERY

Three greats who have passed on! More pastel paintings from my good friend, local artist Andrew Western. Several of Andrew's paintings have also previously appeared in various quiz books of mine.

SIMON & GARFUNKEL ANSWERS: *1. A) Tom & Jerry; 2. B) The Bachelors; 3. The Boxer; 4. A) The Bangles; 5. C) Mrs Robinson; 6. B) I Only Have Eyes For You; 7. B) You Can Call Me Al (number 4); 8. A) Linda Clifford; 9. C) 1990; 10. B) Columbia.*

SIMPLE MINDS are a Scottish rock band formed in the South Side of Glasgow in 1977. Their roots were in the short-lived punk band Johnny & The Self-Abusers. What was regarded as the first serious line up was reached in 1978 - Jim Kerr (vocals), Charlie Burchill (guitar), Mick MacNeil (keyboards), Derek Forbes (bass) and Brian McGee (drums). Simple Minds had 24 Top 40 hits between 1982 and 1998, this included one number one and 7 more Top 10 hits. The band also had 11 Top 40 albums including 5 number ones and 3 more Top 10 successes.

1. Simple Minds got their name from lyrics "He's so simple minded", from which David Bowie song? A) Jean Genie B) The Laughing Gnome C) Life on Mars

2. The first Simple Minds Top 10 hit came in 1985 with their seventh UK hit. What was the song? A) Alive and Kicking B) Don't You (Forget About Me) C) Waterfront

3. In 1979 the band made their first TV appearance, performing *Chelsea Girl* and *Life in a Day* on what renowned music show?
A) The Old Grey Whistle Test B) Later … With Jools Holland C) Ready Steady Go

4. The 6th Simple Minds album was their first to top the charts in 1984. What was the album title? A) New Gold Dream B) Empires and Dance C) Sparkle in the Rain

5. In 1981, Simple Minds switched their record label, moving from Arista to which major label? A) EMI B) Polydor C) Virgin

6. Who were Jim Kerr's two celebrity wives?

7. Which Simple Minds #9 in 1986 opened with these lyrics: "Don't you look back on a big lost world, Crying out tomorrow"?
A) Sanctify Yourself B) All the Things She Said C) Alive and Kicking

8. Brian McGee left the band and was eventually replaced by which man, who went on to be the longest serving Simple Minds drummer?
A) Cherisse Osei B) Mel Gaynor C) Mike Ogletree

9. By 1988, Simple Minds had built their own recording premises in Scotland. What was it called? A) Waterfront B) See the Lights C) Bonnie Wee Studio

10. The only single by Simple Minds to reach #1 was a rewrite of a Celtic folk song, *She Moved Through the* Fair, with new lyrics written about the ongoing war in Northern Ireland. What was the 1989 chart-topper?
A) Belfast Child B) Belfast Boy C) Give Ireland Back to the Irish

Back to SCHOOL

Name the songs with SCHOOL in their titles

A) Chuck Berry (1957)	F) Wings (1977)
B) Jerry Lee Lewis (1959)	G) Spinal Tap (1992)
C) Paul Simon (1972)	H) Bassheads (1992)
D) Alice Cooper (1972)	J) Beverley Knight (1995)
E) Barry Blue (1974)	K) Jurassic 5 (1998)

SIMPLE MINDS ANSWERS: *1. A) Jean Genie; 2. B) Don't You (Forget About Me); 3. A) The Old Grey Whistle Test; 4. C) Sparkle in the Rain; 5. C) Virgin; 6. Chrissie Hynde and Patsy Kensit; 7. B) All the Things She Said; 8. B) Mel Gaynor; 9. C) Bonnie Wee Studio; 10. A) Belfast Boy.* **BACK TO SCHOOL ANSWERS:** *A) School Day; B) High School Confidential; C) Me and Julio Down By the Schoolyard; D) School' Out; E) School Love; F) Girl's School (double A side with Mull of Kintyre): G) Bitch School; H) Back To the Old School; J) Flavour of the Old School; K) Concrete Schoolyard.*

SIMPLY RED are a British soul and pop band formed in Manchester in 1985. Initially The Frantic Elevators, Mick Hucknall (vocals) and manager Elliot Rashman, recruited a band of session musicians; Sylvan Richardson (guitar), Tony Bowers (bass), Fritz McIntyre (keyboards & vocals), Tim Kellett (brass & backing vocals),Chris Joyce (drums), and settled on the name Simply Red. They had 24 Top 40 hits between 1985 and 1999, including a #1 and 7 more Top 10 triumphs. They also had 10 Top 40 albums, including 5 number ones and 3 more Top 10 smashes.

1. Simply Red was signed to what record label in 1985?
A) Capitol   B) Sony   C) Elektra

2. What Albert Hammond & Mike Hazlewood song was a big hit for both The Hollies in 1974 and Simply Red in 1998?
A) Little Arrows   B) The Air That I Breathe   C) Make Me An Island

3. Which Simply Red album was rated as one of the top 100 greatest British albums ever? A) Stars   B) A New Flame   C) Life

4. Which 1989 Simply Red hit, originally a hit for Harold Melvin & The Bluenotes, contains these lyrics: "Don't get so excited, When I come home, A little late at night, You know we only act like children, When we argue fuss and fight"?

5. Which football team did Mick Hucknall try to buy in 1998?
A) Arsenal   B) Liverpool   C) Manchester United

6. In 1995, what song became Simply Red's only number one in the UK?
A) Holding Back the Years   B) Fairground   C) If You Don't Know Me By Now

7. Why was Mick Hucknall bullied at school?
A) His religion   B) His Irish ancestry   C) His hair colour

8. Mick's Sicilian wine, produced near Mount Etna, has received rave reviews. True or False?

9. Sylvan Richardson left the band in 1987. Aziz Ibrahim briefly replaced him, before which Brazilian then joined for 8 years?
A) Heitor Pereira   B) Kenji Suzuki   C) Marcelo Fromer

10. Which prolific Jamaican rhythm section and production duo teamed up with Simply Red to have a #13 hit in 1997 with a cover of Gregory Isaacs' *Night Nurse*?

USING THE CLUES, WHAT WORD APPEARS IN HITS THAT MATCH THESE FACTS?

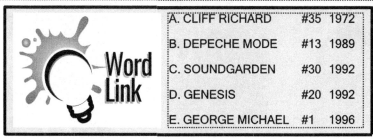

A. CLIFF RICHARD	#35	1972
B. DEPECHE MODE	#13	1989
C. SOUNDGARDEN	#30	1992
D. GENESIS	#20	1992
E. GEORGE MICHAEL	#1	1996

SIMPLY RED ANSWERS: 1. C) Elektra; 2. B) The Air That I Breathe; 3. A) Stars; 4. If You Don't Know Me By Now; 5. C) Manchester United; 6. B) Fairground; 7. C) His hair colour (ginger jokes); 8. True; 9. A) Heitor Pereira; 10. Sly and Robbie.
WORD LINK ANSWERS: JESUS - A) Jesus; B) Personal Jesus; C) Jesus Christ Pose; D) Jesus He Knows Me; E) Jesus To A Child.

FRANK SINATRA *(Francis Albert Sinatra - December 12, 1915 – May 14, 1998) was an American singer and actor. Nicknamed Ol' Blue Eyes. Sinatra was one of the most popular entertainers of the 1940s, 1950s and 1960s. He is among the world's best-selling music artists with an estimated 150 million record sales. A perfectionist, renowned for his style and presence, Sinatra always insisted on recording live with his band. He led a colourful personal life and was involved in some turbulent relationships. Frank had 32 UK Top 10 hits, including three #1's and nine other Top 10 hits. His albums were phenomenally successful with 59 Top 40 successes, including four number ones and thirty-two other Top 10 hits.*

1. Sinatra's first number one came in the first year of pop music charts, 1954. What was the song that was also the title song of a romantic comedy-drama film?
A) Chicago   B) Three Coins in the Fountain   C) Young At Heart

2. Frank played which character in the 1960 heist movie *Ocean's 11*?
A) Danny Ocean   B) Sam Harmon   C) Josh Howard

3. What was Sinatra's 1967 chart-topping duet with his daughter Nancy?
A) These Boots Are Made For Walkin'   B) Jackson   C) Something Stupid

4. Which of these women was never married to Sinatra?
A) Ava Gardner   B) Mia Farrow   C) Lauren Bacall

5. Sinatra was known as the leader of a singing and comedic group known by what name?   A) The Rat Pack   B) The Wrecking Crew   C) Sinatra and Company

6. Frank Sinatra was known to have influenced the success of one particular US president's political campaign. Which president?
A) Richard Nixon   B) Jimmy Carter   C) John F. Kennedy

7. Which song by Sinatra was used in the 1993 film, *Mrs. Doubtfire* during the scene where actor Robin Williams is transformed into an elderly woman?
A) What Now My Love   B) Luck Be A Lady   C) The Way You Look Tonight

8. Which of these, is NOT a nickname used for Frank Sinatra?
A) The Pelvis   B) The Voice   C) The Chairman

9. In 1993 Frank had his last hit single in the UK, a #4 hit with *I've Got You Under My Skin*, which was a duet with which rock band lead vocalist?
A) Phil Collins   B) Mick Jagger   C) Bono

10. Which Sinatra #1 from 1966 includes these lyrics: "And ever since that night, We've been together, Lovers at first sight, In love forever"?

SOME FACES OF FRANK

FRANK SINATRA ANSWERS: *1. B) Three Coins in the Fountain; 2. A) Danny Ocean; 3. C) Something Stupid; 4. C) Lauren Bacall; 5. A) The Rat Pack; 6. C) John F. Kennedy; 7. B) Luck Be A Lady; 8. A) The Pelvis; 9. C) Bono; 10. Strangers in the Night.*

SLADE are an English rock band formed in 1966 in Wolverhampton rising to prominence during the early 70s glam rock era. Slade were the first act to have three singles enter the charts at #1. Slade lined up with Noddy Holder (Lead vocals / Rhythm guitar)); Don Powell (Drums); Jim Lea (Bass) and Dave Hill (Lead guitar). Slade unsuccessfully moved to the US in the mid-70s to try to break into that market. Their fortunes did revive in the 1980s. Their best-selling single, Merry Xmas Everybody has proved to be a perennial seasonal hit. Slade had 25 Top 40 hits, including 6 number ones and 10 more Top 10 hits. Additionally they had 11 Top 40 albums, including 3 #1's and 2 further Top 10 successes.

1. What was the first Slade single to make it to number one in the Top 40 UK charts?
A) Look Wot You Dun   B) Take Me Bak 'Ome   C) Coz I Luv You

2. What is the real first name of Slade's lead singer Noddy Holder?
A) Norman   B) Neil   C) Neville

3. What is the name of the film in which Slade starred in 1975?
A) Flame   B) Far Far Away   C) Stardust

4. At which 1980 music festival did Slade make a surprise comeback, as late replacements for Ozzy Osbourne?   A) Isle of Wight   B) Reading   C) Cheltenham

5. Which American rock band had a #5 hit in the US with the Slade song *Cum On Feel The Noize*?   A) Kiss   B) Quiet Riot   C) Journey

6. Which member of Slade released an album under the name of The Dummies in 1979?   A) Don Powell   B) Dave Hill   C) Jim Lea

7. Which former Animals member was Slade's manager during their early years?
A) Alan Price   B) Chas Chandler   C) Hilton Valentine

8. The last Slade single to reach #1 in the UK contains these lyrics. Name the song. "Does your granny always tell ya, That the old songs are the best".

9. To whom was Slade's 1985 #54 single *Do You Believe In Miracles?* written as a tribute?   A) Andrew Lloyd-Webber   B) Bob Geldof   C) Elton John

10. Slade guitarist Dave Hill was known for his high heeled boots, pudding bowl haircut and a custom built guitar with what word built into its body?
A) Dave the Man   B) Superyob   C) Slayed

Just CAPITAL!

Identify the hit songs that include a CAPITAL CITY in their titles

A. Tulips From .... - Max Bygraves (1958)

B. Drowning in ...... - Mobiles (1982)

C. .... Town - UB40 (1982)

D. In Old ...... - Frank Chacksfield (1956)

E. Poor People of ..... - Winifred Attwell (1956)

F. ...... Calling - The Clash (1979)

G. .... - Fat Les 2000 (2000)

H. Stranger in ...... - Michael Jackson (1996)

J. One Night in .... - Murray Head (1984)

K. ...... - Ultravox (1981)

SLADE ANSWERS: 1. C) Coz I Luv You; 2. C) Neville; 3. A) Flame; 4. B) Reading; 5. B) Quiet Riot; 6. C) Jim Lea; 7. B) Chas Chandler; 8. Merry Christmas Everybody; 9. B) Bob Geldof; 10. B) Superyob.
JUST CAPITAL! ANSWERS: A) Amsterdam; B) Berlin; C) Kingston; D) Lisbon; E) Paris; F) London; G) Jerusalem; H) Moscow; J) Bangkok; K) Vienna.

BITS AND PIECES 2

Yet more pop trivia spanning the decades!

1. The Harry Simeone Chorale took which 19thC hymn into the Top 40 in 1960,1 & 2?

2. Whose debut solo album was *Shepherd Moons*?

3. Which duo had a number one UK hit with *Cinderella Rockefella* in 1968?

4. *Cavatina* was a #13 hit for John Williams in 1979. The Shadows also reached #9 with the melody, but which film used it as its theme?

5. Which word is shared as the title of hits by Rod Stewart, Madonna and Shaggy?

6. Which one hit wonder reached #7 in 1960 with *Angela Jones*?

7. What line precedes "Why, why, why, Delilah" in the Tom Jones #2 hit in 1968?

8. What nationality were Rednex, who had a #1 in 1994 with *Cotton Eye Joe*?

9. What was the title of The Verve's 1997 number one UK hit?

10. What song links the three acts pictured below?

11. What is in brackets after *The Shoop Shoop Song* in the title of Cher's 1991 #1?

12. Rockers Buddy Holly, Eddie Cochran and Ricky Nelson died tragically. Who was the youngest?

13. The Mamas & Papas sung "Every other day of the week is fine" apart from ......?

14. How old was Britney Spears when she had a #1 with *Baby One More Time*?

15. Which prison did Johnny Cash famously sing about in his 1955 song?

16. Which band lined up with Jack Bruce, Eric Clapton, and Ginger Baker?

17. Falco's 1986 #1 UK hit was sung in which language?

18. John Williams, Herbie Flowers, Kevin Peek & Tristan Fry made up which band?

19. In the Dire Straits 1979 #8, *Sultans of Swing*, who "knows all the chords"?

20. During which song did Michael Jackson first perform the moonwalk?

BITS AND PIECES 2 ANSWERS: *1. Onward Christian Soldiers; 2. Enya; 3. Esther & Abi Ofarim; 4.The Deerhunter; 5. Angel; 6. Michael Cox; 7. "My, my, my, Delilah"; 8. Sweden; 9. The Drugs Don't Work; 10. I Only Want To Be With You - Dusty Springfield, The Tourists, Samantha Fox (Sam's title was I Only Wanna Be With You); 11. It's In His Kiss; 12. Eddie Cochran (21); 13. Monday; 14. 16 (in 1999); 15. Folsom Prison; 16. Cream; 17. German; 18. Sky; 19. Guitar George; 20. Billie Jean.*

THE SMALL FACES were an English rock band from London, founded in 1965. The group originally consisted of Steve Marriott, Ronnie Lane, Kenney Jones and Jimmy Winston, with Ian McLagan replacing Winston as the band's keyboardist in 1966. When Marriott left to form Humble Pie, the remaining three members collaborated with Ronnie Wood, his brother Art Wood, Rod Stewart and Kim Gardner, to eventually become the Faces and have much more success. The Small Faces had 14 Top 40 hits, this included a #1 and 6 more Top 10 hits plus a successful re-release of one of them. The band also had four Top 40 albums, including a #1 and a further Top 10 success.

1. With which management impresario did the Small Faces first sign a contract?
A) Don Arden   B) Malcolm Allen   C) Joe Meek

2. The Small Faces only number one record, *All or Nothing*, shared top spot with The Beatles. The only time two bands have shared #1 in the UK charts. True or False?

3. What was The Beatles single that was a joint number one with The Small Faces?
A) Penny Lane   B) Yellow Submarine / Eleanor Rigby   C) Get Back

4. Which member of The Small Faces was affectionately nicknamed 'plonk'?
A) Steve Marriott   B) Kenney Jones   C) Ronnie Lane

5. What was the title of the Small Faces album that reached #1 in 1968?
A) From the Beginning   B) Ogden's Nut Gone Flake   C) Small Faces

6. "Wouldn't it be nice, To get on with me neighbours, But they make it very clear, They've got no room for ravers". Opening lyrics to which Small Faces #2 from 1968?

7. In 1966, The Small Faces moved from Decca to a new label started by Rolling Stones' manager Andrew Loog Oldham and Tony Calder. The new label would eventually owe the band a huge amount in unpaid royalties. What label?
A) Immediate Records   B) Deram Records   C) Sanctuary Records

8. Which Small Faces was a Top 10 hit in both 1967 and 1975?
A) Sha-La-La-La-Lee   B) Whatcha Gonna Do About It?   C) Itchycoo Park

9. Steve Marriott died, aged 44, on 20 April 1991. What was the cause of his early death?   A) Lung cancer   B) House fire   C) Drug overdose

10. On New Years Eve 1968, The Small Faces played together for a final time in the UK. What was the location?
A) Wembley Stadium   B) Highbury Stadium   C) Alexandra Palace

Fiddler's Dram had a number 3 hit in 1969 with which catchy song?

THE SMALL FACES ANSWERS: *1. A) Don Arden; 2. True; 3. B) Yellow Submarine / Eleanor Rigby; 4. C) Ronnie Lane; 5. B) Ogden's Nut Gone Flake; 6. Lazy Sunday; 7. A) Immediate Records; 8. C) Itchycoo Park; 9. B) House fire; 10. C) Alexandra Palace.*
FIDDLER'S DRAM ANSWER: *Day Trip To Bangor (Didn't We Have A Lovely Time).*

THE SMITHS were an English rock band formed in 1982 in Manchester. Their line-up was (Steven) Morrissey (vocals), Johnny Marr (guitar), Andy Rourke (bass), Mike Joyce (drums). An important act from the 80s UK indy music scene, a fusion of 1960s rock and post-punk and a rejection of synth-pop. Internal tensions led to a breakup in 1987, followed by public lawsuits over royalties. The Smiths had 18 Top 40 singles, this included just 3 Top 10 hits. They also had 11 Top 40 albums, including 2 #1 albums and 7 more Top 10 successes. **MORRISSEY** then had 21 Top 40 solo hits, with 5 Top 10 and 10 Top 40 albums including 2 #1 and 5 more Top 10 successes.

1. In October 1982, The Smiths gave their first public performance as support for Blue Rondo à la Turk during a student music and fashion show. Where was the show? A) Old Trafford   B) Maine Road   C) The Ritz, Manchester

2. What was Morrissey famous for carrying on stage and throwing into the crowds, during the early part of The Smiths' career? A) Stink bombs   B) Flowers   C) Shirts

3. Which former band member won a lawsuit against Morrissey and Johnny Marr for over a million pounds in 1996? A) Mike Joyce   B) Andy Rourke   C) Steven Pomfret

4. Who is pictured on the album cover of the *The Queen is Dead* a1986 #2 hit?
A) Alain Delon   B) Terence Stamp   C) Alan Bates

5. The Smiths highest position in the UK singles chart was achieved with in 1992 with a reissue of a 1983 hit. What was the song, and what chart position did it attain?
A) Sheila Take A Bow - 5   B) This Charming Man - 8   C) Panic - 3

6. What was Morrissey's first solo album?
A) Your Arsenal   B) Viva Hate   C) Kill Uncle

7. Which Smiths #10 hit from 1984 included the lyrics: "In my life, Why do I give valuable time, To people who don't care if I live or die?"?
A) What Difference Does It Make   B) Heaven Knows I'm Miserable Now   C) Ask

8. The 'B' side of *Heaven Knows I'm Miserable Now* was *Suffer Little Children*. What is the song about? A) New Testament   B) Moors Murders   C) Dr. Barnardo's

9. Which highest capped, former Republic of Ireland international footballer, is a cousin of Morrissey?   A) Shay Given   B) Steve Staunton   C) Robbie Keane

10. On what album were all of The Smiths hits recorded between 1983 and 1987?
A) WEA   B) Rough Trade   C) HMV

TURTLE POWER... was number one for 4 weeks in 1990. Who were the US hip-hop duo who recorded it?

THE SMITHS & MORRISSEY ANSWERS: *1. C) The Ritz, Manchester; 2. B) Flowers; 3. A) Mike Joyce; 4. A) Alain Delon; 5. B) This Charming Man - 8; 6. B) Viva Hate; 7. B) Heaven Knows I'm Miserable Now; 8. B) Moors Murders (Brady and Hindley); 9. C) Robbie Keane; 10. B) Rough Trade.* **TURTLE POWER ANSWER:** *Partners in Kryme.*

SMOKIE (originally spelt Smokey) are an English rock band from Bradford, Yorkshire. Formed as The Yen and lining up: Chris Norman (lead vocals/rhythm guitar), Terry Uttley (bass/vocals), Alan Silson (lead guitar/vocals), and Ron Kelly (drums), the band had several more name changes. Smokie found success at home and abroad after teaming up with Mike Chapman and Nicky Chinn. They have had a number of line-up changes down the years. Smokie have had 13 Top 40 singles, including 7 Top 10 hits. Additionally they had 3 Top 40 albums, including one Top 10 success.

1. Smokie changed their name from Smokey to avoid a lawsuit from Smokey Robinson and the Miracles. True or False?

2. The lyrics of Smokie's first hit in 1975 included: "A breathless drive on a downtown street, a motorbike ride in the midday heat...". What was title of the #3 hit?
A) If You Think You Know How To Love Me   B) Don't Play Your Rock 'N Roll To Me
C) Something's Been Making Me Blue

3. Smokie had a #5 hit song in 1978 titled *Oh Carol*. Which other singer had a hit with a different song with the same title?   A) Paul Anka   B) Neil Sedaka   C) Emile Ford

4. Smokie covered *Needles and Pins* in 1977 and had a #10 hit. Which British band had previously had a #1 with the song in 1964?
A) Gerry & The Pacemakers   B) The Hollies   C) The Searchers

5. Alan Barton replaced Chris Norman as lead singer in Smokie in 1986. With which chart-topping band had he had previous success?
A) Barron Knights   B) Black Lace   C) Squeeze

6. Smokie had a 1976 #5 hit with *Living Next Door To Alice*. In what year did they team up with comedian Roy 'Chubby' Brown to have a #3 hit with a revised version?
A) 1995   B) 1990   C) 1985

7. At the peak of Smokie's success in 1978, Chris Norman teamed up with which female singer and released a duet single, *Stumblin' In*, that just failed to reach the Top 40?   A) Lulu   B) Elkie Brooks   C) Suzi Quatro

8. Smokie's last solo Top 40 entry came in 1980. It came with a revival of which Bobby Vee song, written by Carole King and Gerry Goffin?
A) Rubber Ball   B) Take Good Care Of My Baby   C) How Many Tears

9. The original Smokie line up was restored for a performance to raise funds for which charity event?   A) Bradford City fire   B) Children in Need   C) Childline

10. Alan Barton was tragically killed when Smokie's tour bus crashed during a hailstorm. Where did the accident happen?   A) Cologne   B) Amsterdam   C) Paris

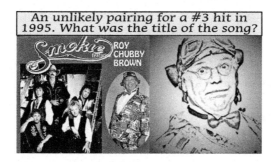

An unlikely pairing for a #3 hit in 1995. What was the title of the song?

SMOKIE ANSWERS: *1. True; 2. A) If You Think You Know How To Love Me; 3. B) Neil Sedaka; 4. C) The Searchers; 5. B) Black Lace; 6. A) 1995; 7. C) Suzi Quatro; 8. B) Take Good Care Of My Baby; 9. A) Bradford City fire (in which 56 people died); 10. A) Cologne.*
SMOKIE feat ROY CHUBBY BROWN ANSWER: *Living Next Door To Alice (Who The F**K Is Alice).*

EIGHTIES NUMBER ONES
WORD SEARCH

Find the 20 acts who had chart-toppers in the 80's, vertically, horizontally or diagonally, forwards or backwards! Their hit songs are listed below.

B	R	O	S	L	I	S	S	T	A	S	F	R	I	E	L	D	O	D	F
A	S	B	H	A	C	U	L	T	U	R	E	C	L	U	B	A	O	R	L
N	H	E	A	P	N	K	M	A	R	N	V	I	S	N	B	W	G	U	Y
G	M	L	Z	H	Q	U	K	R	I	W	R	O	T	Y	K	S	O	B	I
L	Z	I	X	Y	S	S	A	D	R	F	B	O	N	N	W	A	O	M	N
E	A	N	S	L	D	F	R	G	H	O	J	L	K	W	E	U	G	L	G
S	L	D	K	L	J	A	H	G	L	F	C	D	C	U	L	T	A	D	P
B	L	A	G	I	G	H	Y	S	P	H	Y	H	C	H	A	K	J	E	I
E	U	C	R	S	O	O	O	N	P	D	F	G	A	J	V	N	A	M	C
P	O	A	I	N	A	L	H	X	E	M	A	D	N	K	V	X	K	T	K
E	A	R	F	E	G	C	V	B	M	J	D	N	I	A	A	C	D	Q	E
F	O	L	R	L	R	S	R	E	G	O	R	Y	N	N	E	K	T	O	T
B	K	I	N	S	E	M	I	K	E	M	O	R	I	S	S	G	H	B	S
L	Q	S	I	O	A	U	F	E	E	H	A	K	O	I	L	I	L	A	C
A	I	L	C	N	I	D	R	O	W	B	V	D	Z	K	Y	Y	E	D	N
C	V	E	O	B	G	S	M	O	K	E	Y	R	O	B	I	N	S	O	N
K	A	J	L	L	B	A	N	M	P	A	S	W	Y	N	A	F	F	I	T
B	B	L	E	A	C	K	W	H	A	E	M	W	E	A	N	H	I	C	U
O	U	R	I	V	N	B	M	A	W	H	Y	T	T	W	C	A	D	Y	M
X	K	E	B	O	R	S	M	O	R	O	W	Q	A	X	C	H	A	R	S

THE NUMBER ONES:

A) Coward of the County
B) I'm Your Man
C) I Want To Wake Up With You
D) Like A Prayer
E) Heaven Is A Place
F) Only You
G) Too Shy
H) Ride On Time
J) I Owe You Nothing
K) Don't Turn Around
L) Being With You
M) A Little Peace
N) Karma Chameleon
P) I Feel For You
Q) Move Closer
R) The Final Countdown
S) La Bamba
T) I Think We're Alone Now
U) Orinoco Flow
V) Eternal Flame

1. KENNY ROGERS
2. WHAM!
3. BORIS GARDINER
4. FLYING PICKETS
5. KAJAGOOGOO
6. BLACK BOX
7. BROS
8. ASWAD
9. SMOKEY ROBINSON
10. NICOLE
11. CULTURE CLUB
12. CHAKA KHAN
13. PHYLLIS NELSON
14. EUROPE
15. LOS LOBOS
16. TIFFANY
17. ENYA
18. BANGLES
19. BELINDA CARLISLE
20. MADONNA

232

SOUL II SOUL are a British musical collective formed in London in 1988. They won two Grammy Awards, and have been nominated for five Brit Awards—twice for Best British Group. The group initially attracted attention as a sound system run by founder Jazzie B. The official lineup was Jazzie B, Caron Wheeler, Nellie Hooper, Simon Law, Doreen Waddell, Rose Windross, Daddae, Aitch B, and Jazzie Q. Soul II Soul had 13 Top 40 singles, including a #1 and four more Top 10 hits. They also had 5 Top 40 albums in the UK including two number ones and two more reached the Top 10.

1. The breakthrough Soul II Soul single reached #5 in 1989 and featured Caron Wheeler and the Reggae Philharmonic Orchestra. What was the song?
A) Get A Life   B) A Dreamers A Dream   C) Keep On Moving

2. During the late 1980s Jazzie B hosted a show on which radio station ?
A) KISS-FM   B) Radio 1   C) GWR

3. Soul II Soul's first album reached number one in the UK and sold over four million copies worldwide. What was the album title?
A) From The Fridge   B) Club Classics Vol. One   C) Get A Life

4. Soul II Soul had their only UK #1 single in 1989. The lyrics contained these lyrics: "Show me how, decide what you want from me, Tell me, maybe I could be there for you". What was the song?
A) Back To Life (However Do You Want Me)   B) Joy   C) Missing You

5. Marcia Lewis, a cousin of Jazzie B, joined Soul II Soul and the single *Get a Life*, featured her on lead vocals. What chart position did the single reach in the UK chart?
A) 1   B) 2   C) 3

6. In September 1990,a new album titled *A New Decade* reached #1. The album was recorded live at what London venue?
A) Brixton Academy   B) Shepherds Bush Empire   C) Hammersmith Apollo

7. *Joy* reached #4 in the UK charts with yet more personnel changes. Who sung lead vocals on the track?   A) Kofi   B) Richie Stephens   C) Rick Clarke

8. In January 1995, Soul II Soul performed *Papa Was a Rollin' Stone* live on French TV show *Taratata* with which American singer / songwriter?
A) James Brown   B) Al Green   C) Isaac Hayes

9. In the 20th century, when did Soul II Soul officially disband, with each member pursuing a solo career?   A) 1996   B) 1998   C) 1999

10. In 1996 a remixed version of *Keep On Movin'* was released when it was featured in a TV ad campaign for which car?   A) Renault Clio   B) Skoda Yeti   C) Audi A3

A. 1952   B. 1953   C. 1953

Identify the three singers pictured above. What fact links the three of them?

SOUL II SOUL ANSWERS: *1. C) Keep On Moving; 2. A) KISS-FM; 3. B) Club Classics Vol. One; 4. A) Back To Life (However Do You Want Me); 5. C) 3; 6. A) Brixton Academy; 7. B) Richie Stephens; 8. C) Isaac Hayes; 9. B) 1998; 10. A) Renault Clio.* **LINK ANSWERS:** *A) Al Martino; B) Jo Stafford; C) Kay Starr. The first 3 number one records in the UK charts with Here In My Heart, You Belong To Me and Come A-long A-love respectively.*

SPANDAU BALLET were an English new wave band formed in 1979 in Islington. Inspired by post-punk underground dance scene in the 80s as house band for Blitz Kids as The Applause for the new club culture audience. A successful group of the New Romantic era of British pop, part of the Second British Invasion of the US in the 80s. Line up: Gary Kemp (guitar, synthesiser, backing vocals), Martin Kemp (bass), Tony Hadley (vocals), Steve Norman (sax), John Keeble (drums). They had 17 Top 40 hits, including a #1 and 9 more Top 10 successes. They also had 7 Top 40 albums, including a #1 and 4 more Top 10 hits.

1. In 1983, how many weeks did *True* spend at #1 in the UK charts?
A) 8   B) 6   C) 4

2. The name Spandau Ballet comes from ballet dance terminology describing the last performance by a prima ballerina before handing over to an upcoming talent known as the Spandau. True or False?

3. How long did it take for Martin Kemp to teach himself the bass guitar?
A) 3 months   B) 6 months   C) A year

4. Spandau Ballet's debut single *To Cut a Long Story Short* reached #5 in the UK in 1980. Who wrote the song?   A) Martin Kemp   B) Gary Kemp   C) Tony Hadley

5. Kemp has been married to Shirlie Holliman since 1988. She was a former backing singer for Wham! and one half of which 1980s pop duo?
A) Dollar   B) Pepsi & Shirlie   C) Mel & Kim

6. Which Spandau Ballet hit includes the lyrics: "listening to Marvin all night long"?
A) Gold   B) True   C) Lifeline

7. Who was the original manager for Spandau Ballet?
A) Steve Dagger   B) Jeff Jacobs   C) Mack Werner

8. Which electronic musician produced Spandau Ballet's first Top 5 hit, *To Cut A Long Story Short*?   A) Richard James Burgess   B) John Keeble   C) Robert James Elms

9. Spandau Ballet guitarist Gary Kemp appeared in which Kevin Costner film as Sy Spector?   A) Robin Hood: Prince of Thieves   B) Waterworld   C) The Bodyguard

10. The last UK Top 10 single for Spandau Ballet came with a #6 in 1986. What was the song?   A) Fight For Ourselves   B) I'll Fly For You   C) Through the Barricades

Gary and Martin Kemp appear as Ronnie and Reggie Kray in the 1990 British biographical crime drama film The Krays directed by Peter Medak

SPANDAU BALLET ANSWERS: *1. C) 4; 2. False (A friend of the band, Robert Elms saw a phrase which he saw written on a wall on a weekend trip to Berlin: "Rudolf Hess, all alone, dancing the Spandau Ballet"; 3. A) 3 months; 4. B) Gary Kemp; 5. B) Pepsi & Shirlie; 6. B) True; 7. A) Steve Dagger; 8. A) Richard James Burgess; 9. C) The Bodyguard; 10. C) Through the Barricades.*

DUSTY SPRINGFIELD (*Mary Isobel Catherine Bernadette O'Brien OBE). Born at West Hampstead on 16 April 1939 – died at Henley-on-Thames on 2 March 1999. Dusty was an English singer whose career spanned over five decades. With her distinctive mezzo-soprano sound, she was a significant singer of blue-eyed soul, pop and dramatic ballads, with French chanson, country, and jazz also in her repertoire. Initially in The Lana Sisters, then The Springfields who had 5 Top 40 hits. Dusty had 20 solo Top 40 singles, including a #1 and 10 more Top 10 hits. She also had 10 Top 40 albums, including 4 Top 10 successes.*

1. In 1962, The Springfields became the first UK group to reach the US charts with which song that reached #20?
A) Breakaway   B) Silver Threads and Golden Needles   C) Island of Dreams

2. The chorus of Dusty's first UK hit, a #4 in 1963 included these lyrics: "You stopped and smiled at me, asked if I'd care to dance. I fell into your open arms and I didn't stand a chance". What was the song?

3. Only one of Dusty Springfield's solo hits made #1 in the UK. What was the song that topped the charts in 1966?

4. In 1964, Dusty Springfield had a #6 US hit with *Wishin' and Hopin'*. However, the song was a #13 hit in the UK for which band?
A) The Rockin' Berries   B) The Merseybeats   C) The Searchers

5. Dusty's 1968 #9 hit *Son of a Preacher Man* was featured on the soundtrack for which 1994 Quentin Tarantino film?
A) Pulp Fiction   B) Reservoir Dogs   C) Natural Born Killers

6. *What Have I Done to Deserve This?* returned Dusty to the UK Top 10 in 1987. Who which duo did she record the #2 song?
A) The Everly Brothers   B) The Pet Shop Boys   C) Simon & Garfunkel

7. In the 1970s Dusty had a 5 year relationship with Norma Tanega. With what song is Norma best associated in the UK - a #22 hit in 1966?

8. What Clive Westlake song did Dusty take to #4 in 1968?
A) I Close My Eyes and Count To Ten   B) Some Of Your Lovin'   C) Goin' Back

9. Dusty Springfield died at the young age of fifty-nine in 1999. By special permission, her OBE was presented to Dusty in hospital shortly before she died. What illness claimed her life?   A) Heart disease   B) Brain tumour   C) Breast cancer

10. Dusty Springfield was inducted into the Rock and Roll Hall of Fame two weeks after her death. Which star helped induct her into the Hall of Fame, declaring: "I'm biased, but I just think she was the greatest white singer there ever has been ... every song she sang, she claimed as her own."

Lana Sisters (Dusty left)

The Springfields

DUSTY SPRINGFIELD ANSWERS: 1. B) Silver Threads and Golden Needles (not a UK hit); 2. I Only Want To Be With You; 3. You Don't Have To Say You Love Me; 4. B) The Merseybeats; 5. A) Pulp Fiction; 6. B) The Pet Shop Boys; 7. Walkin' My Cat Named Dog; 8. A) I Close My Eyes and Count To Ten; 9. C) Breast cancer; 10. Elton John.

BRUCE SPRINGSTEEN *(Born Long Beach, New Jersey as Bruce Frederick Joseph Springsteen on September 23, 1949) is an American singer, songwriter, and musician. One of the originators of the heartland rock style of music, combining mainstream rock musical style with narrative songs about working class American life. During a career that has spanned six decades, Springsteen has become known for his poetic, socially conscious lyrics and energetic stage performances. He has been nicknamed 'The Boss'. He had 20 Top 40 hits in the UK; this includes 4 Top 10 hits. 'The Boss' also had 14 Top 40 albums, including 4 number ones and 5 more Top 10 successes.*

1. In 1964, Bruce Springsteen was inspired by The Beatles on The Ed Sullivan Show and bought his first guitar at the Western Auto Appliance Store. How much did the guitar cost?   A) $149.95   B) $79.95   C) $18.95

2. Which Springsteen song became a #6 hit in 1976 when Manfred Mann's Earth Band recorded it?   A) Do Wah Diddy Diddy   B) Blinded By the Light   C) Might Quinn

3. Which 1985 #4 Bruce Springsteen hit featured future *Friends* star Courteney Cox in the promotional video?   A) Glory Days   B) Dancing In the Dark   C) I'm On Fire

4. With his first attempt to compose a song for a film, Springsteen won an Academy Award for Best Original Song. What was the song?
A) Streets of Philadelphia   B) Dead Man Walkin'   C) The Wedding Singer

5. The 1996 UK number 26 hit, *The Ghost of Tom Joad*, is based on a character from which classic American novel?
A) To Kill a Mockingbird   B) The Grapes of Wrath   C) Catcher In the Rye

6. Which 1985 hit contains these lyrics: "Got in a little hometown jam, So they put a rifle in my hand, Sent me off to a foreign land, To go and kill the yellow man"?
A) Born To Run   B) Born In the USA   C) Glory Days

7. Bruce Springsteen performed live on stage with which rock band during the 1997 MTV Video Music Awards?   A) U2   B) Rolling Stones   C) The Wallflowers

8. When he dissolved the E Street Band in 1989, The Boss gave each member $2m as a severance payment. True or False?

9. What type of guitar is Bruce Springsteen holding on the cover of *Born to Run*?
A) Fender Telecaster   B) Fender Stratocaster   C) Fender Esquire

10 *Fire* was a Springsteen written song that he envisioned to be sung by Elvis. The song was a 1978 #2 hit in the US but only reached #34 in the UK, but which female group had the hit?   A) The Pointer Sisters   B) The Supremes   C) Sisters of Mercy

Bruce Springsteen by Andrew Western

Bruce Springsteen performing with another legend, Roy Orbison on a Black and White Night

BRUCE SPRINGSTEEN ANSWERS: *1. C) $18.95; 2. B) Blinded By the Light; 3. B) Dancing In the Dark; 4. A) Streets of Philadelphia; 5. B) The Grapes of Wrath; 6. B) Born In the USA; 7. C) The Wallflowers; 8. True; 9. C) Fender Esquire; 10. A) The Pointer Sisters.*

LISA STANSFIELD (Born Lisa Jane Stansfield on 11 April 1966 in Manchester. Lisa is an English singer, songwriter, and actress, her career began in 1980 when she won the singing competition Search for a Star. Stansfield has won numerous awards, including three Brit Awards, two Ivor Novello Awards, a Billboard Music Award, World Music Award, ASCAP Award, Women's World Award, Silver Clef Award and two DMC Awards. Including collaborations, Lisa had 18 Top 40 singles, this included 2 number ones and 6 more Top 10 singles; she also had four hit albums reaching #2,3,6 & 2 respectively.

1. In 1983, Lisa Stansfield co-hosted which children's TV programme as well as appearing on another children's TV series, The Krankies Klub?
A) Razzamatazz   B) Crackerjack   C) Blue Peter

2. In 1986, Arista issued *On Fire*. Just as the single was climbing the charts it was withdrawn by the record company in the wake of which disaster?
A) King's Cross underground fire   B) Bradford City fire   C) Kegworth air disaster

3. Lisa Stansfield's first chart hit was *People Hold On*, a #11 in 1989. With whom did she share the billing on the record label?   A) Blue Zone   B) Band Aid II   C) Coldcut

4. The 1989 album *Affection* received acclaim from music critics, and was commercially successful. Which single from the album was Lisa's only UK number one hit?   A) All Woman   B) Live Together   C) All Around the World

5. Stansfield was a part of Band-Aid II, a charity supergroup founded to raise money for anti-poverty efforts in Ethiopia. recording *Do They Know It's Christmas?*, which topped the UK Singles Chart for three weeks. True or False?

6. Lisa was part of the *Five Live EP* (Freddie Mercury tribute concert) at Wembley in 1992. Which song did she sing with George Michael and Queen on the EP?
A) Somebody To Love   B) These Are The Days Of Our Lives   C) Calling You

7. Name the Lisa Stansfield #10 hit from 1992 that includes these lyrics: "What did I do my darling? That made you send me running, Told you to cast me down and throw me out, What can I tell you honey, if I don't know what I've done"

8. Which Lisa Stansfield co-written song was the theme song for the film *Indecent Proposal*, starring Robert Redford and Demi Moore and was a #8 hit in 1993?
A) In All the Right Places   B) So Natural   C) Little Bit Of Heaven

9. In 1999, Stansfield made her film debut. She played Joan Woodcock in which Nick Mead-directed film, that also starred Hugo Speer?
A) Bank Robber   B) Parting Shots   C) Swing

10. With whom did Lisa Stansfield re-record *People Hold On* in 1997 and have a #4 hit?   A) Divine   B) The Dirty Rotten Scoundrels   C) The O'Jays

THE HITS OF SQUEEZE

The band's founding members in March 1974 were Chris Difford (guitar, vocals, lyrics), and Glenn Tilbrook (vocals, guitar, music), and soon added Jools Holland (keyboards) and Paul Gunn (drums) to form an actual band. The group performed under several names, most frequently "Captain Trundlow's Sky Company" or "Skyco", before selecting the band name "Squeeze" as a facetious tribute to the Velvet Underground's oft-derided 1973 album Squeeze. Gilson Lavis replaced Gunn on drums, and Harry Kakoulli joined on bass in 1975.

#				#		
#19	Take Me I'm Yours	Apr 1978		#4	Labelled With Love	Oct 1981
#2	Cool For Cats	Mar 1979		#16	Hourglass	Aug 1987
#2	Up The Junction	Jun 1979		#39	Third Rail	Jul 1993
#24	Slap And Tickle	Sep 1979		#36	This Summer	Sep 1995
#17	Another Nail In My Heart	Mar 1980		#27	Heaven Knows	Jun 1996
#35	Is That Love	May 1981		#32	This Summer (remix)	Aug 1996

LISA STANSFIELD ANSWERS: *1. A) Razzamatazz; 2. A) King's Cross underground fire; 3. C) Coldcut; 4. C) All Around the World; 5. True (After Band Aid in 1984, Band Aid II followed in 1989); 6. B) These Are The Days Of Our Lives; 7. Someday (I'm Coming Back); 8. A) In All the Right Places; 9. C) Swing; 10. B) The Dirty Rotten Scoundrels.*

ALVIN STARDUST /SHANE FENTON (Born Bernard William Jewry in Muswell Hill on 27 September 1942 – died in Ifold, West Sussex on 23 October 2014). As Shane Fenton in the 1960s, Jewry was pretty successful in the pre-Beatles era. After Shane Fenton & The Fentones broke up he worked in music management and played small venues with his first wife Iris Caldwell. He became better known in the 1970s and 1980s as Alvin Stardust, a character he in the glam rock era. Jewry had 4 Top 40 hits as Shane Fenton and 11 Top 40 hits as Alvin Stardust, including one #1 and 6 further Top 10 hits. Stardust also had 2 Top 40 albums, including one Top 10 success.

1. Bernard Jewry wasn't the original Shane Fenton, who had died of rheumatic fever at just 17 years of age. True or False?

2. Shane Fenton's highest chart placing was #19. What was the song?
A) I'm A Moody Guy   B) Walk Away   C) Cindy's Birthday

3. The Fentones had two singles that bubbled just outside the Top 40. *The Breeze and I* was one, what was the other?   A) The Mexican   B) The Roman   C) The Greek

4. Shane Fenton & The Fentones appeared in which Michael Winner film in 1962?
A) Some Like It Cool   B) The Cool Mikado   C) Play It Cool

5. Alvin Stardust materialised in 1973. Which singer / songwriter actually recorded the first hit, *My Coo Ca Choo*, a track that Bernard Jewry lip-synched to on *Top Of The Pops*?   A) Chris Andrews   B) Peter Shelley   C) Roger Cook

6. What was Alvin Stardust's only UK number one hit?
A) My Coo Ca Choo   B) Jealous Mind   C) Red Dress

be smart... be safe

7. With which road safety campaign was Alvin Stardust involved in 1976?
A) Green Cross Code   B) Clunk-Click Every Trip   C) Drink Drive

8. Stardust had a #4 hit in 1981, with a song that Nat 'King' Cole had taken to #2 28 years earlier. What song includes these lyrics:" You'll find a love you can share, One you can call your own, Just close your eyes you'll be there, You'll never be alone"?
A) When I Fall In Love   B) Let There Be Love   C) Pretend

9. In 1995, Alvin Stardust joined the cast of which soap for 9 months, playing Greg Anderson?   A) Hollyoaks   B) Coronation Street   C) Home and Away

10. On which renowned Christmas TV show did Alvin Stardust appear in 1981?
A) The Two Ronnies   B) Morecambe & Wise   C) Only Fools & Horses

SHANE FENTON / ALVIN STARDUST ANSWERS: *1. True (Johnny Theakston was the original Shane Fenton); 2. C) Cindy's Birthday; 3. A) The Mexican; 4. C) Play It Cool; 5. B) Peter Shelley (Bernard Jewry recorded every other Alvin Stardust track); 6. B) Jealous Mind; 7. A) Green Cross Code; 8. C) Pretend; 9. A) Hollyoaks; 10. B) Morecambe & Wise.*

RINGO STARR *(Sir Richard Starkey MBE (born in Dingle, Liverpool on 7 July 1940), is an English musician, singer, songwriter and actor. He achieved international fame as Beatles drummer. Starr occasionally sang lead vocals. Starr was in another Liverpool group, Rory Storm and the Hurricanes, after moderate success he quit and replaced Pete Best in The Beatles in 1962. Apart from Beatles' films, Starr has acted in numerous others. Many TV appearances. First solo hit in 1971. Toured with several variations of Ringo Starr & His All-Starr Band he Ringo had five solo Top 40 singles, 4 of them reaching the Top 10. He also had three Top 40 albums, three of those reaching the Top 10.*

1. *I Wanna Be You Man* was written for Ringo as a track on the album *With the Beatles*. However it was released as a single and reached #12 by which UK rock band in 1963?   A) Pretty Things   B) Rolling Stones   C) The Small Faces

2. The last song released by The Beatles featuring Starr on lead vocals was a song that he had written himself. It appeared on the 1969 *Abbey Road* album. What was the song's title?   A) Flying   B) Don't Pass Me By   C) Octopus's Garden

3. What was Ringo's childhood nickname?   A) Lazarus   B) Roman   C) Schnoz

4. What was the first band co-founded by Ringo?   A) Rory Storm & The Hurricanes   B) Eddie Miles Band   C) The Quarrymen

5. In 1974 Ringo had a #4 hit with a song that had previously been a #3 hit for Johnny Burnette in 1961. What was the song?
A) Dreamin'   B) Rockabilly Boogie C) You're Sixteen

6. What was the title of Ringo's first album that reached #7 in 1970?
A) Sentimental Journey   B) Beaucoups of Blues   C) Ringo

7. Which children's series did Ringo narrate from 1984 to 1986?
A) The Magic Roundabout   B) Ivor the Engine   C) Thomas & Friends

8. What musical instrument is Ringo holding on the cover of *Sgt. Pepper's Lonely Hearts Club Band*?   A) Tambourine   B) Trumpet   C) Triangle

9. Who is Ringo's drummer son who has played with, amongst others, The Who and the Spencer Davis Group?   A) Zak Starkey   B) Alan White   C) Phil Rudd

10. On the set of which 1981 film did Ringo meet his second wife Barbara Bach?
A) The Unseen   B) Caveman   C) Up the Academy

The Georgia Satellites covered Ringo's song Don't Pass Me By on their 1988 album Open All Night.

RINGO STARR ANSWERS: *1. B) Rolling Stones; 2. C) Octopus's Garden; 3. A) Lazarus (he was a sickly child and had life threatening illnesses); 4. B) Eddie Miles Band; 5. C) You're Sixteen; 6. A) Sentimental Journey; 7. C) Thomas & Friends; 8. B) Trumpet; 9. A) Zak Starkey; 10. B) Caveman.*

STATUS QUO are an English rock band that formed in 1962. The group originated in London as The Scorpions and was founded by Francis Rossi and Alan Lancaster while they were still schoolboys. After a number of lineup changes, which included the introduction of Rick Parfitt in 1967, the band became The Status Quo in 1967 and Status Quo in 1969. The familiar early line up: Rossi (vocals/lead guitar); Lancaster (bass, vocals), Rick Parfitt (vocals/rhythm guitar), John Coghlan (drums) then Andy Bown (keyboards). Many changes followed down the years. Quo had 50 Top 40 hits, including a #1 and 21 other Top 10 hits. Also, 4 #1 albums and 15 more Top10 hits.

1. *Rockin' All Over the World* has become a signature tune of Quo. It was written by John Fogerty, who was the front man of which US rock band?
A) Creedence Clearwater Revival   B) The Doors   C) Buffalo Springfield

2. Status Quo had just one number one hit. What is the 1974 chart-topper that includes these lyrics: "I have all the ways you see, To keep you guessing, stop your messing with me, You'll be back to find your way, Again again again again"?

3. In 1973, what became the first Status Quo album to reach the Top 10?
A) Hello! B) Quo   C) Piledriver

4. Status Quo opened *Live Aid* at Wembley in 1985 with which song?
A) Caroline   B) Rockin' All Over the World   C) Whatever You Want

5. Jeff Rich on drums and Rhino Edwards on bass both joined Quo in 1984 from which band?   A) Climax Blues Band   B) Ten Years After   C) Juicy Lucy

6. Which singer co-wrote Status Quo's second hit *Ice In the Sun* which reached #8 in 1968?   A) Tommy Steele   B) Adam Faith   C) Marty Wilde

7. What position in the UK singles chart did *What You're Proposin'* (1980), *In the Army Now* (1986) and *Anniversary Waltz Part 1* (1990) all reach?   A) 1   B) 2   C) 3

8. In 1996 Quo joined forces with which legendary band to have a #24 hit with *Fun, Fun, Fun*?   A) The Beach Boys   B) The Searchers   C) Fleetwood Mac

9. Status Quo were awarded a Brit Award for outstanding contribution to music in 1981. True or False?

10. The Doors *Roadhouse Blues* was included on the *Piledriver* album and was a strong part of Quo's stage act. Who sung the lead vocal?
A) John Coghlan   B) Rick Parfitt   C) Alan Lancaster

WHO ARE THEY?

This singing group had 9 Top 40 singles between 1953 and 1956, including three number ones - Broken Wings, I See the Moon & Finger of Suspicion (with Dickie Valentine). Can you name them?

STATUS QUO ANSWERS: *1. A) Creedence Clearwater Revival; 2. Down Down; 3. C) Piledriver; 4. B) Rockin' All Over the World; 5. A) Climax Blues Band; 6. C) Marty Wilde; 7. B) 2; 8. A) The Beach Boys; 9. False (it was 1991); 10. C) Alan Lancaster.*
WHO ARE THEY ANSWER: *The Stargazers.*

TOMMY STEELE *(Sir Thomas Hicks, OBE, born IN Bermondsey on 17 December 1936), is an English entertainer, regarded as Britain's first teen idol and rock and roll star. As a child, Steele spent time in hospital for porphyria. After being discovered at the 2i's Coffee Bar in Soho, London. By the 1960s, Steele was an all-round entertainer, appearing in West End theatre productions and starring in musical films. He is also a songwriter, author and sculptor. Steele recorded 17 Top 40 hit singles, including one #1 and 6 more Top 10 hits. He also had 3 successful albums, two reaching number one and the other #5.*

1. Tommy Steele's only number one had been a chart-topper for Guy Mitchell the week previously in January 1957! What was the song?
A) Butterfingers   B) Handful of Songs   C) Singing the Blues

2. Tommy Steele started out as a member of which skiffle group?
A) The Vipers   B) Lonnie Donegan   C) The Chesternuts

3. Tommy Steele fell in love rock 'n' roll when he visited the US as a merchant seaman, and saw which legend performing?
A) Elvis Presley   B) Chuck Berry   C) Buddy Holly

4. In the picture below, Tommy Steele is pictured with a well-known statue that he sculpted. What is it called, and in which city would you find it?

5. *Little White Bull* was a #6 hit in 1959, in which film soundtrack was the song included?   A) Waltz of the Toreadors   B) Tommy the Toreador   C) Ferdinand the Bull

6. What Tommy Steele #5 from 1960 was a former Harry Champion song and includes these lyrics: "It was like a steam boat funnel, or a railway arch, or the Blackwall tunnel"?   A) What A Mouth   B) Butterfingers   C) Water Water

7. When Eamonn Andrews requested a meeting with Tommy Steele, apparently to discuss a forthcoming appearance on *Crackerjack*, at the BBC TV Theatre, what was the real purpose of the meeting?

8. Steele wrote many songs with songwriting collaborators, Lionel Bart and Mike Pratt. In which private detective TV series did Mike Pratt star in 26 episodes from 1969 to 1970?   A) Shoestring   B) Randall & Hopkirk (Deceased)   C) Bergerac

9. To whom was Tommy Steele married in 1960?
A) Joyce Baker   B) Maureen Tyler   C) Ann Donoghue

10. What 1963 stage musical, based on H.G. Wells's 1905 novel *Kipps: The Story of a Simple Soul*, starred Tommy Steele, who then went on to star in a film version four years later?   A) Half a Sixpence   B) The Happiest Millionaire   C) Finian's Rainbow

TOMMY STEELE ANSWERS: *1. C) Singing the Blues; 2. A) The Vipers (with Wally Whyton); 3. C) Buddy Holly (in Norfolk, Virginia); 4. Eleanor Rigby, which he sculpted and donated to the City of Liverpool as a tribute to the Beatles; 5. B) Tommy the Toreador; 6. A) What A Mouth; 7. To surprise Tommy Steele for This Is Your Life; 8. B) Randall & Hopkirk (Deceased); 9. C) Ann Donoghue; 10. A) Half a Sixpence.*

CAT STEVENS *(Yusuf Islam, born in Marleybone, London as Steven Demetre Georgiou; 21 July 1948), commonly known as Cat Stevens, Yusuf, and Yusuf / Cat Stevens, is a British singer-songwriter and multi-instrumentalist. His musical style consists of folk, pop, rock, and, later in his career, Islamic music. Stevens converted to Islam in December 1977, and adopted the name Yusuf Islam the following year. In 1979, he auctioned all of his guitars for charity, and left his musical career to devote himself to educational and philanthropic causes in the Muslim community. Cat Stevens had 9 Top 40 hits, 4 of them reaching the Top 10. Also had 10 Top 40 albums, 7 of them Top 10.*

1. One of Cat Stevens songs was included on a double sided number one hit for Rod Stewart in 1977. Ten years earlier it had been a #18 for P.P. Arnold. Name the song.
A) Father and Son   B) The First Cut Is the Deepest   C) Moon Shadow

2. Cat Stevens' last UK single hit was a #19 in 1974. Who wrote the song?
A) Sam Cooke   B) Cat Stevens   C) Elton John

3. Cat Stevens highest charting single was a #2 in 1967. What was the song that contained these lyrics: "There's a five minute break and that's all you take, For a cup of cold coffee and a piece of cake"?

4. Which hit song, a 1997 #2 for Boyzone, is about a chat between two relatives, one giving advice to the other?   A) Words   B) No Matter What   C) Father and Son

5. In 1976, Stevens nearly drowned off the coast of Malibu, California. He said that he shouted, "Oh, God! If you save me I will work for you." Immediately a wave appeared and carried him back to shore. True or False?

6. Cat Stevens' 1972 recording of the hymn *Morning Has Broken* reached #9 in the UK charts. Who arranged the song and played piano on the track?
A) Elton John   B) Billy Joel   C) Rick Wakeman

7. In 1969 Stevens was close to death and admitted to the King Edward VII Hospital, Midhurst, Sussex. He spent months recuperating followed by a year's convalescence before he recovered from what?   A) Tuberculosis   B) Angina   C) Hepatitis

8. A track off of Stevens' 1967 album, *New Masters*, earned him back-to-back ASCAP "Songwriter of the Year" awards, almost 40 years later. What was the song?
A) I'm Gonna Be King   B) Moonstone   C) The First Cut Is the Deepest

9. *Tea for the Tillerman* was Cat Stevens 4th studio album, released in 1970. Who created the artwork featured on the record's cover?
A) Mick Jagger   B) Cat Stevens   C) Andy Warhol

10. Which Stevens 1970 #8 hit, with a madrigal sound unlike most music played on pop radio, was about an American girlfriend at the time?
A) Lady D'Arbanville   B) Can't Keep It In   C) A Bad Night

CAT STEVENS ANSWERS: *1. B) The First Cut Is the Deepest; 2. A) Sam Cooke; 3. Matthew and Son; 4. C) Father and Son; 5. True; 6. C) Rick Wakeman; 7. A) Tuberculosis; 8. C) The First Cut is the Deepest; 9. B) Cat Stevens; 10. A) Lady D'Arbanville (about Patti D'Arbanville).*

SHAKIN' STEVENS (Michael Barratt (born in Cardiff, Wales on 4 March 1948), is a Welsh singer and songwriter. He was the UK's biggest-selling singles artist of the 1980s. His recording and performing career began in the late 1960s, although it was not until 1980 that his commercial success began. His most successful songs were nostalgia hits, evoking the sound of 1950s rock and roll and pop. In the late 1960s his official occupation was a milkman. Shaky had 32 Top 40 hits, including 4 number ones and 11 more Top 10 hits. He also had 7 Top 40 albums, including a number one and 3 other Top 10 successes.

1. In 1977, after seven years touring and recording, Shaky landed one of the 3 lead roles in a new West End musical *Elvis!*, Playing Elvis in his 'middle' years. Who were the other two singers who played Elvis in other stages of his life?   A) Tim Whitnall / P.J. Proby   B) Ral Donner / Russell Watson   C) Alexander Bar / Bogdan Kominowski

2. Shaky finally had a minor hit with his 11th single in the UK. What song reached a modest number #24 in 1980?   A) It's Raining   B) Marie, Marie   C) Hot Dog

3. The first time Shakin' Stevens hit the top spot in the charts was with which song that had been a #1 for Rosemary Clooney in 1954?
A) This Ole House   B) Mambo Italiano   C) Where Will the Baby's Dimple Be?

4. Shakin' Stevens 1984 #5 hit *Teardrops*, featured which guitar legend?
A) Albert Lee   B) Eric Clapton   C) Hank Marvin

5. Stevens had another #1 in 1981. This time the song was a cover of a song that was a Top 10 hit for both Jim Lowe and Frankie Vaughan in 1954. What was the song?   A) The Garden of Eden   B) Green Door   C) Give Me the Moonlight

6. With whom did Shaky have a #5 hit in 1984 singing *A Rockin' Good Way*?
A) Katherine Jenkins   B) Cerys Matthews   C) Bonnie Tyler

7. In 1985, Shakin' Stevens was able to secure a Christmas Number 1 hit that has proved to be perennially popular every festive season since? What is the song?
A) Last Christmas   B) Merry Xmas Everybody   C) Merry Christmas Everyone

8. With which famous drummer did Shakin' Stevens team up with on the #37 hit *Radio* in 1992?   A) Phil Collins   B) Roger Taylor   C) Ringo Starr

9. In the 1990s Stevens took a lengthy break from recording and was shocked by a court ruling relating to unpaid royalties from the *Legend* album. To whom did he have to make a substantial payout?   A) The Sunsets   B) Dave Edmunds   C) Freya Miller

10. Which product did Shakin' Stevens promote in a 1990s advertising campaign?

refreshes the parts other beers **cannot reach.**

ROD STEWART *(Sir Roderick David Stewart CBE (born Highgate, London on 10 January 1945) is a British rock and pop singer and songwriter. He is of Scottish and English ancestry. With his distinctive raspy singing voice, Stewart is among the best-selling music artists of all time. Stewart's music career began in 1962 when he busked with a harmonica. In 1963: he joined The Dimensions; in 1964: Long John Baldry and the All Stars; 1967, the Jeff Beck Group; then the Faces in 1969, also maintaining a solo career. Rod had 47 Top 40 hits, including 6 #1's and 21 more Top 10 hits. He also had 25 Top 40 albums, including 7 No. 1's and 15 further Top 10 successes.*

1. Rod joined the annual Campaign for Nuclear Disarmament, Aldermaston Marches from 1961 to 1963 and was arrested on three occasions when he took part in sit-ins at Trafalgar Square and Whitehall. True or False?

2. Rod Stewart had his first No 1 album in 1971. What was its title?
A) Never a Dull Moment   B) Sing It Again Rod   C) Every Picture Tells a Story

3. Stewart was the uncredited lead singer on a 1972 #3 hit single, *In a Broken Dream*. What was the name of the Australian rock band?
A) Nick Cave & The Bad Seeds   B) Python Lee Jackson   C) AC/DC

4. Rod Stewart's first number one single in the UK also arrived in 1971? What was the song?   A) Maggie May   B) You Wear It Well   C) I Don't Want To Talk About It

5. To which charity did Rod give profits from his 1978 #1, *Do Ya Think I'm Sexy*? A) Cancer Research UK   B) RSPCA   C) UNICEF

6. Famous ladies' man Rod, has had how many children by five different mothers? A) 8   B) 6   C) 5

7. On the cover of Rod Stewart's 1974 #1 album *Smiler*, Rod's image is set against what background?   A) Polka Dot   B) Tartan   C) Stars

8. What 2 repeated words are missing from these lyrics from a 1978 Rod Stewart #5 hit: "… …. in your satin shoes, … …., are you still in school?, … …., you're makin' me a fool"

9. In 1990, the *Vagabond Heart* album continued Stewart's renewal and inspiration. The lead single, *It Takes Two*, reached #5. It was a duet, sung with whom?
A) Tina Turner   B) Mick Jagger   C) The Scottish World Cup Football Squad

10. The Sutherland Brothers *Sailing* became Rod's biggest selling single, and was a #1 in 1975. A year later it re-entered the charts and reached #3. What caused the second wave of interest in the song?
A) Falklands War   B) Theme for BBC TV series   C) Charity single RNLI

NAME THESE SINGING STEWARTS
They all had hits in the 20ᵗʰ century

ROD STEWART ANSWERS: *1. True; 2. C) Every Picture Tells a Story; 3. B) Python Lee Jackson; 4. A) Maggie May; 5. C) UNICEF; 6. A) 8; 7. B) Tartan; 8. Hot Legs; 9. Tina Turner; 10. B) Theme for BBC TV series (about HMS Ark Royal).* **NAME THESE SINGING STEWARTS ANSWERS:** *A) Andy; B) Al; C) Amii; D) Dave; E) Jermaine.*

STING (Gordon Matthew Thomas Sumner CBE, born Wallsend on 2 October 1951), is an English musician and actor. He was the frontman, songwriter and bassist for new wave rock band The Police from 1977 to their breakup in 1986. (See separate quiz for The Police). He launched a solo career in 1985 and has included elements of rock, jazz, reggae, classical, new-age, and world beat in his music. Sting performed jazz in the evening, weekends and during breaks from college and gained his nickname after his habit of wearing a black and yellow jumper with hooped stripes. After The Police, Sting had 20 Top 40 singles between 1982 and 1999, including 2 Top 10 hits. He also had 9 Top 40 albums, including 3 #1's and 5 more Top 10.

1. Sting has had just one solo Top 10 single. It was a #9 in 1994. What was the song?   A) Spread a Little Happiness   B) Russians   C) When We Dance

2. In 1999 Sting included these lyrics in a song that reached #13: "I'm a bat and you're the cave, You're The Beach and I'm a wave". What is the song title?
A) Brand New Day   B) If I Ever Lose My Faith In You   C) Englishman in New York

3. *If You Love Somebody Set Them Free* was a #26 hit in 1985, inspired by a haunted house. True or False?

4. Which other two stars joined Sting on the 1994 #2 hit *All For Love* taken from the soundtrack of *The Three Musketeers*?

5. The music video for which song, directed by Kevin Godley, features a gold silhouette of Sting singing the song while walking through a dark village at night containing features such as a red telephone box and a red pillar box?
A) Fields of Gold   B) Demolition Man   C) Seven Days

6. Sting has occasionally worked as an actor. In which 1998 film did he play JD, a bar owner who was the father of Eddy, one of the main characters?
A) Lock, Stock and Two Smoking Barrels   B) Waking Ned   C) Deep Impact

7. What was Sting's connection with the Dire Straits 1985 #4 hit *Money For Nothing*?

8. As a child, he was inspired to divert from the shipyard prospects to a more glamorous life, when someone waved to him from a Rolls Royce. Who was it?
A) Jackie Milburn   B) The Queen Mother   C) Harold Wilson

9. *Fields of Gold* was covered by Eva Cassidy on her 1998 #1 album. What was the album titled?   A) Imagine   B) American Tune   C) Songbird

10. Sting decided to leave the Police while onstage during a concert in 1983 at which New York City venue, because playing that venue was "[Mount] Everest"?
A) Shea Stadium   B) Carnegie Hall   C) Central Park

EVERYDAY - Name a hit song title for every day of the week

A) SUNDAY	SMALL FACES (1968)
B) MONDAY	DURAN DURAN (1984)
C) TUESDAY	POGUES (1993)
D) WEDNESDAY	UNDERTONES (1980)
E) THURSDAY	DAVID BOWIE (1999)
F) FRIDAY	EASYBEATS (1966)
G) SATURDAY	WHIGFIELD (1994)

STING ANSWERS: *1. C) When We Dance; 2. A) Brand New Day; 3. True (Sting was living in a former 18th-century pub he felt was haunted); 4. Bryan Adams and Rod Stewart; 5. A) Fields of Gold; 6. A) Lock, Stock and Two Smoking Barrels; 7. Co-wrote song and sung the falsetto parts on the single; 8. B) The Queen Mother; 9. C) Songbird; 10. A) Shea Stadium.*
EVERYDAY ANSWERS: *A) Lazy Sunday; B) New Moon On Monday; C) Tuesday Morning; D) Wednesday Week; E) Thursday's Child; F) Friday On My Mind; G) Saturday Night.*

THE STRANGLERS *are an English rock band who emerged via the punk rock scene. Formed as the Guildford Stranglers in 1974, they built a following in pub rock scene. They explored a variety of musical styles, from new wave, art rock, gothic rock to sophisti-pop in the 80s. Line up: Jet Black (drums), Jean-Jacques Burnel (vocals/bass), Hugh Cornwell (vocals/guitar), Hans Wärmling (keyboard/guitar), replaced by Dave Greenfield within a year. The Stranglers had 22 Top 40 hits, 7 of them reaching the Top 10. They also had 16 Top 40 albums, including 8 Top 10 successes.*

1. The first Stranglers Top 40 hit was a #8 success in 1977. It contained these lyrics. Name the song. "Well I got the notion girl that you got some suntan lotion in that bottle of yours, Spread it all over my peelin' skin baby".
A) Golden Brown   B) No More Heroes   C) Peaches

2. At a gig in Battersea Park, London in 1978, The Stranglers caused a great deal of police and tabloid upset, by featuring a group of what, as part of their stage show to promote their #18 hit *Nice 'N Sleazy*?   A) Strippers   B) Cowboys   C) Policemen

3. The Stranglers highest charting single, *Golden Brown*, reached number two in 1981 and was an alleged ode to what drug?   A) Cocaine   B) Cannabis   C) Heroin

4. In August 1990, who abruptly left The Stranglers to pursue a solo career, following the band's failure to attain a tour in the US?
A) Jet Black   B) Hugh Cornwell   C) Jean-Jacques Burnel

5. The Stranglers fifth album, a #8 hit, but widely considered an artistic and commercial failure, was a concept album exploring religion and a link between religious phenomena and extraterrestrial visitors. What was the album's title?
A) The Gospel According to the Meninblack   B) La Folie   C) Feline

6. Which Ray Davies song, a #2 for The Kinks in 1964, was covered by The Stranglers in 1988 and reached #7 in the charts?
A) You Really Got Me   B) All Day and All Of The Night   C) Waterloo Sunset

7.Before forming The Stranglers in his mid-30s, Jet Black (real name Brian Duffy) was a successful businessman, who at one point, owned a fleet of ice cream vans and an off-licence. True or False?

8. Before The Stranglers achieved major success, for which major American punk act did they open in live concerts in 1976?   A) Sex Pistols   B) Devo   C) Patti Smith

9. *(Get a) Grip (on Yourself)* was the bands first single. It reached #44 in 1977. It was re-released in 1989 as *Grip '89*, what chart position did it achieve second time?
A) 44   B) 33   C) 22

10. Which of these Stranglers songs is the odd one out .... Being sung ONLY in English?   A) European Female   B) Don't Bring Harry   C) La Folie

---

NAME THESE SONGS, WITH 'MIDNIGHT' IN THEIR TITLES?

1. Midnight ___ ___ (Bon Jovi 1997 #4)
2. Midnight ___ ___ ___ (Maria Muldaur 1974 #21)
3. Midnight ___ ___ ___ ___ ___ (Meat Loaf 1983 #17)
4. Midnight ___ ___ ___ (Gladys Knight & Pips 1976 #10)
5. Midnight ___ ___ (Kenny Ball & Jazzmen 1961 #2)

THE STRANGLERS ANSWERS: *1. C) Peaches; 2. A) Strippers; 3. C) Heroin; 4. C) Jean-Jacques Burnel; 5. A) The Gospel According to the Meninblack; 6. B) All Day and All Of The Night; 7. True; 8. C) Patti Smith; 9. B) 33; 10. A) European Female.*
MIDNIGHT SONGS ANSWERS: *1. Midnight in Chelsea; 2. Midnight at the Oasis; 3. Midnight at the Lost and Found; 4. Midnight Train To Georgia; 5. Midnight In Moscow.*

246

BIG JIM SULLIVAN *(Born James George Tomkins, 14 February 1941 – 2 October 2012). Best known as a top session guitarist. In the 1960s and 1970s he was one of the most in-demand studio musicians in the UK, and performed on around 750 charting singles over his career, including 54 UK Number One hits. In his young days he played with Vince Taylor & The Playboys, the Vince Eager Band and most successfully with Marty Wilde & The Wildcats (who had instrumental chart success as the Krew Kats). Gave guitar lessons to near-neighbour Ritchie Blackmore. In 1969 he played in Tom Jones band and from 1978, the James Last Orchestra. Released many albums of his own and fronted the band Tiger.*

NUMBER ONE UK SINGLES FEATURING BIG JIM SULLIVAN ON GUITAR

1961. Petula Clark – *Sailor;* Eden Kane – *Well I Ask You;* Danny Williams – *Moon River;* Frankie Vaughan *–Tower of Strength.*

1962. Mike Sarne – *Come Outside;* Frank Ifield – *Remember You;* Frank Ifield – *Lovesick Blues.*

1963. Jet Harris & Tony Meehan - *Diamonds;* Frank Ifield – *Wayward Wind;* Frank Ifield – *Confessin';* Brian Poole & The Tremeloes - *Do You Love Me.*

1964. The Bachelors – *Diane;* Cilla Black – *Anyone Who Had a Heart.* Peter & Gordon – *A World Without Love;* The Four Pennies – *Juliet;* Cilla Black – *You're My World;* Georgie Fame – *Yeh Yeh.*

1965. The Seekers – *I'll Never Find Another You;* Tom Jones – *It's Not Unusual* (not the main guitar); Jackie Trent – *Where Are You Now (My Love);* Sandie Shaw – *Long Live Love;* The Walker Brothers – *Make It Easy on Yourself;* Ken Dodd – *Tears;* The Seekers – *The Carnival Is Over.*

1966. The Overlanders – *Michelle;* 1966 The Walker Brothers – *The Sun Ain't Gonna Shine Anymore;* Dusty Springfield – *You Don't Have to Say You Love Me;* Chris Farlowe – *Out of Time;* Tom Jones – *Green, Green Grass of Home.*

1967. Engelbert Humperdinck – *Release Me;* Petula Clark - *This Is My Song;* Sandie Shaw – *Puppet on a String;* The Tremeloes - *Silence is Golden;* Engelbert Humperdinck – *The Last Waltz;* Long John Baldry – *Let The Heartaches Begin.*

1968. Esther and Abi Ofarim – Cinderella Rockafella; Dave Dee, Dozy, Beaky, Mick and Tich – *The Legend of Xanadu;* Des O'Connor – *I Pretend;* The Scaffold – *Lily The Pink;* Marmalade – *Ob-La-Di, Ob-La-Da.*

1969. Peter Sarsedt - *Where Do You Go To My Lovely;* Thunderclap Newman – *Something in the Air;* Jane Birkin and Serge Gainsbourg – *Je t'aime... moi non-plus;* Rolf Harris – *Two Little Boys.*

1970. Dana – *All Kinds of Everything.*

1971. Middle of the Road – *Chirpy Chirpy Cheep Cheep;* Benny Hill – *Ernie (The Fastest Milkman in the West);* New Seekers – *I'd Like to Teach the World to Sing.*

1972. Gilbert O'Sullivan – *Clair;* **1973.** Gilbert O'Sullivan – *Get Down;* **1974.** Alvin Stardust – *Jealous Mind;* **1975.** Pilot – *January.*

*Some of the 750 singles that Big Jim played on include these: **1959** Marty Wilde – Bad Boy, **1961** Krew Kats – Trambone, Samovar, Peak Hour, Jack's Good, The Bat. Michael Cox – Sweet Little Sixteen, **1962** John Barry – James Bond Theme (Vic Flick played lead guitar but Sullivan played on the record and devised the walking-step introduction). **1963** Bern Elliott and the Fenmen – Money (That's What I Want), **1964** P.J. Proby – Hold Me and Together. Dave Berry – The Crying Game, Freddie and the Dreamers – I Love You Baby. **1965** Gerry & The Pacemakers – Ferry Cross the Mersey. **1971** Cliff Richard – Silvery Rain. **1972** Gilbert O'Sullivan – Alone Again (Naturally), Tom Jones – The Young New Mexican Puppeteer. **1974** Alvin Stardust – Jealous Mind.*

BARBRA STREISAND (Barbara Joan 'Barbra' Streisand born Brooklyn, New York on April 24, 1942) is an American singer and actress. Streisand is one of the last surviving stars from the Golden Age of Hollywood. She began her career by performing in nightclubs and Broadway theatres in the early 1960s. Barbra has received numerous accolades, both on record and on screen. Streisand had 16 Top 40 hits, either as a soloist or in duos, including a #1 and 6 more Top 10 hits. She also had 17 Top 40 albums, including 4 #1's and 3 more Top 10 successes.

1. Streisand's first husband was an actor with leading roles in films such as *M*A*S*H*. Who was husband No. 1? A) Alan Alda B) Donald Sutherland C) Elliott Gould

2. Barbra's first television appearance was in 1961. On which US late-night talk show did she appear? A) Ed Sullivan Show B) Tonight Show C) Steve Allen Show

3. At the 1969 Academy Awards, Barbra Streisand won an Oscar for Best Actress. Her performance in which film earned her the award?
A) Funny Girl B) Yentl C) A Star Is Born

4. In 1978, Barbra Streisand was nominated for Best Pop Female Vocal Performance at the Grammy Awards for *You Don't Bring Me Flowers*. The #5 UK hit song was performed as a duet with which singer?
A) Don Johnson B) Neil Diamond C) Barry Gibb

5. What was Streisand's only UK #1 hit single?
A) Woman In Love B) Evergreen C) Second Hand Rose

6. A UK #3 hit was the lead single on two 1997 albums, *Higher Ground* and *Let's Talk About Love*. With whom did Streisand duet on the song, *No More Tears (Enough Is Enough)*? A) Donna Summer B) Madonna C) Celine Dion

7. Streisand's concert fundraising events helped propel which President into office, later being introduced by the President at his inauguration in 1993.
A) Bill Clinton B) Ronald Reagan C) George W Bush

8. In 1973, Barbra Streisand starred in a multi-nominated romantic drama film. She also had a #31 UK hit with the title song of which Sydney Pollack directed film?
A) The Prince of Tides B) Hello Dolly C) The Way We Were

9. Barbra Streisand teamed up with Don Johnson in 1988 to have a #16 hit with *Till I Loved You*. On which musical concept album about an artist, was it the love theme?
A) Goya B) Constable C) Cezanne

10. Which 1997 # 10 includes these lyrics: "We started over coffee, we started out as friends, It's funny how from simple things, the best things begin"? A) If You Ever Leave Me B) I Finally Found Someone C) As If We Never Said Goodbye

BARBRA STREISAND ANSWERS: *1. C) Elliott Gould; 2. Tonight Show; 3. A) Funny Girl; 4. B) Neil Diamond; 5. A) Woman In Love; 6. C) Celine Dion; 7. Bill Clinton; 8. C) The Way We Were; 9. A) Goya; 10. B) I Finally Found Someone.*

THE STYLISTICS *are an American soul vocal group that achieved their greatest chart success in the 70s. The Stylistics were created from two Philadelphia groups, The Percussions and The Monarchs in 1968. The line up was Russell Thompkins Jr., Herb Murrell, Airrion Love, James Smith and James Dunn. All of their US hits were ballads characterised by the falsetto of Russell Thompkins Jr. and the production of Thom Bell. The Stylistics had 16 Top 40 hits, including a #1 and 9 more Top 10 hits. They also had 8 Top 40 albums, including 2 numbers ones and one other Top 10 smashes.*

1. Which song gave The Stylistics their first UK hit in 1972, reaching #13?
A) I'm Stone In Love With You   B) Betcha By Golly Wow   C) Peek-a-Boo

2. In 1975, The Stylistics hit number one in the British pop charts for the first time with which song?   A) You Make Me Feel Brand New   B) Sing Baby Sing   C) Can't Give You Anything (But My Love)

3. According to The Stylistics' #5 hit song from 1975, what is the saddest word?
A) Goodbye   B) Sorry   C) Na-Na

4. In 1976, The Stylistics had a UK #4 with a cover of which song that was a #1 for Elvis Presley in 1962 and a #3 for Andy Williams in 1972?   A) Can't Take My Eyes Off You   B) Can't Help Falling In Love   C) Can't Buy Me Love

5. In 1980, who became the first original member of The Stylistics to leave the group?   A) James Dunn   B) James Smith   C) Russell Thompkins, Jr.

6. What Stylistics #3 from 1975 contains these lyrics: "Ain't we got it made, our love song has no end, We're not only lovers we are friends"?

7. Producer Thom Bell stopped working with the Stylistics in 1974, and the split proved commercially difficult for the group in the U.S. Eventually they turned to a man who had had a UK #3 hit with *The Hustle* in 1975. Who was he?
A) Van McCoy   B) Isaac Hayes   C) Quincy Jones

8. The Stylistics were inducted into The Philadelphia Music Alliance Walk of Fame in what year?   A) 1990   B) 1994   C) 1998

9. On what label did The Stylistics record all their singles and albums fro 1972-1976?
A) H&L   B) Polydor   C) Avco

10. In 1979, The Stylistics had small parts playing conservative army officers in which film, directed by Miloš Forman?
A) Hair   B) One Flew Over the Cuckoo's Nest   C) Amadeus

THE MYSTERY SINGER

Our mystery singer was born in Tivoli, Italy, but was a citizen of San Marino. His one hit, Too Good, written by Doc Pomus and Mort Shuman, reached # 19 on the UK singles chart in January 1960. It was the only chart success for this singer and his brothers despite his popularity, especially with the girls, with his stage shows!

THE STYLISTICS ANSWERS: *1. B) Betcha By Golly Wow; 2. C) Can't Give You Anything (But My Love); 3. C) Na-Na; 4. B) Can't Help Falling In Love; 5. A) James Dunn (followed by James Smith later in 1980); 6. Sing Baby Sing; 7. A) Van McCoy; 8. B) 1994; 9. C) Avco; 10. A) Hair.* **MYSTERY SINGER ANSWER:** *Little Tony (and his Brothers).*

DONNA SUMMER *(LaDonna Adrian Gaines, born Boston, Massachusetts on December 31, 1948, died at Naples, Florida on May 17, 2012). Summer was an American singer and songwriter, raised in the Boston neighbourhood of Mission Hill. Her father was a butcher, her mother a schoolteacher. Influenced by the counterculture of the 60s. became lead singer of a psychedelic rock band, Crow, and moved to New York City. She gained prominence in the disco era of the 70s and was known as the 'Queen of Disco', as her music gained a global following. Donna had 29 Top 40 hits, including a #1 and 9 more Top 10 hits. She also had 12 Top 40 albums, including 2 Top 10 successes.*

1. Donna landed the part of Sheila and agreed to take the role in the Munich production of which stage show, and moved to Germany in 1968?
A) Miss Saigon   B) Hair   C) Oh! Calcutta!

2. What became Donna Summer's first UK hit, a #4 success in 1976?
A) Love To Love You Baby   B) Could It Be Magic   C) Hot Stuff

3. Bruce Springsteen originally wrote his own 1984 #16 hit, *Cover Me*, for Donna Summer. True or False

4. On what 1979 #3 hit single did Donna Summer team up with Barbra Streisand?

5. Which fairy tale inspired Donna Summer's 1977 concept album *Once Upon A Time*?   A) Cinderella   B) Snow White   C) Hansel and Gretel

6. Donna Summer and her husband Bruce Sudano wrote *Starting Over Again* which was #1 in the US Hot Country Songs (Billboard) charts. Who had the hit in 1980?
A) Reba McEntire   B) Olivia Newton-John   C) Dolly Parton

7. For which 1977 adventure film, based on a Peter Benchley novel, did Donna sing the theme song and have a #5 hit in the UK?   A) Jaws   B) The Deep   C) The Island

8. Donna Summer had one number one in the UK. These are the opening lyrics to what song: "Ooh it's so good, it's so good, It's so good, it's so good, It's so good"?

9. Donna Summer's 1979 number 11, *Hot Stuff*, was released with new lyrics by a top football club in 1998 and reached number 9 in the UK. Which team had the hit?
A) Tottenham Hotspur   B) Chelsea   C) Arsenal

10. Donna Summer's 1983, #25 hit, *She Works Hard For the Money*, became an anthem for which cause?

WHO IS SHE?

This lady was half of an act that had a number one hit in 1973. Who is she, what was the act and what was the song?

DONNA SUMMER ANSWERS: *1. B) Hair; 2. A) Love To Love You Baby; 3. True; 4. No More Tears (Enough Is Enough); 5. Cinderella; 6. C) Dolly Parton; 7. B) The Deep (Down Deep Inside); 8. I Feel Love; 9. C) Arsenal; 10. Women's rights.*
WHO IS SHE? ANSWER: *Dianne Lee of Peters and Lee who had a #1 with Welcome Home.*

THE SUPREMES (AKA Diana Ross & the Supremes) were a US female singing group and a top act of Motown Records in the 60s. Founded 1959 as the Primettes in Detroit, Michigan. The most commercially successful Motown act and most successful US vocal group. Familiar line-up was Florence Ballard, Mary Wilson and Diana Ross. In 1967, Motown boss Berry Gordy renamed them Diana Ross & the Supremes, and replaced Ballard with Cindy Birdsong. In 1970, Ross went solo and was replaced by Jean Terrell. In the mid-70s, the lineup changed again; but the group were disbanded in 1977. The Supremes had 29 Top 40 hits, including a #1 and 12 more Top 10. Also 16 albums including 3 #1's and 5 more Top 10 hits.

1. Which song, penned by the team of Holland/Dozier/Holland was the first UK hit single for The Supremes, reaching #3 in 1964?
A) Where Did Our Love Go   B) Stop In the Name of Love   C) Buttered Popcorn

2. The second Supremes single was also their only UK #1 hit. What was the song?
A) You Can't Hurry Love   B) Baby Love   C) You Keep Me Hangin' On

3. Florence Ballard' was fired by Berry Gordy. Ballard's alcoholism had led to her missing performances and recording sessions. After being fired in 1967 she struggled with poverty and depression and died of a coronary thrombosis at what early age?
A) 38   B) 32   C) 28

4. While onstage in 1970, Diana Ross announced she was leaving the Supremes and introduced her replacement, Jean Terrell. At which Las Vegas hotel did this event take place?   A) Golden Nugget   B) Stardust   C) Frontier

5. The Supremes had 3 UK hits, *I'm Gonna Make You Love Me, I Second That Emotion* and *Why (Must We Fall In Love)* in 1969 / 1970 with which other Tamla-Motown act?   A) Four Tops   B) Temptations   C) Marvelettes

6. In 1972 The Supremes had a top 10 UK hit that included these lyrics: "And my way no road is too rough to travel, We'll walk barefoot on life's gravel together". Can you name the song?   A) Floy Joy   B) Bad Weather   C) Automatically Sunshine

7. The Supremes issued an 8 track tribute album in 1965 that failed to chart in the UK. To which star was the record dedicated?
A) Stevie Wonder   B) Sam Cooke   C) Ray Charles

8. The Supremes had a #5 hit in 1971 with *Nathan Jones*. Which female group covered the song in 1988 and had a #15 hit?
A) Bananarama   B) Pointer Sisters   C) En Vogue

9. The Supremes recorded an album of UK 60s hits including *How Do You Do It?, World Without Love, A Hard Day's Night* and *Bits and Pieces*. True or False?

10. Mary Wilson was the constant member of the Supremes. In 1977 she decided to end the group and dissolve the name. Discounting splinter groups, which city witnessed the final performance of the Supremes?
A) London   B) Paris   C) New York

NAME THE TITLE OF THE NUMBER 3 HIT FROM 1999
The clue is 'lyrics'!

THE SUPREMES ANSWERS: *1. A) Where Did Our Love Go; 2. B) Baby Love; 3. B) 32; 4. C) Frontier; 5. B) Temptations; 6. C) Automatically Sunshine; 7. B) Sam Cooke; 8. A) Bananarama; 9. True (A Little Bit of Liverpool, it was not a success); 10. A) London.*
TITLE OF THE 1999 HIT ANSWER: *That Don't Impress Me Much by Shania Twain.*

THE SWEET (often shortened to just Sweet), are a British glam rock band that rose to prominence in the 1970s. Originally called The Sweetshop the band was formed in London in 1968. Their best known line-up consisted of lead vocalist Brian Connolly, bass player Steve Priest, guitarist Andy Scott, and drummer Mick Tucker. Connolly left the group in 1979 to go solo, the remaining members continued as a trio until disbanding in 1981. Various forms of The Sweet have continued. They had 15 Top 40 hits, including a number one and 9 other Top 10 hits. They also had two Top 40 albums.

1. On what label did Sweet record all their hits until 1976?
A) Polydor   B) RCA   C) Polygram

2. Between 1971 and 1974 which songwriting duo wrote 12 of Sweet's hits?
A) Greenaway / Cook   B) Goffin / King   C) Chapman / Chinn

3. At what number did *Co-Co, Hell Raiser, Ballroom Blitz, Teenage Rampage* and *Fox on the Run* all peak in the UK?   A) 2   B) 3   C) 4

4. Lead singer Brian Connolly was fostered at the age of two, it was supposed at the time that his foster father was his real father, in addition to being the father to another son, who went on to play which famous TV detective?
A) Jim Taggart   B) Hamish McBeth   C) John Rebus

5. A 1971 #33 from Sweet was about a famous inventor. It included these lyrics: "Well, he knew darned well, That he could find the only way, To talk across the USA, Telephone, telephone". Who was the inventor?
A) Elisha Gray   B) Guglielmo Marconi   C) Alexander Graham Bell

6. The opening to *Ballroom Blitz* opens with a voice asking "Are you ready ...., ..., ..." What are the three names?
A) Steve, Andy, Mick   B) Brian, Steve, Andy   C) Andy, Brian, Mick

7. Which actor and singer was briefly manager of Sweet in 1967 and was responsible for recommending them to record producer Phil Wainman?
A) David Essex   B) Adam Faith   C) Paul Nicholas

8. On which 1973 Christmas TV show did bassist Steve Priest get complaints appearing replete in a German military uniform, Hitler moustache and a swastika armband?   A) Morecambe & Wise   B) Top of the Pops   C) Ready Steady Go

9. In 1974 Brian Connolly's throat was badly injured and he was under treatment from a Harley Street specialist. What caused the problem that gave him severe problems with singing?   A) A throat infection   B) A street fight   C) Tonsilitis

10. Sweet undertook a short tour of the UK and performed their last live show at which Glasgow venue on 20 March 1981?   A) University   B) Empire   C) Alhambra

DANCE THE NIGHT AWAY

Just one Top 10 hit, a #4 in 1988. Who are they?

SWEET ANSWERS: *1. B) RCA; 2. Chapman / Chinn; 3. A) 2; 4. A) Jim Taggart (Mark McManus was assumed to be his brother); 5. C) Alexander Graham Bell; 6. A) Steve, Andy, Mick; 7. C) Paul Nicholas; 8. B) Top of the Pops; 9. B) A street fight (a throat infection officially!); 10. A) Glasgow Empire.* **DANCE THE NIGHT AWAY ANSWER:** *The Mavericks.*

T. REX were an English rock band, formed in 1967 by singer-songwriter / guitarist Marc Bolan. Initially Tyrannosaurus Rex a duo with Steve Peregrin Took, they released 4 albums under this name —three psychedelic folk and one mellow psychedelic rock. In 1969, Bolan began to change the band's style towards electric rock, and shortened their name. Bassist Steve Currie and drummer Bill Legend and Mickey Finn (percussion) were recruited. T. Rex had 19 Top 40 hits, including 4 #1 and 6 more Top 10 hits. They also had 17 Top 40 Albums, including 3 #1's and 5 more Top 10 successes.

1. What kind of shows gave Marc Bolan 3D vision in the 1972 #1, *Telegram Sam*?
A) Alligator shoes   B) Automatic shoes   C) Blue suede shoes

2. The first eight T. Rex singles all reached the Top 2 in the UK charts. True or False?

3. What was the first T. Rex UK #1?

4. Which Beatle directed the 1972 concert film starring T. Rex and Elton John?   A) John   B) Paul   C) George   D) Ringo

5. On which 1986 TV show did Marc Bolan perform, whilst standing on a white swan?   A) Top of the Pops   B) Ready, Steady Go!   C) Supersonic

6. Who replaced Steve Peregrin Took in Tyrannosaurus Rex in 1969?
A) Mickey Finn   B) Bill Legend   C) Herbie Flowers

7. What was the first T. Rex album to reach the Top 20?
A) Electric Warrior   B) T. Rex   C) Unicorn

8. Which 1976 #13 hit bridged the centuries when it was memorably featured in the 2000 smash hit film *Billy Elliott* as a dance routine with Jamie Bell and Julie Walters?
A) The Groover   B) I Love To Boogie   C) Children of the Revolution

9. These lyrics are taken from *Summer Deep*, which appeared on which 1971 T.Rex #7 album: "A coat of grapes is on my back again, I ride upon my zebra, Pterodactyl beak hat on my brow, The truth is like a stranger"?   A) Unicorn   B) Tanx   C) T. Rex

10. Marc Bolan was killed when a car being driven by his girlfriend Gloria Jones, crashed into tree early in the morning at Gipsy Lane on Queens Ride, Barnes. In what year did this tragedy happen?   A) 1977   B) 1978   C) 1979

ARMY INTELLIGENCE

Fill in the 'Army' missing in action!

TITLE	ARTIST	YEAR
1. Are Friends Electric	?????	1979
2. Here Comes the War	?????	1993
3. ?????	Elvis Costello & Attractions	1979
4. ?????	Status Quo	1986
5. ?????	Andy Cameron	1978
6. ?????	Babylon Zoo	1996

T. REX ANSWERS: 1. B) Automatic shoes; 2. True; 3. Hot Love; 4. D) Ringo; 5. C) Supersonic; 6. A) Mickey Finn; 7. B) T. Rex; 8. B) I Love To Boogie; 9. C) T. Rex; 10. A) 1977 (16 September). ARMY INTELLIGENCE ANSWERS: 1. Tubeway Army; 2. New Model Army; 3. Oliver's Army; 4. In The Army Now; 5. Ally's Tartan Army; 6. Animal Army.

TAKE THAT *are an English pop group formed in Manchester in 1990, consisting of Gary Barlow, Howard Donald, Jason Orange, Mark Owen and Robbie Williams. Barlow is the group's lead singer and primary songwriter. Owen and Williams initially provided backing vocals and Donald and Orange served mainly as dancers. Robbie Williams went solo in 1995. On 13 February 1996, Take That disbanded; they had had 15 Top 40 hits in the 20th century, this included 8 #1's and 5 more Top 10 hits. They also had 5 Top 40 albums including 3 #1's and one other Top 10 success.*

1. Take That's first Top 40 hit was *Promises* in 1971, What number did it reach in the UK singles chart?   A) 8   B) 18   C) 38

2. What was the title of Take That's first album, released in 1992, that reached #2? A) Take That and Party   B) Everybody Changes   C) Nobody Else

3. *It Only Takes A Minute* was Take That's first Top 10 hit, reaching #7 in 1992. The song was written by Jonathan King. True or False?

4. What was the name of the break-dancing crew that Jason Orange and Howard Donald formed before they joined Take That?
A) Beat Pop   B) Street Beat   C) Street Madness

5. Who duetted with Take That on their 1993 number one, *Relight My Fire*?
A) Cilla Black   B) Lulu   C) Tracy Chapman

6. Who sung lead vocals on the 1993 #1 *Babe*, written by Gary Barlow?
A) Robbie Williams   B) Gary Barlow   C) Mark Owen

7. Take That's last studio album to be recorded before they disbanded in 1996 was *Nobody Else*. The cover of the #1 album was a parody of which famous album artwork?   A) Sgt. Pepper's Lonely Hearts Club Band - Beatles   B) Dark Side of the Moon - Pink Floyd   C) Rumours - Fleetwood Mac

8. Which Gary Barlow written #1 from 1995 opens with these lyrics: "I guess now it's time for me to give up I feel it's time, Got a picture of you beside me got your lipstick mark still on your coffee cup"?   A) Sure   B) Back For Good   C) Never Forget

9. Who sung the lead vocals on *Never Forget* a Take That #1 in 1995?
A) Robbie Williams   B) Jason Orange   C) Howard Donald

10. Which Barry Manilow song featuring Robbie Williams singing lead vocals, reach #3 in the UK in 1992?   A) Could It Be Magic   B) Can't Smile Without You   C) Mandy

Actor / Singer from the 1960s

Von Ryan's Express (1965)

The Great Escape (1963)

1. Who starred with Frank Sinatra & Steve McQueen, Richard Attenborough etc in 2 epic war films?

2. How many of his 7 UK Top 40 hits from 1961-1963 can you name?

TAKE THAT ANSWERS: *1. C) 38; 2. A) Take That and Party; 3. False (Originally a Tavares US hit, covered by Jonathan King in 1976 as 100 Ton and a Feather); 4. B) Street Beat; 5. B) Lulu; 6. C) Mark Owen; 7. A) Sgt. Pepper's Lonely Hearts Club Band - Beatles; 8. B) Back For Good; 9. C) Howard Donald; 10. A) Could It Be Magic. **ACTOR / SINGER OF THE 1960s ANSWERS:** 1) John Leyton; 2. Johnny Remember Me #1, Wild Wind #2, Son This Is She #15, Lone Rider #40, Lonely City #14, Cupboard Love #22, I'll Cut Your Tail Off #36.*

TEARS FOR FEARS *are an English pop rock band formed in Bath, England, in 1981 by Roland Orzabal (Born in Portsmouth on 22 August 1961) and Curt Smith (Born in Bath on 24 June 1961). Founded after the dissolution of their first band, the mod-influenced Graduate, Tears for Fears became a new wave synthesizer band of the early 1980s, and attained international chart success. Smith and Orzabal then had an acrimonious split in 1991 which lasted for nine years. Tears For Fears had 16 Top 40 hits between 1982 and 1995, including 7 Top 10 hits. They also had 5 Top 10 albums including 2 #1's.*

1. In 1981, Orzabal and Smith became session musicians for the new wave band Neon, where they first met future the Tears for Fears drummer. Who was he?
A) Manny Elias   B) Bobby Graham   C) Dave Grohl

2. Who was a member of Tears for Fears, co-writer many of their early hits, and musically contributing on synthesizers, drum machines, organ, pianos and backing vocals on their first three albums?   A) Gary Numan   B) Dave Bates   C) Ian Stanley

3. Tears For fears' first two singles *Suffer the Children* and *Pale Shelter (You Don't Give Me Love)* both missed out, but the third single hit #3 in the UK charts in 1982. What was the song?   A) Change   B) Mad World   C) Pale Shelter

4. In 1983, the first Tears For Fears album hit the jackpot, and reached the top of the UK album charts. What was the album's title?
A) The Hurting   B) Seeds Of Love   C) Tears Roll Down

5. The second album from Tears For Fears in 1985, *Songs from the Big Chair*, the album was derived from a TV film about a woman with multiple personality disorder who only feels safe when she is sitting in her analyst's "big chair". What was the name of the TV film?   A) Polly   B) Sybil   C) Miss Tibbs

6. How many hit singles on the *Songs from the Big Chair* album?   A) 3   B) 4   C) 5

7. Which #4 hit from 1984 was completed with power chords, heavy percussion, a synth bass solo and a vocal-sounding synth riff, and a lengthy guitar solo, unusual for Tears for Fears?   A) Everybody Wants To Rule the World   B) Shout   C) Change

8. The fourth studio album from TFF reached #5 in 1993. What was the album's title?
A) Raoul and the Kings of Spain   B) Elemental   C) The Tipping Point

9. What was the title of the TFF reworked single released in May 1986 as the theme song for the Sport Aid campaign, becoming the band's sixth top 5 hit in 1986?
A) Run For Your Life   B) Run Run Away   C) Everybody Wants To Run the World

10. Which female singer was featured on the 1989 TFF #26 single, *Woman in Chains*?   A) Oleta Adams   B) Beverley Craven   C) Joan Armatrading

A. UNREALISTIC AIR HAG	F. ALVIN BREWS LITURGY
B. LIBRARY WOMAN	G. AGILE LEVEL POP
C. SLEEPY SILVER	H. WESTERN VIDEO
D. BERTIE NYLON	J. CHESTER POISON
E. BOOKERS LIKE	K.. NERO TOSSES

TEARS FOR FEARS ANSWERS: 1. A) Manny Elias; 2. C) Ian Stanley; 3. B) Mad World; 4. A) The Hurting; 5. B) Sybil; 6. C) 5 - Mothers Talk, Shout, Everybody Wants to Rule the World, Head over Heels, and I Believe; 7. B) Shout; 8. B) Elemental; 9. C) Everybody Wants To Run the World; 10. A) Oleta Adams. **ANAGRAM ACTS 2 ANSWERS:** *A) Christina Aguilera; B) Barry Manilow; C) Elvis Presley; D) Bonnie Tyler; E) Elkie Brooks; F) Traveling Wilburys; G) Village People; H) Stone Roses.*

THE TEMPTATIONS *are a US vocal group from Detroit, Michigan. They were very successful with singles and albums on Motown Records in the 60s and 70s, selling tens of millions of records. The Temptations are one of the most successful groups in popular music. Featuring five male vocalists and dancers (occasionally with fewer or more members), the group formed in 1960 in Detroit under the name the Elgins. The Temptations had 20 Top 40 UK hit singles 5 of those were Top 10 hits. They also had 14 Top 40 albums, 1 #1 and1 other Top 10 success.*

1. Which of these members was a founding member of The Temptations?
A) David Ruffin   B) Ron Tyson   C) Otis Williams

2. In 1967, which member of the group began demanding special treatment as lead singer, riding to and from gigs in a private mink-lined limousine instead of joining the group in their limousine? A) David Ruffin   B) Paul Williams   C) Eddie Kendricks

3. Who was David Ruffin's brother who had a string of UK hits including *What Becomes of the Brokenhearted* and *Farewell Is a Lonely Sound*?

4. What is the very first word of the lyrics that lead singer Eddie Kendricks sings on the #8 hit *Just My Imagination (Running Away With Me)* in 1971?
A) Just   B) Each   C) Soon

5. Who wrote *My Girl*, which became the Temptations signature song and was a #43 hit in 1965 and a #2 smash hit in 1992?
A) Otis Williams   B) Smokey Robinson   C) Russell Thompkins Jnr.

6. What song originally performed by The Undisputed Truth in 1972, became a Grammy-award winning cover by The Temptations later the same year, and was a hit for Was Not Was in 1990?
A) Papa Was a Rollin' Stone   B) Get Ready   C) You're My Everything

7. With whom did the Temptations have a #10 hit in 1991 with *The Motown Song*?
A) Diana Ross & The Supremes   B) Four Tops   C) Rod Stewart

8. How many UK Top 40 hits did the Temptations share the billing with Diana Ross & the Supremes?   A) 2   B) 3   C) 4

9. Which Temptations member died in 1973 in Detroit, aged 34, from a gunshot wound; his death being ruled as suicide?
A) Paul Williams   B) Otis Williams   C) Dennis Edwards

10. Who left the Temptations in 1993 after twenty-two years, following a disagreement?   A) Ali Woodson   B) Ron Tyson   C) Richard Street

THE WURZELS - PRIDE OF THE WEST COUNTRY

Cuz I got a brand new combine harvester

An' I'll give you the key

Come on now let's get together

In perfect harmony

Name the three songs that The Wurzels took into the UK charts in 1976/7?

The author with Wurzels Pete and Tommy at Ashton Gate Stadium

THE TEMPTATIONS ANSWERS: *1. C) Otis Williams; 2. A) David Ruffin; 3. Jimmy Ruffin; 4. B) Each; 5. B) Smokey Robinson; 6. A) Papa Was a Rollin' Stone; 7. C) Rod Stewart; 8. B) 3; 9. A) Paul Williams; 10. C) Richard Street.*
THE WURZELS ANSWERS: *1. The Combine Harvester (Brand New Key), I Am A Cider Drinker (Paloma Blanca), Farmer Bill's Cowman (I Was Kaiser Bill's Batman).*

10cc is an English rock band, formed in Stockport, England, in 1972. The group initially consisted of four musicians – Graham Gouldman, Eric Stewart, Kevin Godley and Lol Crème. The group had two songwriting teams; Stewart & Gouldman predominantly pop and Godley & Creme predominantly experimental. Most of the band's records were recorded at their own Strawberry Studios in Stockport and Dorking, most engineered by Stewart. 10cc had 13 Top 40 hits, including 3 #1's and 8 more Top 10 hits. They also had 12 Top 40 albums, including 8 Top 10 successes.

1. Eric Stewart was lead singer with which band who had a #2 hit with *A Groovy Kind of Love* in 1966? A) Genesis B) The Mindbenders C) Mud

2. Graham Gouldman wrote many hits including, *Heart Full of Soul*, *Evil Hearted You* and *For Your Love* for The Yardbirds. True or False?

3. In 1970, with Gouldman in New York, Godley, Creme and Stewart recorded a song as Hotlegs, that began life as a test of drum layering, at the new Strawberry Studios mixing desk. The song climbed to No. 2 in the UK charts and became a worldwide hit, what was its title? A) I'm Mandy Fly Me B) Neanderthal Man C) Donna

4. In 1972–73 10cc co-produced and played on two albums, *Solitaire* and *The Tra-La Days Are Over*, with which star? A) Paul Anka B) Andy Williams C) Neil Sedaka

5. What was the debut 10cc single, a #2 in 1972, which shared its title with a hit song by Ritchie Valens and Marty Wilde in 1959? A) Donna B) Sea of Love C) Bad Boy

6. 10cc's first five singles were issued on UK Records. Who owned the label?
A) Mickie Most B) Jonathan King C) Tony Hatch

7. Name the three 10cc number one hits in the UK.

8. 10cc accompanied whom on their 1975 number eight hit *Blue Guitar*?
A) The Hollies B) Duane Eddy C) Justin Hayward & John Lodge

9. The last major 10cc hit was a #1 in 1978. What was the song that included these lyrics: "Well he looked down at my silver chain, He said "I'll give you one dollar, I said you've got to be jokin' man, It was a present from me mother"?

10. Which Godley & Crème single reached #3 in the UK in 1981?
A) Under Your Thumb B) Wedding Bells C) Cry

THE LIVING YEARS Mike + The Mechanics	Mike Rutherford – rhythm guitar, bass guitar Paul Carrack – lead vocals Paul Young – backing vocals Adrian Lee – keyboards Peter Van Hooke – drums
(Writers: B.A. Robertson / Mike Rutherford)	Additional personnel
Every generation Blames the one before And all of their frustrations Come beating on your door I know that I'm a prisoner To all my Father held so dear I know that I'm a hostage To all his hopes and fears I just wish I could have told him in the living years	Sal Gallina – keyboards BA Robertson – keyboards Alan Murphy – guitar Martin Ditcham – percussion Luís Jardim – percussion Christopher Neil – backing vocals Alan Carvell – backing vocals Choir: Child and adult studio musicians, recorded in NYC studio separately

10cc ANSWERS: *1. B) The Mindbenders; 2. True; 3. B) Neanderthal Man; 4. C) Neil Sedaka; 5. A) Donna; 6. B) Jonathan King; 7. Rubber Bullets, I'm Not In Love and Dreadlock Holiday; 8. C) Justin Hayward & John Lodge; 9. Dreadlock Holiday; 10. A) Under Your Thumb (the other two reached #7 and #19 respectively).*

TEXAS are a Scottish alternative rock band from Glasgow. They were founded in 1986 by Johnny McElhone (ex- Altered Images on bass, guitar & keyboards) and Sharleen Spiteri (lead vocals). In their hit years the band were completed by: Richard Hynd (drums), Eddie Campbell (keyboards) and Ally McErlaine - guitar. Texas made their performing debut in March 1988 at the University of Dundee. They took their name from the 1984 Wim Wenders movie Paris, Texas. Texas had 14 Top 40 singles between 1989 and 1999, 8 of them reached the Top 10. They also had five Top 40 albums, including 2 #1's and another Top 10 success.

1. In 1989, the Texas debut single was a top-ten hit in the UK, and peaked in the top ten of many other European countries. What was its title?
A) I Don't Want A Lover   B) Alone With You   C) Tired Of Being Alone

2. Texas's debut album, containing the hit single, reached the Top 3 in the UK. All tracks were written by Sharleen Spiteri and Johnny McElhone but what was the title of the album?   A) Mother's Heaven   B) Southside   C) Ricks Road

3. The band's fortunes increased in 1997 with the release of an album, which entered at the top of the UK albums chart and became their biggest seller. To date it has been certified six times platinum in the United Kingdom. What is its title?
A) Parallel Lines   B) Rock Hard   C) White on Blonde

4. In 1992 Texas had a #19 hit with a classic track, *Tired Of Being Alone*, which had been a #4 hit for its writer in 1971. Who had the original hit?
A) Bill Withers   B) Al Green   C) Marvin Gaye

5. Following an endorsement by the presenter of the Channel 4 show *TFI Friday* in 1997, Texas had an international hit with *Say What You Want*. Who was the presenter that gave their career a boost?
A) Chris Evans   B) Tony Blackburn   C) Noel Edmonds

6. How many of the tracks on White on Blonde reached the UK Top 10?
A) 3   B) 4   C) 5

7. *Put Your Arms Around Me*, released in 1997, peaked at No. 10. In 1998, the song was featured in which film starring Drew Barrymore?
A) Ever After: A Cinderella Story   B) E.T.   C) Charlie's Angels

8. Which Texas 1999 #5 single opened with these lyrics: "I'm tired of telling the story, Tired of telling it your way, Yeah I know what I saw, I know that I found the floor"?
A) When We Are Together   B) Summer Son   C) In Our Lifetime

9. For what type of vocal range is Sharleen Spiteri known?
A) Mezzo-Soprano   B) Soprano   C) Contralto

10. Sharleen Spiteri's mother Vilma was a singing window-cleaner. True or False?

Who am I?

MORE POINTS FOR QUICK IDENTIFICATION

5 points –I was born on June 3, 1950 in Detroit, Michigan

4 points – My niece was a Twin Peaks icon

3 points – I was in Happy Days

2 points – I play a bass guitar

*1 point – My biggest hits were number ones.
Can the Can and Devil Gate Drive*

TEXAS ANSWERS: *1. A) I Don't Want A Lover; 2. B) Southside; 3. C) White on Blonde; 4. B) Al Green; 5. A) Chris Evans; 6. C) 5; 7. A) Ever After: A Cinderella Story; 8. B) Summer Son; 9. C) Contralto; 10. False (she was a window DRESSER).*
WHO AM I ANSWER: *Suzi Quatro.*

20 HITS FROM UK CHARTS FROM THE FIFTIES TO THE NINETIES. NAME THE ACTS WHO HAD THE HITS.

THE LAST LETTER TO ANSWER 1 WILL BE THE FIRST LETTER OF ANSWER 2 AND SO ON UNTIL THE LAST LETTER TO ANSWER 20 SHOULD BE THE FIRST ANSWER TO ANSWER 1 - TO COMPLETE THE CHAIN. EXTRA PICTURE CLUES AT BOTTOM OF PAGE.

1. My Way (1977)

2. I Can't Get You Out Of My Mind (1977)

3. I Won't Let the Sun Go Down On Me (1984)

4. In the Midnight Hour (1965)

5. Who Killed Bambi? (1979)

6. Roses Are Red (1962)

7. (How Much Is) That Doggie In the Window (1953)

8. Rock Me Gently (1974)

9. The Girl Is Mine (1982)

10. Stand Up For Your Love Rights (1988)

11. Them Girls Them Girls (1994)

12. Under Your Thumb (1981)

13. (Take A Little) Piece Of My Heart (1992)

14. My Baby Just Cares For Me (1987)

15. Jig A Jag (1971)

16. I'm In the Mood For Dancing

17. Leap Up and Down (Wave Your Knickers In the Air (1971)

18. Black Velvet (1990)

19. Let There Be Drums (1961)

20. Miss You Like Crazy (1989)

A. - - - - - / - - - - - - - -

B. - - - - - - / - - - - - - -

C. - - - / - - - - - - - -

D. - - - - - - / - - - - - - -

E. - - - - - - - / - - - - -

F. - - - - - - / - - - - - - -

G. - - - - / - - - -

H. - - - - / - - -

J. - - - - - - - / - - - - - - - & - - - - / - - - - - - - - -

K. - - - -

L. - - - & - - -

M. - - - - - - & - - - - -

N. - - - - / - - - - - - - -

P. - - - - / - - - - - -

Q. - - - - / - - / - - - -

R. - - - - - -

S. - - / - - - - - - -

T. - - - - - - - / - - - - -

U. - - - - - / - - - - - -

V. - - - - - - - / - - - -

PICTURE CLUES

CHAIN QUIZ ANSWERS: A. Elvis Presley; B) Yvonne Elliman; C) Nik Kershaw; D) Wilson Pickett; E)Tenpole Tudor; F) Ronnie Carroll; G) Lita Roza; H) Andy Kim; J) Michael Jackson & Paul McCartney; K) Yazz; L) Zig & Zag; M) Godley & Creme; N) Erma Franklin; P) Nina Simone; Q) East of Eden; R) Nolans; S) St. Cecilia; T) Alannah Myles; U) Sandy Nelson; V) Natalie Cole.

259

THIN LIZZY are an Irish hard rock band formed in Dublin in 1969. Their music reflects a wide range of influences, including blues, soul music, psychedelic rock and traditional Irish folk music, but is generally classified as hard rock or sometimes heavy metal. Two of the founding members, drummer Brian Downey and bass guitarist, lead vocalist and principal songwriter Phil Lynott, met while still in school. Lynott led the group throughout their recording career of twelve studio albums, writing most of the material. Guitarist Gary Moore had a few stints with the band. Thin Lizzy had 15 Top 40 hits, including 4 Top 10 hits; they also had 12 Top 40 albums, including 8 Top 10 smash hits.

1. Thin Lizzy's name comes from a character in which comic?
A) The Eagle   B) The Beano   C) The Dandy

2. The first Thin Lizzy hit in 1973 reached #6. It included these lyrics, but what was the title: " I went unto my chamber, all for to take a slumber, I dreamt of gold and jewels and for sure it was no wonder"?

3. Which Thin Lizzy #2 album cover from 1978 is pictured below?

Who opened for Thin Lizzy at Slane Festival, Dublin, in 1981?
A) U2   B) The Clash   C) Electric Light Orchestra

4. Which 1999 teen comedy film featured Thin Lizzy's songs *Jailbreak* & *The Boys Are Back In Town*? A) Detroit Rock City   B) Debt Collector   C) Dazed and Confused

5. Phil Lynott and who were the only constant members of Thin Lizzy through 1984?
A) John Sykes   B) Brian Downey   C) Scott Gorham

6. What name did Thin Lizzy assume when they recorded the *Tribute To Deep Purple* album in 1972?   A) Purple People Eaters   B) Mauve   C) Funky Junction

7. In early 1977 with whom did Thin Lizzy tour? A) Queen   B) Bob Seger   C) Mud

8. Thin Lizzy regrouped for a one-off performance in 1986. Who was on lead vocals?
A) Robert Plant   B) Gary Moore   C) Bob Geldof

9. Which Thin Lizzy band member died in January 1986?
A) Michael Lee   B) Phil Lynott   C) John Sykes

10. Where was a bronze statue placed in honour of Phil Lynott?
A) Belfast   B) Dublin   C) Kilkenny

HITS OF THE THREE DEGREES

The Three Degrees had 11 Top 40 hits. Can you match the 10 songs below with the highest chart position that they reached (as listed)?

1. Year Of Decision	6. Toast Of Love	A. 9	F. 3
2. TSOP (The Sound of Philadelphia)	7. Giving Up, Giving In	B. 10	G. 1
3. When Will I See You Again	8. Woman In Love	C. 40	H. 12
4. Get Your Love Back	9. The Runner	D. 36	J. 13
5. Take Good Care Of Yourself	10. Long Lost Lover	E. 34	K. 22

THIN LIZZY ANSWERS: *1. C) The Dandy; 2. Whiskey in the Jar; 3. Live and dangerous; 4. A) Detroit Rock City; 5. B) Brian Downey; 6. C) Funky Junction; 7. A) Queen; 8. C) Bob Geldof; 9. B) Phil Lynott; 10. B) Dublin.*
THREE DEGREES HITS ANSWERS: *1J; 2K; 3G; 4E; 5A; 6D; 7H; 8F; 9B; 10C.*

THE TREMELOES *(Formerly Brian Poole & The Tremeloes) are are an English beat group founded in 1958 in Dagenham, Essex. They initially found success in the British Invasion era with lead singer Brian Poole, before his departure in 1966. The band had further success as a four-piece. The original band was: Brian Poole (lead vocals), Rick West (lead guitar), Alan Blakley (rhythm guitar/ keyboards), Alan Howard (bass) & Dave Munden (drums). With Brian they had 8 Top 40 hits, including a #1 and 3 other Top 10 hits. Then, as The Tremeloes they had 13 Top 40 hits, including a #1 and 6 more Top 10 hits. They had just one Top 20 album (in 1967).*

1. The band were called Tremoloes but the name was changed because of a spelling mistake in an East London newspaper advertisement. True or False?

2. On New Year's Day, 1962, Decca Records, looking for one beat group, auditioned Brian Poole and the Tremeloes and another band from Liverpool. The Tremeloes were selected, but who were the Liverpool band they rejected?
A) Searchers   B) Beatles   C) Gerry & The Pacemakers

3. Brian Poole and the Tremeloes first charted in the UK in July 1963. They had a #4 hit with which Isley Brothers song that the Beatles included on their first British LP, *Please Please Me*?   A) Shout   B) Twist and Shout   C) This Old Heart Of Mine

4. The only #1 the band had before Brian Poole left to go solo, was a 1963 cover of which Contours US hit?
A) Do You Love Me   B) Whole Lotta Woman   C) I Can Dance

5. Brian Poole left in 1966, followed by Alan Howard. Who was the new bass player / vocalist, who would be the father of a singer who would have a #1 in 1991?
A) Eddie Jones   B) Bob Benham   C) Len 'Chip' Hawkes

6. After *Blessed* and *Good Day Sunshine* missed the charts The Tremeloes hit the jackpot with a #4, *Here Comes My Baby*. Who wrote the song?
A) Cat Stevens   B) Paul McCartney   C) Paul Simon

7. Riccardo Del Turco's *Uno tranquillo (One quiet man)*, was translated into English and became another #4 UK hit for The Tremeloes - with what title?
A) Hello World   B) My Little Lady   C) Suddenly You Love Me

8. Brian Poole's daughters Karen and Shelly had a string of hits in the late nineties, staring with a 1996 hit *I Am, I Feel*. What was their performing name?
A) Alisha's Attic   B) Cleopatra   C) Poppy Girls

9. Len Hawkes & Alan Blakley wrote a song that was a #2 hit for The Tremeloes in 1969. The opening lyrics are: "I picture the rain on windows, And I think of home. I wonder if you remember, Did you ever know". What is the song title?
A) Hello Buddy   B) By the Way   C) (Call Me) Number One

10. The Tremeloes recorded a song that they shelved, but eventually it was recorded by Jeff Christie and released with the original Tremeloes backing - and was a #1. What was the song?   A) Mellow Yellow   B) Yellow River   C) Big Yellow Taxi

THE TREMELOES ANSWERS: *1. True; 2. B) Beatles; 3. B) Twist and Shout; 4. A) Do You Love Me; 5. C) Len 'Chip' Hawkes (father of Chesney Hawkes); 6. A) Cat Stevens; 7. C) Suddenly You Love Me; 8. A) Alisha's Attic; 9. C) (Call Me) Number One; 10. B) Yellow River.*

TINA TURNER *(born Anna Mae Bullock; November 26, 1939) is an American-born Swiss singer and actress. Referred to as the 'Queen of Rock 'n' Roll', she rose to prominence as the lead singer of the Ike and Tina Turner Revue. Launched a successful career as a soloist after an acrimonious split, both on and off the stage. Turner is one of the best-selling recording artists, noted for her 'swagger, sensuality, gravelly vocals and unstoppable energy', along with her famous legs. Tina has appeared on 32 UK Top 40 singles; in a duet, as a soloist and as a main part of a charity single. She has not had a #1, but has amassed 11 Top 10 hits. Her 8 albums all reached the Top 10, two of them being chart toppers.*

1. Which 1984 Tina Turner single, written by Mark Knopfler, is about an exotic dancer and features a Jeff Beck guitar solo?
A) Let's Stay Together   B) Typical Male   C) Private Dancer

2. The songs *Steamy Windows* and *Look Me In the Heart* were tracks on which Tina Turner 1989 #1 album?   A) Private Dancer   B) Foreign Affair   C) Simply the Best

3. In which 1985 post-apocalyptic film did Tina Turner play the role of Aunt Entity, alongside Mel Gibson?

4. What is the title of the 1993 semi-autobiographical film, starring Angela Bassett, about Tina Turner's turbulent life?
A) Simply the Best   B) Girl From Nutbush   C) What's Love Got To Do With It

5. With whom did Tina Turner perform *Hot Legs* on *Saturday Night Live* in 1981?
A) Mick Jagger   B) Rod Stewart   C) Bryan Adams

6. Tina Turner sung the theme song for the Bond film *Goldeneye* in 1995. Who wrote the song that charted at #10 in the UK?
A) Bono / The Edge   B) Terry Britten / Graham Lyle   C) John Barry

7. *The Best* was a #5 hit for Tina Turner in 1989. It had originally been recorded a year earlier as an album track by which Welsh singer?
A) Mary Hopkin   B) Cerys Matthews   C) Bonnie Tyler

8. What role did Tina Turner play in the 1975 British satirical operetta fantasy drama film *Tommy* written and directed by Ken Russell, based upon The Who's 1969 rock opera album?   A) Nora Walker   B) The Acid Queen   C) Sally Simpson

9. What song, twice a hit for Tina in 1973 and 1991, includes these lyrics: "Twenty-five was the speed limit, Motorcycle not allowed in it, You go t'the store on Fridays, You go to church on Sundays"?

10. On what 1985 charity #1 did Tina sing a solo in a supergroup with artistes like: Lionel Richie, Stevie Wonder, Paul Simon, Kenny Rogers and Diana Ross?
A) USA For Africa   B) Band Aid II   C) Rokestra

TINA TURNER ANSWERS: *1. C) Private Dancer; 2. B) Foreign Affair; 3. Mad Max: Beyond the Thunderdome; 4. What's Love Got To Do With It; 5. B) Rod Stewart; 6. A) Bono / The Edge; 7. C) Bonnie Tyler; 8. B) The Acid Queen; 9. Nutbush City Limits (initially with Ike, then as a solo act); 10. A) USA For Africa.*

2 UNLIMITED are a Belgian/Dutch dance music act, founded by Belgian producers/songwriters Jean-Paul De Coster & Phil Wilde in 1991 in Antwerp, Belgium. From 1991 to 1996, Dutch rapper Ray Slijngaard & Dutch vocalist Anita Doth fronted the act. 2 Unlimited enjoyed worldwide success, less so with mainstream recognition in the US, but several tracks became popular themes in the NBA and NHL. 2 Unlimited had 14 Top 40 singles, including a #1 and 7 other Top 10 hits. They also recorded 4 Top 40 albums, including 2 #1's.

1. Jean-Paul De Coster and Phil Wilde met in their home city in Belgium and created 2 Unlimited in their studio. Where was their hometown?
A) Brussels   B) Antwerp   C) Liege

2. De Coster and Wilde's first collaboration resulted in a 1990 #7 hit single in the UK. Under what name did they release the hit record *Don't Miss The Party Line*?
A) Coster Living   B) Ray Slijngaard and Anita Doth   C) Bizz Nizz

3. What label issued all of the 2 Unlimited singles in the UK?
A) PWL Continental   B) Mercury   C) PolyGram

4. 2 Unlimited had a #1 hit in 1993 with *No Limit*. How many copies did it sell in the UK?   A) Over 500,000   B) 300,000   C) 200,000

5. 2 Unlimited had a number one album in 1993. What was it's title?
A) That's the Limit   B) Limited   C) N Limits

6. The British music press were very critical of 2 Unlimited and gave them what cruel name?   A) 2 Untalented   B) 2 Unrated   C) 2 Uncouth

7. What 2 Unlimited #6 from 1994 includes these lyrics: "The booming system which plays in places, Move your system, change these spaces, When I'm on the mic you can't refuse, No one ever came to preach, I came to amuse"

8. In 1996 Slijngaard and Doth asked for more creative input. They also felt that they were not getting a fair share of the huge amount of money being earned by the project. No agreement was reached, so who left?
A) Slijngaard   B) Doth   C) Both Slijngaard & Doth

9. As they still owned the rights to the name 2 Unlimited, De Coster and Wilde recruited two new Dutch singers, Romy van Ooijen and Marjon van Iwaarden. What was their only Top 40 hit in 1998?
A) Do What's Good For me   B) Wanna Get Up   C) Here I Go

10. A final album in 1998 featuring new singers Romy and Marjon was not released in the UK and proved to be the last output from 2 Unlimited. What was the album's title?
A) II   B) III   C) IV

BOBBY GRAHAM (born Robert Francis Neate, 11 March 1940 – 14 September 2009) was an English session drummer, composer, arranger and record producer. Graham played on over 15,000 titles, including: *You Really Got Me, All Day And All Of The Night* and *Tired of Waiting For You* by The Kinks, *Downtown* by Petula Clark, *Green Green Grass of Home* by Tom Jones, *Gloria* and *Baby Please Don't Go* by Them (ft. Van Morrison), *"I Only Want to Be with You* by Dusty Springfield, *I Believe* by The Bachelors, *Glad All Over* and *Bits and Pieces* by The Dave Clark Five. In 1962 Graham was offered the drummers seat in The Beatles, but declined! Lucky Ringo!

2 UNLIMITED ANSWERS: 1. B) Antwerp; 2. C) Bizz Nizz; 3. A) PWL Continental; 4. A) Over 500,000; 5. C) No Limits; 6. A) 2 Untalented; 7. Let the Beat Control Your Body; 8. C) Both Slijngaard and Doth; 9. B) Wanna Get Up; 10.II.

UB40 *are an English reggae and pop band, formed in December 1978 in Birmingham. In 1984 were nominated for the Brit Award for Best British Group, their ethnic make-up is diverse and the line-up stable for nearly 29 years, from March 1979. Ali Campbell (lead vocals), Jimmy Brown (drums), Robin Campbell (guitar), Earl Falconer (bass), Norman Hassan (percussion), and Brian Travers (sax). UB40 had 37 Top 40 hits, including 3 number ones and 14 further Top 10 hits. They also had 17 Top 40 albums, including 2 number ones and 8 other Top 10 successes.*

1. The band selected the name UB40 when they formed in 1978, but what was the origin of the name? A) Reference no. on unemployment benefit forms B) Initials and age of a favourite reggae artist C) Postcode where the Campbell brothers lived

2. UB40's first gig was held at a pub in Kings Heath, Birmingham on February 1979. What was the name of the pub?
A) The Covered Wagon B) The Hare and Hounds C) The Crown

3. A double-A side single *King / Food for Thought* was the debut single for UB40, it reached #4 in the UK chart. Who was *King* written about?
A) Martin Luther King B) Billie Jean King C) King Henry VIII

4. Which 1990 #4 includes these lyrics: "And when I am king, Surely I would need a queen, And a palace and everything, yeah, And now I am king …"?

5. In 1985, UB40 teamed up with which female singer to take the 1965 Sonny & Cher #1 hit *I Got You Babe* to the top of the charts again?
A) Lulu B) Annie Lennox C) Chrissie Hynde

6. UB40 took Neil Diamond's *Red Red Wine* to #1 in 1983. With which other Neil Diamond song did they had a Top 40 hit in 1998?
A) Sweet Caroline B) Holly Holy C) Cracklin' Rosie

7. On 11 June 1988, UB40 performed at a tribute concert at Wembley for whom?

8. UB40's first album, *Signing Off* was recorded in a bedsit in Birmingham and was produced by Bob Lamb. What was featured on the cover? A) Unemployment benefit form B) Picture of the band's signatures C) Picture of a dole office

9. In 1995 they covered the Stevie Wonder song *Superstition* for which Eddie Murphy film? A) Beverly Hills Cop III B) Vampire In Brooklyn C) The Golden Child

10. According to *Blood & Fire*, the autobiography of Ali and Robin Campbell, UB40 didn't actually make any money from their album 'Labour Of Love' which sold 10 million copies worldwide and had 4 UK top 40 singles. True or False?

NAME THE WILBURYS - Supergroup to match with their Wilbury aliases!

TRAVELING WILBURYS

A)	Nelson Wilbury	1.	Jeff Lynne
B)	Charlie T Wilbury Jr	2.	Tom Petty
C)	Otis Wilbury	3.	George Harrison
D)	Lucky Wilbury	4.	Roy Orbison
E)	Lefty Wilbury	5.	Bob Dylan

UB40 ANSWERS: *1. A) Reference no. on unemployment benefit forms; 2. B) The Hare and Hounds; 3. A) Martin Luther King; 4. Kingston Town; 5. C) Chrissie Hynde; 6. B) Holly Holy; 7. Nelson Mandela; 8. A) Unemployment benefit form; 9. B) Vampire In Brooklyn; 10. True.*
NAME THE WILBURYS ANSWERS: *A3, B2, C1, D5, E4.*

ULTRAVOX *were a British new wave band, formed in London in April 1974 as Tiger Lily. From 1974 until 1979, singer John Foxx was frontman and the main driving force until he left the band in March 1979. Midge Ure took over as lead singer and guitarist. Ure revitalised the band and steered it to commercial chart success lasting until 1987, at which time the group disbanded. The band's best-known line-up was Ure, Billy Currie (keyboards), Chris Cross (bass) and Warren Cann (drums). A new line-up, led by Currie, formed 1992, but had limited success. Ultravox had 17 Top 40 singles, including 3 Top 10 hits. They also had 7 Top 40 albums, all of them reaching the Top 10.*

1. On which record label did Ultravox have record of their hits?
A) Chrysalis   B) Pye   C) Philips

2. The fourth Ultravox album, the first with Midge Ure, spawned the first four hit singles for the band. What was the title of the album?
A) Systems of Romance   B) Vienna   C) Ultravox!

3. The first Ultravox Top 10 hit, a #2 in 1981, opened with these words. "The feeling has gone, only you and I, It means nothing to me, This means nothing to me". Name the song with a European capital city title.

4. Midge Ure co-wrote Band Aid's *Do They Know It's Christmas* with Bob Geldof. True or False?

5. Midge Ure had some success with semi-glam outfit Slik and Glen Matlock's The Rich Kids. In 1979, he temporarily played with which hard rock band on their American tour?   A) Blue Oyster Cult   B) Thin Lizzy   C) Whitesnake

6. Billy Currie and Midge Ure met while collaborating on a studio-based band which was fronted by New Romantic icon and nightclub impresario Steve Strange. What was the band?   A) Heaven 17   B) The Human League   C) Visage

7. In 1982, Ultravox teamed up with which famous producer to make the album *Quartet*, which peaked at # 6 in the UK and included four future Top 20 hit singles?
A) George Martin   B) Norrie Paramor   C) Nile Rodgers

8. "Give us this day, All that you showed me, The power and the glory, 'Til my kingdom come". More powerful Ultravox lyrics. Name the uplifting #11 hit from 1982?

9. When Ultravox were touring in 1984 they had how many keyboards on stage?
A) 12   B) 17   C) 22

10. Without any other original members, Billy Currie reformed Ultravox again in 1992 which vocalist fronted the band to record the album Revelation?
A) Tony Fenelle   B) Sam Blue   C) John Foxx

MIDGE URE HAD 6 SOLO TOP 40 HITS. CAN YOU UNRAVEL THE ANAGRAMS TO FIND THE TITLES?

1. GERT NORSE (#9 in 1982)

2. HAIFA SEAFRONT (#39 in 1983)

3. I WAIFS (#1 in 1985)

4. ANTHEM RECITALIST (#28 in 1985)

5. ALLOWED FLITCH (#27 in 1986)

6. CHORD COLLATED (#17 in 1991)

ULTRAVOX ANSWERS: *1. A) Chrysalis; 2. B) Vienna (The band's name had an exclamation mark in the early years); 3. Vienna; 4. True; 5. B) Thin Lizzy (replacing Gary Moore); 6. B) The Human League; 7. A) George Martin; 8. Hymn; 9. C) 22; 10. A) Tony Fenelle.*
MIDGE URE ANSWERS: *1. No Regrets; 2. After A Fashion; 3. If I Was; 4. That Certain Smile; 5. Call Of the Wild; 6. Cold Cold Heart.*

U2 are an Irish rock band from Dublin, formed in 1976. The group consists of Bono (lead vocals & rhythm guitar), the Edge (lead guitar, keyboards, & backing vocals), Adam Clayton (bass guitar), and Larry Mullen Jr. (drums & percussion). Initially rooted in post-punk, their style has evolved, yet has maintained an anthemic quality. Popular in live concerts, U2 have staged several ambitious and elaborate tours. U2 had 26 Top 40 singles, including 3 #1's and 17 Top 10 hits. They also had 14 Top 40 albums, including 7 number ones and 3 more Top 10 successes.

1. What Dublin school did the members of U2 attend?
A) Dublin Grammar   B) Liffy College   C) Mount Temple Comprehensive

2. Who was Bono's (Paul Hewson's) best man when he married Alison Stewart in 1982?   A) The Edge (David Evans)   B) Adam Clayton   C) Larry Mullen Jr.

3. What song provided U2 with their first Top 10 hit, reaching #10 in 1983?
A) Fire   B) Gloria   C) New Year's Day

4. Which song from *Achtung Baby* was a #12 hit in 1992, re-mixed, and became a #8 hit the following month?   A) Even Better Than the Real Thing   B) One   C) The Fly

5. With whom did U2 record the 1989 #4 hit?
A) Buddy Guy   B) B.B. King   C) Stevie Ray Vaughan

6. Which song did Bono write as a second part to a John Lennon song?
A) Heartland   B) God Part II   C) All I Want Is You

7. Who duetted with U2 on the *Zooropa* album track, *The Wanderer*?
A) Dion   B) Johnny Cash   C) Francis Rossi

8. The last U2 single in the 20th century reached #3 in the charts in 1998. What was its title that includes these lyrics: "Baby's got blue skies up ahead, But in this I'm a rain cloud, You know she likes a dry kind of love"?

9. Which two members of U2 participated in the *Band Aid* project to raise money for the 1983–85 famine in Ethiopia?
A) Bono and The Edge   B) Bono and Adam Clayton   C) Bono and Larry Mullen Jr.

10. Which 1987 U2 album was critically acclaimed, topped charts in over 20 countries, had 3 Top 10 UK singles, and was fastest-selling album in British history?
A) Rattle and Hum   B) The Joshua Tree   C) Pop

CAN YOU NAME THESE UK NUMBER ONE HITMAKERS?

A) 1960   B) 1966   C) 1968   D) 1983

They all had one number one, in the years shown. Name the artistes and the songs that reached #1.

Number one hits from the last year of every decade in the 20th century. Name all of the artistes who attained the coveted top spot in the UK charts!

NUMBER ONES

1959

1. What Do You Want To Make Those Eyes At Me For?

2. Here Comes Summer

3. Side Saddle

4. Only Sixteen

5. Smoke Gets In Your Eyes

6. The Day The Rains Came

7. Dream Lover

8. As I Love You

9. Travellin' Light

10. One Night

1969

1. Ob-La-Di-Ob-La-Da

2. Sugar Sugar

3. Blackberry Way

4. (If Paradise Is) Half As Nice

5. Where Do You Go To My Lovely

6. Israelites

7. Dizzy

8. Something In the Air

9. Je Taime … Moi Non Plus

10. I'll Never Fall In Love Again

1979

1. Y.M.C.A.

2. Hit Me With Your Rhythm Stick

3. I Will Survive

4. Bright Eyes

5. Ring My Bell

6. Video Killed the Radio Star

7. One Day At A Time

8. When You're In Love With A Beautiful Woman

9. Another Brick In the Wall

10. I Don't Like Mondays

1989

1. Ride On Time

2. Especially For You

3. Something's Gotten Hold Of My Heart

4. Ferry Cross the Mersey

5. Sealed With A Kiss

6. You'll Never Stop Me Loving You

7. Swing the Mood

8. You Got It (Th Right Stuff)

9. Hang On To Your Heart

10. Back To Life (However Do You Want Me)

1999

1. I Have A Dream / Seasons In the Sun

2. Millennium Prayer

3. Lift Me Up

4. Keep On Movin'

5. Genie In A Bottle

6. We're Going To Ibiza!

7. When You Say Nothing At All

8. Livin' La Vida Loca

9. Perfect Moment

10. Fly Away

NUMBER ONES ANSWERS: 1959: *1. Emile Ford & The Checkmates; 2. Jerry Keller; 3. Russ Conway; 4. Craig Douglas; 5. The Platters; 6. Jane Morgan; 7. Bobby Darin; 8. Shirley Bassey; 9. Cliff Richard & The Shadows; 10. Elvis Presley.* **1969**: *1. Marmalade; 2. The Archies; 3. The Move; 4. Amen Corner; 5. Peter Sarsedt; 6. Desmond Dekker & The Aces; 7. Tommy Roe; 8. Thunderclap Newman; 9. Jane Birkin & Serge Gainsbourg; 10. Bobbie Gentry.* **1979**: *1. Village People; 2. Ian Dury & The Blockheads; 3. Gloria Gaynor; 4. Art Garfunkel; 5. Anita Ward; 6. Buggles; 7. Lena Martell; 8. Dr. Hook; 9. Pink Floyd; 10. Boomtown Rats.* **1989**: *1. Black Box; 2. Jason Donovan & Kylie Minogue; 3. Marc Almond feat Gene Pitney; 4. The Christians, Holly Johnson, Paul McCartney, Gerry Marsden and Stock Aitken Waterman; 5. Jason Donovan; 6. Sonia; 7. Jive Bunny & The Mastermixers; 8. New Kids On The Block; 9. Kylie Minogue; 10. Soul II Soul.* **1999**: *1. Westlife; 2. Cliff Richard; 3. Geri Halliwell; 4. Five; 5. Christina Aguilera; 6. Vengaboys; 7. Ronan Keating; 8. Ricky Martin; 9. Martine McCutcheon; 10. Lenny Kravitz.*

FRANKIE VAUGHAN CBE DL (born Islington, Liverpool as Frank Fruim Abelson on 3 February 1928 – died High Wycombe on 17 September 1999). Frankie was an English singer and actor who recorded more than 80 easy listening and traditional pop singles in his lifetime. He was known as 'Mr. Moonlight' after his signature song Give Me the Moonlight, Give Me the Girl. He came from a family of Russian Jewish descent, and derived his stage surname from his grandmother, she called him "Frank my 'number one' grandson", but her Russian accent made "one" sound like "Vaughan". Frankie had 30 Top 40 hits, including two number ones and 9 more Top 10 hits. He also had two Top 20 albums, one reaching #6.

1. Frankie Vaughan's first hit was a #11 in 1954, later to be covered in 1990 by rock band They Might Be Giants. The title was the name of which Turkish city, formerly called Constantinople? A) Ankara B) Istanbul C) Izmir

2. Frankie Vaughan starred in a 1960 film, *Let's Make Love*, with which Hollywood legend? A) Marilyn Monroe B) Jane Russell C) Bette Davis

3. Frankie Vaughan was a major contributor to which association?
A) Dr. Barnardos B) British Red Cross C) National Association of Boys Clubs

4. For which TV show was Frankie 'surprised' by Eamonn Andrews in 1974 and Michael Aspel in 1994?

5. In 1961, Frankie Vaughan covered a Burt Bacharach & Bob Hilliard song, originally performed by Gene McDaniels, and took it to number one in the UK. What was the song? A) Tower of Strength B) Any Day Now C) Three Wheels On My Wagon

6. With whom did Frankie Vaughan team up to have two Top 10 hits with *Gotta Have Something In the Bank Frank* in 1957 and *Come Softly To Me* in 1959?
A) The Beverley Sisters B) The Shepherd Sisters C) The Kaye Sisters

7. In 1964, three versions of the theme song from a new musical were in the UK charts, by Louis Armstrong, Kenny Ball and Frankie Vaughan. What is the song that Frankie took to #18 which contains these lyrics: "I feel the room swayin', While the band's playin', One of our old favourite songs from way back when …"?

8. Frankie Vaughan starred in a 1959 British drama film, directed by Herbert Wilcox, and also starring Anne Heywood and Tony Britton. Vaughan had a #5 hit with the title song from which film? A) The Heart Of A Man B) Garden of Eden C) Kewpie Doll

9. Shakin' Stevens had a #1 in 1981 with which song that had been a #2 for Frankie Vaughan 25 years earlier? A) This Ole House B) Garden Of Eden C) Green Door

10. Frankie Vaughan was awarded an OBE in 1965. This was upgraded to a CBE in what year? A) 1997 B) 1996 C) 1995

BIRTH NAMES

Can you name the lucky seven singers who changed their birth names and found success?

A) Eilleen Regina Edwards

B) Ellen Naomi Cohen

C) Roberta Joan Anderson

D) Eithne Ni Braona

E) Patricia Mae Andrzejewski

F) Gaynor Sullivan

G) Mary Isobel Catherine Bernadette O'Brien

FRANKIE VAUGHAN ANSWERS: *1. B) Istanbul (not Constantinople); 2. A) Marilyn Monroe; 3. C) National Association of Boys Clubs; 4. This Is Your Life; 5. A) Tower of Strength; 6. C) Kaye Sisters; 7. Hello Dolly; 8. A) The Heart Of A Man; 9. C) Green Door; 10. B) 1996.*
BIRTH NAMES ANSWERS: *A) Shania Twain; B) Mama Cass; C) Joni Mitchell; D) Enya; E) Pat Benatar; F) Bonnie Tyler; G) Dusty Springfield.*

BOBBY VEE *(born Fargo, North Dakota as Robert Thomas Velline on April 30, 1943 – died Rogers, Minnesota, October 24, 2016). Bobby Vee was an American singer who was a teen idol in the early 1960s and also appeared in a few films. His parents were Sydney Ronald Velline (a chef, pianist and fiddle player) and Saima Cecelia Tapanila, from a family of Norwegian and Finnish heritage.In the early 1980s, Vee moved his family from Los Angeles to near St. Cloud, Minnesota, where he and Karen organised annual fundraising concerts to provide music and arts facilities for local children. Bobby Vee had 10 Top 40 hits in the UK, seven of them reaching the Top 10. He also had seven Top 40 albums, five of those reaching the Top 10.*

1. Bobby Vee's first big break came in 1959 when he was 15 and responded to a local radio appeal for acts to play at the Fargo Winter Dance Party, when three of their scheduled acts were all tragically killed. Who were the tragic trio?

2. Bobby Vee's first UK hit in 1961 was which Gene Pitney co-written song, that was also a Top 10 hit for Marty Wilde? A) Bad Boy B) Rubber Ball C) Sea Of Love

3. Bobby Vee's backing band changed their name to The Strangers due to a clash with which established band?
A) The Shadows   B) The Searchers   C) The Ventures

4. Bobby Vee's second single release was a cover of Adam Faith's *What Do You Want*. True or False?

5. In 1959, Elston Gunn briefly toured with Bobby Vee and his band. Who later became famous as whom? A) Neil Young B) Jackson Browne C) Bob Dylan

6. Which 1961 #3 hit contains these lyrics: "And if you should discover, That you don't really love her, Just send my baby back home to me …"?
A) Run To Him   B) Take Good Care Of My Baby   C) How Many Tears

7. Bobby Vee was scheduled to appear in Dallas, Texas on 22nd November 1963. Why was the concert cancelled?

8. What is the name of the company that Bobby Vee set up in an old bank building in St Joseph, Minnesota to help aspiring entertainers, and still continues?
A) Roadhouse Productions   B) The Vee Sign   C) Bobby Tomorrow

9. In 1963 Bobby Vee had another #3 hit in the UK with which song written by Benjamin Weisman, Dorothy Wayne, and Marilyn Garrett?
A) Sharing You   B) Run To Him   C) The Night Has A Thousand Eyes

10. Crickets Sonny Curtis and Jerry Allison wrote a song just after Buddy Holly died. It was a #26 hit for The Crickets, but covered by Bobby Vee, the song became a #4 UK hit for Bobby Vee in 1961 and a #2 for Leo Sayer in 1980. Name that tune!

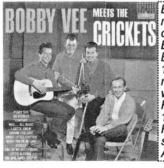

Bobby Vee had numerous connections with Buddy Holly. After Buddy;s death in 1959 Bobby recorded an album with the Crickets. Reissued on CD in 1991. If you love Rock and Roll - seek it out. It s on Amazon Music.

BOBBY VEE ANSWERS: *1. Buddy Holly, Ritchie Valens and The Big Bopper; 2. B) Rubber Ball; 3. A) The Shadows; 4. True; 5. C) Bob Dylan; 6. B) Take Good Care Of My Baby; 7. President John F. Kennedy was assassinated in Dallas that day; 8. A) Roadhouse Productions; 9. C) The Night Has A Thousand Eyes; 10. More Than I Can Say.*

GENE VINCENT (*Born Norfolk, Virginia as Vincent Eugene Craddock on February 11, 1935 – died Newhall, California, October 12, 1971). Vincent was an American musicial rock 'n' roll and rockabilly pioneer. He was inducted into the Rock and Roll and Rockabilly Halls of Fame. A dispute with the US tax authorities and the American Musicians' Union over payments to his band, and his having sold the band's equipment to pay a tax bill led Vincent to leave the United States for Europe. His singles chart record does not reflect the major contribution that he made in the early days of Rock 'n' Roll. Gene had 12 Top 40 singles, incredibly none of them reached the Top 10. He had just one Top 20 album.*

1. In 1952, Gene enlisted in the United States Navy, at the age of seventeen. As he was under the age of enlistment, his parents signed the forms allowing him to enter. What service did he join? A) US Marine Corps B) US Navy C) US Army

2. What was the name of Gene Vincent's backing group in the early years?
A) The Jordanaires B) The Blue Caps C) The Bluesbreakers

3. In 1955, why did Vincent have to spend months in hospital?
A) Polio B) Tuberculosis C) Shattered leg after motorcycle accident

4. Who was lead guitarist in Gene Vincent's backing group?
A) James Burton B) Scotty Moore C) Cliff Gallup

5. What was Gene Vincent's most famous song. It was self composed and reached #16 in the singles chart, amazingly the highest placing he ever achieved?
A) Rocky Road Blues B) Be-Bop-A-Lula C) Say Mama

6. *Dance To the Bop, Bluejean Bop, Anna Annabelle* and *Baby Blue* and *Race With the Devil* are all rock 'n' roll classics but none, entered the UK charts. True or False?

7. Who released a 1977 tribute song, *Sweet Gene Vincent*, on their album *New Boots and Panties!!* ? A) Ian Dury & The Blockheads B) The Jam C) The Skids

Two Rock 'n' Roll greats - Cochran & Vincent

8. On April 16,1960 Gene was travelling in a private-hire taxi in Chippenham, which was involved in a high speed crash, he broke his ribs and collarbone and further damaged his weakened leg. Who died in the crash?
A) Johnny Kidd B) Marc Bolan C) Eddie Cochran

9. Which Al Dexter song, was a hit for both Dexter and for Bing Crosby with the Andrews Sisters, in the forties before being a #15 hit for Gene Vincent in 1961?
A) Pistol Packin' Mama B) She She Little Sheila C) Wild Cat

10. On December 15, 1959, Vincent appeared on his first appearance in England on which Jack Good TV show. He wore black leather, gloves, and a medallion, and stood in a hunched posture. A) Oh, Boy! B) Boy Meets Girl C) Six-Five Special

GENE VINCENT ANSWERS: *1. B) US Navy; 2. B) The Blue Caps; 3. C) Shattered leg after motorcycle accident; 4. C) Cliff Gallup; 5. B) Be-Bop-A-Lula; 6. False - Race With the Devil got to #28; 7. A) Ian Dury & The Blockheads; 8. C) Eddie Cochran; 9. A) Pistol Packin' Mama; 10. B) Boy Meets Girl.*

THE WALKER BROTHERS *were an American pop group of the 1960s and 1970s comprising Noel Scott Engel (known professionally as Scott Walker), John Joseph Maus (John Walker) and Gary Leeds (Gary Walker). Formed in 1964, they adopted the 'Walker Brothers' name as a show business touch even though the members were all unrelated. They moved to the UK in 1965 and provided a unique counterpoint to the British Invasion by achieving much more success in the UK than in their home country, even in a period when British bands such as The Beatles dominated the US charts. The Walker brothers had 10 Top 40 hits, including a #1 and 2 more Top 10 hits. They also had Five Top 10 albums.*

1. Scott Engel was the bass player with which instrumental band, who had a minor hit with *Let's Go* in 1962, before joining the Walker Brothers?
A) The Ventures   B) The Crossfires   C) The Routers

2. The Walker Brothers debut single, *Pretty Girls Everywhere*, flopped, despite an appearance on which TV pop music show?
A) Top Of the Pops   B) Thank Your Lucky Stars   C) Ready Steady Go!

3. Their first chart single *Love Her*, a #20 hit, was originally an Everly Brothers 'B' side. How many musicians made the Wall of Sound' backing under Jack Nitzsche's supervision?   A) 38   B) 28   C) 18

4. What role did Scott Walker play in the 1979 *Muppet Movie*?
A) Lew Lord   B) Doc Hopper   C) Snake Walker

5. *Make It Easy On Yourself*, written by Bacharach/David, became the first Walker Brothers number one in 1965. What song did it knock off the top spot?
A) (I Can't Get No) Satisfaction   B) I Got You Babe   C) Like a Rolling Star

6. John Maus (John Walker) was a child star who was a friend of Ritchie Valens, and was an honorary pallbearer at Valens' funeral. True or False?

7. The Walker Brothers had a 1966 #34 hit with the title song of which UK adventure crime mystery film starring Richard Johnson as Hugh 'Bulldog' Drummond?
A) Some Girls Do   B) Deadlier Than the Male   C) Calling Bulldog Drummond

8. The first of five Walker Brothers Top Top 10 albums reached #3 in 1965, what was its title?   A) Portrait   B) Images   C)Take It Easy With the Walker Brothers

9. The Walker Brothers all had solo Top 40 UK hits, which of them had hits with the following songs   A) Twinkie Lee   B) Annabella   C) Lights Of Cincinatti

10. What song took the Walker Brother to #7 in 1976 after a nine year absence from the charts?   A) Walking In the Rain   B) No Regrets   C) Stay With Me Baby

THE WALKER BROTHERS ANSWERS: *1. C) The Routers; 2. B) Thank Your Lucky Stars; 3. A) 38; 4. C) Snake Walker; 5. A) (I Can't Get No) Satisfaction (Rolling Stones); 6. True; 7. B) Deadlier Than the Male; 8. C) Take It Easy With the Walker Brothers; 9. A) Gary B) John C) Scott; 10. B) No Regrets.*

DIONNE WARWICK *(born East Orange, New Jersey on December 12, 1940) is an American singer, actress, and television host. During her career, she has sold more than 100 million records worldwide. She has won many awards, including 6 Grammy Awards. Warwick was inducted into the Hollywood Walk of Fame, the Grammy Hall of Fame, the R&B Music Hall of Fame and the Apollo Theatre Walk of Fame. Many of her songs were covered, thus much reducing her hit singles in the UK compared to the US. A former Goodwill Ambassador for the UN's Food and Agriculture Organisation. Dionne Warwick had 10 Top 40 hits, including 4 Top 10 recordings. She also had 9 Top 40 albums, including 4 Top 10 successes.*

1. Many of Dionne Warwick's family were members of which family gospel group and RCA recording artists, who performed throughout the New York area?
A) Wings of Heaven   B) Grace Gospel Singers   C) Drinkard Singers

2. Dionne, and another singer, left the gospel group to go solo as recording artistes. Whilst not as successful here, who was the other soloist who had hits like *Whatcha Gonna Do About It* and the original of *Just One Look*, covered by The Hollies?
A) Doris Troy   B) Irma Thomas   C) Mary Wells

3. Dionne sung the title song of a 1968 film and recorded a #28 hit with the song. The film starred Barbara Parkins, but what is its title?
A) Valley Of the Dolls   B) Barefoot in the Park   C) Rosemary's Baby

4. In the title of her 1968 #8 hit single, to which US city was Dionne Warwick seeking directions?   A) Los Angeles   B) San Jose   C) Detroit

5. Together with Elton John, Stevie Wonder and Gladys Knight, on behalf of which charity did Dionne record *That's What Friends Are For*, a 1985 hit that was previously recorded by Rod Stewart in 1982?
A) Cancer Research   B) Sickle Cell Society   C) Aids Research & Prevention

6. Which major singing star, who was to tragically die at 48, was Dionne Warwick a first cousin?   A) Michael Jackson   B) Natalie Cole   C) Whitney Houston

7. Dionne Warwick's highest chart placing in the UK was #2 with *Heartbreaker* in 1982 . Who wrote the song?
A) The Bee Gees   B) Dolly Parton   C) Roger Cook & Roger Greenaway

8. The follow up to *Heartbreaker* also reached the UK Top 10. Written by the same songwriters, what was the title of the song?
A) Then Came You   B) All the Love in the World   C) You Can Have Him

9. Dionne's first US Top 10 hit, *Anyone Who Had A Heart* just failed to reach the Top 40 in the UK, but a cover version by which English singer topped the charts?

10. Which Dionne Warwick 1964 #9 hit contains these lyrics: "... So let me hide, The tears and the sadness you gave me, When you said goodbye"
A) Walk On By   B) You'll Never Get To Heaven   C) Alfie

THE HIPPY HIPPY SHAKE

In the 1988 film Cocktail one of the flair bar tending routines with Tom Cruise and Bryan Brown has The Hippy Hippy Shake by the Georgia Satellites providing the soundtrack. Chan Romero wrote the song and had a US hit with the song when he was aged just 17: but who had a number two hit in the UK with the song in 1963?

DIONNE WARWICK ANSWERS: *1. C) Drinkard Singers; 2. A) Doris Troy; 3. A) Valley of the Dolls; 4. B) San Jose; 5. C) Aids Research & Prevention; 6. C) Whitney Houston; 7. A) The Bee Gees; 8. B) All the Love in the World; 9. Cilla Black; 10. A) Walk On By.*
THE HIPPY HIPPY SHAKE ANSWER: *The Swinging Blue Jeans.*

PAUL WELLER / STYLE COUNCIL *(The Style Council were a British band formed in late 1982 by Weller, former singer, songwriter and guitarist with The Jam, and keyboardist Mick Talbot, former member of Dexys Midnight Runners.The band enabled Weller to take his music in a more soulful direction. The Style Council split in 1989, and Paul Weller established himself as a solo artist with his eponymous 1992 album. Style Council had 15 Top 40 singles, including 7 Top 10 hits. 7 albums, including 1 number one and 4 more Top 10. Paul Weller had 17 Top 40 singles, including 3 Top 10 hits. He also had 6 Top 40 albums with 1 number 1 and 4 more Top 10 successes.*

1. What is Paul Weller's real name? A) Paul Weller   B) John Weller   C) Ian Smith

2. Which band did Paul Weller see perform live, inspiring him to form a band?
A) Oasis   B) Status Quo   C) U2

3. Which acid house classic did Paul Weller cover in 1989?
A) Promised Land   B) We Call It Acieed   C) It's Alright

4. For which member of Band Aid did Paul Weller stand in on a Top Of the Pops appearance? A) Sting   B) Boy George   C) Bono

5. Which famous artist painted the cover of the 1995 album *Stanley Road*?   A) Francis Bacon   B) Peter Blake   C) David Hockney

6. What was the first solo Paul Weller album to reach #1 in the UK?
A) Stanley Road   B) Heliocentric   C) Heavy Soul

7. What was the name of the Labour Party supporting project that Paul Weller was part of in the 1980s?   A) Red Rock   B) Red Wedge   C) Red Mole

8. What was Paul Weller's nickname in the 1970s & 1980s?
A) Mr Woking   B) Pope of Mope   C) The Modfather

9. What was the title of Paul Weller's second album, released in 1993, that produced three hit singles?   A) Wild Wood   B) Paul Weller   C) Live Wood

10. In the late 1980s, Weller was increasingly interested in which organisation?
A) Greenpeace   B) Carbon 180   C) CND

LUCKY 13 STYLE COUNCIL HITS.
MATCH THE SONG WITH ITS HIGHEST CHART POSITION

1. Speak Like A Child	A. 3
2. Money Go Round (Part 1)	B. 4
3. Long Hot Summer / Paris Match	C. 5
4. My Ever Changing Moods	D. 6
5. Shout To The Top	E. 7
6 Walls Come Tumbling Down	F. 9
7 Come To Milton Keynes	G. 11
8. The Lodgers	H. 13
9. Have You Ever Had It Blue	J. 14
10. It Didn't Matter	K. 20
11. Wanted	L. 23
12 Life At A Top People's Health Far	M. 27
13. Promised Land	N. 28

PAUL WELLER ANSWERS: *1. B) John Weller; 2. B) Status Quo; 3. A) Promised Land; 4. C) Bono; 5. B) Peter Blake; 6. A) Stanley Road; 7. B) Red Wedge; 8. C) The Modfather; 9. A) Wild Wood; 10. C) CND.* **LUCKY 13 STYLE COUNCIL HITS ANSWERS:** *1B; 2G; 3A; 4C; 5E; 6D; 7L; 8H; 9J; 10F; 11K; 12N; 13M.*

WHAM! were an English pop duo formed in Bushey in 1981. The duo consisted of George Michael (born East Finchley as Georgios Kyriacos Panayiotou; 25 June 1963 – died Goring-on-Thames, 25 December 2016), and Andrew Ridgeley (born Windlesham, 26 January 1963). One of the most commercially successful pop acts of the 1980s, selling more than 30 million certified records worldwide from 1982 to 1986. Wham! Had 10 Top 40 hits, including 4 number ones and the other 6 all reached the Top 10. They also had 4 Top 40 albums including 2 #1 and 2 other Top 10 successes.

1. What was the first Wham! hit single, a #3 in 1982?
A) Young Guns (Go For It) B) Wham Rap! C) Bad Boys

2. The lyrics from what smash hit from Wham! frequently uses the word "Jitterbug"?

3. Which subsequently perennial Christmas hit single, originally issued in 1984, had all of its royalties handed to Band Aid?

4. Which Wham! number one was credited to Wham! Featuring George Michael?
A) I'm Your Man B) Everything She Wants C) Careless Whisper

5. After one album, the duo signed with which record label?
A) Epic Records/CBS B) Capitol Music Group C) Decca Records

6. Andrew Ridgeley was ordered to leave the official party at the end of the Live Aid concert in 1985 because of his wild behaviour. True or False?

7. Wham!'s backing singers were Dee C. Lee and Shirlie Holliman, with which act did Shirlie gain some chart success in the mid-eighties?
A) Centrefold B) The Dooleys C) Pepsi & Shirlie

8. Which Wham! 1985 #1 was written very quickly by George Michael, the whole of the first verse and chorus in five minutes on an internal flight in America during the Whamamerica! Tour? A) I'm Your Man B) Freedom C) The Edge Of Heaven

9. In 1986 Wham! Played their farewell concert in front of 72,000 fans at which venue? A) The Rose Bowl B) Wembley Stadium C) Glastonbury

10. After the breakup, Ridgeley moved to Monaco and tried his hand at what sport?
A) Skiing B) Formula Three Motor Racing C) Ice Hockey

LIFE'S BEEN GOOD!

Joe Walsh had a #14 hit with Life's Been Good in 1977. Which American rock band, formed in Los Angeles in 1971, did Joe join in 1975, and with whom he is still performing.

WHAM! ANSWERS: *1. A) Young Guns (Go For It); 2. Wake Me Up Before You Go Go; 3. Last Christmas; 4. C) Careless Whisper; 5. A) Epic Records/CBS; 6. True; 7. C) Pepsi & Shirlie; 8. A) I'm Your Man; 9. B) Wembley Stadium; 10. B) Formula Three Motor Racing.*
LIFE'S BEEN GOOD ANSWER: *The Eagles.*

BARRY WHITE *(Born Galveston, Texas as Barry Eugene Carter on September 12, 1944 – died Los Angeles on July 4, 2003) He was an American singer and songwriter, known for his bass voice and romantic image, particularly in the 70s. Barry came from humble beginnings, worked hard and achieved success in a notoriously cutthroat industry. He was overweight for most of his adult life and suffered related health problems. White remains a popular icon, remembered for his love ballads and as the singer who openly celebrated love through his art and music. Barry White had 17 Top 40 hit singles in the UK, including one #1 and 5 more Top 10 hits. He also had 8 Top 40 albums, including 2 Top 10 successes.*

1. By what nickname was Barry White affectionately known?
A) The Walrus of Love   B) The Whale of Love   C) The Weasel of Love

2. White was jailed for four months at the age of 16 for stealing $30,000 worth of Cadillac tyres (equivalent to about $300,000 in 2022). In prison, he listened to an Elvis Presley song on the radio, which he credited with changing his life. What was the song?   A) Jailhouse Rock   B) It's Now Or Never   C) In the Ghetto

3. In 1972, Barry White got his big break producing a girl group he had discovered in the imitative style of The Supremes. What was the name of the group who had two UK Top 20 singles?   A) Whiter Than White   B) Love Unlimited   C) The Exciters

4. In 1973, White created a 40-piece orchestral group, originally as a backing band for his girl-group. However, he released *Love's Theme* in 1974 and it reached #10 in the UK. What was the name of the orchestra?
A) Love Unlimited   B) Boston Pops   C) Simon Park

5. What was Barry White's only number one in the UK?   A) You're the First, the Last, My Everything   B) Let the Music Play   C) Never Never Gonna Give You Up

6. Which animated TV series featured Barry White in two episodes?
A) The Flintstones   B) South Park   C) The Simpsons

7. In 1974, White married for the second time, who was the singer he married and with whom he had four children?
A) Glodean James   B) Katherine Denton   C) Karyn White

8. Which Barry White #5 hit contains these lyrics: "Stay right there, right there, don't you move, You don't know what I'm going through …"?

9. Barry White had his only 1970s Top 10 UK album in 1974. What was its title?
A) Let the Music Play   B) Can't Get Enough   C) Heart and Soul

10. While touring in August 1999, White was forced to cancel a month of tour dates owing to exhaustion, high blood pressure and a hectic schedule. With which band was he touring?   A) Kool & The Gang   B) The Gap Band   C) Earth, Wind & Fire

WHAT'S MY NAME?

> I was born in Exeter in 1942.

> In the early 1960s, I was a member of The Kestrels with Roger Greenaway and Roger Cook.

> I joined the Ivy League who metamorphosed into the Flower Pot Men.

> I sang lead vocals on several one-hit wonder songs under different group names including, Edison Lighthouse's *Love Grows (Where My Rosemary Goes)*; White Plains *My Baby Loves Lovin*; the Pipkins' *Gimme Dat Ding*; and First Class' *Beach Baby*.

> I also sang lead vocals on Brotherhood of Man's *United We Stand*

> I recorded as a session harmony singer with Elton John on the songs *Levon* and *Tiny Dancer*

BARRY WHITE ANSWERS: *1. A) The Walrus of Love; 2. B) It's Now Or Never; 3. B) Love Unlimited; 4. A) Love Unlimited; 5. A) You're the First, the Last, My Everything; 6. C) The Simpsons; 7. A) Glodean James; 8. What Am I Gonna Do With You; 9. B) Can't Get Enough; 10. C) Earth, Wind & Fire.* **WHAT'S MY NAME ANSWER:** *Tony Burrows.*

1. Cliff Richard & The Drifters had a hit with *Livin' Lovin' Doll?*

2. When was *Bohemian Rhapsody* by Queen first released?

3. Madonna's lowest chart placing for her singles was No.16, when did both *Oh Father* and *Take a Bow* only reach that position in the Top 40?

4. Bryan Adams' *(Everything I Do) I Do It For You* top for 16 weeks.

5. The Carpenters on *Top of the World.*

6. The Beatles asked *Ain't She Sweet.*

7. Swiss duo Yello took *The Race* to number seven.

8. *Killing Me Softly With His Song* was a big it for Roberta Flack.

9. Billy Joel introduced us to his *Uptown Girl.*

10. John Travolta and Olivia Newton-John told each other *You're the One that I Want for the* second time.

11. The Rockin' Berries informed us that *He's In Town.*

12. Boney M had a Christmas number one with *Mary's Boy Child.*

13. Mike Sarne invited Wendy Richard to *Come Outside.*

14. The Surfaris had a *Wipe Out.*

15. 2 Unlimited had *No Limit.*

16. Level 42 gave us *Lessons in Love.*

17. The Rolling Stones had this memorable cover designed by Michael Cooper for their 1967 album, *Their Satanic Majesties Request.*

18. *Drummer Man* by Tonight was beating its way up the charts.

19. *The Guitar Man* by Bread was drawing the crowd and playing so loud.

20. The underrated Pat Benatar was *All Fired Up.*

DECADE DIAGNOSIS ANSWERS: *1. 1950s; 2. 1970s; 3. 1990s; 4. 1990s; 5. 1970s; 6. 1960s; 7. 1980s; 8. 1970s; 9. 1980s; 10. 1990s (reissued in 1998); 11. 1960s; 12. 1970s; 13. 1960s; 14. 1960s; 15. 1990s; 16. 1980s; 17. 1960s; 18. 1970s; 19. 1970s; 20. 1980s.*

THE WHO are an English rock band formed in London in 1964. Their classic lineup consisted of Roger Daltrey (lead singer), Pete Townshend (guitar/singer), John Entwistle (bass / singer), and Keith Moon (drums). Considered one of the most influential rock bands of the 20th century. Their contributions include developing the Marshall Stack, large PA systems, using synthesizers, Entwistle and Moon's influential playing styles, Townshend's feedback and power chord guitar technique, and the development of the rock opera. The Who had 24 UK Top 40 singles, including 14 Top 10 hits. They also had 19 Top 40 albums, including a #1 and 12 further Top 10 hits.

1. The Who's early roots were as an instrumental band who played Shadows and Ventures music. What was their name?
A) The Detours   B) The Silhouettes   C) The Fast Lane

2. Roger Daltrey was inducted into the Rock and Roll Hall of Fame in 1990, he had solo success and appeared on both the small and large screen. What was his only solo Top 10 hit in 1973?   A) Thinking   B) Giving It All Away   C) After the Fire

3. Pete Townshend particularly admired which early British Rock and Roll track?
A) Shakin' All Over By Johnny Kidd/Pirates   B) Move It by Cliff Richard/Drifters
C) Brand New Cadillac by Vince Taylor/Playboys

4. Which hotel chain banned The Who for life in 1967, after Keith Moon allegedly drove a Lincoln Continental into the hotel's swimming pool in Michigan?
A) Hilton   B) Marriott International   C) Holiday Inn

5. Roger Daltrey was temporarily sacked by the band in 1965 when he threw amphetamines down the toilet and assaulted which band member?
A) Keith Moon   B) John Entwistle   C) Pete Townshend

6. The Who were known for destroying their instruments during a performance. This was initiated in 1964 when Pete accidentally broke the head of his guitar on a low pub stage ceiling. Angered by the audience's laughter, he smashed the guitar on the stage, picked up another guitar and continued the show. Where did this happen?
A) Oldfield, Greenford   B) Goldhawk, Shepherd's Bush   C) Railway, Wealdstone

7. Keith Moon attended a party at Paul McCartney's house to celebrate which singer's birthday, hours before he died from after taking 32 tablets of clomethiazole, prescribed to combat his alcohol withdrawal?
A) Eddie Cochran   B) Buddy Holly   C) Rick Nelson

8. The Who did not have a UK number one hit single. Their highest chart position was #2, achieved with which 1965 recording?
A) My Generation   B) Substitute   C) Happy Jack

9. A) What was the first Who album, recorded in 1980 after Keith Moon's death?
B) Who played drums on the album?

10. Which member of The Who was Nicknamed 'The Ox' and 'Thunderfingers'?

THE WHO ANSWERS: 1. A) The Detours; 2. B) Giving It All Away; 3. B) Move It by Cliff Richard/Drifters; 4. C) Holiday Inn; 5. A) Keith Moon; 6. C) Railway, Wealdstone; 7. B) Buddy Holly; 8. A) My Generation; 9. A) Face Dances; B) Kenney Jones; 10. John Entwistle.

KIM WILDE (born Chiswick, London as Kim Smith, 18 November 1960). The daughter of singer Marty Wilde and Joyce Baker, a member of the Vernons Girls. Kim is an English pop singer, DJ and TV presenter. Worldwide, Wilde has sold over 10 million albums and 20 million singles. She was the most-charted British female solo act of the 1980s. Starting in 1998, while still active in music, she has branched into an alternative career as a landscape gardener, which has included presenting gardening shows on the BBC and Channel 4. Kim Wilde had 19 Top 40 singles, this included 7 Top 10 hits. Additionally she had 6 Top 40 albums, including 2 Top 10 successes.

1. Kim Wilde's first hit single was written by her father, Marty, and her brother Ricky. What was the name of the song that reached #2 in the UK in 1981?
A) Chequered Love   B) Water On Glass   C) Kids In America

2. In 1983, what Best Brit Award was handed to Kim Wilde?
A) Female Solo Artist   B) Newcomer   C) Best Original Song

3. Which record company, headed by Mickie Most, gave Kim Wilde her first recording contract?   A) RAK   B) MCA   C) RCA

4. In 1994 Kim Wilde toured Australia and Japan. What was the name of the tour?
A) Wilde Tour Party   B) Greatest Hits Concert Tour   C) Hang On! Tour

5. What former Supremes and Vanilla Fudge hit from the sixties, was covered by Kim Wilde in 1986 and reached #2 in the UK charts?
A) Baby Love   B) You Keep Me Hangin' On   C) Reflections

6. What nickname did Kim Wilde have in the 1980s?
A) The Monroe of Pop   B) The Dors of Pop   C) The Bardot of Pop

7. In 1987 Kim Wilde duetted on the old Brenda Lee hit, *Rockin' Around the Christmas Tree* and had a #3 hit with which comedian, actor and director?
A) Mel Smith   B) Rowan Atkinson   C) Ben Elton

8. On which major tour was Kim Wilde the support act in 1988?   A) Crazy Nights World Tour (Kiss)   B) Bad Tour (Michael Jackson)   C) Faith Tour (George Michael)

9. Which song from *Saturday Night Fever*, originally a hit for Yvonne Elliman, provided Kim Wilde with her last Top 40 success, a #12 hit in 1993?
A) More Than A Woman   B) Manhattan Skyline   C) If I Can't Have You

10. On which 1987 charity single, a #1 hit, did Kim Wilde perform?
A) Ferry Aid - Let It Be   B) Justice Collective - He Ain't Heavy, He's My Brother
C) Reaching Out - Rock Therapy

NAME THESE 50s/60s HITMAKERS

A) 11 HITS	B) 4 HITS	C) 8 HITS	D) 6 HITS	E) 9 HITS
INC. HOLD ME	INC. LET'S DANCE	INC. LET'S TWIST AGAIN	INC. GUITAR BOOGIE SHUFFLE	INC. MY SPECIAL ANGEL

KIM WILDE ANSWERS: 1. C) Kids In America; 2. A) Female Solo artist; 3. A) RAK;
4. B) Greatest Hits Concert Tour; 5. B) You Keep Me Hangin' On; 6. C) The Bardot of Pop;
7. A) Mel Smith; 8. B) Bad Tour (Michael Jackson); 9. C) If I Can't Have You; 10. A) Ferry Aid - Let It Be (Supporting the Zeebrugge Disaster Fund).
NAME THE 50s/60s HIT MAKERS ANSWERS: A) P J Proby; B) Chris Montez; C) Chubby Checker; D) Bert Weedon; F) Malcolm Vaughan.

MARTY WILDE MBE (born Reginald Leonard Smith; 15 April 1939 is an English singer and songwriter. He was among the first generation of British pop stars to emulate American rock and roll, scoring several late 1950s /early sixties hit singles with covers of US hits backed by his band, The Wildcats. During the 1960s and 1970s, Wilde continued to record and, with Ronnie Scott, he co-wrote hit singles for others whilst continuing to write and tour. He is the father of pop singer Kim Wilde and co-wrote many of her hit singles too. Marty Wilde had 12 Top 40 hit singles, including 6 Top 10 hits.

1. What year was Reg Patterson performing at London's Condor Club when he was spotted by impresario Larry Parnes and turned into Marty Wilde?
A) 1957   B) 1958   C) 1959

2. Marty Wilde had three unsuccessful singles before he hit number #4 with his fourth single. The song was a cover of a US hit by Jody Reynolds, what was its title?
A) Honeycomb   B) Endless Sleep   C) Oh-Oh, I'm Falling In Love Again

3. On what music TV programme was Marty Wilde a resident alongside Cliff Richard and the Dallas Boys?   A) Boy Meets Girls   B) 6.5 Special   C) Oh Boy!

4. The Wildcats were; Big Jim Sullivan, Brian Bennett, Liquorice Locking and Tony Belcher. In 1961, Brian Bennett left the band, followed by Liquorice Locking the following year. Which top instrumental band did they both join?

5. In 1959 Marty had his biggest hit, a #2 song written by Pomus/Shuman. The original version by Dion & The Belmonts and another by Craig Douglas also reached the charts. What was the song?   A) A Teenager In Love   B) Bad Boy   C) Donna

6. On which ABC TV show was Marty Wilde principal male singer with guests like Eddie Cochran and Adam Faith?   A) Oh Boy!   B) Discs-a-Gogo   C) Boy Meets Girls

7. Marty Wilde co-wrote several hit songs, which artistes had hits with:
A) I'm A Tiger   B) Ice In the Sun   C) Jesamine

8. Marty Wilde was included on the *Group Scene 1964* tour with acts like The Ronettes, Dave Berry, The Swing Blue Jeans. Who were top of the bill?
A) The Beatles   B) The Rolling Stones   C) The Shadows

9. After his marriage in 1960 and a surge in Cliff Richard's career, Marty's popularity declined, but he had a #9 hit with a cover of a Booby Vee song that reached #4. What was the song?   A) Rubber Ball   B) Little Girl   C) Tomorrow's Clown

10. In 1961 Marty appeared as a Rock 'n' Roll star in which musical at Her Majesty's Theatre?   A) Guys & Dolls   B) Bye Bye Birdie   C) The Boy Friend

MARTY WILDE ANSWERS: 1. A) 1957; 2. B) Endless Sleep; 3. C) Oh Boy!; 4. The Shadows; 5. A) A Teenager In Love; 6. C) Boy Meets Girls; 7. A) Lulu; B) Status Quo; C) The Casuals; 8. B) The Rolling Stones; 9. A) Rubber Ball; 10. B) Bye Bye Birdie.

ANDY WILLIAMS *(Born Howard Andrew Williams at Wall Lake, Iowa on 3 December 1927 - died Branson, Missouri, 25 September 2012 (aged 84) was an American singer and TV star. His brothers and he formed the Williams Brothers quartet. Williams was signed to Cadence Records, run by conductor Archie Bleyer. He was nominated for six Grammy Awards. He hosted The Andy Williams Show, a popular television variety show, from 1962 to 1971, along with numerous other TV specials. The Andy Williams Show won three Emmy awards. He sold more than 45 million records worldwide. Andy Williams had 20 Top 40 UK singles, including one #1 and 8 more Top 10 hits. He also had 24 Top 40 albums, including three #1's and 7 more Top 10 hits.*

1. Andy Williams' only UK number one came in 1957 with a cover of a Charlie Gracie song, it was his first UK hit. What was the song that topped the charts?
A) Stranger On the Shore   B) Can't Get Used To Losing You   C) Butterfly

2. The Andy Williams TV show ran from 1962 to 1971. Which group catapulted to fame after regularly appearing on the show?
A) The Osmonds   B) The Carpenters   C) The Partridge Family

3. Andy Williams had 3 big UK hit singles in 1963, 1968 and 1970, whose titles all began with the word "Can't". Can you name them?

4. Andy Williams sung the Henry Mancini & Johnny Mercer Oscar winning song, from the film *Breakfast At Tiffany's*, at the Academy Awards ceremony in 1962.
A) What was the song? and B) Who had a #1 hit in the UK with the song?

5. In 1966 Andy Williams performed at the opening of at which famous Las Vegas hotel and Casino and headlined there for 20 years after?
A) Casino Royale   B) Caesar's Palace   C) Planet Hollywood

6. At the 1968 funeral of which icon of modern American liberalism, did Andy Williams sing the *Battle Hymn of the Republic* and Schubert's *Ave Maria*?
A) Robert F. Kennedy   B) Adlai E. Stevenson   C) Dwight D. Eisenhower

7. In 1994 which Andy Williams 1969 #19 hit was sung over the closing credits of which Danny Boyle film? A) Sunshine   B) Trainspotting   C) Shallow Grave

8. Andy Williams last hit of the 20th century, a #9 success, has a title about melodies for observing what?

9. What 1925 song with the original title of *Ke Kali Nei Aua (Waiting There for Thee)* was sung by Elvis Presley in the 1961 film *Blue Hawaii*, was a minor 1965 UK hit for Julie Rogers and provided Andy Williams with a US hit in 1958?

10. Which Chopin inspired, Neil Sedaka / Phil Cody written song, gave Andy Williams a #4 UK hit in 1973 and The Carpenters a #32 hit in 1975?
A) Solitaire   B) Love Will Keep Us Together   C) Laughter In the Rain

WHAT IS THE FOUR LETTER WORD?

What word appears in hits that match the following details? Leroy Van Dyke #5 in 1962, Val Doonican #3 in 1964, Seekers #10 in 1966, The Four Tops #3 in 1967, Daniel Boone #17 in 1971, David Ruffin #11 in 1976

ANDY WILLIAMS ANSWERS: *1. C) Butterfly; 2. A) The Osmonds; 3. Can't Get Used To Losing You #2, Can't Take My Eyes Off You #5 and Can't Help Falling In Love #3; 4. A) Moon River; B) Danny Williams; 5. B) Caesar's Palace; 6. Robert F. Kennedy; 7. C) Shallow Grave; 8. Music To Watch Girls By; 9. Hawaiian Wedding Song; 10. A) Solitaire. **WHAT IS THE FOUR LETTER WORD ANSWERS**: The word is **WALK**. Walk on By, Walk Tall, Walk With Me, Walk Away Renee, Daddy Don't You Walk So Fast; Walk Away From Love.*

ROBBIE WILLIAMS (Robert Peter Williams, born Stoke-on-Trent on 13 February 1974) is an English singer and songwriter. In 1990, 16-year-old Williams was the youngest member to join Take That, where he found fame from 1990 to 1995. Williams' use of alcohol and cocaine brought him into conflict with band manager Nigel Martin-Smith. In November 1994, Williams's drug abuse had escalated; he had a near drug overdose the night before the group was scheduled to perform at the MTV Europe Music Awards. He agreed to quit and left the group in July 1995. Williams then went on to achieve massive commercial success after launching a solo career in 1996. In the 20th century Robbie had 10 Top 20 hits, including 2 #1's and 7 further Top 10 hits. He also had 2 smash hit #1 albums.

1. Take That disbanded 7 months after Robbie Williams left, on 13 February 1996. Which was also what milestone in Robbie's life?
A) Start of relationship with Mel C   B) His 22nd birthday   C) His first single released

2. Robbie Williams debut album in 1997 produced five hit singles, including *Angels*. What was the name of the album?
A) Life thru a Lens   B) I've Been Expecting You   C) Everything Changes

3. In 1996 with members of whom did the Press photograph Robbie Williams partying at the Glastonbury Festival?   A) Manic Street Fighter   B) Foo Fighters   C) Oasis

4. When Robbie was younger, of which football club social club was his dad, Peter, the licensee?   A) Stoke City   B) Port Vale   C) Crewe Alexandra

5. With whom did Robbie Williams co-write many of his songs?

6. What links: the logo of TV's *The Saint*, the spectacles of *The Two Ronnies*, the skip dance pose of Morecambe and Wise and the coat of arms of Burslem?

7. To what record label did Robbie Williams sign in 1996?
A) Chrysalis Records   B) Snapper Music   C) Network Records

8. In 1996 Robbie Williams appeared in the background, using a telephone, in which TV pub?   A) The Rovers Return   B) The Queen Victoria   C) The Woolpack

9. Which Adam & The Ants hit did Robbie Williams feature as a 'B' side of *No Regrets* in 1998?   A) Stand and Deliver   B) Antmusic   C) Prince Charming

10. What was the name of Robbie Williams' first solo tour in 1997?   A) Show Off Must Go On Tour   B) Ego Has Landed Tour   C) One More for the Rogue Tour

THE TURTLES *are an American rock band formed in Los Angeles, California in 1965, whose best-known lineup included Howard Kaylan, Mark Volman, Al Nichol, Chuck Portz, Jim Tucker and Don Murray.*

NAME THE THREE TOP 20 HITS RECORDED BY THE TURTLES IN 1967/8

ROBBIE WILLIAMS ANSWERS: *1. B) His 22nd birthday; 2. A) Life thru a Lens; 3. C) Oasis; 4. B) Port Vale; 5. Guy Chambers; 6. All Robbie Williams tattoos; 7. Chrysalis Records; 8. B) The Queen Victoria; 9. B) Antmusic; 10. A) Show Off Must Go On Tour.*
TURTLES HITS ANSWERS: *Happy Together #12, She'd Rather Be With Me #4, Elenore #7.*

PICTURE LAST IS FIRST!

Identify the acts. The last letter of the first answer is first letter of the second answer and so on. Finally, the last letter of answer 20 is the first letter of the first answer to complete the circle!

Don't Laugh At Me
#3 – 1954

Venus In Blue Jeans
#4 – 1962

The Last Farewell
#2 – 1975

Black Betty
#7 – 1977

Love Changes Everything
#2 – 1989

Always and Forever
#20 – 1995

Dippety Day
#13 – 1978

Cool For Cats
#2 – 1979

Pearl's A Singer
#8 – 1977

Frankie
#1 – 1985

The Last Waltz
#1 – 1967

My Sharona
#6 – 1979

Everything I Own
#1 – 1974

Well I Ask You
#1 – 1961

I Don't Wanna Dance
#1 – 1982

Nellie the Elephant
#4 – 1984

The Logical Song
#7 – 1979

This Is My Song
#1 – 1967

Sukiyaki
#6 – 1963

D.I.S.C.O.
#2 – 1980

PICTURE LAST IS FIRST ANSWERS: A) Norman Wisdom; B) Mark Wynter; C) Roger Whittaker; D) Ram Jam; E) Michael Ball; F) Luther Vandross; G) Smurfs; H) Squeeze; J) Elkie Brooks; K) Sister Sledge; L) Engelbert Humperdinck; M) Knack; N) Ken Boothe; P) Eden Kane; R) Eddy Grant; S) Toy Dolls; T) Supertramp; U) Petula Clark; V) Kyu Sakomoto; W) Ottawan.

STEVIE WONDER *(Stevland Hardaway Morris (neé Judkins; May 13, 1950). Blind since shortly after his birth, Wonder is an American singer-songwriter, regarded as a pioneer and influence by musicians across a range of genres. Wonder's use of synthesizers and other electronic musical instruments in the 70s reshaped R&B conventions. He helped drive these genres into the album era. His albums are cohesive and consistent, including socially conscious statements with complex compositions. Wonder had 39 Top 40 hits, including two number ones and 17 other Top 10 hits. He also had 17 Top 40 albums, 9 of those reaching the Top 10.*

1. Stevie Wonder joined Motown at 12 years of age, by what name was he known in before 1964? A) Small Wonder   B) Little Stevie Wonder   C) Tiny Dancer

2. Stevie had his first UK hit in 1966. What song reached #14 in the charts?
A) Blowin' in the Wind   B) A Place in the Sun   C) Uptight (Everything's Alright)

3. One of Wonder's two number ones was a duet with Paul McCartney in 1982. What was the song that took them to the top?
A) Ebony and Ivory   B) Say, Say, Say   C) The Girl Is Mine

4. Which Smokey Robinson & The Miracles number one hit in 1970 was co-written by Stevie Wonder?   A) Tears Of A Clown   B) The Tracks Of My Tears   C) Shop Around

5. What instrument did Stevie Wonder play on The Eurythmics 1985 # 1 hit *There Must Be An Angel (Playing With My Heart)*?
A) Percussion   B) Harmonica   C) Keyboards

6. What 1973 Stevie Wonder album produced two big UK hits, *Superstition* and *You Are The Sunshine Of My Life*?
A) Innervisions   B) Talking Book   C) Songs In the Key of Life

7. What Stevie Wonder #2 UK hit from 1977 opens with these lyrics: "Music is a world within itself, With a language we all understand, With an equal opportunity, For all to sing, dance and clap their hands"?

8. In 1980, Stevie Wonder, known as an activist for political causes, led a campaign to establish who's birthday as a federal holiday in the US?
A) John F. Kennedy   B) Ralph Abernathy   C) Martin Luther King Jr.

9. What song from the 1976 album, *Songs in the Key of Life* was only a minor hit for Stevie Wonder in the UK but became a #4 for David Parton in 1977?
A) Isn't She Lovely   B) Pastime Paradise   C) Knocks Me Off My Feet

10. What was Stevie Wonder's only solo number one in the UK?

WHAT CHART STATISTIC LINKS ALL OF THESE 1980S SINGLES?

A. AND THE BEAT GOES ON - THE WHISPERS
B. DANCE YOURSELF DIZZY - LIQUID GOLD
C. ZOOM - FAT LARRY'S BAND
D. WELCOME TO THE PLEASURE DOME - FRANKIE GOES TO HOLLYWOOD
E. ONLY YOU - YAZOO
F. ABRACADABRA - STEVE MILLER BAND

STEVIE WONDER ANSWERS: *1. B) Little Stevie Wonder; 2. C) Uptight (Everything's Alright); 3. A) Ebony and Ivory; 4. A) Tears Of A Clown; 5. B) Harmonica; 6. B) Talking Book; 7. Sir Duke; 8. C) Martin Luther King Jr.; 9. A) Isn't She Lovely; 10. I Just Called To Say I Love You.*
CHART STATISTIC ANSWER: *All 6 songs reached number two in the UK charts.*

ROY WOOD *(born in Kitts Green, Birmingham on 8 November 1946) is an English musician and singer-songwriter. He was particularly successful in the 1960s and 1970s as member and co-founder of the Move, Electric Light Orchestra and Wizzard. As a songwriter, he contributed a number of hits to the repertoire of these bands. Altogether he had more than 20 singles in the UK Singles Chart under various guises, including three UK No. 1 hits - The Move had 10 Top 40 hits, including a #1 and 6 further Top 10 hits. Roy Wood had four Top 40 solo hits, including one Top 10 hit. Wizzard had 8 Top 40 hits, including two #1's.*

Below are listed 21 hit singles involving Roy Wood. All you have to do is to state whether the song was a hit for The Move, Roy Wood or Wizzard.

1. ANGEL FINGERS

2. ARE YOU READY TO ROCK

3. BALL PARK INCIDENT

4. BLACKBERRY WAY

5. BRONTOSAURUS

6. CALIFORNIA MAN

7. CHINATOWN

8. CURLY

9. DEAR ELAINE

10. FIRE BRIGADE

11. FLOWERS IN THE RAIN

12. FOREVER

13. GOING DOWN THE ROAD

14. I CAN HEAR THE GRASS GROW

15. I WISH IT COULD BE CHRISTMAS EVERYDAY

16. NIGHT OF FEAR

17. OH WHAT A SHAME

18. ROCK 'N' ROLL WINTER

19. SEE MY BABY JIVE

20. THIS IS THE STORY OF MY LOVE

21. TONIGHT

ROY WOOD ANSWERS: 1. Wizzard; 2. Wizzard; 3. Wizzard; 4. The Move; 5. The Move; 6. The Move; 7. The Move; 8. The Move; 9. Roy Wood; 10. The Move; 11. The Move; 12. Roy Wood; 13. Roy Wood; 14. The Move; 15. Wizzard; 16. The Move; 17. Roy Wood; 18. Wizzard; 19. Wizzard; 20. Wizzard; 21. The Move.

ZZ TOP is an American rock band formed in 1969 in Houston, Texas. They comprised vocalist-guitarist Billy Gibbons, born December 16, 1949; drummer Frank Beard, born June 11, 1949; and vocalist-bassist Dusty Hill, May 19, 1949 – July 28, 2021. ZZ Top developed a signature sound based on Gibbons' blues guitar style and Hill and Beard's rhythm section. Popular for their live performances, sly and humorous lyrics, and matching appearances of Gibbons and Hill. ZZ Top formed after the demise of Moving Sidewalks. Thy had 10 UK Top 40 singles, including 2 Top 10 hits. Their albums were very successful, 6 Top 40, 5 reached the Top 10.

1. Which Elvis Presley hit from 1964 was covered by ZZ Top in 1992 and reached the UK Top 10?   A) Devil In Disguise   B) Viva Las Vegas   C) Jailhouse Rock

2. What three fashion features immediately identified Dusty and Billy?

3. ZZ Top become renowned in North America for their live act, including which 1976/7 tour which was a critical and commercial success?
A) Worldwide Texas Tour   B) Worldwide Oklahoma Tour   C) Worldwide Kansas Tour

4. In 1973, ZZ Top had a minor US hit with a song about the Chicken Shack, a notorious brothel in Texas. The song won a silver disc in the UK, what was its title?
A) Beer Drinkers and Hell Raisers   B) La Grange   C) Cheap Sunglasses

5. ZZ Top had their first UK hit in 1983. It reached #10 and won a silver disc. What is the song's title?   A) Gimme All Your Lovin'   B) Sharp Dressed Man   C) Legs

6. Which band were inducted into the Rock and Roll Hall of Fame by ZZ Top in 1993?
A) Jimi Hendrix Experience   B) Creedence Clearwater Revival   C) Cream

7. In 1977, Dusty Hill spent 3 months working in a normal job, he just wanted to "feel normal" and "ground himself" after years spent performing. He even wore a name tag that just said "Joe". Where did Dusty work?
A) McDonald's   B) Dallas/Fort Worth International Airport   C) Walmart

8. In 1994, ZZ Top signed a $35m record deal and released the million-selling album, *Antenna*. Which label did they join?   A) Warner Bros   B) London   C) RCA

9. In 1997, ZZ Top performed *Tush* and *Legs* at half-time during which major sporting event?   A) Super Bowl XXXI   B) The Rose Bowl   C) BCS National Championship

10. In 1980, ZZ Top visited the UK and performed on the BBC show *The Old Grey Whistle Test*. They shared the studio with which English group, whom Billy Gibbons felt "were great"?   A) ELO   B) OMD   C) XTC

THE EYES HAVE IT!

Name the acts who had these hit song titles that included the word 'Eyes'

A) Blue Eyes (1968)

B. My Eyes Adored You (1975)

C. Lyin' Eyes (1975)

D. Bette Davis Eyes (1981)

E. In Your Eyes (1983)

F. Eyes Without A Face (1984)

G. We Close Our Eyes (1985)

H. Old Red Eyes Is Back (1992)

J. Eyes Of Blue (1996)

K. My Father's Eyes (1998)

ZZ TOP ANSWERS: 1. B) Viva Las Vegas; 2. They wore sunglasses, hats and long beards; 3. A) Worldwide Texas Tour; 4. B) La Grange; 5. A) Gimme All Your Lovin'; 6. C) Cream; 7. B) Dallas/Fort Worth International Airport; 8. C) RCA; 9. A) Super Bowl XXXI; 10. B) OMD (Orchestral Manoeuvres in the Dark. THE EYES HAVE IT ANSWERS: A) Don Partridge; B) Frankie Valli; C) The Eagles; D) Kim Carnes; E) George Benson; F) Billy Idol; G) Go West; H) The Beautiful South; J) Paul Carrack; K) Eric Clapton.

OTHER MRM QUIZ BOOKS
AVAILABLE FROM AMAZON

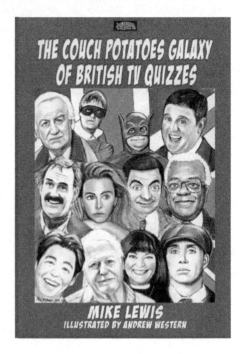

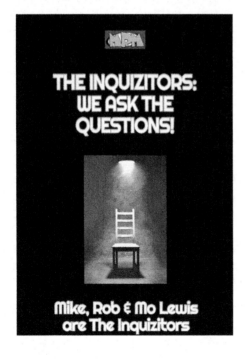

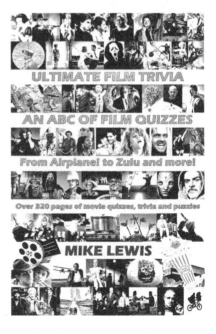

SCRIBBLES

Credits

This quiz book, is my fifth, and probably my last, to be published by Amazon in the last two years. The book covers a favourite subject of mine - popular music of the 20th century.

First of all my thanks to my long suffering wife Mo who has put up with many months of solitude, whilst I have battled to get this book completed.

My gratitude also to my son Rob, who has spent hours proof checking most of the pages. If you find any errors (which I am sure you will) it is most likely pages that I have checked myself.

I have also once again included many pastel paintings by my friend Andrew Western. The black and white prints do not do them full justice, but his talent still clearly shines through.

I have drawn enormously upon a few websites;

Wikipedia

everyhit.co.uk

IMDB

My thanks to them, and a few more too, for some invaluable information.

Thanks also to Amazon for publishing the work and distributing the book throughout the UK and beyond, so competently.

Printed in Great Britain
by Amazon

31500559R00163